Machines
and Liberty

A PORTRAIT OF EUROPE
EDITORS: MARY R. PRICE AND DONALD LINDSAY

A Portrait of Europe 1789–1914

Machines
and Liberty

Martin Roberts

Oxford University Press · 1972

Oxford University Press, Ely House, London W.1

GLASGOW NEW YORK TORONTO MELBOURNE WELLINGTON
CAPE TOWN IBADAN NAIROBI DAR ES SALAAM LUSAKA ADDIS ABABA
DELHI BOMBAY CALCUTTA MADRAS KARACHI LAHORE DACCA
KUALA LUMPUR SINGAPORE HONG KONG TOKYO

Photoset by BAS Printers Limited, Wallop, Hampshire,
and printed in Great Britain at the University Press, Oxford,
by Vivian Ridler, Printer to the University.

Editors' Preface

Recently there have been marked changes in the methods of teaching history and in our conception of what it is possible for young historians to experience and enjoy in school. The changes are designed to encourage them to make use of sources very early, to penetrate as deeply as they can into historical topics, to enjoy discovering for themselves what life was like in the past, and to develop their own individual interests. All this has had a very stimulating, in many cases, a re-vitalizing effect upon our presentation of the subject in school, and not least upon our attitude to the kind of books we need. There must now be few places where pupils are provided with only a single book for a year's work. Instead they are introduced to a multiplicity of publications dealing with separate topics, movements, and personalities, and the study of history is much enriched for them.

In view of this trend it may be asked if there is any place today for a series of background books such as these. Are they not quite outmoded and useless, if not positively harmful? We do not think so, for we are convinced that, if historical knowledge, at any level, is to be of lasting value and interest, such knowledge must not be piecemeal, but in the end set in a firm framework. Thus in addition to books dealing with separate topics young historians need books which will help to create this framework. It is not sufficient to relate topics solely to the history of our own country; historians will want books about the larger units with which their own country is particularly and obviously linked, about Europe in the first place, and ultimately about the world.

In these new Portrait books we have tried to avoid the superficiality of a brief chronological recital of events, and instead have chosen to highlight significant movements and people. Above all we have, wherever possible, introduced in the text and in the illustrations the sources of history, believing that this is one of the best ways to kindle the minds and imagination of the readers.

M.R.P.
D.D.L.

Author's Preface

To my pupils and colleagues at Brays Grove

One of my chief aims in writing this book was to attempt to show to pupils that however important past politics and economics may be they are by no means the only valid areas of historical study. I felt that a genuinely balanced Portrait of Europe in the nineteenth century could only be achieved if it included some reference to aspects like social conditions, the arts, religion, science and leisure activities. The style and content have been moulded by two considerations. The vocabulary is intended to be such that the average 'O' level candidate can take it in his stride. At the same time, I have included concepts which should stretch the most able pupils. I hope therefore that the book will not only prove a useful text for the 'O' level examination but also a stimulating introduction for sixth form work.

I have been helped by many friends and colleagues amongst whom I should like especially to thank Miss Sylvia Newton for her advice on the musical section. My greatest debt is to Christopher Black of the University of Glasgow who read the original text and whose rigorous and sometimes caustic criticism has done much to improve both content and style. Two heads are better than one when it comes to making recommendations for further reading so the bibliography is a joint effort. I am most grateful to Ray Marriott of the History Department of Leeds Grammar School for his prompt and judicious co-operation. I should like to thank Mrs. A. Fritchley whose ability to transform my vile handwriting into immaculate typescript never ceases to amaze me.

Finally my grateful thanks to my wife Diana and my colleague Roger Smith who have undertaken the tedious task of proof-reading with their usual good humour.

Any errors and omissions remain of course my entire responsibility.

M.R.

Contents

Acknowledgements

Black and white photographs are reproduced by kind permission of the following:
Albright-Knox Art Gallery, 246; Baines: *History of Cotton Manufacture*, 1835, 91; Bibliotheque Nationale, Paris, 213, 342; Bildarchiv Foto Marburg, 237 (top left); Bodleian Library, Oxford, 135, 155, 207; Calcographie du Louvre, 57; J. Allan Cash, 297; Courtauld Institute of Art, 301; Deutsche Fotothek, Dresden, 99; Deutsches Museum, Munchen, 83 (top), 267; La Documentation Française—Phototheque, 25, 27, 28, 29, 32, 35 (top), 37, 43, 52, 54, 58, 62, 64, 98, 105, 113, 117, 118, 140, 141, 145, 153, 158, 180, 209, 210, 250; Federico Arborio Mella, 244 (top); Flammarion, 241; Greater London Council, 237 (bottom); Heeresgeschichtlichen Museum, Vienna, 217; The Hispanic Society of America, 59; The Illustrated London News, 245; Krupp, 84 (top), 85 (top); Mansell Collection, 10, 21, 35 (bottom), 38 (bottom), 69, 74, 77 (bottom), 80, 81, 90, 93, 95, 100, 101, 115, 121, 127, 129, 130, 150, 269 (top), 172, 176, 182, 193, 237 (top right), 240 (bottom), 254, 261, 264, 291, 292, 293, 300, 318, 324, 336; Mary Evans Picture Library, 83 (bottom), 198; Military Museum, Beograd-Kalemegdor, 328; Museo Centrale del Risorgimento, 169 (bottom), 170; National Army Museum, 320, 323; National Maritime Museum, 49, 322; Novosti Press Agency, 221; Osterreichische Nationalbibliothek, 47, 63, 163; The Parker Gallery, 309; Photographie Bulloz, 38, 40, 41 (top); Radio Times Hulton Picture Library, 41 (bottom), 71, 75, 77 (top), 96, 102, 124, 137, 173, 216, 240 (top), 244 (bottom), 248, 249, 252, 263, 266, 269, 298 (top), 307, 310, 348; Reunion des Musées Nationaux, Versailles, 55, 148, 149; H. Roger-Viollet, 298; Roy Round, 290; Snark International, 199, 203, 211, 212, 219 (top); Dr. Franz Stoedner, 78, 84 (bottom), 301 (top); The Tate Gallery, London, 66; Times Newspapers, 89; Ullstein Bilderdienst, 186, 219, 317, 346; Vickers Ltd., 329.
Colour photographs are reproduced by kind permission of the Reunion des Musées Nationaux, Louvre, facing p. 288; and the National Gallery, facing pp. 289, 312, 313.

List of Maps

Chapter 1
Europe in 1789

In 1789 the population of Europe (excluding Russia) was approximately 140 million. Today it is more than 430 million. In 1789 there was only one town, London, with more than a million inhabitants. Today there are more than thirty. Then, between 80 per cent and 90 per cent of the European population made their living from the land. The corresponding figure today is between 30 per cent and 40 per cent. The vast majority of this population was illiterate, education being usually confined to a minority of the rich and privileged. Almost all Europeans were religious—overwhelmingly Christian with some small groups of Muslims in the Balkans—though the number of educated who were critical of religious beliefs was increasing. They were also poor in a way which today we find hard to imagine. Real hunger and physical suffering were always close. The good life for too many was dependent on the good harvest, and weather conditions caused harvests to vary considerably from year to year. Europeans in the late eighteenth century were physically smaller than we are. For instance, of the army conscripts from the Genoa area between 1792 and 1799, 72 per cent were less than 5 ft. 2 in. high. Life expectancy was also much less, 20–35 years in 1800 against 60–75 years today. The fastest form of land transport was the government dispatch rider galloping with his diplomatic messages from capital to capital. Ordinary people made do with the carter and his great wagon moving at walking pace when he was not held up by the poor conditions of the roads. Ocean transport—the sailing ship—was often speedier, but, at the mercy of the wind and weather, no more reliable. European life, therefore, remained intensely local. There was no instant news. Even the news of the fall of the Bastille took a fortnight to reach the citizens of Peronne—a mere 83 miles from Paris. Thus, while our modern European life is mainly urban, secular, fast-moving, prosperous, and healthy, in the 1780s it was rural, religious, slow-moving, and close to poverty and death (see opposite).

As can be seen from maps 1a and 1b (pp. 12 and 13), the political divisions of Europe in 1789 were also very different from those of today. Only in Western Europe have the boundaries of the major states remained generally stable. In Central and Eastern Europe, some names are familiar but little else. The forms of government

Rural life in eighteenth-century France

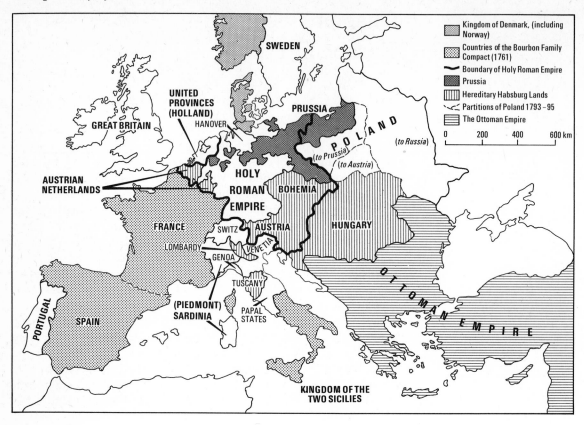

Legend:
- Kingdom of Denmark, (including Norway)
- Countries of the Bourbon Family Compact (1761)
- Boundary of Holy Roman Empire
- Prussia
- Hereditary Habsburg Lands
- Partitions of Poland 1793–95
- The Ottoman Empire

0   200   400   600 km

SWEDEN

UNITED PROVINCES (HOLLAND)
HANOVER
GREAT BRITAIN
PRUSSIA
POLAND
(to Russia)
(to Prussia)
(to Austria)
HOLY ROMAN EMPIRE
BOHEMIA
AUSTRIAN NETHERLANDS
FRANCE
SWITZ
AUSTRIA
HUNGARY
LOMBARDY
VENETIA
GENOA
TUSCANY
(PIEDMONT) SARDINIA
PAPAL STATES
OTTOMAN EMPIRE
PORTUGAL
SPAIN
KINGDOM OF THE TWO SICILIES

Map 1a Europe in 1789

were also quite different. Starting in the south-west of the continent, Spain and Portugal were hereditary monarchies, whose days of greatness lay in the past. Both countries had built up huge overseas empires in the sixteenth century but, in the seventeenth century, had been unable to compete economically with their northern neighbours, Holland, France, and Britain. By the eighteenth century, they were stagnant, economically, socially, and politically. Their kings ruled in an uneasy alliance with their nobility, whose social position was unchallenged and who often ruled their immense estates like petty kings. 'The Dukes of Medina Sidonia', a French visitor observed, 'reign like lions in the forest whose roar frightens away whatever might approach'. In both countries, the Catholic church was rich, powerful, and intolerant, and the peasantry (the mass of the population) was superstitious and wedded to medieval farming methods. There was only a tiny middle class, especially in Spain. The good Spaniard despised men of business and much of Spanish commerce was handled by Frenchmen. Plague, moreover, had caused great loss of life and economic disruption in eighteenth-century Spain. Neither Spain nor Portugal played a major part in

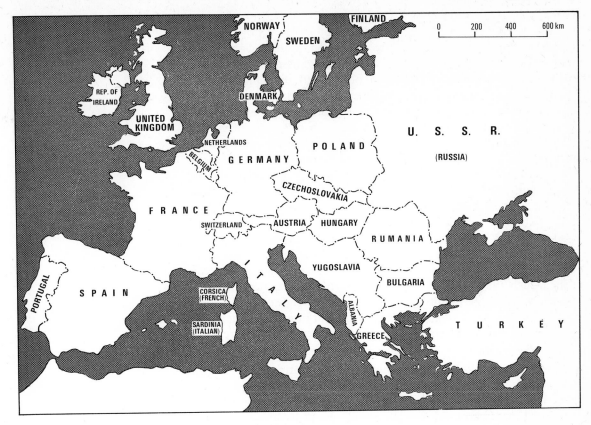

NORWAY FINLAND SWEDEN DENMARK REP. OF IRELAND UNITED KINGDOM NETHERLANDS BELGIUM GERMANY POLAND U. S. S. R. (RUSSIA) CZECHOSLOVAKIA FRANCE SWITZERLAND AUSTRIA HUNGARY RUMANIA ITALY YUGOSLAVIA BULGARIA PORTUGAL SPAIN CORSICA (FRENCH) SARDINIA (ITALIAN) ALBANIA GREECE TURKEY

0   200   400   600 km

Map 1b Europe in 1970

European politics though Portugal, for trading reasons, tended to ally herself to Britain while Spain, because of Bourbon family links, tended to ally herself to France.

France, a land rich in natural resources, with a population of more than 27,000,000, a flourishing international trade, an energetic and ambitious middle class, a strong army and increasingly effective navy, should unquestionably have been the most powerful nation of Europe. At the end of the seventeenth century she had been able to fight the whole of Europe single-handed and stand a good chance of winning. However, a series of disastrous wars occurred between 1701 and 1783. As a result of these, the French lost an empire to the British and spent huge sums of money which their government could not afford. At the end of the War of American Independence —during which the French helped the Americans against the British—the government of Louis XVI was bankrupt.

There were a number of ways in which this financial situation could have been righted but none were politically easy. The vital reform was the abolition of the privileges of the nobility and clergy which enabled them—the two richest classes in the country—to go

13

virtually tax-free. The nobles, however, were in no mood to be bullied. Louis XIV had edged them out of political power, their social position was challenged by the rising middle classes and they were bent on using the financial embarrassment of the government to recover their old political power and to maintain their social position. Other groups in France were also discontented. The educated middle classes regarded the despotism of Louis XV and Louis XVI as inefficient, unfair and often absurd. The privileges of the nobility and their snobbery seemed intolerable. With increasing vigour, they demanded that they should be consulted in the running of the country. The French peasantry, though better off than their counterparts elsewhere in Europe, were also restless. Having enjoyed a steadily rising standard of living for most of the eighteenth century, they had been affected by an economic depression which, by 1787, was serious and rapidly worsening. As bread prices soared, they became acutely aware how burdensome were the traditional feudal dues which they owed to the nobility and the tithe which they owed to the clergy. Within the major towns of France which were rapidly growing during the eighteenth century, there were the beginnings of an industrial working class which, like the peasantry, was driven near starvation by the economic depression. They too were restive.

The system of government which was attempting to cope with this society in ferment was quite unsuited to its task. It was still very much the monarchy created by Louis XIV (1661–1715) a masterful man who loved the job of ruling and had made efficient government in France dependent on a man of his stamp. His successors, however, were not up to the job. Louis XV preferred hunting and women, Louis XVI hunting and the locksmith's craft to the business of government. Both presided over frivolous courts, the intrigues of which ensured the rapid disgrace of those ministers who might have been capable of carrying out the reforms necessary for the well-being of France and the survival of the monarchy. The machinery of government proved increasingly incapable of fulfilling its essential tasks, including the collection of taxes. In the provinces, the key government officials, the Intendants, struggled with less and less success to enforce their orders from Paris and to break down the fantastic medley of rights and privileges, many of them dating back to the Middle Ages, which characterized provincial France. In the 1780s the government of Louis XVI was bent on reform but it had neither the authority nor the prestige to rally any considerable section of the population behind it.

To the north of France lay the Austrian Netherlands, geographically the equivalent of modern Belgium. Here there were social tensions similar to those of France. A privileged and powerful clergy and nobility, which included 'merchant princes', felt themselves threatened by a reforming government and an expanding middle class, which was demanding a more democratic government and an end to outdated privileges. In 1787, the Austrian Emperor Joseph II, the most thoroughgoing reformer of all the monarchs of this time, reorganized the administration of the Netherlands from top to bottom, reducing the powers of the nobility, the clergy, and some of the merchants in the process. The result was a nation-wide revolt against Austrian rule which then developed into a bitter struggle between the privileged and the unprivileged. This twofold conflict was in progress when the French Revolution broke out.

The neighbouring United Provinces (Holland) was a republic in name but in practice virtually a monarchy owing to the exceptional position of the Orange family, which provided the *Stadholder* (Head of State). The greatest trading nation of Europe after Britain, her merchant princes were politically extremely powerful. As in Belgium, however, the 1780s were years of revolt. A Patriot party emerged which wished to weaken the power of the Orange family and to aid the Americans in their war against the British. It was eventually suppressed by the old order and its mainly middle-class leaders driven into exile.

Across the Channel Great Britain, which at this time included the whole of Ireland, looked less flourishing than in fact she was. After a century of unbroken success in foreign wars, she had recently been beaten in humiliating fashion in the American War of Independence and was without an ally. Unique among the major states of Europe in that the power of her kings was clearly limited by a parliament which represented some of the people (albeit mainly the noble and the rich), there were widespread demands that the powers of the king should be further lessened and parliament reformed. Nonetheless by 1789 Britain was much the most powerful trading nation in Europe. Such had been her strategic gains in the eighteenth century and the power of her navy that, despite the setback of the American War, she had a stranglehold on world trade. Her population stood at about 14,500,000 and was rising fast. Her enterprising traders and businessmen were given ample scope by her governments. In fact the decade 1780–90 proved to be one of the most important in her history because it was the period of 'take-off' of the Industrial Revolution which was to make her the workshop of the world in the following century. The vast resources at her disposal became clear in the long and desperate struggle against France between 1793 and 1815.

In the far north of Europe lay a Sweden (which at this time controlled northern Finland) and a Denmark which controlled Norway. Both were monarchies with powerful aristocracies.

Sweden, a major European power in the seventeenth century, had been catastrophically defeated after Charles XII had invaded Russia in 1708 and never again played an important part in European history. Her chief ambition was to gain control of Norway from Denmark which, for her part, was scheming to win the southern provinces of Sweden and thus gain control of the entrance to the Baltic.

South of Denmark was the political confusion known as the Holy Roman Empire. Voltaire's comment that it was 'neither Holy, Roman, nor an Empire' was very apt. Its origins lay deep in the Middle Ages but by the eighteenth century it had lost all political meaning. It was made up of 365 separate states—electorates, principalities, duchies, imperial free cities, bishoprics—of all shapes and sizes. The two most powerful states of the area—Austria and Prussia—lay both inside and outside its boundaries. In theory, the Holy Roman Emperor was elected; in practice he was always the Emperor of Austria. In theory, the rulers of all the separate states owed their authority to the Emperor; in practice they were quite independent. The great majority of the 21,000,000 inhabitants were German speaking but as yet there was very little sense of German nationhood.

The northern part of the Empire was dominated by Prussia, a kingdom of 76,000 square miles and 5,500,000 inhabitants, more feared by her neighbours than her size seemed to warrant. Her reputation was due to the remarkable reign, from 1740 to 1786, of Frederick II (the Great) who added the Austrian province of Silesia and a large slice of Poland to his dominions by crafty diplomacy and brilliant use of his excellent army. However, like Louis XIV of France, he created a system of government which needed a man like himself at its head if it was to work. During the reign of his successor, his nephew Frederick William II (1786–97), the system clogged up and neither the army nor the administration functioned with its former efficiency. Few, however, noticed the change and it was not until Napoleon destroyed the famous army on the battlefield of Jena in 1806 that Prussia awoke to the realities of her situation.

Prussia's chief enemy and the major power of Central Europe was the Austrian Empire which, ruled for centuries by the House of Hapsburg, stretched over 280,000 square miles from Bavaria to the Balkans and contained more than 24,000,000 inhabitants of many different races. This size and variety made it a particularly difficult state to rule. Between 1780 and 1790 the Emperor Joseph II, a highly intelligent man, attempted to modernize and unify his far-flung realms. However, he went too far too fast, insisting on fighting a war against the Turks while carrying out major and unpopular internal reforms. He upset the Catholic Church, the Austrian and Hungarian nobility and, as we have seen, the Austrian Netherlands. Though his reforms were intended to benefit the peasants and serfs, their immediate effect was to puzzle and scare them. When he died in 1790, the Empire seemed on the verge of disintegration. The main job of his successor, Leopold II, was to salvage the dynasty by cancelling almost all Joseph's reform schemes.

The Austrian Empire also stretched down into the Italian peninsula which, like Germany, was a collection of small states. The Tyrol and Lombardy were part of the Austrian Empire and Habsburg relatives ruled in other states in Northern Italy. A band of territory running north-east from Rome across the centre of Italy, the Papal States, was ruled by the Pope, and Bourbon relatives of the kings of France and Spain controlled Southern Italy and Sicily (the Kingdom of the Two Sicilies). Only three areas were ruled by Italians—the kingdom of Piedmont in the north-west (which also included the island of Sardinia), the nearby republic of Genoa and the republic of Venice in the north-east. Piedmont was a rising power under the vigorous rule of the House of Savoy. In contrast, Genoa and Venice had decayed after centuries of commerical prosperity and political power. Like the Germans, the Italians possessed a common language and a common culture. Otherwise unity was non-existent.

To the north of Austria and east of Prussia lay Poland, still a large state of 188,000 square miles and more than 7,000,000 inhabitants but only two-thirds of her size before the First Partition of Poland in 1772. This cynical carve-up by Prussia, Russia, and Austria had inspired a new sense of national purpose among the Poles. The weakness of former years had been due to the anarchy and self-indulgence of the nobility, who had used their powers of veto in the Diet (assembly) to paralyse the government. In 1788 the famous Four Years Diet met to reform the constitution and give power to the popular king, Stanislas Augustus, to strengthen and modernize the country. Her powerful neighbours watched this process with concern. The last thing they wanted was a revived and unified Poland. By the Second and Third Partitions of 1793 and 1795, they wiped the state of Poland off the map.

Much the most powerful nation of Eastern Europe was Russia, stretching from the Baltic to the Black Sea and deep into Asia, with at least 35,000,000 inhabitants and an army of 500,000 men. Catherine the Great, Tsarina from 1762 to 1796, considerably increased Russian territory at the expense of the Poles and the Turks and the powers of the monarchy and nobility at the expense of the Russian peasantry. More than 90 per cent of the Russian population were either peasants or serfs, living for the most part in conditions of desperate poverty, and the main weight of the heavy taxation needed by Catherine to pay for her successful wars fell upon them, the class least able to pay. Rural Russia, therefore, was disrupted by a succession of peasant risings, the most serious of which, Pugachev's Rising of 1773–4, was directed against Catherine's government as well as the local nobility. Thereafter, Catherine formed a close alliance with her nobility, further increasing their legal powers so that, while in most other parts of Europe serfdom was disappearing, in Russia it grew. 'The formerly free peasants of the Ukraine', wrote an English visitor in 1784, 'have lately undergone a deplorable change and have been reduced by an edict of the present Empress, to the servile condition of her other subjects'. Catherine set the Russian monarchy on its nineteenth-century course. Most of her successors followed her example, pursuing a belligerent foreign policy while refusing to consider any major internal reforms. The eventual twentieth-century consequence of such a political tradition was the annihilation of the monarchy and everything that it stood for.

The south-east of Europe, including the Danube basin, the Balkans and Greece, was part of the Ottoman Empire. The Ottoman Turks, having captured Constantinople in 1453, continued to press north and west into Europe for the next two centuries, almost capturing Vienna in 1683. Their defeat outside the Austrian capital was in fact the beginning of their decline, and by 1789 their Empire, though still very large, was weak. The Sultan was becoming increasingly a figurehead and the authority of his government was often ignored in the outlying parts of his realms where the local 'pashas' ruled like petty kings. In Constantinople itself the government was disrupted by harem intrigue, by the corruption of the Janissaries (the Sultan's bodyguard which in earlier days had been of legendary courage and discipline) and by the refusal of a succession of Sultans and Grand Viziers (the chief ministers) to agree on the necessary reforms. The Turks were Muslims and their rule was hated by their Christian subjects in Europe. Between 1768 and 1792 Russia, by a series of victories in the Black Sea area, displayed Turkey's weakness to the world. The Eastern Question—or just how and by whom south-east Europe was to be ruled once the Turkish Empire disintegrated—was to become the most long-lasting and difficult problem of European diplomacy in the nineteenth century.

Finally, in the mountain fastness of Switzerland lay a republic made up of a federation of cantons controlled by a minority of rich townsmen. In 1768 a middle-class revolt overthrew this minority and stayed in power until 1782 when the old order was restored with the help of the French.

Taking Europe as a whole, though there were republics like Venice and Genoa, hereditary kingdoms and empires were the rule. Moreover though in Britain, in Sweden, and in Poland the powers of the individual monarchies were limited by assemblies of nobles, over most of the continent monarchies were absolute; i.e. in theory the ruler recognized no limits to his power except the laws of God and the traditions of his country.

By the standards of our own age, European society of the 1780s was very stable. The way of life of most Europeans—except in Britain and parts of Western Europe—hardly differed from that of their fathers and grandfathers. European society remained hierarchic; that is one in which each section of society knew its place and generally kept to it. Outside the towns, which were usually market-towns serving the locality, the basic community consisted of lord, priest, and peasant.

Since the middle of the eighteenth century, however, there had been signs of important changes—intellectual, social, and political. In the previous century, science and mathematics had made rapid progress thanks to the genius of men like the French philosopher and mathematician, Descartes, and the English physicist, Newton. The success of scientists in explaining many hitherto mysterious aspects of the universe gave rise to a more general confidence among educated Europeans in the power of human reason. An intellectual movement known as the Enlightenment developed in France inspired by writers like Montesquieu, Diderot, and Voltaire. They believed that if reason, rather than superstition or old customs, directed human affairs, mankind would make rapid progress towards prosperity and happiness. In their eyes most European institutions, especially the French ones which they knew most about, existed only because they were traditional, and were best abolished. Major obstacles to progress, they felt, were the Catholic Church and a privileged and idle nobility. A powerful development of 'enlightened' thinking was provided by another Frenchman, Rousseau. He believed that the society of his time was corrupt because it was artificial, that the best society was one in which men could approach most closely the condition of 'the noble savage' and rule themselves in freedom and equality. 'Man is born free and everywhere he is in chains', began *The Social Contract*, his most famous work. Here he argued that in any community, power should come only through the expression of the 'general will' of the community, and that the ideal community would be one of equals. To him, the traditional and absolute power of hereditary kings and the social privileges of a hereditary nobility were intolerable. Rousseau was a writer of exceptional eloquence and, with the writers of the Enlightenment, created a new climate of opinion. By 1789 educated men in Western

Europe tended to be critical of the society round about them and to find great inspiration in the Rousseauesque slogans of 'Liberty, Equality, Fraternity' and 'the sovereign people'.

The most significant social change in the second half of the eighteenth century was the increasing size and political awareness of the middle classes, a mainly urban group of businessmen, government officials, professional men, and shopkeepers, often referred to as 'the bourgeoisie'. In Western Europe especially, they were growing richer, more educated and, influenced by the ideas of the Enlightenment, ever less ready to tolerate absolutism and noble privilege. An event which gave them much encouragement was the successful American Revolution against British rule in 1776. Here a mainly bourgeois group of colonists threw off the hated rule of George III in the name of liberty and the Rights of Man. Their struggle captured the imagination of Europe. In his old age, the French Comte de Ségur recalled those days. 'The bravery of these new republicans (the American colonists) won esteem in all parts of Europe and enlisted the sympathies of the friends of justice and humanity. . . . Soon the American envoys arrived in Paris. . . . It would be difficult to express the enthusiasm with which they were welcomed in France into the midst of an old monarchy—these envoys of a people in revolt against their king.'

The American revolution was one of a series of revolts on both sides of the Atlantic which showed that 'the age of absolutism' was drawing to its close. Geneva in Switzerland had revolted against its urban nobility in 1768, reformers were active in Britain in the 1760s, 1770s and 1780s; there were revolts in the Austrian Netherlands and the United Provinces in the 1780s. In all these movements there was a strong bourgeois element. Finally, in 1789, came the French Revolution, in its size, its violence, and its consequences far vaster than any revolt that preceded it. Almost simultaneously an economic revolution was occurring in Britain which was to transform the economy firstly of Europe and then of the world. Only after this double revolution did the age of absolutism really give way to the age of revolution.

1789 was a year of great optimism, especially in France. 'In a few days time', wrote an Orleans priest that year, 'I shall be 98 years old. No day in my life has been as happy as that which I now see dawning. O Blessed Sun beneath which so many virtues have sprung up.'

*Lafayette, one of the many
Frenchmen who fought
alongside the American
colonists and who was to play
a leading part in the French
Revolution, lying wounded
during the American War of
Independence*

Chapter 2
The French Revolution

Perhaps the most significant thing about the French Revolution was that it did not remain French for very long. Though the English had executed one king in 1649 and deposed another in 1688, and though the Americans had rejected royal authority in the name of the Rights of Man in 1776, the rulers of continental Europe could safely ignore these events as distant, curiously Anglo-Saxon affairs. They could not, however, ignore the French, who not only proclaimed the ideals of Liberty, Fraternity and Equality but, from 1793, marched their armies across Europe carrying these slogans with them. Much of the history of Europe and of the world in the nineteenth and twentieth centuries is contained in the attempts of different societies to work out how they can best achieve liberty and equality, and the outstanding question of the twentieth century remains: how can the different nations of the world best achieve genuine fraternity? The problems posed by the French revolution-aries remain very much our problems and are still dangerously far from solution.

The last chapter described some of the difficulties of the French monarchy in the eighteenth century and the considerable tension that had developed in French society by 1789. Many intelligent observers predicted a major policitical explosion as a result of these tensions, but few if any imagined that a social upheaval unprece-dented in European history was near at hand. Arthur Young, an English agricultural expert who travelled extensively in France between 1787 and 1790, declared in 1788 that France was 'on the verge of some great revolution in government', but that this revolution 'would add to the scale of the nobility and clergy'. Since the nobility was swept away and the clergy radically changed by the French Revolution, Young was in one sense quite wrong. In another, however, he was right. The French Revolution began in fact as 'a revolt of the aristocracy', which was determined to add substantially to its political power. As Chateaubriand, author and politician, was later to put it, 'the patricians began the revolution and the plebeians completed it'. What no one realized in 1789, the patric-ians (or aristocrats) least of all, was the power of the plebeians (or lower classes). The aristocratic revolt, occurring at a time of serious economic depression, merely unleashed the pent-up forces of popular revolution.

The sequence of events in France between 1787 and 1799 is dramatic and very complicated. The following summary may provide a useful, if rough, guide through the maze. The aristocratic revolt provided the opportunity for the mainly middle-class leaders of the popular revolution to seize political power, which they used in the name of the people or nation. Their control was threatened first by lack of co-operation from the king, then by foreign and civil war, by divisions in their own ranks, and by a disillusioned working class. After twelve years of constantly changing governments, war, internal anarchy, and economic distress, most Frenchmen were only too pleased to accept the dictatorship of Napoleon Bonaparte who was prepared to safeguard the economic and social gains made by the middle classes and peasantry since 1789 as long as his own authority was unquestioned.

The details of the story are these. In 1787 Calonne, Controller-General of Finance, having discovered that the government was in debt to the tune of 112,000,000 *livres*, decided on drastic remedies including a tax on land to be paid by all landowners, nobles, and clergymen as well as peasants. Knowing that such a measure was bound to cause a political crisis, he persuaded Louis XVI to summon the most eminent men of the kingdom (the Notables) to discuss his policy. From Calonne's point of view, the Assembly of Notables was not a success. They distrusted him and secured his dismissal and the appointment of Cardinal de Brienne, one of their number, as his successor. Brienne found, however, that he could do little to modify Calonne's economic proposals, and before they separated the Notables suggested, first that the Paris *Parlement* should be consulted and secondly that the States-General, a body which represented the three estates of the realm—the nobility, the clergy, and the rest—and had not met since 1614, should be summoned to advise on the serious state of the country. The aristocratic revolt really began when Brienne referred his economic proposals to the Paris *Parlement*. The French *parlements*—primarily judicial assemblies in Paris and the provinces—were mainly noble in membership and had come increasingly to be centres of aristocratic resistance to royal government. The Paris *Parlement* of 1787 was no exception. It rejected Brienne's proposals and, like the Notables, demanded the summoning of the States-General. In May 1788 Lamoignon, Brienne's lieutenant, faced by the determined opposition of the Paris *parlements* backed by the provincial *parlements*, suspended them all in an attempt to crush their resistance for ever. Popular riots, however, took place all over France because the *parlements* seemed to represent the liberties of all Frenchmen against the tyranny of the king. In Rouen and Grenoble the army, called in to restore order, went over to the rioters. Louis had to give way. Brienne and Lamoignon were dismissed. A Swiss banker,

Necker, became Controller-General and the States-General was summoned to meet at Versailles in May 1789.

In the autumn and winter 1788–9 there was a most significant change in the popular mood. Whereas in the summer of 1788 the nobility was popular, by the spring of 1789 it was deeply distrusted. The basic cause of this change of mood was the demand of the nobility led by the Paris *Parlement* that the forthcoming States-General should be made up, as in 1614, of the three orders, each with the same number of deputies debating and voting in separate assemblies. Since the nobility would dominate the clergy as well as their own assembly, the Third Estate, representing the vast majority of the population, would always be outvoted by the privileged. The leaders of the Third Estate, however, were no longer prepared to be pushed around. Their feelings were best expressed by Siéyès, unsuccessful abbot turned political thinker, in his pamphlet *Qu'est ce que le Tiers État?* published in February 1789. 'What is the Third Estate?' he wrote, 'everything. What has it been until now? Nothing. What does it ask? To be something'. As for the nobility, it was a class 'assuredly foreign to the nation because of its do-nothing idleness'. The divide between the privileged orders and the rest of the nation became even more apparent after the election to the States-General and the completion, by the electors, of their lists of grievances (*cahiers de doléances*) which their representatives were to submit to the king. Though there was a wide measure of agreement between all the orders that major administrative and political reforms were urgently required, the nobility and clergy generally defended their traditional privileges while the Third Estate gave highest priority to the abolition of just these privileges—tithes, local monopolies, local judicial rights, hunting rights, feudal dues, and immunity from taxation. In May 1789, therefore, the men elected to represent the Third Estate arrived at Versailles determined to secure reforms and as suspicious of the privileged orders as they were of the monarchy. As Siéyès put it: 'The deputies of the clergy and the nobility have nothing in common with the National Representatives, so no alliance is possible among the three orders in the States-General.'

Furthermore, in the spring and summer of 1789 France was in ferment for economic as well as for political reasons. The agricultural depression was deepening, bread prices rising, and both the rural peasantry and Parisian working classes increasingly desperate. The tumultuous events of the next few months only make sense against this economic background.

The States-General got off to a bad start. Although the king had allowed the Third Estate to send 610 deputies while the nobles and clergy sent only 300 each, he insisted that the Estates

The Opening of the States-General at Versailles in May 1789. Here is the French Monarchy in all its glory for almost the last time. Louis XVI sits on the dais surrounded by members of the royal family. In front of him below the dais, royal officials including Necker sit at a table. In the foreground with their backs towards us are the clergy, opposite them the nobility. The Third Estate are on the right, facing the king

met and voted by order, thus ensuring that the Third Estate was outvoted. A long opening speech by Necker failed to mention any need for constitutional reforms and the court ceremonial constantly reminded the representatives of the Third Estate of their social inferiority. From the first, however, they refused to meet on their own. After six weeks wrangling they went further and on 17 June declared themselves the National Assembly. This was the first really revolutionary gesture, as the British ambassador of the time rightly noted. 'If his Majesty once gives his decided approbation to the proceedings of the Third Estate,' he wrote home, 'it will be little short of laying his Crown at their feet.' Louis, deeply upset by the recent death of his eldest son, took no immediate action, however, and three days later the National Assembly went further still. Finding themselves shut out of their usual meeting place (owing almost certainly to the inefficiency of royal officials) and suspecting a plot against them, the deputies sheltered from the rain in an indoor tennis-court and there took the famous oath 'that all members of this assembly shall never separate but assemble wherever circumstances shall demand, until the constitution of the kingdom is established and fixed upon solid foundations'. By this time many of the clergy and some of the nobility had joined the Assembly, but Louis, spurred on by his younger brother, the Comte d'Artois, and by his Austrian wife, Marie Antoinette, now resolved on firm action. An open confrontation occurred on 23 June, one of the key moments of the Revolution. At a royal session, surrounded by troops, Louis outlined his reform proposals, declared the resolutions of the National Assembly null and void, and ordered the estates to separate and meet in future by order. He met with open defiance. When the Grand Master of Ceremonies ordered the Third Estate to disperse, Bailly, President of the National Assembly, replied, 'the assembled nation cannot receive orders', and Mirabeau, the most fearless speaker of them all, retorted 'Go and tell those who sent you that we shall not stir from our seats unless forced by bayonets.' No bayonets appeared. Louis's reaction to the news of their defiance was merely, 'Oh well—the devil with it, let them stay.' The monarchy, and the privileged orders, had lost another vital round.

July saw the last serious attempt by the court, led by the Comte d'Artois, to stop the Revolution in its tracks. Loyal troops were concentrated near Paris and Versailles and on 11 July Necker, who

Map 2 Paris during the Revolution

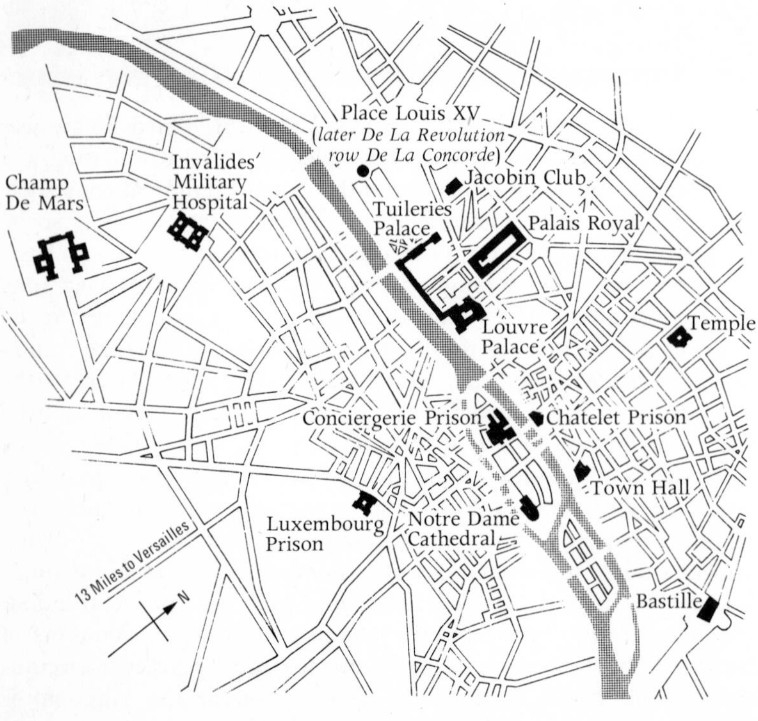

*The Taking of the Bastille:
a fortress which looks much
more formidable than in fact it
was*

had done his best to persuade the king to co-operate with the
Assembly, was sent into exile. The suppression of the Assembly by
force seemed imminent. The citizens of Paris, however, now
intervened. The capital, some twelve miles from Versailles, was the
centre of extreme revolutionary thinking. Suffering from large-
scale unemployment, its ferocious crowd was quite ready to take the
law into its own hands. The news of Necker's dismissal led to a
frenzied search for arms and ammunition for the defence of the city
against royal troops. One possible source of ammunition was the
Bastille, a grim fortress with a reputation as the place where the
kings of France entombed their political prisoners. (See map 2.)
On 14 July, after confused negotiations between the prison governor
and the mob, firing broke out and, with the help of a few professional soldiers with some cannon the fortress with its tiny garrison
was taken and its governor lynched. The Bastille had no military
importance and contained no political prisoners. Its fall, however, was of immense significance. Not only did it symbolize all
that was detestable about the old regime, but its capture showed
those who were planning to suppress the National Assembly that
they also had Paris to reckon with. Necker was recalled. The Comte
d'Artois left the country. The king had no alternative but to accept

the National Assembly on its own terms.

Meanwhile, revolution had spread to the provinces. Throughout the spring and summer the French countryside had been alive with rumours. Arthur Young, travelling in July, came across a peasant woman who told him 'something was to be done by some great folk for such poor ones as she. She did not know how and who but God send us better for the taille (the traditional tax) and manorial dues are crushing us'. Reports of events in Paris and of royal troop movements suggested that 'the great ones' had fallen out and created a panic among the peasantry that the nobles were coming to avenge themselves on the people. In some areas, unemployment had created bands of vagrants whose existence added to these fears.

An Incident during the Great Fear: one noble gets round the angry peasantry by giving them a good meal

In July and August these anxieties built up into an extraordinary series of events, known as 'the Great Fear', when the peasantry in every part of the country turned on their former lords, burning their chateaux and destroying the manorial registers which listed the feudal dues. In a dramatic debate on the night of 4 August the landowners of the National Assembly surrendered most of their feudal and financial privileges, an action which was less generous than it looked since they were merely recognizing accomplished facts. Attempts by the landowners to gain compensation for their lost privileges proved hopeless in the face of mass peasant resistance. Thus the French peasantry intervened in the events of 1789 with massive effect. They had been revolutionary because

29

of the weight of feudal dues and of taxes. Feudal dues were now abolished and taxes would henceforward be imposed by a revolutionary government. After 1789, when it was not passive, the peasantry tended to be anti-revolutionary.

The last dramatic event in 1789 was once more Paris-centred. The National Assembly had not been able to do anything about the bread shortage and by the end of the summer many Parisian families were starving. On 5 October a vast throng of Parisian women marched to Versailles imagining that the king, or someone, would provide them with bread. They were in an ugly mood. 'We have had such dreadful doings', reported an English visitor to Versailles. 'A set of wretches forced themselves into the chateau, screaming 'The Queen's head, down with the Queen. Let Louis abdicate. Long live the Duke of Orleans (one of Louis's younger brothers, known to favour the revolution). He will give us bread.' One of the guards defending the Queen's apartments was killed and others assaulted.' The upshot of this incident was the moving of the royal family from Versailles to Paris. Henceforward, Louis was the virtual prisoner of his capital which was far more revolutionary than any other part of France. This 'March of the Women' took place some fifteen months after Louis had originally bowed to the pressure of an aristocracy in revolt and had agreed to summon the States-General. The aristocracy had believed that the Third Estate would follow them wherever they led. Obviously they were sadly mistaken. By October 1789 the leading nobles were in exile, the old privileges had been swept away, and the king was an unwilling partner of a confident and mainly middle-class assembly. The next phase of the revolution would show whether this inexperienced body could cope with the problems of government which it had inherited.

It set to work with energy, determination and high ideals. Before they left Versailles for Paris with the King, the deputies had set down their main principles in the famous Declaration of the Rights of Man and Citizen. It was a superbly written document. 'The representatives of the French people,' it begins, 'organized in the National Assembly, considering that ignorance, forgetfulness or the contempt of the rights of man are the sole causes of public misfortunes and of the corruption of government, have resolved to set forth in a solemn declaration, the natural, inalienable and sacred rights of man, in order that such a declaration, continually before all members of the social body, may be a perpetual reminder of their rights and duties.' The right to liberty was a central theme. No citizen could be arrested and held without trial. There must be freedom of conscience and of the press. Equality was important too. The law must be the same for all citizens, and there could be no taxation privileges. In the appointment of public officials, merit alone must count. With its stress on liberty and equality, the

Declaration of the Rights of Man had a tremendous influence in the next century wherever an educated class felt itself trodden down by a tyrant king or arrogant nobility. In a sense it was the manifesto of the revolutionary bourgeoisie and, though it claimed to speak for all peoples, it tended to reflect the interests of its middle-class and male authors. Though it emphasized the right to property, it said nothing about the right to work. Though it stressed the importance of merit in promotion, it said nothing about the right to education. Though it insisted on equality before the law, it said nothing about the right of every citizen to have the vote. Women's rights were ignored.

The Declaration was followed by two years of radical reform directed by the Assembly, which now called itself the Constituent Assembly since it saw its main job as providing France with a constitution. Louis XVI became 'King of the French', was provided with an annual income, and allowed to appoint ministers, ambassadors and generals. He was also given 'the suspensive veto' by the use of which he could delay laws up to a period of four years. Ultimate power, however, no longer belonged to the king but to the Assembly which alone could make law. It was to be elected every two years and a complicated method of voting ensured that it would be composed of men of property. Citizens were divided into the active and the passive according to the level of tax they paid. The latter, the poorest section of the community, who did not pay enough tax, took no part in the primary elections. In the secondary elections which chose the deputies for the Assembly, an even higher tax-level limited the right to vote to 1 per cent of the population. In order to stand as a deputy, one had to pay a higher rate still. 'In place of Commons, Nobles and Clergy', remarked one cynic, 'we have now the Rich, the Richer and the Richest.' The men of '89 believed passionately in the representative principle, but they were no democrats.

The French administration was transformed. The old inefficient patchwork of local government which had been such an obstacle to progress was replaced by eighty-three departments of similar size and extensive powers. A network of judicial tribunals replaced the parlements and local courts of nobility and clergy. The old tolls and other economic barriers were abolished and complete free trade encouraged internally. Throughout the period of revolution, labour unrest was frequent and often serious. The Assembly met it more with repression than sympathy. The public work-shops which had been opened in Paris in 1789, to provide work for the unemployed, were closed in 1791, and in the same year the 'Loi Chapelier' forbade workers to combine in unions.

The extent to which France was reconstructed by the revolution-

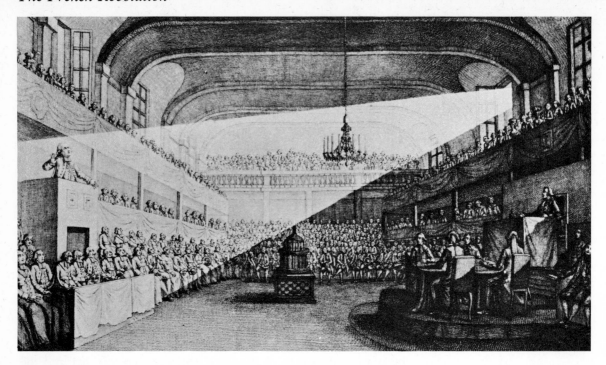

aries of the Constituent Assembly was remarkable, but their achievement was marred by three failures. They were unable to solve the financial problems they had inherited. They caused great bitterness by their reforms of the French Catholic Church, and they never won the whole-hearted co-operation of Louis XVI. The inadequacy of the old financial system had been a major cause of the revolution and the 'men of '89' swept it completely away. The old confusion of *taille*, *gabelle*, *aides* and so on was replaced by a land tax which was to be backed up by a new type of income tax. However, the revenue from these new taxes proved too small to meet the costs of government, partly because of the immensity of these costs and partly because the peasantry refused to pay. The gap was made up by the nationalization and sale by public auction of the vast estates of the Catholic Church. Interest-bearing notes— *assignats*—were issued to finance this scheme and before long became accepted as bank notes. For a short time, *assignats* solved the financial problems of the government but, in the long run, they led to runaway inflation, economic distress and popular unrest.

The great mass of the French clergy had not seemed unduly alarmed either by the nationalization of church lands or by the abolition of the tithe. The great riches of the Church, concentrated in the hands of a few clerical princes, had been a source of conflict within the Church for years. The Civil Constitution of the Clergy managed however to turn the great majority of priests against the

Abbot Gregory is the first priest to take the oath of loyalty to the new constitution. The building in which the Constituent Assembly met is the old riding school of Louis XV which was both uncomfortable and acoustically deplorable

Revolution. The aim of this Constitution, drawn up by the Assembly in the summer of 1790, was to make the clergy salaried civil servants and reorganize the administration of the Church. The Assembly would have been wise to proceed cautiously since the measure would greatly reduce the independence of the Church and bring into the open the knotty problem of the relationship between the State, the Church, and the Pope. Two articles of the Constitution were particularly hard for traditional Catholics to stomach. Article 19 stated: 'A new bishop may not write to the Pope for confirmation', and Article 21: 'Before consecration, a priest-elect must take a solemn oath "to be faithful to the nation, to the law and to the king and to maintain with all his power the constitution decreed by the National Assembly".' Many of the clergy felt that they were being asked to be Frenchmen before they were allowed to be Catholics.

Too many of the deputies, however, were disciples of Voltaire, with nothing but contempt for the clergy and the claims of the Pope. The Constitution, which reduced the number of bishops from 135 to 83 and deprived hundreds of priests of their livings, was rushed through without formal consultation with the clergy and in total disregard of Pope Pius VI. As a consequence, the Church was hopelessly split. Those priests who refused to take the oath of loyalty to the Constitution were suspended by the Assembly, those who did were suspended by the Pope. In fact only seven bishops and a third of the priests eventually took the oath and the 'non-Jurors' (those who refused to swear) came increasingly to be leaders of resistance to the revolution, especially in country districts.

The Civil Constitution of the Clergy also set the king more firmly against the revolution. Louis was a stupid man with little interest in politics. What he understood of the revolution he did not like, but up to 1790 he was prepared to co-operate half-heartedly with the new Assembly. He was, however, a sincere Catholic. The Civil Constitution appalled him and he came to listen more readily to Marie Antoinette's schemes for a flight from France and a triumphant return at the head of an army of *emigré* nobles and Austrians to crush the revolution and all its works. The only effective link between the Assembly and the Court was the Comte de Mirabeau, the outstanding politician of the first years of the Revolution. Born an aristocrat, he had scandalized his fellow-nobles so much by making off with another man's wife and running up huge debts that they would have nothing to do with him. He therefore got himself elected as a deputy of the Third Estate and won immortality by his defiance of Louis's commands in the tense days of June 1789. He soon came to dominate the Constituent Assembly by his powers of oratory and clear grasp of essentials. France, he believed, needed a constitutional monarchy with a strong central government if she was to survive such troubled times. The Assembly was in danger of taking too much power from the king while giving too much to the provinces. Both monarchy and country would face the gravest danger if the uneasy co-operation of king and assembly ever broke down and he devoted much of his energies to acting as a go-between. He was, however, a rogue whom few could trust. He continued to run up huge debts and supplied Louis with political information in return for a salary. Marie Antoinette loathed him and the Assembly grew suspicious of his activities. Yet as long as he lived, the co-operation continued. His death in April 1791 was a disaster for Louis. 'I carry with me', he said on his deathbed, 'the last rags of the monarchy.' And so it proved. Two months after his death, Louis gave way to Marie Antoinette and decided on flight. The plan was characteristically bungled. The royal coach was intercepted at Varennes close to the border of the Austrian Nether-lands and escorted by the National Guard back to the capital, where it was greeted with spits, jeers, or stony silence. Though Louis and his family were not actually imprisoned for more than a year, Varennes marked the end of the monarchy as a political force.

Constitutional monarchy had failed because the monarch would not accept the spirit of the constitution, and the revolutionary leaders began reluctantly to accept that France must become a republic. The doom of Louis and his wife was finally sealed by the war which, as we shall see, broke out between *Prussia* and *Austria* on one side, and *France* on the other, in April 1792. From the first, the royal family behaved with absurd foolhardiness. The Queen, sister of the Austrian Emperor, kept up a secret correspondence with the Austrian court. In June 1792, as the untrained French armies fell back before the invaders, Louis dismissed numbers of the popular Girondin government. Simultaneously, the Duke of Brunswick, commander of the enemy forces, issued the following warning to the people of Paris, 'If the least violence be done to Their Majesties, if their security, preservation and liberty be not provided for immediately, then the rulers of Austria and Prussia will exact an exemplary and ever memorable vengeance by delivering the city of Paris to military punishment and total destruction.' The Brunswick Manifesto had the opposite effect to that intended. The Tuileries Palace was assaulted and the king taken into custody. The revolutionary government declared him deposed and in 1792 brought him to trial as a traitor. There was no doubt that he was guilty since an iron chest found in the Tuileries full of documents made clear the extent of his intrigues against the revolution since 1789. Louis, however, won much sympathy by the honesty and simplicity of his replies to the prosecutor and, though the Assembly was almost unanimous in finding him guilty, it proved bitterly divided over whether he should die. A great speech by Robespierre, leader of the

The Execution of Louis: he attempts to speak to the crowd but the drums drown his words

Marie Antoinette on her way to the guillotine. The sketch is by J-L David

Jacobin faction, finally swung opinion in favour of the death penalty: 'Because the country must live', he declared, 'Louis must die.'

Louis's bearing on the scaffold on 21 January 1793 was worthy of a greater man. The Abbé Edgeworth, who accompanied him on his last journey from prison, left this description: 'I saw him cross the breadth of the scaffold with a firm foot, silence by his look alone ten or fifteen drums placed opposite me and, in a voice so loud that it must have been heard on the banks of the Seine, pronounce distinctly these memorable words: "I die innocent of all the crimes laid to my charge; I pardon those who have occasioned my death and I pray to God that the blood you are about to shed may never be visited on France".' The drums then drowned his words, the executioners went quickly about their business and, when the head was held aloft, thousands of hats were thrown in the air by the cheering crowd.

It is impossible not to feel sorry for Louis, for he was a well-meaning man caught up in a situation of incredible difficulty. In character, however, he could hardly have been less suited to his situation. Slow-witted, lazy, and indecisive, he was also sly and his attempts to double-cross the revolutionary assembly in a time of acute national danger led directly to his death. From 1787 onwards, there seems scarcely to have been a time when he heeded the right advice. His wife, who had been the cause of so many of his troubles, was also guillotined, with much popular rejoicing, in October 1793. Their only surviving son died of tuberculosis in 1795 after a harsh imprisonment. The Comte de Provence, the eldest exiled brother of Louis XVI, then proclaimed himself Louis XVIII. He would have to wait another twenty years before he could set foot again in France.

In August 1791, two months after the flight to Varennes, the Constituent Assembly dissolved itself and, after new elections, an assembly known as the Legislative Assembly came into existence. Since the Constituent Assembly had decreed that none of its members could be re-elected, the new governing body was comparatively inexperienced. Before long two major factions appeared among the revolutionary leaders, the Girondins and the Jacobins. As their name suggests, the Girondins were provincials, many of them coming from the area round Bordeaux, the great port on the Gironde estuary. They were idealists, brilliant orators full of optimism for the future of the Revolution in France and in Europe. Politically however, they were lightweights, with none of the sagacity, patience, and ruthlessness to succeed in such dangerous times. The Jacobins, who took their name from the old Parisian abbey which was taken over as an extreme revolutionary club, emerged as the main rivals of the Girondins over whom they enjoyed two important advantages. They possessed well-organized support in Paris itself and an able and ruthless leadership including such men as Robespierre and Marat.

In the autumn of 1791 and the spring of 1792 the Girondins were dominant in the Legislative Assembly. It was they who blithely led France to war first against Austria and Prussia and then against most of the continent. Once serious fighting began, however, they were seldom masters of events. The demands of war only intensified the already intense problems of the monarchy, the clergy and the economy. The closeness of Paris to the attacking armies made the capital specially nervy and the Convention—the new assembly formed in 1792 to cope with the war—was increasingly influenced by the mood of the *sans-culottes*, the street-army of artisans and shop-keepers which had already made its presence felt when it had stormed the Bastille in 1789. It was the *sans-culottes* who stormed the Tuileries palace after the Brunswick Manifesto. When in September the enemy captured Verdun, the strongest fortress on the northern frontier of France, they turned on the inmates of the Parisian prisons searching for 'informers' in an atmosphere of panic and revenge and indiscriminately massacred more than a thousand of them (the so-called September Massacres). They were an unpredictable and horribly violent force.

Though the war situation temporarily improved, the economic situation worsened and the Girondin ministers passed a series of economic measures which made them specially unpopular in Paris.

The September Massacres

The trial and execution of the king showed the increasing power of Robespierre and the Jacobins. In the spring of 1793 the French armies were once again in retreat and Dumouriez, their most famous general, deserted to the enemy. Rumour and panic once more stalked the Paris streets. Food prices soared and the value of *assignats* plummeted downwards. On 2 June a carefully disciplined force of *sans-culottes*, led and organized by Jacobins, surrounded the Assembly. Thirty-one of the leading Girondins were arrested and executed after a summary trial. In the provinces, their supporters were dispatched with similar ruthlessness.

The *coup d'état* of 2 June 1793 heralded the most heroic yet the most terrible phase of the Revolution. What was at stake was far more than which particular group should control the Convention. The whole revolution was threatened. The revolutionary armies facing the invaders were demoralized. Through civil war, more than half the French provinces were controlled by anti-revolutionary forces. There was economic chaos, the Convention was bewildered and Paris crazed with fear and excitement. This challenge inspired a tremendous response. Twenty years later an official of Napoleon's declining empire recalled the 'good old days' of 'a government of passionate Jacobins, wearing rough woollen cloth, and wooden shoes who lived on simple bread and bad beer and went to sleep on mattresses on the floor of their meeting halls when they were too tired to work and deliberate further. Those were the kind of men who saved France.'

After the *coup d'état*, the Jacobins steadily increased their hold on the machinery of government. Two special committees, the

Committee of General Security and the Committee of Public Safety, had already been established to control day to day events. Under the Jacobins the Committee of Public Safety emerged as the effective government of the country. Of this remarkable committee of powerful men which usually met every morning at 8 o'clock in the Tuileries Palace and worked late into the night, the most striking was Robespierre. He, more than any other man, characterized the period of Jacobin Terror and has either fascinated or sickened historians ever since. He came to power by violence, stayed in power by a policy of terror, and ended his life on the guillotine. Yet he saved the Revolution. He deserves the closest attention.

After a brilliant school career in his home town of Arras, Maximilien Robespierre followed in his father's footsteps and became a lawyer. Having gained a reputation as one who would go to enormous trouble to help the poor in legal difficulties, he was elected as a deputy of the Third Estate in 1789. A frequent speaker in the National and Constituent Assemblies, he soon became a leading member of the Jacobin club. He achieved national fame by his bitter and solitary opposition to the Girondins' call for war in 1792 and by his successful demand for the death penalty on Louis. He was not an attractive personality. Somewhat reptilian in appearance, he was a dandy in a prim kind of way, taking the greatest care with his dress. As a politician, however, he was outstanding. His revolutionary beliefs, which he drew from Rousseau, were clear, consistent, and held with a determination that was fanatical, even by the standards of the time. The Revolution, he

A Jacobin Club in Toulon: There was a network of Jacobin clubs throughout the country by 1793

Robespierre

believed, was the greatest advance in human history and therefore virtuous. Its defeat would be the triumph of evil. In its defence, therefore, any means were justifiable. Though a man of the greatest honesty, with a genuine capacity for friendship, there was iron in his soul. He never doubted that he was right. In July 1793 he jotted down what he thought should be the Jacobin programme:

> What is our aim? 'It is to use the Constitution for the benefit of the people. What are the obstacles to the achievement of freedom? The war at home and abroad. By what means can the foreign war be ended? By placing republican generals at the head of our armies and by punishing those who have betrayed us. How can we end the Civil War? By punishing traitors and conspirators, especially those deputies and administrators who are to blame . . . and by making a terrible example of all the criminals who have outraged liberty and spilt the blood of patriots.

He was a great but terrifying man.

The foreign war was immediately taken in hand. The Convention decreed total mobilization and Carnot, an ex-army engineer and organizer of genius, made sure that this vast supply of manpower was rapidly transformed into adequately trained and well-equipped armies. By the autumn France had more than a million men under arms. State-controlled factories turned out a regular supply of arms and ammunition. Jacobin representatives, headed by Saint-Just, the youngest member of the C.P.S., toured the fronts, inspiring the troops and goading on the generals (the penalty of failure was death!). In less than a year all the invaders were driven from French soil. The civil war was brought under control equally quickly. The most serious revolt, that of La Vendée, was crushed after bitter fighting and resistance elsewhere collapsed.

By a law of December 1793, all the French provinces were brought more firmly under the control of Paris. A further series of laws aimed to restore economic order. Maximum prices were fixed on basic foodstuffs to try to beat inflation and some stability was brought to the much devalued *assignat*. A new constitution and radical policies for education, industry and poor relief were drafted to be put into effect when the present crisis was over.

By any standards, the Jacobin achievement of the autumn and winter of 1793 was stupendous but it was not without cost. France had known 'terror' before the Jacobins came to power but they converted it into an instrument of policy. As Robespierre put it, Jacobin rule was 'virtue, without which intimidation is disastrous, and intimidation, without which virtue has no power'. Special and speedy judicial powers were given to the Revolutionary Tribunal, and in their thousands opponents of the Jacobins, mostly real though some imagined, were hurried to their deaths as a result of the Jacobin Terror. Paris was the centre of activity but the most brutal episodes took place elsewhere. The rebels of Lyons who surrendered after a two-month siege were mown down by firing squads, while at Nantes Carrier took to drowning his victims in the river Loire. Jacobin savagery matched Jacobin heroism.

No society, however, could live at such a pitch for long and by the spring of 1794 the Jacobins found opposition mounting against them despite their successes. On the one hand a number of experienced politicians led by Danton felt that the Terror had lasted long enough, on the other a group of *sans-culottes*, led by Hébert, wanted to begin a de-christianization campaign of which Robespierre in particular deeply disapproved. The Jacobins, however, had lost none of their skill and ruthlessness. They struck twice in quick succession. The Hébertists were guillotined on 25 March, the Dantonists on 5 April 1794. 'Infamous Robespierre', declared Danton as he passed Robespierre's home on his way to the scaffold, 'you will follow me before long', and so it proved. In these two purges, the Jacobins had sown the seeds of their own destruction. Robespierre seemed to be losing his sense of reality. While to everyone else the crisis was obviously over, he continued to see traitors everywhere. He spent much of his time developing a new religion of the Supreme Being, and lost his dominance of the C.P.S. and the Convention. In an attempt to recapture this dominance, he made some fatal errors. By the Law of Prairial (Prairial was the name given by the new revolutionary calendar to the month of May/June) he so widened the definition of treason that few could feel safe. He also stepped up the Terror, 1,376 people being guillotined in Paris alone between 10 June and 27 July. Then, on 26 July, he made a powerful but vague speech to the Convention, threatening enemies of the Revolution, wherever they might be. This drove a terrified Convention into action. The following day Robespierre's attempts to gain a hearing were greeted with boos and cries of 'Down with the tyrant'. His voice eventually failed him. 'Danton's blood is choking him', cried an unknown voice. In scenes of pandemonium, the Convention voted that Robespierre and his colleagues be arrested. The *sans-culottes*, disillusioned by the failure of the Jacobins to control the economy and by the execution of Hébert, failed to come to their aid. While the Convention was able to muster 6,000 troops, the Jacobins could only find 3,000 who melted away when they discovered the odds. Robespierre tried and failed to commit suicide. With his brother, Saint-Just and eighteen other associates he was guillotined on 28 July. Seventy-one followed the next day, the last and largest blood-letting session of the Revolution.

The great days of the Revolution were over. The new leaders muddled through mounting economic chaos marked by a catastrophic fall in the value of the *assignats*, serious rioting in Paris and a

The Guillotine : the method of execution most used by the Jacobins. It was more efficient and less painful than previous methods. Ironically, its inventor, Dr. Guillotin, died on his own invention during the Reign of Terror

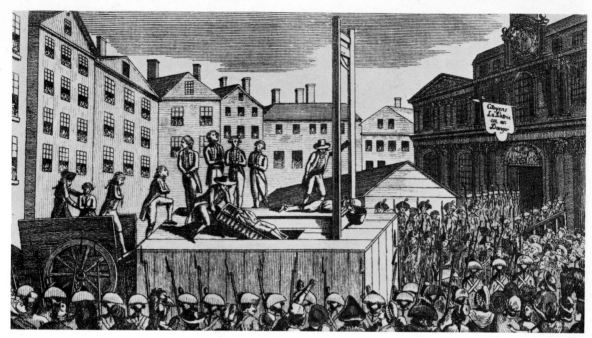

The Guillotine in action : nine young noblemen being executed in Paris during the Reign of Terror

vicious anti-Jacobin campaign in the provinces to another constitution in 1795. All taxpayers voted to elect deputies to two Chambers. These Chambers then elected five Directors who were supposed to provide the strong day to day government which France so urgently needed. The failure of the Directors to provide this strong government led eventually to the dictatorship of Napoleon.

The Revolutionary War 1792–5

Meanwhile the first phase of the Revolutionary War had ended (see map 3, p. 42). The Girondins had declared war on Austria and Prussia in 1792 partly because of the army of exiled nobility gathering in the Austrian Netherlands, partly because of the encouragement that the rulers of these states seemed to be giving Louis XVI, and partly because they wished to liberate the peoples of Europe from their despotic monarchies. There seemed little reason why Europe should take the French war effort seriously. Her army was apparently leaderless since the senior officers had been drawn almost exclusively from the nobility. Her navy was in an even worse state as its effectiveness depended on the minor nobility of Normandy and Brittany, among the most bitter enemies of the Revolution. Britain's Prime Minister, the Younger Pitt, was a cautious man but he had no doubt that French resistance would soon collapse. The first skirmishes fulfilled his expectations. The raw French troops simply ran away. The Austrians and Prussians advanced into French territory and it was not until 20 September,

Danton

41

Map 3 The Revolutionary Wars 1792–1801

at Valmy, that they suffered their first minor setback owing mainly to some excellent French artillery. The Duke of Brunswick, commander of the joint Austro-Prussian forces, was elderly and very cautious. After Valmy, he retired to the Austrian Netherlands and allowed the French, reinforced and gathering confidence, to take the offensive. Dumouriez swept into the Austrian Netherlands, won a major victory at Jemappes in November 1792 and occupied Brussels. The main consequence of his success was to bring Britain and Holland, alarmed by the conquest of the vital strategic area of the Austrian Netherlands, into the First Coalition against France.

In the face of such formidable opposition, Dumouriez's triumph was short-lived. Girondin war-planning worked only with difficulty and, by spring 1793, relations between the general and the government were very bad. When his second offensive against the Austrians went wrong at Neerwinden (18 March) Dumouriez tried to persuade his troops to march on Paris. When they refused, he deserted to the enemy. The Coalition then launched a concerted attack, the Spaniards across the Pyrenees, the Piedmontese across the Alps, the Prussians across the Rhine, the Austrians from the Netherlands and Britain from the Channel and the Mediterranean. It was these attacks which the Jacobins faced in the summer and autumn of 1793. Carnot, 'the organiser of victory', concentrated first on the northern threat. The battle of Hondschoote saved Dunkirk from the British, the battle of Wattignies, Maubeuge from the Austrians. The other frontiers were then cleared by the enthusiastic and increasingly efficient republican levies. In 1794 the French armies took the offensive. Victory at Fleurus (June 1794) opened the road again to Brussels. By October the Rhine and the Pyrenees had been crossed. By the end of the year, Holland was occupied. The First Coalition then fell apart. In April 1795 Prussia made peace by the Treaty of Basel, handing over the left bank of the Rhine to the French. A month later, by the Treaty of the Hague, the Dutch changed sides. At the end of 1795 only Austria, Piedmont, and Britain were left to face a nation of considerable military might which, having conducted a determined defence of its borders, now sought to satisfy the appetite for conquest which its recent successes had aroused.

Jemappes : the end of the battle. The defeated Austrians try to escape from the French cavalry across a canal

Chapter 3
Napoleon

In November 1790, Edmund Burke's *Reflections on the French Revolution* were published. He was one of the few Britons to disapprove of the Revolution from its start. He argued that the French, by their whole-hearted attack on so many long-established traditions, were undermining the social fabric of their nation. A few sinister and irresponsible men were leading the swinish multitude towards chaos in the name of reason and liberty. After more violence and bloodshed, he prophesied, a military dictatorship would emerge which would rivet onto the French a despotism more efficient and terrible than anything they had experienced under their kings. This prophecy proved accurate. The military dictator who emerged, just ten years after the Revolution began, was Napoleon Bonaparte.

Early Years

Napoleon was born in 1769, the second son of Charles and Letizia Bonaparte, minor nobility of the disorderly island of Corsica. The islanders, having won their independence from Genoa, had been annexed by the French in 1768 and their leader, Paoli, driven into exile. Napoleon, therefore, was a French citizen by birth. We know little about his childhood except that he was a domineering and troublesome child whose quick wits impressed his first teachers. He also impressed his father who decided that Napoleon, the second son, should be educated for a military career rather than Joseph, the eldest. On the strength of his French nationality and Corsican nobility, he won a French military scholarship to colleges first at Autun and then at Brienne.

Brienne was an important stage in his life. It laid the foundation of his military career and powerfully moulded his character. He was the first Corsican to hold such a scholarship and his Corsican accent and attitudes set him apart from the other pupils. He was also stocky and these characteristics seem to have made him an object of some ridicule. With his teachers, however, he gained a good reputation because of his intelligence and readiness to work hard. His final report read as follows: 'Constitution and health excellent; character, obedient, amenable, honest, and grateful; conduct, perfectly regular; he has throughout distinguished himself by his steady work in mathematics. He knows his history and geography quite well.

Fencing and dancing very poor.' In 1784 he did a course at the École Militaire in one year which usually took two or three and became a lieutenant in the artillery while still in his teens. Until 1792, he divided his time between Auxonne, where he mastered the most modern artillery techniques, and Corsica, where he became deeply involved in political feuds which eventually ended with him and his family being expelled from the island.

He welcomed the Revolution with rapture. The events of 1789 opened up hitherto undreamt of opportunities to restless and ambitious young men such as he. Under the old regime, his relatively humble background would have prevented him rising to the highest position in the French army. Now the sky was the limit. In the struggle between the Girondins and the Jacobins, he backed the Jacobins. He also began to develop a valuable flair for being in the right place at the right time. In 1793 he was in the Toulon area when the British fleet under Admiral Hood sailed in to aid the royalist rebels of this important naval base. The republican artillerymen were either sick or wounded, and being temporarily in command of the artillery he moved and used his guns to such effect that the English were cleared out of the harbour and the royalists forced to surrender. This success won him the friendship of Augustin Robespierre, the brother of Maximilien, and he was marked out for promotion. Even at this early stage, he made no secret of his ambition. As the cynical and experienced General Dugommier observed soon after the Toulon affair: 'Even if his country were to be ungrateful to him, this officer would see to his own advancement.'

The fall of the Jacobins cost him a month in prison in the south of France and then, finding himself unemployed, he made for Paris, assuming rightly that there the best jobs were to be had. He joined the circle of Barras, a political adventurer who had played an active part in the overthrow of the Jacobins and was now a leading figure in the capital. Barras soon needed an artillery expert. The Parisian *sans-culottes*, desperate again because of food shortages, took to the streets against the government. They outnumbered the troops that Barras could muster four to one but Bonaparte's guns were decisive. Brother Joseph received this matter of fact description of a very nasty moment: 'We disposed our troops; the enemy attacked us at the Tuileries. We killed large numbers of them. They killed 30 of our men and wounded 60. We have disarmed the sections and all is quiet. As usual, I haven't a scratch.' In this so-called 'whiff of grapeshot' incident, Napoleon managed to kill more than 300 rioters. His contempt for mob action was henceforth total.

He had also managed to further improve his prospects. The grateful Barras first obtained for him the rank of general and then in 1796 the command of the Army of Italy. He also introduced

Napoleon to his first wife Josephine de Beauharnais, whom he married just forty-eight hours before he left Paris to take up his new command.

The projected Italian campaign of 1796–7 was to be a minor part of a general French offensive against Austria to complete the collapse of the First Coalition and make further gains in the Rhineland. The Army of Italy, 40,000 strong and poorly equipped, was the Cinderella of the French armies. Yet what followed was one of the most successful campaigns in the history of warfare. By the spring of 1797 Europe was uncomfortably aware that a general the equal of Marlborough, Caesar, or even Alexander the Great commanded the French army in Italy. The key to Napoleon's military success was his intelligence and his energy. His studies at Brienne and Auxonne had not been wasted and he put his mastery of new artillery methods to devastating tactical use. He perfected the art of rapid marching and surprise attack. He was also a master of detail who left nothing to chance. His military theory was years in advance of any of his opponents' and, combined with rapid powers of decision and supreme self-confidence, it was irresistible. He was fortunate too in his soldiers, though he complained bitterly about their lack of discipline and equipment. They were very daring. 'They gamble with death with a smile on their lips', he reported back to the Directory. 'Their courage is only equalled by the cheerfulness with which they face forced marches of the hardest kind.' The subordinate commanders, Berthier and Masséna in particular, were of the highest calibre.

When he arrived to take up command, the morale of the Army of Italy was low. A succession of poor commanders had inspired the suspicion that generals from Paris owed their promotion less to ability than to intrigue. Napoleon quickly overcome these feelings. This is how Massena reported his first impressions of the new commander: 'He asked us where our divisions were stationed, how they were equipped, what was the spirit and fighting value of each corps. He gave us our marching orders and announced that tomorrow he would inspect the whole army and the day after tomorrow that it would march and deliver battle against the enemy. He spoke with such dignity, precision and competence that his generals retired with the conviction that at last they had a real leader.'

Their confidence was not misplaced. The Army of Italy marched eastward at the end of March 1796. Within a month the Piedmontese (Piedmont was still part of the First Coalition) were so confused by the rapid marching and savage attacks of the French that they made peace, having lost three battles—Montenotte, Mondovi, and Cherasco—in quick succession. Without delay Bonaparte continued

The French Army campaigning. A typical scene during Napoleon's early campaigns. His soldiers were often a scruffy bunch. The supply wagons in the background are no doubt full of food looted from the surrounding countryside

his advance against the main enemy, Austria. By 3 June he had reached Verona, covering 150 miles in not much more than a month and capturing Milan while doing so. The sheer speed of his advance—the most rapid in the history of warfare before the coming of motor transport—so dumbfounded the Austrians that having been swept off the bridge across the River Adda at Lodi by a heroic frontal attack led by Massena and Berthier, they fell back on their huge fortress of Mantua (see map 3, p. 42).

At this point Napoleon, to his annoyance, was diverted southwards by the Directory to counter British influence in Central Italy. A lightning campaign in June and July brought this area to heel and he returned to Mantua, forcing its surrender in January 1797, having fought off relieving Austrian armies at Castiglione, Arcola, and Rivoli. Again the Directors diverted him southwards and another lightning campaign extracted the favourable Treaty of Tolentino from the Pope. In the late spring of 1797 the French armies marched swiftly across Venetia, up the Isonzo valley and deep into Austrian territory. They met little resistance since the Austrians, now virtually isolated, were resolved on peace. Negotiations began at Leoben in May and were completed at Campo Formio in October 1797. In these negotiations Napoleon showed himself to be more than just a brilliant soldier. His diplomacy was brutally effective. In order that the Austrians should tolerate vast French gains, he offered to compensate the Emperor Francis with Venice, which had remained neutral throughout the war. French troops occupied Venetia and 'liberated' the city from its aristocratic government. Having planted a tree of liberty in the great square of St. Mark and placed a copy of the Declaration of the Rights of Man beneath the paw of the Venetian Lion, the French handed the city over to the Austrian enemy, the leader of the crusade against revolutionary France since 1792! In return, France gained Lombardy and the Austrian Netherlands and was allowed to settle the Rhineland and the rest of Italy as she pleased.

Since France had been clamouring both for glory and peace, Napoleon returned home a national hero. Behind the scenes, however, the Directors were far less pleased. Bonaparte had shown too much independence from the start of the campaign and as he achieved success after success he became less ready to do what his political masters told him. He made little attempt to conceal this reluctance. 'For the moment', he wrote home sharply, 'here in Italy, diplomacy is a business for soldiers'. In the peace negotiations with Austria, he hurried through the preliminaries so that when the official diplomats of the Directory arrived they had to accept accomplished facts. There was little, however, that the Directors could do to discipline the over-powerful general. Their support in the assemblies had been whittled away in election after election. In September 1797, only a *coup d'état* had kept them in power and the general who had carried out the necessary purge of the assemblies had been nominated by Napoleon, himself still absent in Italy. Thus the French government was increasingly dependent on the French army and the star of the army was Bonaparte.

It was with relief, therefore, that the Directors saw him depart for Egypt in 1798. After the humiliation of Piedmont and Austria, only one member of the First Coalition remained to be brought to her knees—Britain. Since war had been declared in 1793, neither side had gained a clear advantage. British attempts to aid the royalists in France from 1793 to 1795 had been defeated, but these defeats had been balanced by naval victories in 1794 (the Glorious First of June) and 1797 (Cape St. Vincent). Britain also survived a serious grain shortage, a financial crisis and, in 1797, naval mutinies at Spithead and the Nore. Napoleon's 1798 plan to defeat Britain was of characteristic imagination and daring. The enemy's strength, he argued, was her Mediterranean and Asiatic commerce. Seize Egypt and at one blow this commerce would be dislocated, and India, the brightest jewel in the British imperial crown, would be within his grasp. Apart from these strategic considerations, Napoleon found the lure of the East irresistible. Had not the Italian campaign shown him to be a second Alexander and had not Alexander's phalanxes trodden the shores of the Indian Ocean? 'This little Europe', he proclaimed, 'is too small a field. Real fame can only be won in the East.'

The morning after the Battle of the Nile. The triumphant British ships surrounded by battered and burning French hulks

The Egyptian expedition sailed from Toulon in May 1798. After eluding the British fleet under the command of Nelson more by luck than judgement and capturing Malta, it landed at Alexandria at the end of June. Conditions were dramatically different from those in Italy. The heat and poverty of the countryside made the march on Cairo desperately hard since the army tried to live off the land. Not surprisingly, there were many casualties. 'Some men', wrote one officer, 'were so tired that they threw away their packs. Some died of thirst, others of hunger and heat; some, seeing the sufferings of their comrades, blew out their brains, others threw themselves into the Nile and perished in the water.' Napoleon, however, was undaunted. Pushing southward down the Nile, he threatened Cairo and brought the Mameluke rulers of Egypt with their famous cavalry to battle in the shadow of the pyramids. It proved to be less a battle than a massacre, the French losing ten men killed as they broke the power of the Mamelukes for ever. A week later, however, Nelson, having chased vainly round the Mediterranean in search of the French fleet, at last tracked it down in Aboukir Bay at the mouth of the Nile. Though it was nearly nightfall when the French fleet was sighted, he attacked without hesitation and by dawn the next morning the French fleet was destroyed. For Napoleon, it was a devastating setback. He was cut off completely from Europe and further major conquests in the East were out of the question. He decided to fight his way northward round the Mediterranean. Palestine and Syria were his first targets but his route was blocked by the city of Acre, surrounded on three sides by the sea and reinforced by the British fleet under Sir Sidney Smith. Here Bonaparte met his first defeat, his assault on 7 May 1799 being repulsed with heavy losses. As he turned his weakened army back towards Egypt, failure brought out a cruel streak in him. 3,000 prisoners were massacred on his orders and those French soldiers so seriously wounded that they seemed unlikely to survive the march were given fatal doses of opium. Once back in Egypt, he abandoned his army and, dodging the British fleets in a flotilla of swift-sailing frigates, got back safely to France.

He returned to a discontented country. The wide-ranging ambitions of France had scared Russia, Sweden, and Turkey into joining Britain and Austria to form the Second Coalition and, during Napoleon's absence in Egypt, the armies of this coalition, led by two excellent generals, the Austrian Archduke Charles in Germany and the Russian Suvorov in Italy, had inflicted heavy defeats on the French—the first since 1793. Inside France, the authority of the Directory, never very strong, had almost disappeared in the atmosphere of defeat. Of the Egyptian expedition, much had been heard about the victory of the Pyramids, little about the defeats at Aboukir Bay and Acre. So Napoleon was as popular as ever. There were a number of plotters working to overthrow the Directory. The most skilful and experienced of these was Siéyès, that 'mole of the revolution' as Robespierre had contemptuously described him, who was still burrowing away in search of the perfect constitution. He was now sure that France needed a single strong man at the centre of government whose power would be held in check by elected assemblies. After considering two other politically minded generals he approached Napoleon and between them they engineered the *coup d'état* of Brumaire (November 1799) which finally overthrew the Directory and made Napoleon First Consul of France.

This *coup d'état* demonstrated more of the Bonaparte luck than of the Bonaparte genius and had its comic moments. In order that power could be seized without bloodshed, the two existing assemblies—the Council of the Ancients and the Council of the 500—had to be persuaded to vote for the new Siéyès-Bonaparte constitution. Because of popular disturbances, both assemblies had moved from Paris to St. Cloud and were there surrounded by Bonaparte's troops. The Ancients gave him no trouble after he had addressed a fierce speech to them insisting on his patriotic duty to save France from the corruption and defeatism that were spreading everywhere. He ended with a clear threat. 'If anyone calls for my outlawry, then the thunderbolt of war will crush him to the earth. Remember that I march hand in hand with the God of War!' The 500, however, were a tougher proposition altogether. 'Down with the dictator', 'Outlaw him', were the cries that greeted him as he entered. In the face of such hostility, the conqueror of the Mamelukes lost his nerve and allowed himself to be driven from the chamber. The *coup d'état* was only saved by the quick wits of his younger brother, Lucien, President of the Chamber on that day. By declaring the debate adjourned, he prevented the deputies from outlawing his brother and then called in the troops to clear the chamber. At 9 p.m. the same evening, the Council of Ancients, with a handful of the 500, declared the five Directors to be replaced by three Consuls, Bonaparte, Siéyès and Ducos. Before long this trio issued a proclamation. 'The Revolution is established upon the principles which began it; it is ended.'

The Consulate

Only force could maintain the new regime and Napoleon controlled the army. Very quickly he made it clear that, as First Consul, he was not going to be anybody's partner. Within a year, he had so manipulated Siéyès' original constitution that he was dictator in all but name. As Siéyès himself pointed out to the Senate, it was a chamber made up increasingly of Bonaparte nominees: 'Gentlemen, you have got a master—a man who knows everything, wants everything and can do everything.' In 1800, few Frenchmen were bothered by the concentration of so much power in the hands of one man. Their experiences since 1789 made them yearn for a strong government at home and an honourable peace abroad. Napoleon seemed to be the best guarantee of both.

During the period of the Consulate (1799–1804) he gave his subjects very much what they wanted. As we shall see later in the chapter, the Consulate proved not only a period of strong government but of remarkably constructive and generally popular reforms true to the spirit of the early years of the Revolution. He was also able to win a more than honourable peace. In 1799 the armies of the Second Coalition were pressing in on the frontiers of France, and to relieve this pressure the First Consul planned a two-pronged offensive, himself attacking along the familiar routes of N. Italy

The Crossing of the St. Bernard: an incident in the campaign against the Austrians which ended at Marengo. The big problem was to get the heavy cannons over the icy pass which was continuously threatened by avalanches

while Moreau should strike across S. Germany. In a confused campaign, he was remarkably lucky. He lost contact with the Austrian army and dispatched part of his forces under Desaix to relieve Massena who was besieged in Genoa. Almost at once, he found himself face to face with a larger Austrian army at Marengo and was on the point of defeat when Desaix, having heard the distant sounds of battle, returned on his own initiative and transformed defeat into brilliant victory (see map 3, p. 42). Desaix, however, was killed on the battlefield and Napoleon at once issued an 'official' and totally inaccurate account of the battle which portrayed the experienced First Consul master-minding a brilliant victory ably served by loyal subordinates, the most courageous, alas, dying in the thick of the fighting. A much more clear-cut victory by Moreau at Hohenlinden brought the Austrians to terms. By the Treaty of Luneville, 1801, France gained the Rhine frontier that she had sought since 1793 but demanded no further territory in Italy. Once again, only Britain remained fighting, but even on her own, she was a formidable enemy. Her navy seized Malta in 1800, sank the Danish fleet at Copenhagen in 1801, to keep the Baltic open to British shipping, and finally secured the surrender of the remnants of the French army in Egypt. There was, however, much war-weariness in Britain and peace negotiations begun in 1801 led to the Peace of Amiens (March 1802) whereby Britain accepted French domination of Western Europe in return for some overseas gains (Ceylon, Trinidad).

Napoleon was now idolized more than ever. A group of friends proposed that he should be made First Consul for life and a plebiscite showed that 3,500,000 of the population agreed with them while only 8,000 did not. In 1804, a plot against his life was discovered which involved *emigré* nobles in Germany. Napoleon retaliated by having the Duke d' Enghien, the leading *emigré* noble in Germany, kidnapped and executed as an example to other would-be plotters, although Enghien had nothing to do with the original conspiracy. Europe was horried, but not so France. In May 1804 the Senate declared Napoleon to be hereditary Emperor of the French. Another plebiscite showed that another vast majority were in favour. The following December, in the presence of Pope Pius VII, standing in a large central space in Notre Dame specially created by destroying two altars and a choir screen, he crowned himself Emperor using an ancient crown reputedly that of Charlemagne (see colour plate facing p. 288).

It is worth pausing here to consider how it was that a Corsican nobody had been able to rise to be Emperor of the French and the terror of all Europe. There is no getting away from the fact that Napoleon was a man of rare ability. He had a mind of exceptional clarity and range which enabled him to understand and solve rapidly any problem whether military, diplomatic, constitutional, or administrative. He also possessed unusual physical and mental energy and a magnetic personality which enabled him to dominate in any situation. To these qualities were added a vast ambition and a self-confidence unfettered by any religious, moral, or philosophical scruples. Nonetheless, able though he was, Fortune helped him greatly. The Revolution occurred just in time to give men of his talent opportunities which their parents had never possessed. He was lucky to be in Toulon in 1793, to meet Barras in 1795, to escape Nelson in the Mediterranean in 1798–9, and to be in Paris again when the Directory was on its last legs. Fortune smiled upon him as it smiled on few others and he came to believe that behind him lay a god of Destiny and that, whatever the odds, he could not fail.

The Empire

The story goes that the great composer Beethoven, who like many young Germans had greeted the French Revolution and the triumph of the young Napoleon with rejoicing and had dedicated his 'Eroica' Symphony to the First Consul, was so infuriated by the news of the imperial coronation that he tore the dedication from the score and replaced it with 'to the memory of a great man'. He was quite justified. 1804 marks an important turning point in Napoleon's career. It was not that he had yet made his greatest conquests. It was rather that before 1804, however ruthless, ambitious, and

cynical he may have been, his actions were, for the most part, in the interests of France, and if one accepted that the French Revolution had more to offer Europe than the old despotism, in the interests of Europe too. So Beethoven and thousands like him believed. The imperial crown was, in contrast, a symbol of personal and family power which suggested privilege and tyranny and insulted the memories of the men of '89 and of the Jacobins. After 1804, the energies of France and Europe were increasingly consumed not to achieve a set of principles, revolutionary or otherwise, but to satisfy the extraordinary personal ambition of Napoleon and the family ambition of the numerous and demanding Bonaparte clan.

In its first years, the Empire went from strength to strength. Just one year and sixteen days after the Peace of Amiens had been signed, Britain and France were at war again. Neither side had fulfilled its part of the peace terms, and so deep was the distrust between the two nations that no real settlement was possible. Napoleon affected to despise the English as 'a nation of shop-keepers', but he realized their power. As Mme. de Stael, an unfriendly critic, noted, the English 'have found the means of being honest as well as successful, a thing which Bonaparte would have us regard as impossible'. The British navy now dominated the sea as the French army dominated the land and, in Nelson, it too had a commander of genius. The Emperor, however, was ready with his master plan. 'The Channel', he declared, 'is a mere ditch and will be crossed as soon as someone has the courage to attempt it.' 'Let us be master of the straits for six hours', he asked his admirals, 'and we shall be masters of the world.' Following the Emperor's instructions, Villeneuve, admiral of the Toulon fleet, was able to dodge Nelson's blockade and lure him away from European waters to the West Indies. He then tried to get back to obtain temporary mastery

The fleet that never sailed. The ships to carry the army across the Channel wait at Boulogne

Austerlitz 1805: Just before his greatest victory Napoleon on the white horse gives his final orders to his marshals

of the Channel so that Napoleon with his Grand Army could make a safe landing on the English coast. Nelson, in the West Indies, guessed what was afoot and got a message back to the Admiralty in London by means of a fast frigate. Villeneuve was headed away from the Channel by Admiral Calder in an apparently indecisive engagement off Cape Finisterre. It was quite decisive for Napoleon who realized that the essential naval escort was not going to get through. Cursing the unfortunate Villeneuve—who was to commit suicide after Nelson had destroyed his combined French and Spanish fleet off Cape Trafalgar in October 1805—Napoleon called off the invasion scheme on 3 September and marched on the Austrians.

In 1803, France's only enemy had been Britain. By 1805, Napoleon's ambitions seemed so vast that Austria and Russia joined the Third Coalition for their own protection (see map 4). They were hit by a thunderbolt. The French army, 172,000 strong, marched eastward in seven great columns from the Channel coast, averaging 15 miles per day. An Austrian army, making its leisurely way to take up defensive positions in Western Bavaria, was surprised, surrounded and forced to surrender with 27,000 men at Ulm. Napoleon at once occupied Vienna and marched north to attack the main Austro-Russian army before the Prussians made up their minds to join the Coalition. On 2 December 1805, his army of 72,000 met 86,000 Austrians and Russians at Austerlitz. Here he

Map 4 Napoleon's Campaigns of 1805–7 and 1809

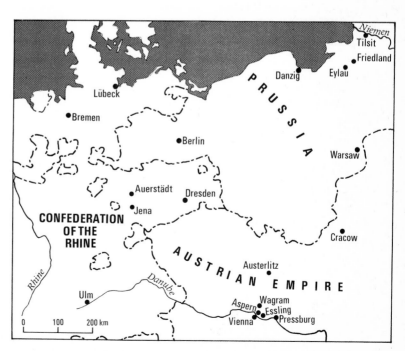

won a textbook victory. As he had foreseen, the enemy tried to outflank him on his right and cut him off from Vienna. As they moved he struck straight at their centre, temporarily weakened by the flanking move, and cut it in two. Over 20,000 of the enemy were killed against only 900 Frenchmen. While Alexander retreated tearfully towards Russia, Francis of Austria had peace terms dictated to him at Pressburg. Austria lost all her remaining Italian lands and some too in Germany. Napoleon then reorganized the western half of Germany into the Confederation of the Rhine. Francis of Austria declared the Holy Roman Empire to be ended and the Confederation recognized Napoleon as its Protector. This was too much for Prussia, which had previously hesitated from joining the Coalition against France. Absurdly over-confident, the Prussian armies marched without waiting for their Russian allies and, on the same day, 14 October 1806, one was destroyed by Napoleon at Jena and another by Davout at Auerstadt. Napoleon then chased after the Russians. In February 1807 they fought him to a standstill at Eylau in East Prussia and withdrew in good order. In May, however, they were completely defeated at Friedland and Alexander too sought peace. By the Treaty of Tilsit signed in July 1807 after secret negotiations between the two Emperors on a raft moored in the River Niemen, Europe was virtually partitioned between France and Russia, with France grabbing much the greater share. Russia was to take Finland from Sweden and part of Prussian Poland. The rest of Prussian Poland became the Grand Duchy of Warsaw, the Prussian provinces on the Rhine the Kingdom of Westphalia, both these areas under French rule. Prussia in fact lost a third of her territory with about half her population. Tilsit suitably completed the most successful of Napoleon's campaigns. In less than two years, he had broken the three most powerful military nations in Europe. As a result, he was master of more of the continent than any ruler since the Roman Emperors. He was only thirty-eight (see map 5).

Less than eight years later, however, he was the life-prisoner of the British on the isolated granite island of St. Helena, 5,000 miles from Europe. His fall was even more dramatic than his rise. Although Tilsit marks the height of his power, some of the seeds of disaster had already been sown. After the failure of his 1805 invasion scheme, Napoleon had resolved to blockade Britain into surrender. Two sets of decrees, the first issued from Berlin in 1806, the second from Milan in 1807, set up the Continental System, the aim of which was to prevent any part of Europe importing British goods. Such a ban, he argued, would so disrupt British industry that the government would have to make peace. As he put it to his brother Louis, 'I mean to conquer the sea by the land'. The scheme, however, backfired. Britain did suffer, particularly in 1811,

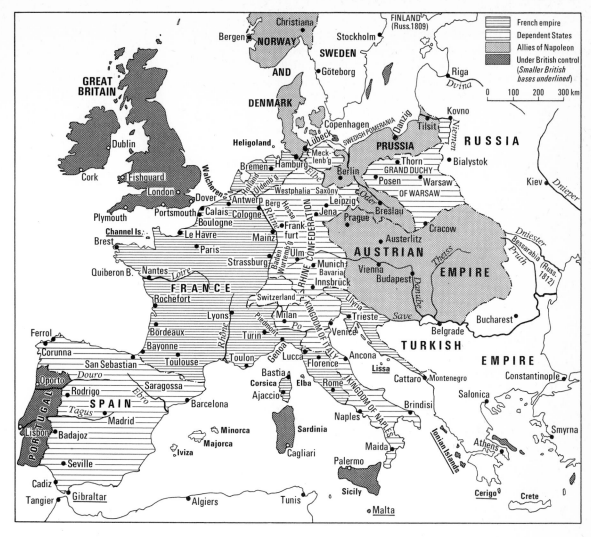

Map key:
- French empire
- Dependent States
- Allies of Napoleon
- Under British control (*Smaller British bases underlined*)

0   100   200   300 km

Map 5 Europe after Tilsit

Tilsit 1807 : in the privacy of tents moored in the middle of the River Niemen, Napoleon and Alexander of Russia divide up Europe between them

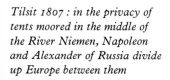

but managed to develop new markets outside Europe. The System also had the effect of causing a serious economic depression in Europe which affected the French as badly as anyone. Those nations with traditional trading links with Britain—Portugal, Belgium, Holland, and the Baltic States—had to be continually bullied to keep the System going. There was an enormous amount of smuggling. The French army continued to march in British boots and the Emperor was eventually forced to issue licences to trade with Britain in order to raise much needed money! The overall result was to lose support for France in areas of Europe where previously she had been popular.

The need to make the Continental System effective took the French into Spain and Portugal—with disastrous results. In 1808 Napoleon decided that the quarrelsome and incompetent royal family of Spain could be replaced by his brother Joseph. At Bayonne, King Charles and Prince Ferdinand were persuaded, by a mixture of bribes and threats, to give up their positions, and Joseph was despatched to Madrid. The government of the Spanish Bourbons had been so bad that Napoleon assumed that the Spanish would immediately welcome a Bonaparte king. He was quite wrong, as Joseph soon found to his cost. 'The fact is', he wrote back to his brother, 'not a single Spaniard is on my side, except the few who are travelling with me.' The Spanish were outraged by the treatment handed out to their ancient royal family by the upstart Bonapartes and revolts against Joseph broke out all over the country. On 22 July 1808, the first clear defeat of a French army since Napoleon became First Consul occurred at Baylen when Dupont was forced to surrender with 18,000 men. The Emperor refused, however, to accept that there were any serious problems in Spain. 'Nothing was

A British view of the Continental System. The caption of this cartoon of 1807 was 'The Giant Commerce overwhelming the Pigmy Blockade!!'

The War in Spain portrayed in all its horror by the Spanish painter Goya. Here French soldiers massacre Spaniards 'with or without reason'

ever so stupid, inept or cowardly', he fumed on hearing the Baylen news, and crossed the Pyrenees himself to put matters right. In a lightning campaign, he destroyed the Spanish regular armies, drove a small British force under Sir John Moore in headlong retreat to Corunna and returned to Paris convinced that Spain was settled. He was wrong again. The Spanish took to guerrilla tactics in a country particularly suited to this type of warfare. A small British army based on Lisbon and commanded by Sir Arthur Wellesley, the future Duke of Wellington, refused to be driven into the sea and, after 1810, probed more and more persistently into Spain (see map 6a, p. 60). From 1809 onwards, Napoleon was in desperate need for soldiers to fight in other parts of Europe, yet about 250,000 French troops were tied down in a vicious and unwinnable war south of the Pyrenees. This was 'the Spanish Ulcer' which, as Napoleon later acknowledged, drained away so much of his Empire's strength. (See above.)

The news of Baylen echoed round Europe. 'It is clear', wrote a Prussian minister, 'that luck is leaving Bonaparte and that his frightful career has reached its zenith. Europe can be saved through

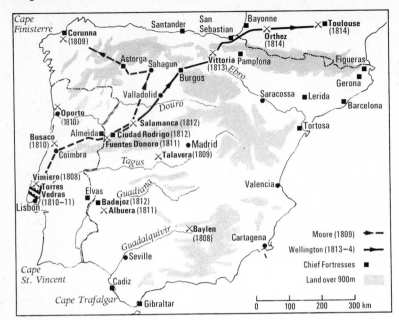

Spain, if Europe still has the courage and determination to save itself.' The Austrians, eager to avenge the humiliation of Austerlitz, declared war again in 1809. The Archduke Charles badly mauled the French at Aspern but was defeated at Wagram (see map 4, p. 55). The Emperor Francis, without allies, had to seek peace. By the Treaty of Schonbrunn he had to cede further lands to the French. He also agreed that his daughter Marie Louise should become Napoleon's second wife, replacing the childless Josephine whom he had coldly divorced. As one commentator of the time brutally put it, 'The Austrian heifer is sacrificed to the Minotaur.' The Austrians, however, were not unduly dispirited. The 1809 campaign had shown the French armies and their general to be much less terrifying than before. Let by the wily Count Metternich, they bided their time.

Metternich had been Austrian ambassador in Paris and had studied the Emperor carefully. Napoleon, he decided, was a gambler who could not resist staking everything on a final throw. That throw was made in 1812 and the prize was Russia. At Tilsit, Napoleon had mesmerized Tsar Alexander by the force of his personality but later Franco-Russian relations deteriorated. In Poland, Turkey, and Sweden the interests of the two countries were in conflict and Alexander tended increasingly to ignore the Continental System. In June 1812 Napoleon lost patience and declared war, proclaiming, 'I have come to finish off once and for all the colossus of the barbarian north.' Though he was well aware of the immensity of his task, of the size of the country and the harshness

Map 6b The Russian Campaign

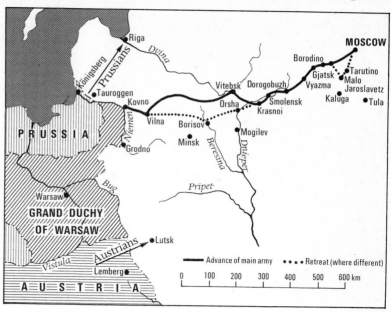

of the Russian climate, of the toughness of the Russian armies and of the real possibility of revolts in Europe during his absence, he did not doubt that he would succeed. His huge army of 600,000 men would defeat the Russians in a series of conclusive victories and Alexander would be forced to make peace long before summer turned to autumn. Things turned out very differently. His army was great only in numbers. Less than half of it was French and it proved raw, indisciplined, and prone to desertion. It was so big, moreover, that the Russians, greatly outnumbered, had no option but to retreat and avoid the open battle which Napoleon so desired. Both armies stumbled deeper and deeper into Russia (see map 6b). Surely, the French asked themselves, the Russians would make a stand at Vilna? Vilna was occupied without a struggle. At Vitebsk? Vitebsk was deserted when the French rode in. At historic Smolensk? The Russian rearguard slipped out of the burnt-out shell of Smolensk just in time to avoid capture by the encircling French. The whole advance was marked by uncharacteristic dithering by Napoleon and by incompetence among his marshals. It was now mid-August and the Emperor's Chiefs of Staff urged him to turn home without delay. The Grand Army had been reduced by death and desertion to less than 200,000 and a clear-cut victory before the onset of winter seemed less and less likely. Napoleon, however, was convinced that the Russians must defend Moscow, less than 200 miles away. The capture of Moscow must bring Alexander to terms. So the advance east continued. At last,

on the banks of the River Moskova, with the village of Borodino in the centre of their line, the Russians stood to defend their capital. In the bloodiest battle he had ever fought, Napoleon just managed to drive them from their position and continue their retreat but at the cost of 32,000 French casualties. On 14 September the French entered Moscow. It too was empty and before long in flames—lit perhaps on the orders of the retreating Russian governor. Still no word came from Alexander in St. Petersburg and on 19 October Napoleon finally brought himself to retreat.

He had waited too long. Fresh Russian armies barred the southern route home and the French were forced back on the route that had been devastated on the march east. Though the rest of October was quite mild, and November too, the lack of food and constant harrassment of the Cossacks made the retreat a nightmare from the start. Only the famous Imperial Guard held the French army together. As one Russian observer put it, 'the Guard with Napoleon passed through our Cossacks like a 100-gun ship through a fishing-fleet.' With December came really terrible cold with frosts of 30 degrees. What was left of the army became a desperate rabble. On 6 December Napoleon hurried away by coach for Paris and, eight days later, Marshal Ney, whose heroic leadership of the rearguard won him the title 'the bravest of the brave', crossed

The Retreat from Moscow: the Emperor's sledge is surrounded by demoralized troops. On the left some soldiers have made a fire, in the centre others carve up a horse to cook and eat. The ground is littered with men dead or dying from cold and on the right a dead man is being stripped of all his clothes

the Niemen with less than a sixteenth of the original army. 'General Famine and General Winter', wrote Ney to his wife, 'rather than Russian bullets, have conquered the Grand Army.' What he might have added, but did not because he was very loyal and rather stupid, was General Bonaparte's terrible over-confidence and mis-calculations.

Before long, a Fourth Coalition of European states was formed to follow up this remarkable Russian victory. It was a formidable alliance. Britain controlled the seas and had a fine army operating in the Spanish Peninsula. The Russians had a huge army and the knowledge that they could outfight the French. Austria was more than ready to fight again, and a reformed and revitalized Prussia was thirsting to avenge the terrible defeat of Jena. Other minor European states joined the Big Four, and for almost the first time since the French Revolution the ordinary people, sick of the constant demands made upon them by French conscription-officers and tax-collectors, backed the despotic monarchs against the French.

Napoleon, however, remained astonishingly optimistic. Refusing to negotiate, he raised yet another army and fought to hold onto Germany. He was victorious at Dresden but, nearly encircled at Leipzig, was only able to extricate himself with half his army, leaving 60,000 to surrender. As he fell back towards Paris, fighting a brilliant defensive action, Wellington, with the British army, crossed the Pyrenees and advanced on Toulouse. The French, unused to fighting within their own borders and worn out by the Emperor's insatiable demands for more men and more money, had had enough. As Allied troops neared Paris his ministers and marshals deserted him and on 6 April 1814 he abdicated.

The victorious allies enter Paris in triumph in 1814

The Hundred Days : Napoleon is greeted by the citizens of Grenoble with tremendous enthusiasm

The Hundred Days

Europe heaved a sigh of relief—but prematurely. There was one further remarkable episode in the life of this extraordinary man before the continent was really rid of him. While the victorious Coalition met at Vienna to sort out post-Napoleonic Europe, and Louis XVIII, the brother of Louis XVI who had entered France with the Coalition armies, tried to re-establish royal authority, Napoleon was given the Mediterranean island of Elba to keep him happy in his enforced retirement. This was Tsar Alexander's idea and not a good one. Ten months after his abdication, Napoleon slipped away from Elba with a handful of followers and landed on the south coast of France.

The period known as 'the 100 days' had begun. When he started his march north, he had less than a thousand men, but the Bourbon regime crumbled before him. 'Kill your Emperor if you wish', he said, and advanced unarmed in his familiar grey coat towards the battalion barring his entrance into Grenoble. 'Vive l'Empereur' they cried and joined his march. Marshal Ney, having cheerfully told Louis XVIII that he would bring Napoleon back to Paris in a cage, went back to his old commander after an emotional meeting at Lyons. (This action was to cost him his life.) Louis hurriedly fled from the capital and on 20 March Napoleon was carried up the steps of the Tuileries Palace by a vast and cheering crowd.

Since the armies of the Coalition had not disbanded, his chances of survival were very slim. His best hope lay in winning a quick victory at the expense of one of the armies before he was encircled by overwhelming numbers. He therefore marched on Brussels with an army of 130,000 men, aiming to defeat the British and Prussians before they could be reinforced by the Russians and Austrians. He nearly did. While Ney and Wellington fought each other to a standstill at Quatre Bras, Napoleon savaged the Prussians at Ligny. Both the British and Prussians fell back towards Brussels, but Napoleon fatally miscalculated the direction of the Prussian retreat and sent 20,000 men on a wild-goose chase after them. With a depleted army, he prepared to attack Wellington who had taken up a strong position near the village of Waterloo, defending the main road to Brussels. As usual, he was very confident. 'I tell you that Wellington is a bad general, that the English are bad troops and that it will be a picnic', he declared as he prepared his offensive. It proved to be a bitterly contested battle. 'The most desperate business I ever was in and never was so near being beat' is how Wellington put it.

The British just managed to repulse wave after wave of French attacks and were about to counter-attack themselves when the Prussians arrived in the late afternoon. Then the French were routed and Napoleon, finding on his return to Paris that support had melted away, placed himself at the mercy of the British. The last six years of his life were spent in failing health on St. Helena with a small band of faithful retainers, writing his Memoirs and quarrelling with the island's governor.

Napoleon: *For and Against*

For France, the consequences of Napoleon's sixteen years of power were very mixed. During the Consulate (1799–1804) he did much that was to the lasting benefit of the French people. During this period, under his direction, a series of major reforms were carried out. After 1800 some of the financial problems which had haunted France throughout the eighteenth century were solved by the creation of the Bank of France which strictly controlled the issue of money, established a sound currency and helped to give the country much-needed financial stability. The local government system, established by the Constituent Assembly in 1790, was modified in that elected councils were replaced by prefects for the departments, sub-prefects for the district and mayors for the communes, all appointed by the government. This system proved so durable that it is still in existence.

French education was transformed. An educated nation, Napoleon believed, was a strong nation. Forty-five *lycées* or secondary schools with 6,400 places were financed by state scholarships and, by 1813, 6,000 former pupils from the *lycées* were studying at the Imperial University. The *lycées* and the university were specially designed for future leaders and the curriculum strictly controlled by a Director of Public Instruction. 'Till children are taught whether they ought to be Republicans or

After Waterloo. Napoleon surrendered to the British and was taken across the Channel aboard H.M.S. Bellerophon before being transferred to another ship for the long voyage to St. Helena

Monarchists or Catholics or Unbelievers', wrote Napoleon, 'there may indeed be a state but it cannot become a nation.' Female education was, in contrast, a matter of little importance. 'We ask not that girls should think,' he commented, 'but that they should believe.' Their education was left to the religious orders.

Napoleon himself was not religious. He was convinced, however, that the ordinary man needed religion and that no ruler could afford to ignore the religion of his subjects if he wished to maintain social order. 'If I were governing Jews', he said, 'I should restore the Temple of Solomon.' Since he was governing Catholics, he worked hard to improve relations with the Papacy. The result was the Concordat of 1801, a diplomatic triumph for Napoleon since Pope Pius VII, in return for Catholicism being recognized as 'the religion of the great majority of the citizens', accepted the essentials of the Civil Constitution of the Clergy. Though religious problems continued to plague France throughout the nineteenth century, the Concordat survived until 1905.

The most impressive of the reforms, however, was the Civil Code which laid down precisely and systematically the legal rights and duties of every French citizien. It was the work of a skilled committee of professional lawyers building on foundations laid by the Constituent Assembly and urged on by the dynamic First Consul. When it was completed Napoleon said that he was prouder of it than of all his forty military victories. It was followed by Criminal and Commercial Codes which were inspired by the same kind of rational and orderly thinking which made French law and administration the envy of Europe.

There is no denying that Napoleon did much for France, but not without heavy cost. If he was a brilliant administrator, he was also a vindictive autocrat with a vulgar streak. The Empire was maintained by an extensive system of spies and informers presided over by Fouché, the brutal Minister of Police. Press censorship was complete and opponents of the government were continually harassed. Such tyrannical methods upset many Frenchmen, so did Napoleon's creation of the Legion of Honour, and of the Imperial Court with Imperial honours. Another source of criticism, both inside and outside France, was the way Napoleon advanced his own family. The Bonapartes were a greedy and difficult bunch and caused him much exasperation. 'From the way they talk', he once exploded, 'you'd think that I'd mismanaged my father's inheritance.' In fact he looked after them well. Joseph became King, first of Naples, then of Spain. Louis became King of Holland and Jerome King of Westphalia. All his sisters married into the best European aristocracy and his stepson, Eugène de Beauharnais, became Viceroy of Italy. Apart from Eugène, they were not worth the trouble and cost him much support.

Altogether, the Empire was a tawdry and often ludicrous affair, and in its last years the Emperor was obviously not the man he had been. Even before 1805, he had suffered two nervous crises brought on by overwork. It seems that his exceptional nervous vitality burnt him out and he aged early. After 1805 he put on weight and found it less easy to do without sleep. After his return from Moscow, those who knew him well found that he no longer possessed his former capacity for work and for decisions.

Yet he could never admit that even to himself. His ambitions, far from declining, grew ever more colossal. 'God', he told the Spaniards, 'has given me the will and the force to overcome all obstacles', and he believed it. As early as 1806 his Minister of Marine, Decrès, had noted privately, 'The Emperor is mad and will destroy us all'. At a conservative estimate, his wars killed or maimed a million Frenchmen and rather more than a million non-Frenchmen. Perhaps his most appropriate epitaph was written by another great French general, Marshal Foch: 'Napoleon forgot that a man cannot be God; that above the individual is the nation, and above mankind the moral law; he forgot that war is not the highest aim, for peace is above war.'

Chapter 4
Economic Revolution

'Whereas in France, the hurricane of revolution swept the country, there passed through England a quieter, but no less powerful upheaval. The sleepy evolution of the period of manufacture was turned into a veritable "storm and stress" period of production.' So wrote Frederick Engels, son of a German cotton-manufacturer and one of the earliest students of industrial conditions in England. He was describing the second, economic part of the double revolution which began to transform European life in the last twenty years of the eighteenth century.

The importance of this economic revolution is hard to exaggerate. It changed the face of Britain by 1800, of most of Europe and the U.S.A. by 1900. It helped to make these areas the economic and, to a large extent, the political masters of the world. By World War I, it had radically altered the way of life and habits of thought of most sections of European society. What is more, the speed of economic and social change begun by this economic revolution has never slackened. Rather it has accelerated, and the society of which we are part is the consequence and continuation of this unending process of accelerating change.

The economic events of the late eighteenth century and nineteenth century in Europe deserve the title 'revolution' because, in this period, for the first time in human history, what some economists refer to as 'the takeoff into self-sustained growth' took place. By this they mean that first in Britain and then elsewhere, an industrial economy developed which caused a rapid and sustained increase in the wealth of these areas and a growing mastery of the natural world. As the nineteenth century passed, more and more of the inhabitants of these advanced economies were taken away from the fear of famine and real poverty which had been their lot from the beginning of time (and remains so still for two-thirds of the world's population). It is only since this economic revolution that most Europeans have come to assume that if they do not find themselves growing better off year by year, something has gone wrong.

There were a number of important characteristics of this self-sustaining and expanding economy. The key industries were manufacturing ones which made use of raw materials from home and abroad and were capable of selling their manufactured articles—clothing, shoes, cannon, locomotives for instance—the world over. Production on an international scale was made increasingly possible by the development of a factory-based instead of a cottage-based system of production, powered by machines instead of by hand. Since factories had to be built and machinery installed before profitable production could begin, individuals with money (capital) to spare, and the readiness to lend it to businessmen over a period of years, were a vital factor. In the early years of the Industrial Revolution in Britain, the new industrial companies were usually owned and financed by a small group of partners with their own capital invested in the business. As time passed, however, new industrial companies both in Europe and Britain took the form of joint-stock companies which raised money for their enterprises by offering shares in their company in return for loans from the general public. Since governments and local authorities showed themselves ready to follow the same financial procedures both to raise money for their own needs and to encourage those industries vital to the national economy, what is best described as a 'capitalist' economy spread through Europe as a result of this revolution. Companies were able to secure the necessary capital by promising to pay interest in proportion to the amount lent out of the profits that they expected to make. More and more of the European public came to buy shares in industrial companies and to receive regular dividends (payments of interest) for their shares. Stock exchanges where company shares are bought and sold, became central features of European business life. Since individuals with money to spare

The London Stock Exchange: the hub of the capitalist world in the nineteenth century

and the readiness to invest their money carefully for future dividends tended to be middle-class—professional men, shopkeepers,
other men of business—and since their thrift and energy inspired
the economic revolution and its capitalist structure, it was the
middle classes, at least to begin with, that this revolution rewarded
both with wealth and with political power.

Though there has been much debate over when exactly the
Industrial Revolution in Britain began, the production figures of
the major sectors of the economy indicate that the decade 1780–90
marks the vital period of 'take-off into self-sustained growth'. The
question why this revolution began in Britain has also caused
considerable discussion. Perhaps Britain's most useful advantage
over her competitors was the worldwide trade and commerce she
had developed in the seventeenth and eighteenth centuries. At the
end of the seventeenth century, Britain had overtaken Holland as
the major commercial power of Europe. During the eighteenth
century, she had successfully beaten off a powerful challenge from
France. This commercial power ensured that in the crucial era of
'take-off' there was plenty of capital available in Britain for industrial investment. It also meant that the British government and
ruling classes were more interested than their continental counterparts in the possibilities of making money by careful investment
and the use of new methods and new machines. There was also
little of the aristocratic snobbery against men who made money
rather than inherited it which was particularly characteristic of
France. As Count Chaptal, a scientist and businessman as well as an
aristocrat, put it in 1819, 'the stupid prejudice which forbids the
French nobility to engage in commerce and relegates the individual
involved in industry to a lower class, has contributed not a little to
arrest the progress of public fortune.' Moreover, in the Stock
Exchange, the Bank of England and the private banks in London
and in the provinces, Britain possessed the financial institutions
necessary for rapid economic advance. The French, in contrast,
were without a national bank until 1800 and regarded joint-stock
companies with grave distrust until well into the nineteenth
century. Britain was also fortunate in that by accidents of geography
and history both the vital raw materials for manufacture and
extensive markets for manufactured goods were easily available.
For instance, the infamous but highly profitable slave trade had
established close links between the ports of Liverpool and Bristol
and the cotton plantations of the U.S.A. These links led directly
to the growth of much the most important manufacturing industry of Britain in the nineteenth century, the cotton industry
of Lancashire. The British trading empire also provided ready
markets for her manufactured goods. India and South America
quickly became major purchasers of British textiles.

18th Century Liverpool: a town which grew rich on the slave trade

In Britain itself coal, the vital source of energy in the first phase of the economic revolution, and iron, the vital metal for the new machines, were easily available. As for the vital machines—the steam engines, the power-looms, the blast furnaces—there were enough British engineers with the inventiveness either to adapt old machines to new needs or to devise new machines. In 1765, for instance, James Watt adapted Newcomen's steam pumping engine by the addition of a separate condenser. The efficiency of the pump was thus radically improved. By further ingenious adaptations, he was able to produce in 1783 an engine which, instead of merely pumping, developed a rotary action and could be used to drive a whole range of machines both stationary and moving. There were also great technical improvements in the British iron industry. Early in the eighteenth century, Darby discovered how iron ore might be smelted with coke rather than with charcoal. The industry, therefore, was freed from its dependence on charcoal which was in increasingly short supply as the English forests disappeared. The Darby process was improved by Smeaton in the 1760s, and in the 1780s Cort's 'puddling' process made available a wrought iron of unprecedented purity.

In the textile industry, a succession of inventions pointed the way towards revolutionary changes in production. Kay's flying shuttle, a gadget attached to the traditional handloom which enabled the weaver to work much faster than before, appeared in 1733. By speeding up the weaving process, it immediately encouraged a search for quicker methods of spinning the yarn that the weavers used. Hargreave's' 'Spinning Jenny' (1764) which enabled one spinner to work a number of spindles, radically speeded up the spinning process which was further mechanized by Arkwright's 'Water Frame' (1775) and Crompton's 'Mule' (1779). Cartwright's power-loom which mechanized the more complex weaving process first appeared in 1784 and, after many modifications, began to be widely introduced into the textile mills during the Napoleonic wars.

The interesting thing about these inventions is that, important though they were, they were the result of ingenuity rather than careful experiment, of craftsmanship more than scientific skill. In 1800 the French were ahead of the British in science and mathematics and no less inventive. The Jacquard silk loom (1804) for instance was a more sophisticated piece of machinery than anything produced at that time in Britain and it was a Frenchman, Carnot, who in the 1820s worked out the scientific explanation of the working of steam engines. Furthermore, throughout the nineteenth century, both the French and the Germans could fairly claim that their scientific and technical education was better than its British equivalent. As a German visitor noted in 1839: 'it cannot but amaze us that a country in which the manufacturing tendencies are predominant, and hence the need to familiarize the people with the sciences and arts which advance these pursuits is evident, the absence of these subjects in the curriculum of youthful education is hardly noticed. It is equally astonishing how much is nonetheless achieved by men lacking any formal education for their professions.' It was not so much that brilliant inventions created new industrial situations but rather that new industrial situations demanded and eventually obtained new machines.

The nature of the British population in the late eighteenth century also contributed to the rapid development of British industry. In the first place it was growing faster than ever before. In 1700 there were about 7,000,000 people in England and Wales. In 1801 there were 9,000,000, in 1831 14,000,000 and in 1851 18,000,000. Secondly, agricultural developments had created landless wage-labourers no longer tied to the land like the Western European peasant or the Eastern European serf. The mass of the British population, landless and increasing, was quicker to move to the manufacturing towns and villages where new jobs were to be had, and the urbanization of Britain proceeded faster and farther than anywhere else in the world in the nineteenth century.

For these reasons industrial development in Britain raced far ahead of the rest of Europe and the world in the first phase of the economic revolution. Exact statistics are hard to come by but in

1830 it would seem that Britain was mining 75 per cent of the continent's coal and manufacturing more than 50 per cent of its cotton goods. In 1860, she was producing 54 per cent of the world's iron and steel. Simultaneously the volume of her trade and commerce rocketed upwards. In 1830 the value of British exports was double the value of the French, which were the next most valuable, although the British population was still appreciably smaller. The title 'the workshop of the world' was fully justified.

This economic revolution, however, proved infectious and, in fits and starts, spread eastwards across the continent. By 1914 only a few wild and primitive areas—parts of Ireland, Spain, Southern Italy and the Balkans for example—remained unaffected by its consequences, and Britain's industrial supremacy was being successfully challenged.

Belgium was the first European country to follow Britain with whom, economically, she had much in common. In 1819, J. C. Symons, an Englishman investigating the state of industry in Europe, noted that 'Belgium from her mineral riches and other topographical facilities, naturally takes the lead in the progress of Continental machinery.' The port of Antwerp was a great international trading centre, and in the valleys of the Sambre and Meuse lay extensive coal deposits. One effect of the Continental System was to stimulate certain Belgian manufacturers to fill the gaps caused by the ban on British exports. The cotton industry of Ghent and the engineering industry of Liège for instance did well out of the Napoleonic wars. After independence had been won from the Dutch in 1830, the Belgian economy expanded fast. Coal production trebled from 2 million tons in 1830 to 6 million in 1850. The number of steam engines employed in industry doubled from 354 in 1830 to 712 in 1838 and almost trebled again to about 2,300 in 1850. An ambitious network of state railways centred on Brussels was constructed in the 1830s and 1840s.

Elsewhere in Europe, industrialization was very patchy before 1840. Certain areas—northern France with textiles, coal, and iron, the Prussian Rhineland with the Ruhr coalfield, and textiles at Elberfeld-Barmen, Habsburg Bohemia with the iron industry at Vitkovice—stood like industrial islands in an agricultural lake (see map 7, p. 79).

The most important single factor in the spread of industry in the next half-century was the building of railways. They provided the speedy and reliable communication over long distances without which the rapid expansion of large-scale manufacturing industries was impossible. They also demanded big powerful steam locomotives and thousands of miles of iron track, thus giving further encouragement to the key industries of the new economy. In

Stephenson's Rocket : victor in the famous Rainhill locomotive trials in 1829

Britain—an island whose major cities were never more than seventy miles from the sea and whose gentle geography had encouraged the construction of a network of canals at the end of the eighteenth century—the need for a new form of transport was not as urgent as on the Continent, and railways were not built until the industrial revolution was well advanced in this country. Nonetheless, it was British engineers who pioneered railway development throughout the world. In a number of British collieries mobile steam engines or locomotives running along rails were being used in the early nineteenth century to haul coal-trucks. The most efficient of these locomotives were those of George Stephenson of Newcastle on Tyne. They were used for the first passenger railway opened between Stockton and Darlington in 1825 and for the much more important line opened between Liverpool and Manchester in 1830, itself a major engineering achievement.

Olive Mount cutting on the Liverpool-Manchester line in 1830

The new machine, unlike any other, captured the imagination of the age. It enabled man to move for the first time faster than any other animal and with its power, noise, and steam, it perfectly symbolized the new industry. Investors all over Europe hastened to put their savings into railway shares, to such an extent indeed that the term 'railway mania' has often been used to describe the two earliest periods of speculation in railway shares in 1835–7 and 1845–7. Though they did not turn out to be a particularly good investment—capital invested in railways in the British Isles was returning only $3\frac{1}{2}$ per cent in 1855—the railways got built. The first French line opened in 1832, the first German in 1835, the first Russian in 1838 and the first Italian in 1839. These were novelties and very short. Major lines quickly followed. The Brussels-Antwerp line, the first of the ambitious Belgian network, was begun in 1836. The following year, the seventy-mile line joining Leipzig and

Dresden in Germany was constructed. Once their economic value was established, European governments were prepared to give them their backing. The Belgian railways were state-controlled from the first; the French state-aided from the 1840s. In 1840, there were 1,800 miles of track in Europe, by 1870, 65,000, and by 1910, when the continental network was virtually complete outside Russia, 172,000 miles. In 1871 the Alps were pierced for the first time by the Mt. Cenis tunnel. In 1888 it became possible to travel from Calais to Constantinople by train, and in 1904 the Trans-Siberian railway was completed. As mileages lengthened, even higher standards of speed, reliability and comfort were set. Sleeping cars appeared in the 1870s, luxury transcontinental expresses in the 1880s and refrigeration cars in the 1890s. It is hard to exaggerate the significance of this new means of transport. Not only were raw materials and manufactured goods sped to their destination and the whole tempo of industrial life accelerated, but distances became less and less an obstacle between men. In 1800 the fastest mail-coach from London to Edinburgh took the best part of 4 days. In 1870 the rail time was down to 12 hours. In 1835, the average day's journey of the German mail coaches was about 28 miles, a distance which the new locomotives could cover in an hour. In the last thirty years of the nineteenth century, ocean transport was also transformed, as wooden sailing ships were finally superseded for carrying both goods and passengers by iron or steel steam ships.

From the technical point of view, the European economic revolution entered a second phase between 1840 and 1870. The age of iron and steam gave way to the age of steel and electricity. Though steel techniques had been improved during the eighteenth century, particularly by Huntsman of Sheffield, production remained very expensive. In 1856, however, Bessemer, son of a Frenchman who had settled in England, perfected a new process which made steel production much cheaper. There was one snag with this process however. It could not cope with phosphoric ore, the type of ore most easily available. Only in 1878 was a way of purifying phosphoric ore discovered through the research work of S. Gilchrist Thomas, a London clerk who studied metallurgy at evening classes, and of his chemist cousin P. C. Gilchrist. Since the British steel industry had made a massive investment in the Bessemer process immediately after 1856, few steelmasters were interested in installing the improved Gilchrist-Thomas method. On the continent, however, where investment in the steel industry came later, the Gilchrist-Thomas process gave a great boost to steel production, particularly in Germany.

The electric dynamo was perfected in 1866 by the veteran German inventor Werner Siemens (see p. 83). Its importance lay in its ability

Above *The Toulouse-Paris express in 1912*

Right *A dining saloon on a French luxury express in the late nineteenth century*

to harness the energy of electricity for industrial and domestic purposes. Electric traction began to replace steam traction and electric lighting to replace gas lighting, especially after the American, Edison, had developed the incandescent filament lamp. In 1884 Sir

Charles Parsons patented the high-speed turbine and dynamo and, also in the 1880s, the Croatian, Tesla, who worked in Vienna and Prague before emigrating to the U.S.A., perfected the means of transmitting electrical current from a central power-plant throughout a given area, thus making possible the public and private use of electricity which today we take for granted.

The Industrial and Commercial expansion of Germany: Borsig's locomotive works in Berlin in the late nineteenth century

The European state which made the greatest use of these new technical developments was Germany. Before 1850 her industrialization had been limited to a few areas like the Ruhr and Silesian coalfields. Progress had been hindered by lack of capital, an inadequate transport system and political disunity. In 1818, however, Prussia, after Austria the most powerful member of the German Confederation, began reforming her economy. An efficient system of roads was constructed, and internal customs duties abolished. At the same time, a customs union, or *Zollverein*, was begun with neighbouring members of the Confederation. By

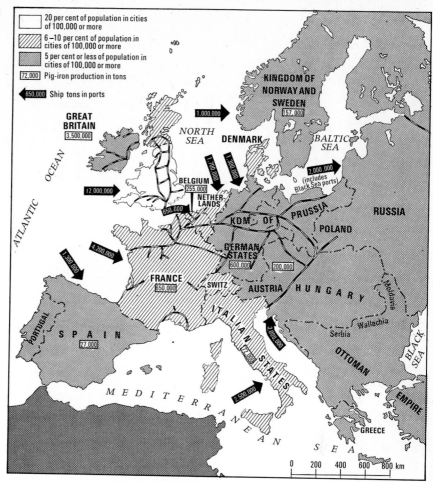

Map 7 The Industrialization of Europe in 1850

1834 the *Zollverein* included 23,500,000 people and stretched across northern and central Germany. It provided the economic base not only for the industrialization of Germany but also its political unification under Prussian leadership. Railway building began in earnest in the 1840s and continued hectically through the 1850s and 1860s. By 1870 the essential financial institutions for industrial growth—national and provincial banks, joint-stock companies—had been created and, with the completion of political unity in 1871, all was set for economic take-off. Between 1871 and 1913 German coal production multiplied more than seven times, from 38,000,000 tons to 279,000,000. Between 1880 and 1910 her steel production multiplied twenty times. By 1900 German electrical engineering was the most advanced in Europe and her chemical industry the world leader. Between 80 and 90 per cent of the world's dyes, for instance, were German-made at the beginning of the twentieth century. Between 1890 and 1914 German exports

The Paris Bourse in the 1860's. French commerce is booming

expanded 300 per cent. Her education and science were better organized to serve the needs of industry than anywhere else in the world, and with the emergence of huge 'cartels', or business corporations, in vital industrial sectors—the Rhenish-Westphalia Coal Syndicate, the A.E.G. electrical combine and the I.G. dye-works for instance—German industry was highly competitive in European and world markets. In the years before World War I, Germany appeared to be challenging Britain successfully for industrial supremacy in Europe.

French industrialization was never so thorough as that in Britain or in Germany. Why this was so is not completely clear. There was no shortage of raw materials in France, nor of good seaports with international trading links, nor of a capitalist class with money to invest, nor of skilful inventors and scientists. Yet the economy never really took off. One reason for this may have been the position of the French peasantry. By 1789 France had developed a flourishing rural economy and was a nation of few cities and many villages. In the French Revolution the peasantry had erupted for a moment and gained the abolition of feudal privileges, and in many cases the ownership of their own plot of land. Since the French population increased more slowly than that of any other single country in Europe, there was not the same landless and rapidly increasing population to make up the labouring force of the new industrial cities. Other reasons may have been the reluctance of French industrialists to produce cheap goods for a mass market rather than luxuries, and the readiness of the French investor to put his money in foreign enterprises as often as domestic ones.

French industrial development was therefore steady rather than spectacular. To begin with, new industry was concentrated in existing big cities like Paris and Lyons and in the textile towns of north-west France and the iron-fields of Alsace-Lorraine. Railway development began in the 1830s but it was not until after the 1848 revolution that a national railway network was constructed. During the Second Empire (1852–71), carefully encouraged by the Emperor Napoleon III, the French economy grew much faster. Unlike the British government which as a rule left its businessmen to prosper or go bankrupt in perfect feedom, the French government actively intervened to encourage those industries which seemed particularly vital. Between 1850 and 1870 iron production trebled, from around 400,000 tons to around 1,200,000 tons. In the same period, there was a fivefold increase in the amount of horsepower used by industrial steam engines. Despite the loss of the valuable iron deposits of Alsace-Lorraine to Germany in 1871, the economy proved very resilient and rapid progress continued through the 1870s. By the end of the century, France was economically the most advanced nation of Europe after Britain, Germany, and Belgium, and maintained a better balance between industry and agriculture than them all.

The last major European power to industrialize was the largest and furthest east—Russia. For much of the nineteenth century, the Russian economy was the most backward in Europe. Though the country possessed immense natural resources—iron ore in the Urals and coal in the Donetz basin for example—these were a long way from the centres of population and communications were frightful. Other obstacles to development were the survival of serfdom until the 1860s, the smallness and political weakness of the Russian middle class, and the lack of interest of the powerful nobility in the new industry. In contrast to Western Europe railways were built in Russia well before serious industrialization began. In 1861 there were already 1,000 miles of track, and by 1880 there were 14,000 miles. Enterprising foreigners like the German Knoop in textiles, the Welshman Hughes in iron, and the Swedish Nobel brothers in oil, pioneered important advances in the 1860s and 1870s, while the government did its utmost to encourage the new industry. In fact the process of industrialization in Russia was as closely directed by the state as anywhere in Europe. It was also created on a large scale. As early as 1880, 45 per cent of Russian factory workers were employed in factories of a thousand or more. Take-off occurred in the 1890s when Count Witte was Minister of Finance. His motto was 'A great power cannot wait', and he channelled two-thirds of government money into economic development. The results were remarkable. Helped by foreign, especially French, capital, the Russian economy grew faster than any other in Europe. In 1900

Count Witte (1849–1915): the man who masterminded Russia's remarkable economic growth between 1890 and 1914

40 per cent of all Russian industry had been created since 1891. After a pause between 1898 and 1906, it picked up again with an annual growth rate of 6 per cent between 1906 and 1914. Between 1880 and 1914, railway mileage increased more than threefold, coal production fourfold, and iron and steel tenfold. The economic foundations of a world industrial power were being laid.

Certain other areas of Europe also enjoyed a high degree of industrialization by the end of the nineteenth century. Northern Italy, with a commercial tradition going back to the Middle Ages, became industrialized in the second half of the century. The main impetus came from Piedmont, and rapid growth took place during the premiership of Cavour (1851–61). In the Habsburg Empire Bohemia developed as the major industrial region after the Vienna area, and in the north of Europe Sweden, richly endowed with metallic ores, was much the most advanced of the Scandinavian countries. By 1914 few parts of the continent remained unaffected by economic revolution. Even mountainous Switzerland had by this time established a reputation as a producer of quality manufactured goods for export.

In order to make clearer how this complicated and massive change occurred, it is worth focussing in more detail on certain major inventors and industrialists.

James Watt

Born in 1736 at Greenock in Scotland, the son of a master carpenter, he soon demonstrated such a talent as a craftsman that it was a common saying among his father's workmen that 'Jamie has gotten a fortune at his fingers' end.' In 1763, when he was established as an instrument maker in Glasgow, he was asked by the University to repair a model a Newcomen's steam engine for pumping water out of coal-mines. He was struck by the inefficiency of the design and became convinced that the addition of a separate condenser would make a much better engine. The problem was that there was no engineer skilful enough to put his ideas into practice and it was not until 1774, when he went into partnership with Matthew Boulton, a Birmingham businessman, that his design could be tested. Boulton was an industrialist of great flair. He owned a large factory at Soho, near Birmingham, where skilled workmen produced quality toys for a vast export market which included most of the major cities of Europe. Realizing the potential of Watt's design, he was ready to devote his considerable engineering resources to developing the engine commercially. It was a most productive partnership. Watt's pumping engine proved as efficient as he claimed and in 1783 he perfected the rotary engine. By 1800 the firm of Boulton and Watt had produced more than 700 pumping engines and more than 300 rotary engines, and their designs were being copied in France, Germany, and the U.S.A.

Thus the fortunate meeting of a craftsman of genius and a brilliant businessman brought about the single most important technological advance of the early industrial revolution.

Werner Siemens

Werner Siemens (1816–1892)

Born in 1816, he was the most talented of the many talented sons of a German farming family. Since his father did not have the means to send him to university, he became a cadet in the Prussian army and gained an excellent technical education at the Engineering and Artillery School in Berlin. His first real interest after leaving school was the process of galvanic gilding and plating. He soon showed his talent for combining invention with good business by securing a patent for this process and then selling it at a handsome profit to a British firm. He then turned to electric telegraphy and, with the financial backing of a cousin, set up a telegraph factory in partnership with Halske, an engineer. His first electric telegraphs failed to function very well and the firm lost its contracts with the Prussian State railways. Undeterred however, Siemens improved his product and won profitable contracts in Russia, Britain, and elsewhere. With the help of his brothers, he established firms in London and St. Petersburg as well as in Berlin, and by 1860 the firm was famous throughout the world for overland and submarine telegraphy. Siemens, however, never allowed his business successes to stop his experimental work, and his greatest single invention— the electric dynamo—was perfected in his sixtieth year and soon developed commercially by Siemens-Halske. In 1880 the firm demonstrated its first electric lift and, the following year, established a factory for making light filament lamps. When he eventually retired, his original firm had merged with its main rival to form the huge electrical cartel A.E.G.

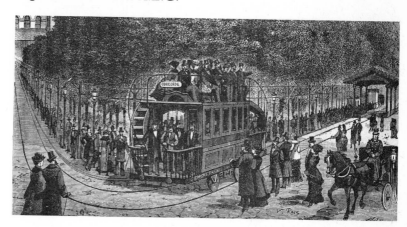

The Siemens electric tram 'Concorde' at the Paris Electrical Exhibition of 1881

Above *The factory Alfred Krupp inherited in 1826*

Below *Part of the organization in Essen which he bequeathed to his successors in 1887*

Siemens's career, spanning the middle of the nineteenth century, demonstrates how a brilliant inventor with a sound technical education and a taste for business could in a lifetime establish a firm with an international reputation and a virtual monopoly in his home country. It also helps to show how Germany was able to develop so fast in the second phase of the economic revolution.

Alfred Krupp

The Krupp family had, for generations, been successful merchants in the small German town of Essen in the valley of the River Ruhr. Friedrick Krupp, Alfred's father, had converted a fulling mill into a foundry and had concentrated on producing high quality steel by a process similar to that of Huntsman in Sheffield. To begin with, he was quite successful but he was struck down by a long lingering illness and when he died, he left his fourteen-year-old son Alfred with a works employing only seven men with no firm contracts. Alfred, however, was energetic and determined. Despite his youth, he travelled widely in Germany, securing enough contracts to keep the steelworks going and learning much about the possibilities of steel in industry. At this time he was running the business virtually single-handed, acting as he put it 'as clerk, letter writer, cashier, smith, smelter, coke-pounder, nightwatchman at the converting furnace and taking on many other jobs'. As the *Zollverein* expanded so did the business, and in 1835 he switched his factory from water-power to steam-power. Nonetheless things were often difficult still and the slump of 1847–8 drove him to melt down the family silver in order to pay his workmen. For Krupp, however, like Cockerill, railways were the salvation. Steel springs and axles were ordered by the Cologne-Minden line and before long cast steel railway-tyres had become a major Krupp product. In the 1850s and 1860s the firm steadily expanded. The Bessemer process did not take him by surprise since his representative in London was a close friend of the inventor. Before long, Krupp was manufacturing cheap steel using the new process. He also began to develop the armaments which were to become the most notorious and profitable products of the House of Krupp. The Prussian victories of 1864, 1866, and 1871 were won with Krupp guns. By 1873 Alfred had won the nickname, 'the Cannon King', and employed 16,000 men. On his death in 1887 he employed more than 70,000, a ten-thousandfold increase on his boyhood inheritance.

His career shows what opportunities were available in this century for a man with energy, guts, and a bit of luck. It also shows the fundamental importance of steel in the German economy in the second half of the century and the advantages war could bring to certain types of business.

Alfred Krupp (1812–1887)

John Cockerill

In 1839 the French poet and novelist, Victor Hugo, wrote the following description of a view of the Meuse valley: 'At the foot of the hills . . . two round balls of fire glared like the eyes of tigers. By the roadside was a frightful dark chimney-stack surmounted by a huge flame. Nearer the entry of the Valley, hidden in the shade, was a mouth of live coal, which suddenly opened and shut and, in the midst of frightful noises spouted forth a tongue of fire.' He was in fact looking at the largest industrial complex in Europe—the factories of John Cockerill at Seraing, Belgium—when the furnaces were being lit.

Cockerill was born in Lancashire but had accompanied his father William to Belgium in 1797 in search of work. By the time he retired in 1813, William, an expert builder of cotton machinery, had built up a prosperous little business in the textile towns of Verviers and Liège which he handed on to his sons. John was a very able organizer and diplomat. He soon established a good relationship with the Dutch king (who had become ruler of Belgium in 1815) and with his backing went into the engineering business. The old castle of Seraing near Liège, which the Cockerills bought from the king, was transformed into an engineering works. What Cockerill did was to copy English designs and sell them throughout Western Europe. An English observer noted that 'Mr. Cockerill often boasts that he has all the new inventions over at Seraing ten days after they come out in England.' Steam engines were followed by steam ships (1820) and by locomotives (1835). After a brief setback when Belgium revolted against the Dutch in 1830, the business forged ahead again with the construction of the Belgian railways. At the time of his death, John Cockerill controlled more than 60 industrial establishments and the joint-stock company formed after his death—Société Anonyme John Cockerill—survives to the present day.

His career demonstrates not only the vitality of the Belgian economy in the early nineteenth century, but also the important part played by Englishmen and English designs in the development of the new industry on the continent.

The Péreire brothers

In the second phase of the economic revolution companies grew bigger, new machines became more complicated and expensive and the amount of money involved in loans and investments multiplied. As important as the inventors or the industrialists were the financiers whose skill lay in finding the money to make possible large-scale industrial expansion. Two of the most enterprising were Emile and Isaac Péreire, members of a small French Jewish banking family of Bordeaux. At the age of twenty-two, Emile became a member of the Paris Stock Exchange and Isaac soon joined him in Paris, working as an accountant. They were both greatly influenced by the ideas of the philosopher Saint-Simon who was one of the earliest to realize the power of the new economy and how much could be achieved in Europe by intelligent banking. In the 1830s and 1840s they concentrated on financing railways in the Paris region. Both the lines from Paris to the northern border and from Paris to Lyons proved successful, and their reputation grew. The government of Napoleon III gave them plenty of scope. They were closely connected with the new national railway network, with gasworks, and with omnibus services. They helped to raise loans for Haussmann's reconstruction of Paris and for the Emperor's wars in the Crimea, Italy, and Mexico. Perhaps their greatest achievement, however, was the creation of the *Credit Mobilier*. This was a type of bank the main aim of which was to sell shares to the public and use the money raised to offer long-term credit either to established companies developing new projects or for floating completely new companies. These banks—the *Credit Foncier* in France, the Darmstadt Bank in Germany, and the *Kreditanstalt* in Austria were of the same type—attracted the savings of the smaller investor and proved immensely popular. Moreover, this type of investment banking was greatly encouraged by new company law in Britain (1855–62) and France (1863–7) which limited the liability of companies in the event of failure. Industrialists were, therefore, more ready to take the risks inevitably involved in embarking on a new project.

For a variety of reasons the Péreire brothers overstretched themselves in the 1860s. The recession of 1866 proved too much for the *Credit Mobilier* which crashed the following year. Nonetheless, their achievement was considerable. They contributed much to French economic progress during the Second Empire and, with the *Credit Mobilier*, they pioneered a type of banking which was to have a profound effect the world over.

All these men—Watt, Boulton, Siemens, Cockerill, Krupp, the Péreires—were of middle-class origin and throughout the period the economic revolution was directed by men of their type. As Marx put it though he was no friend of the bourgeoisie and was writing in 1847 before the second phase of the revolution had really begun:

> the bourgeoisie has created in its rule of the upper classes barely one hundred years old more colossal forces of production than all previous generations put together. Harnessing natural forces to machinery, utilizing chemistry for industry and agriculture, steam navigation, electric telegraph, cultivation of vast tracts of land of the earth's surface, making rivers navigable, conjuring whole populations out of the land. What previous century dreamt that such productive forces slumbered in the lap of social toil?

Chapter 5
Urban and Agricultural Conditions

Urban Conditions

As a consequence of the economic revolution, Europe in 1914 was in many ways a very different place from Europe in 1789. For one thing, there were many more Europeans. Even before the period of economic take-off, the population of the continent was growing fast. Why this was so is still far from clear. It may have been due to a rising birth-rate or to a falling death-rate, or perhaps to a combination of both these factors. A falling death-rate was probably the more significant factor. Certainly two historic killers of the human species—famine and plague—lost much of their force in the eighteenth and nineteenth centuries. Improvements in transport made it generally possible for food to be brought speedily to areas affected by famine, while the black rat, the great plague carrier of Europe, was replaced by the comparatively harmless brown rat. Though the rate of increase has varied greatly, the population of both Europe and the world has continued to grow, with social consequences which have been and remain enormous. In 1750 there were probably about 157 million Europeans including Russians; by 1830 the number had grown to 230,000,000; by 1880 to 320,000,000; and by 1900 to 420,000,000. (In 1960, there were approximately 630,000,000 of whom 214,000,000 were Russians.) During the nineteenth century, the British population almost trebled from 16,000,000 to 45,000,000; so did the German from 24,000,000 to 65,000,000 and the Russian almost quadrupled from 37,000,000 to 140,000,000. In contrast, the French rate of increase over the same period was much slower, with a rise of less than 50 per cent from 27,000,000 to 39,000,000. Across the Atlantic, the population of the U.S.A. enjoyed an eighteenfold increase, from 5,000,000 to 92,000,000, due almost entirely to emigration from Europe.

At the same time, an increasing proportion of this rapidly increasing population became urbanized. In other words, more and more Europeans came to live in towns. In 1789 there were only two really large cities in Europe—London, with about 1,000,000 inhabitants, and Paris, with about 500,000. Even in Western Europe, the overwhelming majority of citizens—80 per cent or more—would be country-dwellers. By 1910 there were seven cities

'The March of Bricks and Mortar': the rapid growth of London as seen by the cartoonist Cruikshank in 1829

with more than 1,000,000 inhabitants and another twenty-three with more than 500,000. Certain towns had had staggering growth rates. In 1800, London's population was 959,000 by 1850, 2,363,000 and by 1910, 4,452,000. Moscow grew even faster: from 250,000 in 1800, to 365,000 in 1850 and to 1,506,000 in 1910. Yet of the major capitals Berlin grew the fastest: 172,000 in 1800 to 419,000 in 1850 and then to 3,730,000 in 1910 (a ninefold increase in 60 years). Major industrial cities mushroomed in the same way. Manchester, at the centre of the Lancashire cotton industry, increased tenfold in one period from about 70,000 to 719,000. Essen, the home town of the Krupp family, was a small market town of little more than 4,000 in 1800. In 1900 it was a city of 295,000. Odessa, one of Russia's main Black Sea ports had 6,000 inhabitants in 1800 and about 500,000 in 1910.

As these figures show, the overall population of industrial cities was increasing at a rate faster than that of the population as a whole. Thus an ever decreasing proportion of Europeans came to earn their living from the land. Somewhere around 1850 the number of Englishmen living in towns began to outnumber those living in the country for the first time. By 1914 the same was true of most of Europe. Of the total British labour force in 1910, just 8 per cent were employed in agriculture; in Germany, the proportion was 34 per cent, in France 43 per cent. The corresponding figure in the

U.S.A. was 32 per cent. When compared with the 80–90 per cent proportion of a century before, these figures indicate an enormous change.

Not only were these industrial cities bigger and faster-growing than any previous urban areas but the social groups within them were different too. As machines, factories, and mass production replaced individual craftsmen working in small shops or in their own cottages, two distinct classes of town-dweller became increasingly apparent. On the one hand, there was a property-owning minority—bankers, industrialists, merchants, professional men, who either owned or invested in the new industrial enterprises—and the vast majority who were employed in the new factories—the industrial working classes—whose only income was the wage they received from their employers. During the nineteenth century, the tension between these classes, which Marx, the founder of modern Communism, described as the 'bourgeoisie' and the 'proletariat', was often considerable and sometimes erupted into violence.

There were many reasons for both the tension and the violence. In the years immediately after 'industrial take-off', while the standard of living of the middle and upper classes rose steadily and obviously, there seems to have been no corresponding increase in the standard of living of the European industrial worker. There has been a long and often bitter debate among economic historians about what exactly happened to the standard of living of the British industrial worker in the period 1780 to 1850. The relevant statistical evidence is hard to handle but suggests that while some workers certainly enjoyed higher real wages than their fathers and grandfathers, others certainly did not, and any general improvement was slow and uncertain.

Factory Industry : spinning with 'mules' 1835. While the woman in the opposite picture can set her own pace, the one in the factory must keep up with the machine. The lad in the bottom right of the picture who is sweeping up beneath the threads works in constant danger from the machinery

Whatever the truth about real wages may be, there is no doubt that the conditions of living for the industrial worker in the new towns and factories were extraordinarily harsh. The new factories were increasingly machine-powered. In the old cottage industry, the craftsman with his own tools set his own pace and his own standards of quality. The new industry, however, functioned at the pace and to the standard of the machine. The power and rhythm of the industrial day became mechanical rather than human. This change had obvious consequences for the industrial worker. Since the longer the machines were working, the greater the factory's production and profits, the working days tended to be very long. Since most factory work tended to be the completion of those parts of the manufacturing process which could not be done mechanically, the factory-worker was often little more than a cog with muscles doing a monotonous job as fast and for as long as possible. As Biedermann, a Leipzig professor, observed of the German textile industry, 'even the weaver's work is becoming much more mechanical; the intelligence which he used to apply to transfer the pattern onto the loom has now passed, to a certain extent, over to the machine; and the benefit which the worker used to derive from this use of his intelligence is now lost to him and rests with the owner of the machine, the commercial employer.'

Displine within industry was severe. The Prussian miners in the first half of the nineteenth century had elaborate regulations which even laid down how miners should greet the mine officials, their social superiors. 'Any infringement of these regulations', a contemporary reported, 'was punished by a fine and, on subsequent occasions by demotion to harder and worse-paid work. Mining boys received instead 4 to 16 lashes with a rope. In order to achieve a deterrent effect, beatings were administered in the presence of the entire work force immediately after prayers and before the pit-descent. On the third infringement, miners were laid off for specific or indefinite periods.' The 1844 rules of a foundry and engineering works in Berlin contained the following: 'Rule 6: No worker may leave his position of work otherwise than for reasons connected with his work. Rule 7: All conversation with fellow-workers is prohibited; if any worker requires information about his work he must turn to the overseer or to the particular fellow-worker designated for the purpose.'

By modern standards, working hours were almost incredibly long. In the Lancashire cotton industry, a fourteen hour day, six days a week (i.e. an eighty-four hour week) was commonplace in the early nineteenth century. The silk industry of Lyons in France worked longer hours still. John Bowring, who was inquiring for the British government into the state of French industry, noted in 1834 that 'the average hours of labour in Lyons are sixteen but when demand is active, it is usual for the weavers to work eighteen or twenty. In summer, they usually rise at 4 a.m. and go to bed at 10 p.m. In the winter they rise at 6 or 7 and go to bed at 11.'

Perhaps the worst feature of the early industrial revolution was the widespread use of women and children in appalling factory conditions. From the employer's viewpoint they were much better than men because they were easier to discipline and could be paid less. In the Lancashire cotton industry 50,000 adult men were employed against 53,000 adult women, 54,000 youths between the ages of 13 and 18, and 24,000 children under the age of 13. A government inquiry into the German state of Saxony discovered that it was 'usual practice to employ even children under ten in factories on normal working days from five in the morning to eight in the evening continuously" and that the government's schemes of providing education within factory hours were made pointless since 'children of such a tender age cannot fail to be so tired and worn out by this unremitting labour that the hours spent in school instruction may be considered as good as wasted.' Here are some French textile workers as described by Villermé, one of the earliest students of the effects of the Industrial Revolution: 'One should see them coming into the town every morning and leaving every evening. Among them are large numbers of women, pale, starving, wading barefoot through the mud—and young children, in greater numbers than the women, just as dirty, just as haggard, covered with rags which are thick with oil splashed over them as they toiled at the looms.'

The long hours, both for adults and children, and the hot, noisy, steaming, sooty and oily atmosphere of most machine-driven

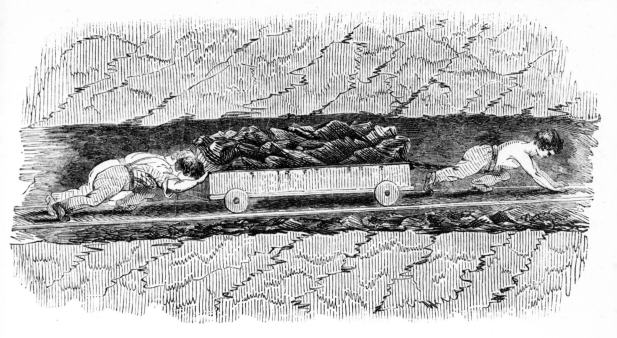

Examples of appalling working conditions.
Above *Trolley boys at work in English coalmines*
Below *An exhausted child at the end of a working day*

factories took their toll on the health of the employees. These are Villermé's comments on the cotton workers of Mulhouse, whom he studied from 1835 to 1840: 'the commonest illnesses are nervous disorders—facial neuralgia, quinsy, and ophthalmia. The children suffer from scrofula in its most hideous forms; and in their earliest years they are decimated by two diseases which are often fatal through neglect—bronchitis in the cold of winter and diarrhoea thoughout the summer and early autumn.' Accidental injury by poorly protected machinery was another real danger.

93

Nonetheless, however terrible the conditions, factory work was better than no work at all. Throughout the nineteenth century, fear of unemployment haunted the European worker. The new economy quickly developed a cyclical character. Years of boom conditions—high production, profits, wages, employment, and investment—would be followed by years of depression with lower production, many workers laid off altogether and lower wages for those still employed. There was a serious depression from 1816–9, immediately after the Napoleonic wars, and further ones in 1825–6, 1836–7, 1839–42, 1846–8, 1857–8 (the first really world-wide financial crisis), 1866–7, 1873–6 and 1893–6. In these hard times, millions of European workers found themselves dependent on what meagre savings they had made when times were better or the various systems of poor relief which European governments provided. None of these was remotely adequate to cope with the problem of widespread temporary unemployment until Bismarck's legislation in Germany in the 1880s. For many workers the only escape from such terrible uncertainty was emigration. One of the first students of emigration, G. Fenenzano, who compared Italian emigration to the U.S.A. with that from other European states, concluded that the most important factors driving a worker from his homeland were

the introduction of machines and the frequency of industrial crises. For instance the American crisis of 1857, after deeply affecting all the most important states of Central Europe, perplexing the well-informed and striking the most important establishments, went on to penetrate far into Scandinavia. When work can be affected in this fashion, suddenly and on a vast scale, it is understandable that the worker thinks of insuring himself against such grave and frequent vicissitudes.

The new industrial towns were often frightful places in which to live (see p. 96). In 1844, Engels described the view from a bridge in the centre of Manchester as follows: 'Below the bridge, you look upon piles of debris, the refuse, filth and offal from the courts of the steep left bank; here each house is parked close behind its neighbour and a piece of each is visible, all black, smoky, crumbling ancient with broken panes and window frames.' Lille, in north-west France, was just as horrific. Here is Adolphe Blanqui's description of some of the housing in 1848:

Only in the depth of the cellars can one appreciate the agonies of those who cannot be allowed out on account of their age or of the cold weather. For the most part, they lie on bare soil or wisps of straw on a rough couch of potato peelings or sand, or on shavings carefully collected during the day's work. The pit in which they languish is bare of any fittings; only those who are best off possess a temperamental stove, a wooden chair, some cooking utensils. 'I may not be rich', an old woman told us, pointing to her neighbour lying full length on the damp cellar floor, 'but at least I've

HERE AND THERE;
OR, EMIGRATION A REMEDY.

The appeal of Emigration: this cartoon of 1849 contrasts the hardships of Europe with the prosperity of the New World

my bundle of straw, thank God!' More than 3,000 of our fellow citizens lead this horrifying existence in the little cellars.

Such housing conditions obviously affected the health of the occupants. Experience of some of the housing in Breslau in Germany brought this comment from Dr. Crocker, the Junior Poor Doctor of the city in 1845:

> The labouring classes live generally in low-lying damp floor-dwellings, in courts, narrow yards and streets. Here often several persons or perhaps a whole family live in one room or in a single bed, and use the room for all domestic duties, so that the air gets fouled while the whole room is seldom aired in winter for reasons of economy. Their diet usually consists of bread and potatoes. These are clearly the two main reasons why scrofula is so widespread here.

The slums of the Fleet Ditch, 1836, a centre of disease in London before sanitary legislation

Moreover, these towns, built as quickly and as cheaply as possible to house a rapidly increasing population, were usually lacking in the basic urban services—sanitation, an adequate water supply, street-cleaning. The inevitable and tragic result of such shortcomings was the reappearance of mass epidemics of contagious (usually water-borne) diseases. Cholera ravaged western and central Europe in 1831–2 and in 1848. Typhoid fever and diphtheria were frequent and murderous visitors. Hardly surprisingly, many workers sought escape from their surroundings by heavy drinking or the taking of opium. The saying went that the quickest way out of Manchester was alcohol.

In these circumstances, it is also hardly surprising that the industrial working class often felt bitterly towards their employers. After a visit to Lancashire in 1835, de Tocqueville, a most perceptive political writer, observed: 'From this foul drain, the greatest stream of human industry flows out to fertilize the whole world. From this filthy sewer pure gold flows. Here humanity attains its most complete development and its most brutish, here civilization works its miracles and civilized man is turned almost into a savage.' To more and more Europeans, it seemed that the tremendous forces unleashed by the economic revolution were bringing wealth and civilization to a minority at the expense of the rest. In the 1830s and 1840s there was a growing sense of class conflict in the major cities of Europe. As a French deputy, St. Marc Girardin, put it in 1831, during a debate in the French assembly: 'Every manufacturer lives in his factory like a colonial planter in the midst of his slaves. The barbarians who menace society are neither in the Caucasus nor in the steppes of Tartary; they are in the suburbs of our industrial cities. . . . The middle class must clearly recognize the nature of the situation, it must know where it stands.'

Working-class reaction to early industrial conditions in Europe took two main forms. The first was a desperate and hopeless attempt to turn back the pages of history by breaking the new machines which seemed to be depriving them of their traditional employment. This type of action is usually known as Luddism after Ned Ludd, the probably mythical leader of the Nottingham machine-breakers of 1811–2. The second and eventually much more successful reaction was to build up combinations or trades unions of workers which, strong in their unity, might obtain better conditions of work from their employers.

In the first half of the nineteenth century, both employers and governments met both reactions with uncompromising hostility. Luddism in Britain during the depressed years from 1810 to 1820 was sternly repressed. In 1813 seventeen workers were hanged at York for machine-breaking activities. In 1819 eleven people lost their lives as a result of the 'Peterloo' massacre in Manchester, when the military forcibly broke up a peaceful, mainly working-class meeting which was demanding political reform. An attempt by agricultural workers in Dorset to form a trades union led to six of them being transported to Australia in 1834. When the bad years of 1838 to 1842 inspired Chartism, a huge working-class political movement, neither the Whig government of Lord Melbourne nor the Tory government of Sir Robert Peel had any policy but to deploy troops in industrial areas and to arrest the main leaders when serious trouble threatened.

In France, successive governments took the same kind of attitude. There were serious outbreaks of Luddism immediately after the Napoleonic Wars. In 1819 the Minister of the Interior wrote to the prefect of the Isère department warning that the introduction of new cutting machines in the textile town of Vienne might lead to trouble. 'You will recognize', his letter continued, 'how important it is that the Administration should display the greatest firmness and energy. If the agitators realize their aims, if a first example of insubordination were not punished with the greatest severity, the consequences might be extremely awkward and we should perhaps see repeated in our own country the excesses that have afflicted England.' When the new machines were in fact ambushed by the Vienne workers and thrown into the River Isère, the prefect at once arrested nineteen of the ringleaders.

As in England, combinations of workers were strongly discouraged. In 1831 an attempt by the Lyons silk workers to establish new ways of negotiating wage rates between employers and employees led to an armed rising which was eventually suppressed

by 20,000 troops. Three years later, an even more serious rising occurred when the government forbade the formation of workers' associations even if they numbered fewer than twenty. The silk-workers threw up barricades round the industrial areas of the city and for nearly a week held them against the army. Considerable bloodshed was necessary before they gave in. Indeed, during the July Monarchy (1830–48) labour relations in France were as bad as any in Europe. The government was uncompromising and the French workers more politically conscious than any of their European counterparts. The Lyons riots were the most famous disturbances but there was trouble in Paris in 1832, 1834, and 1839, and in Lille, Clermont, and Toulouse in 1840. The years 1833 and 1844–6 were bad years for strikes throughout the country. It was, moreover, France alone of the major European countries which, in the nineteenth century, provided class war on a grand scale with thousands rather than hundreds of casualties—during the 'June Days' of 1848 and the Paris Commune of 1871.

Germany was, on the whole more orderly than France, partly because her working population was less politically conscious and partly because major industrialization occurred for the most part in the second half of the century and employers and government were able to learn from British and French mistakes. In the 1840s, however, there were serious disturbances in Silesia and Saxony. In

A worker's rising in Lyons, April 1834. Cavalry and infantry of the French army are repulsed by the citizens of Lyons who are on the left behind the barricades

Silesia, a linen industry which had been one of the most thriving in Europe a century earlier collapsed in the face of machine competition. In 1844 the linen weavers attacked the machines and the private property of their owners. Like the Nottingham stocking makers and the Lyons silk weavers, they were crushed by the army. In neighbouring Saxony, Luddism appeared in 1846 and 1848. The owner of a nail-making factory in the Erz mountains returned to his factory after a visit to a nearby town to find 'the yard full of stones, in the factory buildings nearly all the machines destroyed by axes and crowbars. Most of the stocks had been stolen or thrown into the river.' He at once summoned the military who arrested eighty suspects.

One careful observer of this series of bitter conflicts between employers and workmen was Karl Marx (1818–83). Marx was a German Jew by birth who became deeply interested in philosophical, economic, and political matters while he was still at university. Beginning a career as a journalist, he edited the *Rheinische Zeitung* for a short time before the Prussian authorities exiled him because of his radical political views. The French and Belgian authorities also saw to it that his stays in Paris and Brussels were brief, and in 1849 he was forced to take refuge in England. He lived in terrible poverty in Soho for most of the rest of his life. Much of

Machine-breakers in Bohemia (part of the Habsburg Empire) in 1844

his research work was done in the British Museum and he was buried in Highgate Cemetery. In 1848 Marx, in collaboration with his close friend Frederick Engels, published the *Communist Manifesto*, which is both a programme of political action and an analysis of industrial society. History, Marx was convinced, is the story of struggles between classes. In modern capitalist society, which the Industrial Revolution had brought into existence, the classes locked in combat are the middle class or bourgeoisie and the working class or proletariat. Since the bourgeoisie are only interested in profits, they must exploit the proletarians to the full, holding down their wages and denying them any political power. But though the proletarians will increase in misery, they will grow in numbers and in desperation. Eventually their conditions will become intolerable and they will rise in violent revolution to overthrow capitalism for ever. From this successful revolution the genuine communist society will gradually emerge in which no private property will exist and all will work together in brotherly co-operation for the common good. As long as capitalism survives, the job of communists is to accelerate the coming of the inevitable revolution. The Manifesto ends with the famous appeal: 'The proletarians have nothing to lose but their chains; they have the world to gain. Workers of all countries unite!'

Karl Marx (1818–1883)

Marx was a writer of tremendous power. For millions of working men in Europe and elsewhere, his analysis of the industrial situation rang true and his vision of a communist future was a great inspiration. Though the Manifesto made little impact in the year 1848 itself, it was widely read in the years that followed and Marxist parties sprang up all over the continent. Marxism was particularly strong in Germany before World War I. From Germany it spread to Russia, and after the successful Bolshevik revolution of 1917 to the non-European world. Since Marxist Communism is now the official creed of half the human race, the Communist Manifesto of 1848 must rank as one of the most important publications of the nineteenth century.

Agricultural Conditions

The changes in industry and in urban life during the nineteenth century were so dramatic that they often overshadow other important social changes, in agricultural methods and conditions for instance. Yet during this period the changes in European agriculture were enormous.

In 1789 Europe, still predominantly a rural continent, produced virtually all the food it needed. By 1914, predominantly an industrial continent, it depended on other continents, notably America and

Friedrich Engels (1820–1895). Marx and Engels were lifelong friends and the founders of modern Communism

Australasia, for many of its foodstuffs, although its own European farmers produced far more than they had done a century earlier. In 1789 only Britain and Holland had developed relatively large farms producing commercially for the market and worked by wage-earning agricultural labourers. The rest of the continent was farmed by peasants or serfs who, while owing feudal dues to their landlord either in service or in produce, possessed their own plots of land which they could work for themselves and their families. In much of Europe farming methods had changed little since the Middle Ages and most of the land was owned by kings, noblemen, or the Church. By the First World War, however, commercial farming with high productivity through scientific methods was widespread. Though peasant ownership was also widespread, serfdom, and all feudal dues had been abolished. The great estates of the Church had disappeared and land ownership more widely divided between the social classes.

These changes occurred in stages. The Enclosure movement in England, which made efficient commercial farming possible by enclosing the old open fields and common lands with hedges or fences, occurred between 1760 and 1815. In marked contrast were developments in another part of the British Isles, Ireland. Here a mainly peasant population, renting their plots from other absentee English landlords, were driven into increasing dependence on a single crop, the potato, by a rapid increase in population. The danger of such a dependence was tragically demonstrated when the potato crop failed in 1845 and brought upon Ireland the 'Great Hunger', the greatest single catastrophe in Europe during the nineteenth century.

The French Revolution ended what serfdom still existed in France, broke the hold of the nobility and church on the French countryside and increased the number of peasant proprietors from around 4,000,000 to probably about 6,500,000. France became and stayed a country of small peasant farmers. The average French farm in 1892 was $2\frac{1}{2}$ acres as against the English average of 66 acres. The French armies which marched across Germany between 1793 and 1815 brought many revolutionary practices with them, one of which was to emancipate the serfs of Prussia and most other German states. The ex-serfs had, however, to pay compensation to their former owners as well as high rents, and for the first half of the nineteenth century German peasants were worse off than the French and suffered terribly in the depressed years of 1845–8. In 1848 they played an important part in the first revolutionary disturbances and one of the few concrete results of the 1848–9 revolution was the reduction of their heavy economic burdens. Nonetheless from 1840 to 1870 there was a marked 'flight from the land' in the German states. Many peasants emigrated or moved into the new industrial towns. Between 1865 and 1875 Germany began for the first time to import rather than export food.

In Eastern Europe serfdom was not abolished until the second half of the century. In the Habsburg Empire it was effectively ended after the 1848 revolution. Only small compensation was asked of those serfs who were granted their freedom and, according to a system devised by von Bach, Minister for Domestic Affairs, 3,000,000 peasants were granted plots of land, drawn from 100,000 of the larger estates. Different parts of the Empire began to concentrate on different products—Austria on livestock, Hungary on grain and Bohemia on sugar. Vienna became the chief market of a flourishing agricultural region. The last remaining serfs of Europe—those of Russia and Rumania—were emancipated in the 1860s. In neither country, however, did the social and economic position of the peasantry significantly improve. In Russia it was not until the reforms of Stolypin between 1906 and 1912 that extensive peasant ownership became possible.

The emancipation of the serfs accompanied by the spread of much more scientific farming methods led to a great increase in agricultural productivity. Better ploughs and fertilizers brought hitherto unused land under cultivation. Between 1820 and 1880 the amount of acreage rose under crops from around 364,000,000 to

Russian peasants in 1823

546,000,000 (an increase of 70 per cent). More intensive agricultural methods pioneered in Holland and Britain—enclosures, scientific crop-rotation and selective breeding for instance—brought better yields per acre. Grain production rose between 1820 and 1880 from 2,800 million bushels to 5,040 million (an increase of 78 per cent). Relatively new crops, such as potatoes and sugar beet, began to be grown on a large scale.

In the 1870s and 1880s, however, European agriculture faced an unprecedented challenge. Certain overseas areas like the U.S.A., Argentina, Australia, and New Zealand possessed natural advantages which enabled them to produce food far more economically than Europe. In the U.S.A., for example, the invention of the mechanical reaper and binder multiplied the grain production of the Great Plains so that there was a huge surplus above American needs. In the 1860s and 1870s steamship services across the Atlantic became swifter and more reliable, and consequently, in the 1870s, cheap American grain began to flood into Europe. Moreover in 1867 the first freezing machine had been invented in England, and less than ten years later refrigerated merchant ships were in existence. The first refrigerated cargo of Australian beef was landed in London, and in the 1880s and 1890s cheap refrigerated foodstuffs were shipped to Europe from all quarters of the globe.

In face of this novel situation, European governments had two alternatives. Either they could do nothing and allow foreign competition to swamp their home agriculture. This would mean lower food prices and a higher standard of living for their population. Or they could protect their home agriculture by putting tariffs (thus raising the price) on foreign foods. Britain and Belgium, both advanced manufacturing countries with great confidence in free trade, chose the former alternative; most other European countries chose the latter. The consequences were startling. While France and Germany managed to maintain quite a thriving agricultural sector in which more than a third of the labour force was employed in 1914, British agriculture, once the most flourishing in Europe, was ruined between 1875 and 1900. By 1914 less than a tenth of the labour force was employed in agriculture and Britain was dependent on overseas supplies for her vital foodstuffs. The danger of such dependence in times of war was vividly displayed in 1916 when German U-boats nearly succeeded in starving this island into surrender.

Chapter 6
Reaction and Apparent Peace

The Congress of Vienna

The galaxy of European rulers and diplomats who gathered at Vienna in the autumn of 1814 faced two enormous problems: first, how to dismantle Napoleon's vast empire in a way that would allow a lasting peace; and secondly, how to restore to European society those old, traditional and established ways which had been disrupted by the French Revolution. They dealt quite successfully with the first problem. The second, however, was too much for them. Wherever French armies had marched in Europe after 1793, they had carried with them both the principles of 1789 and the most orderly, efficient, and modern government in the world, best represented by the Code Napoleon. By 1815 the seeds of European liberalism—the set of political beliefs which were inspired by the principles of the French Revolution and which laid special emphasis on the importance of individual freedom and on the limitation of the powers of rulers by an elected assembly—were too deeply sown to be destroyed. In areas where there was a thriving middle class—the Low Countries, the Rhineland, Northern Italy—liberalism grew increasingly influential. It became the predominant political philosophy of the urban middle classes which the economic revolution was to make the most powerful social group in Europe. The period 1815 to 1848 was a period of 'reaction', when the rulers of Europe, especially in central and eastern Europe, did their utmost to maintain society as they knew it and to suffocate all the forces of change, of which liberalism was one of the most powerful. Consequently the continent was shaken by a series of 'liberal' revolutions which clearly demonstrated how inadequate conservative policies were in such changing times.

The Congress of Vienna proved picturesque and dramatic. The Viennese nobility laid on a continuous round of parties and balls; Metternich, Austrian Chancellor and host, had secret agents everywhere; in the middle of the proceedings Napoleon escaped from Elba and had to be defeated again; and twice the victors seemed on the point of war again over the division of the spoils. A key figure of the Congress was Tsar Alexander of Russia, whose enormous army had played the greatest part in defeating the French. He had come to the throne in 1801 after his half crazy father Paul had been murdered in a palace revolution. He was an

The Congress of Vienna. The painter Isambey has grouped together the representatives of the major European states

a *Wellington (Britain)*
b *Metternich (Austria)*
c *Castlereagh (Britain)*
d *Talleyrand (France)*

enigma. 'A riddle of a man who carried his secret with him to the grave' was how the novelist Puskin described him. Sensitive and idealistic, moody and melancholic, he easily fell under the influence of more powerful personalities. Napoleon had held him spellbound at Tilsit in 1807, and at Vienna he was deeply influenced by Baroness von Krudener, a mystic who believed that the days of mankind were numbered and that she had been called by God to save the world with the help of the Russian Tsar. Alexander was, therefore, determined that the peace settlement should fulfil both Russia's interests and his religious ideals, and his army gave him a strong bargaining position.

There were three other outstanding diplomats at the Congress. The first was Lord Castlereagh, the British Foreign Secretary. Britain's main interest lay in cutting France down to size and in preventing Russia getting too strong. Castlereagh safeguarded this interest skilfully and, at the same time, was a force of moderation, doing much to prevent the other allies falling out and to pilot the Congress to a constructive conclusion. The second was Prince Metternich, Austrian Chancellor and the cleverest diplomat of them all. Despite the essential weakness of the Austrian Empire, he managed to restore the Habsburg dynasty to a dominant position in Central Europe. He and Castlereagh saw eye to eye on most issues and co-operated closely throughout the Congress. The third was Talleyrand, representing the Bourbon monarchy of France. Though he was there supposedly as 'an observer', his devious but clear-sighted diplomacy helped to obtain for his country far better terms than might have been expected by one so recently and completely defeated (see p. 105).

The 'Vienna settlement' of 1815 consisted of three separate agreements: the Second Treaty of Paris which dealt with the treatment of France; the Treaty of Vienna which redrew the map of Europe; and the Quadruple Alliance which was intended to maintain the new settlement. The Second Treaty of Paris replaced the First, which had been signed before Napoleon escaped from Elba. As a punishment for supporting the 'Hundred Days' adventure, rather harsher terms were imposed on the French. France lost all her European conquests since 1791, and her boundaries were reduced to those of 1790. An indemnity was demanded and an army of occupation imposed. The most serious territorial losses were outside Europe. Mauritius, St. Lucia, and Tobago went to Britain, part of San Domingo to Spain. All her fortresses in India had to be dismantled. The Great Powers pledged themselves to maintain the restored Bourbon monarchy of Louis XVIII and his successors on the French throne, and looked forward to the day when a reformed Bourbon France could join them in their concerted action to hold revolution at bay.

Map 8 *Europe according to the Vienna Settlement*

The map of Europe redrawn by the Treaty of Vienna differed in many respects from both Napoleon's Europe of 1812 and pre-revolutionary Europe of 1789 (see map 8). There were three principles underlying it: first, France should be prevented from menacing Europe again by the creation of stronger buffer states along France's borders; secondly, the major victorious powers should gain at the expense of France and of the minor powers but never to the extent that the balance of power was seriously disturbed; and thirdly, where possible the old dynasties should be restored. In order to contain France, Piedmont was strengthened by the addition of Genoa (formerly an independent republic), Prussia gained the Rhineland provinces and Holland and Belgium (formerly the Austrian Netherlands) were welded into a single kingdom ruled by the Dutch king. Of the victorious major powers, Britain gained the Cape of Good Hope and Ceylon (from Holland), Heligoland, Malta, and the Ionian islands, as well as the territories she had gained from France. These strategic gains gave Britain, with her immensely strong navy, a virtual stranglehold on world trade. Russia gained Finland from Sweden and Bessarabia from Turkey. She also made considerable gains in Poland, including the city of Warsaw, at the expense of Prussia. As a conciliatory gesture to the Poles, whose independence had been so cynically destroyed by the Partitions of the late eighteenth century, Tsar Alexander declared Poland a kingdom under his protection and granted a constitution. The independence of Poland, however, remained more apparent than real. As compensation to Sweden who had fought with the victorious allies, Finland was replaced by Norway, which had previously belonged to Denmark. To compensate Prussia for her Polish losses, parts of the kingdom of Saxony, which had fought too long for Napoleon, were added to her Rhineland gains. Austria rebuilt her power in Italy either directly as in Lombardy and Venetia, or through members of the Habsburg family as in Parma, Modena, and Tuscany. Thus, like Genoa, the ancient republic of Venice finally lost its independence. 'Republics are no longer in fashion', commented Tsar Alexander. Members of the Bourbon family were restored to Spain and to the Kingdom of Naples as well as to France. The Pope recovered the Papal States. The restoration of these rulers, none of whom were renowned for their popularity, was justified by the principal of 'legitimacy'. This was the brain-child of Talleyrand who, realizing that claims to rule by Divine Right sounded sadly out of date, argued that those with the best legal claim to power were the 'legitimate' rulers. After such stormy years, the best legal claim could usually be made by the old dynasties. One old political organization not to be restored was the Holy Roman Empire. The Napoleonic Confederation of the Rhine was replaced by the German Confederation made up of thirty-eight loosely grouped states including Austria and Prussia. The Confederation had a Diet which, though it met regularly, had no significant powers. Austrian influence throughout the area was strong, and remained so for the next thirty years.

The Vienna settlement had much about it of the ruthless power politics of eighteenth century diplomacy. Smaller peoples—the Norwegians, the Finns, the Poles, the Venetians, the Genoese, and the Saxons, for example—were subjected, without any kind of consultation, to rulers they disliked, usually of a different nationality from themselves, for no better reason than that they were weak and their neighbours were strong. For these reasons, it at once had its critics. Gentz, a perceptive Prussian who took a major part in the negotiations, concluded that the Vienna Congress 'has resulted in nothing but agreements between the great powers of little value for the preservation of the peace of Europe, quite arbitrary alterations in the possessions of the smaller states ... but no great measure for the public order or the general good which might compensate humanity for its long suffering or pacify it in the future'. Thirty years later an even harsher view was stated by Cavour, the Italian who did more than anyone to destroy the Austrian rule this settlement had imposed on his countrymen. 'Resting on no principle, neither of legitimacy nor of national interests nor of popular will, taking account neither of geographical conditions nor of general interests, this august assembly (the Congress of Vienna), acting only by the right of the strongest, erected a political edifice without moral foundation.'

Certainly Cavour was right when he maintained that the 1815 settlement ignored both liberalism and nationalism, the two most powerful forces of the mid-nineteenth century. It is worth noting, however, that since neither of these forces was at all strong so early in the century only a statesman of quite extraordinary foresight could have correctly gauged how quickly they would grow. The Vienna peacemakers did not possess this foresight, but they were neither mere power politicians, nor blind reactionaries. Their experiences had convinced them that war was an evil to be avoided at all costs, and that the old diplomatic methods had been inadequate to prevent it. Through the Quadruple Alliance they attempted to institute regular international 'summit' talks for the first time in modern history, in order that the settlement be maintained and peace preserved. In the words of Article VI of the alliance, Britain, Prussia, Austria, and Russia agreed 'to renew their meetings . . . for the purpose of consulting upon their common interests and for the consideration of the measures . . . which shall be considered most salutary for the repose and prosperity of nations and for the maintenance of the Peace of Europe'. Almost immediately, however, two rival ideas emerged of how peace-keeping should work in practice. The original alliance was Castlereagh's creation, but Tsar Alexander soon produced his own higher sounding scheme. Madame de Krudener had much to do with it. All the rulers of Europe were asked to join the Tsar in a 'Holy Alliance of charity peace and love and to consider themselves all as members of one and the same Christian nation'. 'A high sounding Nothing' was how Metternich described the Tsar's proposal, and Castlereagh dismissed it as 'a sublime piece of mysticism and nonsense'. Nonetheless all the rulers of Europe signed it with the exception of the Prince Regent of Britain, the Sultan of Turkey and the Pope. When the periodic Congresses began to meet it became clear that the Russian view of the duties of the Quadruple Alliance differed considerably from the British. Castlereagh always held that the Congresses should confine their attention to the disputes between states which arose from the Vienna settlement. The Powers should never intervene in the internal affairs of another state even if the most democratic revolution threatened. 'The Alliance of the Great Powers', he wrote in the State Paper of 1820, 'never was intended as a Union for the Government of the World or for the Superintendence of the Internal Affairs of other states.' Tsar Alexander, in contrast, was convinced that revolution was the work of the devil and, like a disease, infectious. It was the Christian duty of the Powers, for their own safety and for the safety of the continent, to intervene and crush revolution wherever it reared its ugly head. Because of this difference of view between the two most powerful nations in Europe, the Congress system came to grief.

The first Congress at Aix-la-Chapelle in 1818 was quite successful, although Metternich and Castlereagh combined to sabotage a scheme of Alexander's to crush the revolutions in Spanish South America. France was invited to join the Alliance and the army of occupation was withdrawn. The second Congress, which met first at Troppau in 1820, was much more stormy. A spate of revolutions in Spain, Italy, and Greece persuaded Austria and Prussia to join Russia in signing the Troppau Protocol, the vital passage of which read: 'if owing to such alterations (revolution) immediate danger threatens other states, the Powers bind themselves by peaceful means or if need be by arms, to bring back the guilty state into the bosom of the Grand Alliance.' Britain refused to have anything to do with such interventionist schemes. The Troppau Protocol was, in Castlereagh's opinion 'destitute of common sense'. At the next Congress, held at Verona in 1822, the Duke of Wellington, acting on instructions from Canning, the new Foreign Secretary, refused, 'come what may', to have anything to do with a French scheme for intervening against the Spanish revolutionaries. This was the virtual end of the Congress system. Canning, that 'malevolent meteor' in Metternich's opinion, refused to send a representative to a congress on Spanish America in 1824, or to the Congress of St. Petersburg in 1825.

It would be wrong, however, to write off the Quadruple Alliance or the Congress System as a complete failure. Though Britain went her own way, and though after 1830 France became another major power hostile to 'interventionist' schemes, the idea that there was a 'concert of Europe', that European statesmen discussed before they threatened, that peace was in the interests of all European nations, helped to create a diplomatic climate which enabled Europe to avoid a major war until 1854. This was the Vienna peacemakers' greatest achievement. After the Treaty of Westphalia (1648), Europe enjoyed less than fifteen years peace, after the Treaty of Utrecht (1713) less than thirty, after the Treaty of Paris (1763) less than twenty and after the Treaty of Versailles (1919) less than twenty. The peacemakers of 1815 deserve some criticism. They also deserve some praise.

Metternich

Thus the first problem of the victorious allies—how to dismantle the Napoleonic Empire and provide a lasting peace—was solved with some success. The attempts to solve the second—how to restore the continent to old, orderly pre-revolutionary ways— provoked a wave of revolutions. Alexander's 'Holy Alliance' was one aspect of reaction after 1815. Much the most skilful and patient enemy of revolution in the period 1815–48, however, was Prince Metternich.

The Austrian Chancellor inspired much hatred in his lifetime. The English poet Browning has an Italian liberal say

'. . . if I pleased to spend
Real wishes on myself—say three
I know at least what one should be.
I would grasp Metternich until
I felt his red wet throat distil
In blood through these two hands.

Moreover, since historians have tended to be sympathetic to liberal values, he has more often appeared a villain than a hero in the pages of history. He was certainly an interesting figure. Born a Rhinelander, he followed his father into the Habsburg Civil Service and soon made his mark as a skilful diplomat. By 1809 he was Austrian ambassador in Paris, where he made a careful study of Napoleon's strengths and weaknesses and played a part in bringing about his defeat. Thereafter he was indispensable to the Habsburgs and indeed, to the monarchs of Prussia and Russia. Until his fall in 1848, he was, without question, the most influential man in Europe.

His diplomatic skills were considerable and his arrogance fantastic. Having outsmarted Napoleon, he was convinced he could outsmart anyone. Gifted with an acute intelligence and wide experience of politics, he reckoned that he understood his own age as no-one else did. 'Men regard me', he wrote to Gentz, 'as a lantern which they approach in order to illuminate a dark night.' More than twenty years later, when the 1848 revolution had driven him to a London exile, he could still write to his daughter, 'during my long career as minister, amongst those who govern, I have been the most capable of governing.' He disliked almost everything that had happened in his lifetime except for developments in literature and in science. 1789 was a terrible year. 'There is only one serious problem in Europe', he wrote in 1832, 'and that is Revolution.' The French had much to answer for. 'Two words are enough to create evil: two words which, because they are empty of all real meaning, enchant the dreamers by their emptiness. These words are "Liberty" and "Equality".' His own age he regarded as a period of transition between two more pleasant eras. 'My life', he reflected, 'coincides with an abominable period. I have come into the world either too soon or too late. . . . I should have been born in 1900 with the twentieth century before me.' His whole career was one of dedicated pessimism. He was convinced that the old order which he championed was doomed, yet with extraordinary skill and patience he fought to keep it alive for as long as he could. The only way revolution could be met was by firm and dexterous repression. For thirty-three years he held it at bay until 1848 overwhelmed him. In his own way, he was a remarkable man.

The Revolutions of 1820–5

The first wave of revolution began in Spain in 1820. The Bourbon king, Ferdinand, who had been restored in 1814, installed the most rigidly reactionary government in Europe although there had been extensive support for liberal ideas in the cities of northern Spain in the years before the restoration. The country also had many problems stemming from the Napoleonic wars, of which politically the most explosive was a large number of able and unemployed young army officers. A contingent ordered by the government to prepare to sail to South America to fight the rebellious colonists mutinied in 1820 and, under the leadership of General Riego, proclaimed the liberal Constitution of 1812 in order to rally support. As Riego tried to rally the south, the northern cities revolted and forced Ferdinand to accept the 1812 constitution.

Revolution proved infectious. In March 1821 army officers and liberal nobility in Portugal succeeded in securing an assembly and constitution from the king and his regent, the English soldier, Marshal Beresford. In Southern Italy, the numerous revolutionary secret societies put their plans into action when they heard the news from Spain. General Pepe, an energetic officer who was known to have his differences with the king, was persuaded to lead the revolt. Since there was deep discontent in the Neapolitan army because of the way Austrian officers were getting the top jobs, most regiments proved ready to follow him. At first the revolutionaries achieved success with almost ludicrous ease, Pepe becoming head of the army and King Ferdinand granting the Constitution of 1812 with the comment 'had he only known that there was such a general desire for a constitution, he'd have granted one earlier'. Piedmont, in north-west Italy, was the next area to be affected. Again secret societies of officers and intellectuals inspired the rising, which was intended not only to secure a constitution but to expel the Austrians from Italy.

'Conflagration', 'earthquakes', 'torrents', were terms used by Metternich to describe these events. In his view the revolts, particularly the Italian ones, threatened the power of the established monarchies throughout Europe. He regarded the demand for Italian unity as particularly dangerous. Italy, he maintained, was only 'a geographical expression' and should remain so. He, therefore, set about suppressing them, with the backing of all the major powers, Britain excepted.

Once organized, the conservative forces proved far too strong for the revolutionaries. In the spring of 1821 the Austrian army marched south, defeated Pepe at Rieti and entered Naples to help Ferdinand re-establish his old despotism. Pepe, with those liberal leaders who escaped imprisonment, disappeared into exile. Much the same happened to Piedmont. An Austrian army defeated the revolutionary leader Santarosa at Novara, many liberals were transported to an Austrian imprisonment and an army of occupation, 12,000 strong, was left in Piedmont. All over Italy liberals were hunted down, many imprisoned and some put to death. At least 2,000 Italians were driven from the peninsula into exile.

The turn of the Spanish came in 1823, when the French decided to intervene on behalf of the Spanish king. The French army crossed the Pyrenees in April and drove the revolutionaries southward. Final resistance ended when Cadiz fell in September. Ferdinand then set about his former opponents with a savagery that the French tried but

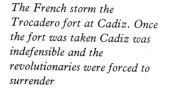

The French storm the Trocadero fort at Cadiz. Once the fort was taken Cadiz was indefensible and the revolutionaries were forced to surrender

failed to restrain. Hundreds were tortured and executed, thousands more imprisoned. Riego was dragged in a basket behind an ass to one of the main squares of Madrid, hung and carved up into five parts each of which was sent for public display to the five towns where he had enjoyed the greatest support. Ferdinand had learnt nothing from his experiences. He soon managed to quarrel with his brother, Don Carlos, leader of a powerful clerical political movement, and internal chaos was the lot of Spain for many years to come.

Only in Portugal did the forces of conservatism fail to win a complete triumph. In a very confused situation, John VI managed to stay on the throne and to maintain some kind of parliamentary government. He was, however, continuously threatened by his second son, Don Miguel (who wanted a more despotic government) and needed British support, supplied by Canning, if he was to remain in control.

By 1824, therefore, the conservative forces in Europe were once more in control. The liberal revolts were, at this stage, the work of a tiny handful of disgruntled nobility, army officers, and intellectuals, whose organization and links with middle classes and peasantry were never strong. Without widespread and passionate popular support, men like Pepe, Riego, and Santarosa were powerless against the combined forces of the Congress states which were organized against them with vigour.

Though the Duc de Berri, nephew of Louis XVIII, had been assassinated in February 1820 and a plot to murder Lord Liverpool's cabinet (the Cato Street Conspiracy), had been discovered almost simultaneously in Britain, no major European power was disrupted in this wave of revolution. In 1825, however, Russia was shaken by the so-called Decembrist revolt. The rule of Alexander had become very harsh. In Poland, hopes that he would allow some genuine self-government had been dashed. In Poland and Western Russia secret societies grew up, influenced by French and Italian ideas. Minor disturbances in 1820 had scared Alexander and caused him to give more and more power to Arakcheyev, an efficient but brutal administrator. By 1825 frustration in Russia and Poland was so great that two societies, the Society of the North led by Prince Troubetzkoy and the Society of the South led by Colonel Pestel, were planning to overthrow the government in 1826. On 13 December 1825, however, Alexander died, and for some time confusion reigned, since Nicholas, the younger brother, though intended by Alexander to succeed, proclaimed his elder brother Constantine as Tsar while Constantine, in Warsaw, proclaimed Nicholas. The Society of the North decided to act but, with no clear plan, dithered when they had Nicholas at their mercy. Loyal troops rounded up the conspirators without difficulty. When the

The conspirators of Cato Street, betrayed by one of their number, are surprised by the authorities

Society of the South began a rebellion a month later, it too was easily suppressed. The young Nicholas, now generally recognized as Tsar, was terribly shocked by the affair and greatly exaggerated the danger. 'Revolution stands on the threshold of Russia', he said, 'but I swear it will never enter Russia while my breath lasts.' Mass arrests followed the revolt. One hundred and twenty were eventually brought to trial, of whom five were executed and many others exiled to Siberia. To prevent further revolts, Nicholas created the Third Section, the first of a long line of secret police organizations. Yet by his brutal treatment of the Decembrists, Nicholas only strengthened the revolutionary cause in Russia. He made them martyrs who were to provide constant inspiration to Russian revolutionaries later in the century.

The Revolutions of 1830–3

The second wave of revolution, from 1830 to 1833, was a more serious affair altogether than its 1820–3 predecessor. It began in France with a revolt against the Bourbon monarchy which had been restored in 1815. Under Louis XVIII the Restoration had got off to a good start. He was old and gouty, without much popular appeal, but during his long exile he had developed much patience and a determination 'to heal the wounds of the revolution'. The charter which he granted at the beginning of the reign accepted the changes in land ownership made during the revolutionary period and reassured the propertied classes which had done well since 1789. It also established a Chamber of Peers and an elected Chamber of Deputies. Louis also allowed most of Napoleon's reforms, including the Concordat, to survive intact. Nonetheless, constitutional monarch though he had to be, Louis consoled himself with the thought that he still retained much more power than his brother-monarch, George III of England. He still had considerable powers of censorship and, most important of all, he could choose his own ministers.

Unfortunately for Louis, his good sense was shared by too few of his supporters, especially those royalists who had returned with him after a long and bitter exile. They let loose their own brand of terror after Napoleon's defeat at Waterloo. At Carcassonne a live eagle (the eagle was Napoleon's symbol) was brought down from the hills and torn to pieces. At Avignon one of Napoleon's Marshals was lynched and, when his coffin was being taken to burial it was seized and his body thrown in the River Rhone. In the years that followed, the extreme royalists, known as the Ultras and led by Louis's younger brother the Comte d'Artois, formed powerful groups in both chambers. They felt that Louis had compromised too much with the Revolution; that a more determined effort should be made to turn the clock back; that the king should be more despotic; that the Catholic Church should be more influential, particularly in education, and that the old aristocracy should recover its former social position. These demands naturally dismayed millions of Frenchmen who were convinced that the revolution had brought real gains. A number of determined liberals were elected to the Chamber of Deputies, and during the years 1815 to 1820 the crucial issues if 1789 to 1793 were debated again with remarkable eloquence. Louis's main aim was to hold the Ultras in check, since he had little doubt that if he gave way to their demands he would have a liberal revolution on his hands. At first he was successful with the help of two able ministers, Richelieu and Decazes, but the assassination (1820) of the Duc de Berri (the King's nephew) played into the Ultras' hands. They secured the dismissal of Decazes for being too soft on the liberals and forced a marked shift

The Coronation of Charles X

in government policy. There was more press censorship, greater clerical influence in education and the French armies were marched into Spain to crush the Spanish liberals.

The death of Louis in 1824 did nothing to halt this trend because he was succeeded by his younger brother, the Comte d'Artois, who became Charles X. Now aged 67, he had not mellowed. The coronation at Rheims took place with all the pageantry of the Middle Ages. The influence of priests seemed everywhere. The theft of religious objects from church—the crime of sacrilege—became punishable with death. Lay teachers at schools and universities were replaced by clerics and press censorship further extended. Furthermore, a scheme to provide adequate compen-

An episode during 'the Three Glorious Days' which drove the Bourbons from Paris in July 1830. A Swiss regiment which has managed to break through a street barricade is counter-attacked by a group of revolutionaries

sation for those nobles dispossessed by the Revolution was so handled that most men of property came to regard Charles X as a menace to their security.

By 1827 the formidable French middle classes had become once again the steadfast opponents of the Bourbon monarchy. A liberal political society, *Aide-toi, le ciel t'aidera* (Help yourself and Heaven will help you), was formed that year which, ably led by Guizot and backed financially by the famous banker Laffitte, played a great part in securing a liberal majority in the Chamber of Deputies in the subsequent election. Charles, however, was not one to compromise. In 1829 he decided the time had come for a showdown with the liberals and appointed three of the most extreme Ultras—Polignac, la Bourdonnaye, and General de Bourmont—as his ministers. To win popular support, a military expedition was sent off to conquer Algeria. Algiers fell on 9 July 1830 but the liberals further increased their majority. The government, therefore, decided on a *coup d'état* and on 25 July published ordinances which dissolved the newly elected chamber, and reduced the electorate from 100,000 to 25,000. At this time Polignac was having repeated visions of the

Virgin Mary who always promised him success. Perhaps it was the assurance of divine aid which caused the government to refrain from taking the slightest precautions before publishing the Ordinances. Most of the army was some distance from the capital and the general responsible for the defence of the city did not know what was going on.

The publication of the Ordinances soon led to barricades being erected in the streets of Paris. The most active revolutionaries were students and working men but they had the support of most of the city (see opposite). Resistance was not fierce. By the evening on 29 July the tricolour flew over Notre Dame and Charles X fled into exile. It proved easier to get rid of the Bourbons than to choose their successor. Many of the young revolutionaries wished for a republic with the veteran revolutionary Lafayette as President. The more experienced politicians like Talleyrand, Thiers, and Lafitte preferred a constitutional monarchy with Louis Philippe, Duc d'Orleans, a member of the old royal family as king. Louis Philippe was acceptable as a candidate because he had always been sympathetic to the 1789 revolution and had even fought for the revolutionary army at Jemappes in 1792. After much negotiation, Lafayette was persuaded to back Louis Philippe, and to the applause of a large crowd, they both appeared at a window of the Town Hall wrapped in a tricolour flag. A few days later, Louis Philippe was recognized as 'King of the French by the Grace of God and the will of the nation'. The power of the assemblies were strengthened and the size of the assembly approximately doubled to 200,000 (out of a population of 35,000,000). This July Revolution was a triumph for the French propertied classes. They had acquired a king who was virtually one of themselves and a constitution which ensured their political dominance.

In 1828 the young Cavour had written prophetically: 'In France the two parties are about to come to a decisive struggle . . . the course of events will drag all Europe in its train.' So it proved. Neighbouring Belgium was greatly excited by the revolution in France. The Belgians resented the rule of the Dutch king imposed on them in 1815 by the Vienna settlement. There were deep tensions between the races. The Dutch Protestants with a long tradition of independence despised the Catholic Belgians who had always been ruled by a foreign power. Though the king did much to stimulate the Belgian economy he tended to place Dutchmen rather than Belgians in public positions and his despotic ways offended the liberals who were growing more numerous as Belgium industrialized.

A group of liberals, meeting in secret, planned a revolt for 25 August. That evening an opera audience took to the streets of Brussels shouting 'down with the Dutch'. Rioters then took control of the capital and the following day the popular demand all over Belgium was for independence. Serious fighting broke out in September but the Brussels people proved solidly revolutionary and managed to hold the barricades against the Dutch troops. By November the Dutch had been driven from most of the country and a National Congress met to draw up a constitution. The main danger now to the revolutionaries lay in the fact that Austria, Prussia, and Russia were all hostile. Since each of these powers were faced with revolutions nearer home and France and Britain were sympathetic the new nation was never seriously threatened from this quarter. The National Congress wanted a constitutional monarchy and, under pressure from Britain, accepted Leopold of Saxe-Coburg, a German prince, as king with the most liberal constitution in Europe. By 1831 Belgian independence was secure and by 1839 it was recognized by most of Europe including the Dutch.

The bloodiest revolution took place in Poland. In November 1830 rumours in Warsaw that Tsar Nicholas was on the point of marching against the French and Belgian revolutionaries sparked off a rebellion which drove the Russian viceroy from the country. The Poles set up a provisional government but were soon divided amongst themselves, the 'Whites' aiming for moderate reform and a compromise with Russia, the 'Reds' for major reforms and complete independence. Tsar Nicholas, however, refused to negotiate. The Russians invaded in overwhelming force and, having won a decisive victory at Ostroleka, laid siege to Warsaw. There the Reds fought on grimly, hoping for French intervention which never came. Nicholas took a terrible revenge. A tenth of Polish lands were confiscated. The Universities of Warsaw and Vilna were closed. Thousands were put to death or imprisoned and thousands more chose to emigrate. Poland became the most tragic country in Europe. In the words of her poet Krasinski: 'the land of graves and crosses. One may know it by the silence of its men and the melancholy of its children.'

From 1815 to 1848 the Germany Confederation was one of the quietest parts of Europe. Momentary disturbances organized by students in 1819 led to the Metternich-inspired Carlsbad decrees which increased press censorship and government control of education. So effective was this repression that the liberal poet Heine could remark sarcastically—'when I was at the top of the St. Gotthard Pass, I heard Germany snoring.' The 1830 revolutions temporarily woke her up. In 1832 journalists, university teachers and students organized a great liberal and national festival at Hambach in Rhenish Bavaria at which, in the presence of more than 25,000 people, the Vienna settlement was severely criticized, particularly as it affected Germany. Metternich acted at once. The

Federal Diet was prevailed upon to pass further repressive measures, the Six Acts, and the Confederation sank back into its previous doze.

The area where Metternich most feared the influence of the French revolution of 1830 was Italy. The news from Paris inspired revolts in north and central Italy which had some immediate success. The provisional liberal governments had, however, no hope of surviving without French aid. Metternich worked with complete success to dissuade the new government of Louis Philippe from providing this aid, and the Austrian army quickly suppressed the various provisional governments. The old rulers were soon back on their thrones and their prisons full of liberals. Cardinal Bernetti in the Papal States took particularly savage reprisals.

Mazzini

Unlike Germany, however, Italy did not go back to sleep. Out of the disasters of 1830 a new liberal champion emerged. Giuseppe Mazzini. He was Genoese, the son of a university professor. Highly intelligent, the authorities found him a problem even while he was still at school. As his headmaster wrote with some exasperation on one of his reports, 'Although a young man of exceptional talent, he is nevertheless very dissipated and often goes out of the building to confer with his friends.' On leaving school, he quickly got mixed up in politics, joining a revolutionary secret society and taking part in the 1830 revolution. He was captured, imprisoned, and exiled. Moving to Marseilles, he founded a new society 'Young Italy' which soon developed offshoots—Young Germany, Young Ireland, Young Europe. He was a theatrical figure. His rooms were full of cigar smoke and canaries and he always dressed in black as 'a mourner for Italy'. As a practical politician, moreover, he was not very effective. After a lifetime spent in organizing ineffective conspiracies to free and unite Italy, he eventually saw an Italy freed and unified in a way he thoroughly despised. What is important about Mazzini is his writings, and his concept of a young liberal and nationalist movement prepared to go to any lengths to free its country. Only when all nations are united and free, Mazzini argued, will peace and progress come to the world. His idealism captured the minds of thousands of young Europeans and gave new fervour and optimism to liberalism between 1830 and 1848. Mazzinian conspiracies might be comic in their ineptitude, but the power of his ideas could not be denied. In Metternich's opinion he was 'the most dangerous man in Europe'.

By 1833, it became clear that the revolutions had effectively divided Europe into two camps. In France and in Belgium conservative regimes had been overthrown by liberal ones, and in Britain, Spain and Portugal, liberalism had made appreciable ground. Elsewhere, in Poland, Italy, and Germany, where the propertied middle classes remained comparatively weak, liberal revolutions had completely failed. Two treaties in 1833–4 further divided the conservative east from the more liberal west of Europe. The Convention of Munchengratz, signed by Austria, Russia and Prussia, agreed that the three states should act together against revolts. 'So long as this union of the three monarchs lasts', wrote Metternich, 'there will be a chance of safety in the world.' The following year France, Britain, Spain, and Portugal signed a Quadruple Alliance which, though mainly concerned with the Spanish peninsula was also intended, in the words of Palmerston the British Foreign Secretary, 'to serve as a counterpoise against the Holy Alliance of the East.'

Chapter 7
The Problem of 'The Beastly Turks'

In the century after 1815 the most explosive diplomatic issue in Europe was the so-called Eastern Question or what should happen to the very considerable area of south-east Europe still under Turkish rule as this rule continued to weaken. It was an extremely complex problem because as early as 1815 five major powers were involved. The Turks, however real their political weakness in the nineteenth century, had a magnificent past and a traditional contempt for Europeans against whom they had fought with such success for so long. They had no intention of surrendering their Empire without a struggle. The Russians, who had made considerable gains at Turkish expense in the eighteenth century, hoped to make the Black Sea a Russian lake and Constantinople a Russian city. The Austrians, though less aggressive than the Russians, were very conscious of the importance of the Danube and the Black Sea as trading routes and reluctant to stand by and watch Russia gaining territory and influence at the expense of the Turks without making corresponding gains themselves. The French had built up a prosperous trade in the eastern Mediterranean and political influence in Egypt, neither of which they wished to see threatened by an expanding Russia. And Britain, whose commercial interests in the eastern Mediterranean were even stronger, was also conscious that Russia was the one power which, by expansion in the Near East, could threaten her Indian Empire.

Certain characteristics of the Balkans added to the complications. From the earliest times, wave after wave of invaders had swept across this mountainous area with the result that its population was extremely varied. The majority were South Slavs, but there was a Latin race, the Roumans, in the lower Danube valley, the Albanians, whose roots went back beyond the Slav invasions of the sixth century A.D., on the Adriatic coast, and, in the south, the Greeks. Among the Slavs themselves, there were important differences. The Bulgars had their own language and folk memories of a great empire which in 910 A.D. stretched from the Black Sea to the Adriatic. Though the Serbs and Croats spoke a similar language, the Serbs used a Cyrillic, the Croats a Latin script. While the Croats were Catholic in religion, the Serbs were Orthodox. Moreover, like the Bulgars, the Serbs remembered a glorious past. Between 1331 and 1355, during the reign of Stefan Dushan, the

Serbian Empire had stretched from Belgrade to northern Greece. Though the great majority of South Slavs had remained Christian despite their conquest by Muslim Turks, the Bosnians, especially the nobility, had become more Turkish than the Turks, fanatical Muslims and bitter oppressors of their Christian peasants. In Macedonia there was also a substantial Muslim population using a dialect of Serbo-Croat which was almost a separate language (see map 9).

Thus it was that not only were there rivalries between Christians and Muslims but also between Christians and Christians, not only between Turks and Slavs but between Slavs and Slavs. The big power rivalries in the eastern Mediterranean made the Eastern Question explosive, the local Balkan rivalries doubly so. It proved too big a problem for the nineteenth century to solve despite the Crimean War, innumerable minor Balkan wars and a succession of diplomatic crises. By 1900 the Balkans had become 'the powder-keg

Map 9 South-east Europe about 1850

of Europe' which, fourteen years later, blew up.

Even before 1815 the deep-seated weakness of the Turkish Empire was clear. Between 1768 and 1792 the Turkish army had suffered a series of defeats at the hands of the Russians, and in the outlying parts of the Empire the authority of the Sultan was so weak that the local pashas (provincial governors) were virtually independent. In the mountains of Western Macedonia, for instance, Ali Pasha, 'the lion of Jannina', ruled as he pleased from 1788 to 1822. In 1799 the first Balkan state won its independence. Set back from the Adriatic lay the tiny country of Montenegro. 'When God finished making the world,' ran an old Balkan ballad, 'He found that He had a good many rocks left in His bag; so He tumbled the whole lot onto a wild and desolate piece of land—and that is how Montenegro was formed.' The Montenegran ruler, Peter I, declared war on the Turks and though his army was tiny won a complete victory. 'In the limestone mountains of Montenegro', went another Balkan saying, 'a small army is beaten and a large one dies of starvation.' The Turks were forced both to recognize the independence of Montenegro and to cede territory to Peter.

Serbian Indepedence

It was against the misrule of the local rulers rather than against the Sultan himself that the first major Slav revolt of the nineteenth century occurred. The Serbs were a race with a proud history, but in 1389 their army and nobility had been destroyed by the Turks on the Field of Blackbirds at Kosovo and their Balkan empire broken. At first, Turkish rule had been efficient and tolerant but, in the seventeenth and eighteenth centuries, it had become corrupt and exacting. The Janissary class was especially powerful in Serbia and its rule led to a deterioration in social and economic conditions. In 1717 an English noblewoman sent home this description of Turkish Serbia. 'We crossed the desert of Serbia, almost quite over-grown with wood, though a country naturally fertile. The inhabit-ants are industrious but the oppression of the peasants is so great they are forced to abandon their houses and neglect their tillage, all they have being a prey to the Janissaries whenever they please to see it.' Another cause of bitterness was the destruction of the Serbian Orthodox Church in 1766. The Sultan placed it directly under the control of the Greek Patriarch of Constantinople and many Serbian priests were replaced by Greeks. What made these conditions hard to bear was the comparative well-being of those Serbians living to the north under the rule of the Austrian Habsburgs.

The inevitable rising came in 1804. Its leader was Black George (Karageorge), so-called because of his black hair. Hoping to persuade the Sultan to grant him some measure of self-government, he first directed the revolt against the local Janissaries but when the Sultan turned down his self-government proposals, he proclaimed a war of independence. At first the Serbs, with their detailed knowledge of the countryside and with some support from Russia, held the advantage, but they were soon hampered by a divided leadership. Russian aid ended in 1812 and the Turks gained the upper hand, driving Karageorge into exile. Savage vengeance by the returning Turks soon led to another rising in 1815, this time planned by Milos Obrenovic. Milos was much shrewder than Karageorge and more successful. Though he was not able to gain complete independence, he made Turkish rule in the northern part of Serbia little more than nominal. Just at the end of this second rising, Karageorge returned from exile and considerably embarras-sed Milos who was negotiating with the Turks. In 1817 he was found murdered in circumstances which threw suspicion on the

The riots at the beginning of the Greek War of Independence. Greek Orthodox priests played a large part in the rising

Obrenovic family. Someone had betrayed him to the Turks with the result that his head was sent from Belgrade to Constantinople as a trophy for the Sultan. The betrayer was almost certainly Milos. A long and bloody feud was thus begun between the Obrenovics and Karageorgevics which haunted Serbian history for more than a century.

Milos continued to rule until 1839 and in this period the foundations of Serbian nationalism were laid. In 1833 he further increased his territories. He improved trade, roads, and education. Scholars studied the Serbian language and literature, and spread a wider understanding of Serbian history and culture. The main problem of the Obrenovics, however, apart from the Karageorgevics, were their mountain chiefs who regarded any government which attempted to reduce their authority and to tax them as the enemy. Without any Turks to plunder, they were only too pleased to take part in family vendettas. Of the nine rulers of Serbia (Yugoslavia) between 1804 and 1945, four were assassinated and four exiled!

Greek Independence

Other Europeans tended to regard the Slavs with disdain. As late as 1868 a Hungarian Count could say to an Austrian Chancellor, 'You look after your barbarians and we will look after ours', and by

127

barbarians mean the Slav populations of their respective lands. So these Serbian revolts aroused little interest in other parts of the continent. The Greek risings which immediately followed were, however, a different matter. Though most Greeks were in fact similar to their Balkan neighbours, brigand chiefs and peasantry loyal only to the Orthodox Church, there was also a class of Greek merchants, diplomats, civil servants, and seamen scattered all over the Turkish Empire. This group, prosperous and educated, with many links with other parts of Europe, were very conscious of the misery of the Greece of their generation compared with the glories of Ancient Greece. They found tremendous inspiration in the French Revolution. Rhigas, an early Greek revolutionary, rewrote the Marseillaise, the French National Anthem, to suit Greek conditions and founded a secret society which combined a study of the Greek past with preparations for a liberal revolution. Societies of this type flourished wherever educated Greeks gathered, the most influential, the 'Philiki Etaireia', or National Society, being founded in 1814 in the Black Sea port of Odessa. This society organized a rising in Moldavia in 1821 led by Prince Ypsilantis. The assumption appears to have been that the Moldavian peasants would be sympathetic to the idea of Greek independence. However, since they disliked their Greek civil servants almost as much as their Turkish rulers, Ypsilantis received little support and was soon defeated.

Meanwhile, a much more formidable rising had taken place in southern Greece, quite different in character from Ypsilantis'. Since 1770 Turkish rule in the area had been maintained, without any permanent success, by a reign of terror of Albanian troops. Internal order was the exception rather than the rule and outlaw chiefs known as 'klephts' were the real masters of much of the region. When Germanos, archbishop of Patras, unfurled the national standard at the monastery of Hagia Lavra on 25 March 1821—a date which the Greeks now celebrate as Independence Day—he did not so much start a war as give unity to a series of minor wars already in progress. The heroes of this war of independence— Kolokotrones and Odysseus the Klepht for instance—had much more in common with Karageorge or Ali Pasha of Januina than with recent national heroes such as George Washington of the U.S.A. or Lafayette of France, or ancient Greek heroes such as Miltiades or Leonidas. Yet such was the fascination of Greece to a Europe educated in the classical tradition of Homer and Thucydides and so persuasive were the revolutionary writings of the Greek educated classes that European liberals took up the cause of Greek independence with an extraordinary enthusiasm.

None spoke out more eloquently than the English poet, Byron.

His visit to Marathon, where in 490 B.C. the Athenians had destroyed the advancing Persian hosts, inspired these lines:

> The mountains look on Marathon,
> And Marathon looks on the sea,
> And musing there an hour alone
> I dream'd that Greece might still be free.

At Thermopylae, 300 Spartans had in 480 B.C. held a narrow defile against 50,000 Persians. Their heroism he recalled:

> Earth render back from out thy breast
> A remnant of our Spartan dead.
> Of the 300 grant but three
> To make a new Thermopylae.

Byron did not merely write. He went to Greece to fight with the revolutionaries. Working hard to raise money and to unite the quarrelling Greek leaders, he died from disease at Missolonghi in 1824. Many young liberals, particularly from Britain and France, were fired by his example and also came to fight.

The war proved a vicious one. The Greeks celebrated their first successes by massacring 8,000 defenceless Turks, who retaliated by massacring the Greeks in Constantinople and by hanging the Patriarch of the Orthodox Church on Easter Sunday from the gates of his palace. They then dumped his body in the sea. The most horrifying incident was on the island of Chios in 1822. At the beginning of the year, Chios had had a population of nearly 100,000. In August, when the Turks had finished with it, only 1,800 were left. 23,000 had been killed and more than 47,000 sold into slavery (see page 293).

Shocked though European opinion was, especially by the Turkish massacres, the statesmen of Europe were most reluctant to intervene against the Sultan. To help the Greeks would be to encourage revolution everywhere. It would be best, Metternich argued, that the revolt 'burn itself out beyond the pale of civilization'. Austria, France and Britain were also reluctant to help the Greeks, lest by weakening the Turkish Empire they would in fact be strengthening Russia.

They changed their attitude after 1824 when the Sultan, despairing of success, called in Mehemet Ali and his stepson Ibrahim to crush the Greeks. Mehemet Ali was Pasha of Egypt, the most powerful of the Sultan's subordinates, with an efficient army and navy. Ibrahim moved in on the Greeks and was on the verge of complete success when the Russians decided to intervene. Britain and France then signed an alliance with the Russians in 1827 and a joint Anglo-French-Russian navy sailed into Greek waters. There

Byron

The Battle of Navarino 1827

was no desire for war with Turkey. This naval force, it was hoped, would persuade the Sultan to negotiate a settlement of the Greek question. A Turkish captain, however, was foolish enough to fire on an allied boat which had approached him in order to parley, and Admiral Codrington, the supreme commander of the allied fleet, destroyed the whole Turkish fleet in the Bay of Navarino. It was, as Wellington, the British Prime Minister, put it, 'an untoward affair', but combined with French and Russian military assistance to the Greeks it secured Greek independence. By the Treaty of Adrianople between Russian and Turkey, Greek independence was recognized. Between 1830 and 1832 the Conference of London worked out the boundaries of the new state and, in 1833, the seventeen-year-old Prince Otto of Bavaria was recognized as king.

Among the Greeks, however, there was much dissatisfaction with the boundaries of the new state. It included only a tiny part of the Greek-speaking area north of the Gulf of Corinth, and the island of Crete remained Turkish. Nor did King Otto prove popular. Most of the top jobs went to Bavarians rather than Greeks, and not until after a bloodless revolution in 1843 did he grant a constitution. Yet there was no great improvement. Successive ministries were always short of money and unable to control brigandage. In 1862 King Otho was forced to abdicate and Britain provided a successor in the person of Prince William George of Denmark, brother-in-law of the Prince of Wales. The passing of time did nothing to reconcile the Greeks with the 1832 boundaries and their demands for further territory brought them into conflict with Bulgaria as well as with Turkey. It took four wars before 1914 and another between 1920 and 1923 before the present boundaries of Greece were settled. Thus, though the setting up of an independent Greek state was hailed with delight throughout Europe, it did little to reduce the political tensions in the Eastern Mediterranean.

Mehemet Ali

In the 1830s and 1840s Tsar Nicholas of Russia pursued a policy of 'peaceful penetration' towards The Turkish Empire (see map 10, p. 135). So strong was Russia's position in relation to the Balkans compared with that of any other European power, his advisers argued, that Turkey was never worth a war. This peaceful policy paid off in 1833 when Sultan Mahmud had to appeal to Nicholas for an alliance. The man who drove the Sultan to such a desperate course was Mehemet Ali. Backed by the French, he wished to build up his authority in Syria and hoped the Sultan would approve his schemes. When he discovered that, on the contrary, the Sultan was planning to reduce his power in Egypt, he sent Ibrahim to march on Constantinople. Ibrahim was the best general in the Turkish Empire. In 1831 and 1832 he won victory after victory. At the battle of Konieh he destroyed the Sultan's last army and Constantinople was at his mercy. The Sultan, in desperation, appealed to Britain for aid. Against the advice of the British ambassador, the British Foreign secretary, Palmerston, refused since he judged the risks to be too great. Only then did Mahmud turn to Russia. 'A drowning man', commented one of his advisers, 'clings to a serpent.' In return for military assistance, Nicholas forced the Turks to sign the Treaty of Unkiar Skelessi (1833) which made the Black Sea virtually a Russian lake. Mehemet Ali and Ibrahim agreed to negotiate and were granted very much what they wanted. British interests had received a serious setback and Palmerston, with the aid of an exceptionally gifted ambassador, Stratford Canning (later Lord Stratford de Redcliffe), set about restoring British influence. Both were resolved—and both were unusually resolute men—that in the event of another such crisis, Britain should be much more positive.

A very similar crisis did occur just six years later, in 1839. The same actors were involved, Sultan Mahmud, Mehemet Ali, and Ibrahim, Russia, Britain, and France. Mahmud was doing his best to weaken Mehemet Ali, and though he was on his death-bed, ordered his army to march against the Egyptian pasha. The results were catastrophic. Ibrahim won a crushing victory at Nezib, Mahmud died and the Turkish fleet deserted to Alexandria. Mehemet Ali, secretly backed by France and faced by an inexperienced youth of sixteen, assumed he could dictate what peace terms he liked. Palmerston, however, went into action. While the British fleet blockaded Alexandria, he proposed a great power conference and, by June 1840, had persuaded Russia, Austria and Prussia to agree that Mehemet Ali should merely be recognized as hereditary pasha of Egypt and pasha of Acre for life. Neither the French nor Mehemet Ali were consulted. 'It was', said Thiers, the French Prime Minister, 'the Waterloo of my diplomacy.' The French government was outraged and, for a moment, considered declaring war on Britain. They soon had second thoughts, and Thiers was replaced by the less aggressive Soult. In the meantime the British fleet bombarded Beirut and Acre, forcing Ibrahim to retreat to Egypt, and the appearance of Admiral Napier off Alexandria persuaded Mehemet Ali to come to the conference table. The result of negotiations, dominated by Palmerston, was the restriction of Mehemet Ali to Egypt and the Straits Convention of 1841. All vessels of war belonging to foreign powers were forbidden to enter the straits between the Black Sea and the Mediterranean. This was a great triumph for Palmerston's diplomacy. The advantage that the Russians had gained by the Treaty of Unkiar-Skelessi was cancelled out and the new Sultan, Abdul Mejid, had great confidence in Britain's friendship. Henceforward, Palmerston and his successors at the Foreign Ministry assumed that the Turkish Empire could and should be propped up against Russian aggression. As Palmerston put it in his forthright way, 'all that we hear every day of the week about the decay of the Turkish Empire and its being a dead body or a sapless trunk and so forth is pure unadulterated nonsense.' Thus Britain was convinced that Turkey was sick but curable, Russia that she was incurable.

The Crimean War

This crucial difference of opinion determined much of the history of the eastern Mediterranean for the rest of the century. In 1844 Tsar Nicholas paid a visit to England, during which he had a long conversation with Aberdeen, Foreign Secretary in Peel's Tory government. Since the Turk was in his opinion a dying man, Nicholas suggested that Britain and Russia should plan ahead for his death. A partition was the obvious solution, he argued. While Russia should take Constantinople, Britain should have Egypt and Crete. Aberdeen was not a forceful man and he allowed Nicholas to leave England with the feeling that though Britain was not keen on his partition scheme, she was unlikely to go to war in defence of Turkey. He underestimated how confident British governments were that the Turkish Empire could be both reformed and revived and how increasingly anti-Russian British public opinion had become in the mid-nineteenth century.

The next Eastern Question crisis did not at first concern Britain. In 1850 a bitter dispute broke out between Catholic and Orthodox priests over the care of the Holy Places in Jerusalem and Bethlehem. The Tsar of Russia had always claimed to protect the interests of Orthodox Christians within the Turkish Empire, while France since the time of the Crusades had posed, when convenient, as the defender of all Christian interests in the Holy Land. As it happened, it suited Napoleon III, the French Emperor, to champion the Catholic cause because he particularly wanted the support of the French Catholic Church at home. Tsar Nicholas loathed Napoleon III partly as an upstart and partly as a Bonaparte. Moreover since 1774 Russia had claimed a special right to protect all Christians within the Turkish Empire, which was now threatened by the French. Britain was drawn into the dispute because both France and Russia asked for her support.

None of the powers either wanted or expected war from what was essentially a trivial issue. Such were the muddles and blunders of the diplomacy of 1853–4 that the Crimean War, the first major European war since 1815, broke out between Russia on the one side and Britain, France and Turkey on the other. The sorry sequence of events was as follows. Tsar Nicholas, confident that Britain would not allow herself to become too deeply involved in the Holy Places affair, sent Prince Menshikov, a haughty and tactless man, to insist on Russia's right to protect Turkish Christians as and when she saw fit. Since the Sultan had already decided in favour of French claims in the Holy Land, this mission only served to enrage the Turks and disturb the French. It also convinced the British that Russia was using the crisis to secure much greater influence within the Turkish Empire. Neither Aberdeen, now Prime Minister in Britain, nor Clarendon, his Foreign Secretary from February 1853, wished for war, but they were not masters of their own house. Palmerston, though officially he had no responsibility whatever for foreign affairs at the time, led a belligerent group within a divided cabinet. The British and French press whipped up a frenzied campaign against the Russian bully. In Constantinople, Lord Stratford de Redcliffe, 'the voice of England in the East' and well-known for his anti-Russian attitude and readiness to meet threat with threat, though he never disobeyed instructions from Aberdeen, certainly gave the Turks the impression that the British government was more resolute than in fact it was. Consequently, the Turks rejected the Russian demands. Nicholas, who still believed that

Britain was no real danger, then took the dangerous step of moving his troops into Moldavia and Wallachia, Turkish territory, to show he meant business. Napoleon III, who had fewer misgivings about a war than Aberdeen and was determined not to lose face, moved the French fleet nearer Constantinople. In June 1853 the British fleet joined the French off the Dardanelles. Even now, war still seemed far off, especially when the powers involved conferred at Vienna on the invitation of the Austrians. By this time, however, British, and to some extent French, public opinion had got out of hand. Russia must give way completely. The Turks too had worked themselves into an aggressive mood. The diplomatic cogs turned too slowly and in October Sultan Abdul Mejid, confident that France and Britain would not desert him now, declared war on Russia when she refused to evacuate Moldavia and Wallachia. 'The beastly Turks have dared to declare war', said an exasperated Clarendon to his wife, but though France and Britain still held back, they had gone too far to retreat without serious loss of face. Their fleets moved closer to Constantinople and when the Russian fleet intercepted and destroyed a Turkish flotilla off Sinope in November 1853, this action appeared to be a deliberate insult to the two Western powers. The British press chose to regard what was in fact an armed encounter between two nations formally at war as a treacherous and brutal massacre and howled for war. Eventually, in March 1854, Britain and France declared war on Russia, their stated aim being to drive Russian troops from Turkish territory and to end Russian claims to any special right to protect Turkish Christians.

The war itself was even more mismanaged than its preliminaries (see map 10). Its most obvious features were the extraordinary stupidity of the commanding officers on both sides and the equally extraordinary courage and patience of the men who suffered on account of their mistakes. Since threats from Austria that she would join the allies if Russia remained in the Danube basin were enough to force a Russian withdrawal, the French and British armies found on their arrival that they had to discover a new area to attack. They chose the Crimean peninsula, the main target being the great naval base of Sebastopol. The allied landing on the northeast coast of the peninsula was badly handled. However Menshikov, the Russian commander, failed to inflict any serious losses. Marching southwards, the British and French infantry forced the crossing of the river Alma with great courage. Their generals, St. Arnaud and Raglan, then missed a golden opportunity of bringing the campaign to a speedy and glorious end. The road to Sebastopol was open, the city virtually defenceless. They decided, however, on a slow circuitous approach instead of a swift direct one. By the time Sebastopol was surrounded, Todleben, the only commander of any

Map 10 The Eastern Mediterranean in the mid-nineteenth century

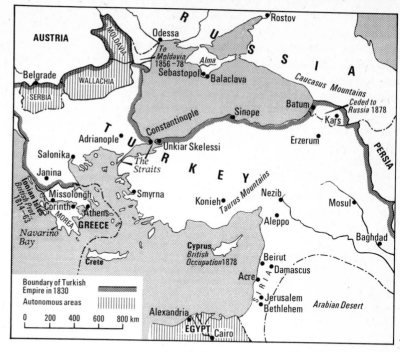

talent on either side, had greatly strengthened the defences and Menshikov, with a reinforced Russian army, stood close by. The allies had to settle for a siege through the long Crimean winter, which proved especially frightful since cholera and dysentery came with the cold. The British army suffered particularly severely, since its supplies and hospital staff proved quite inadequate for the conditions. Fortunately, the scandalous situation did not

'The Supply Problem': Punch cartoon 1855

"WELL, JACK! HERE'S GOOD NEWS FROM HOME. WE'RE TO HAVE A MEDAL."
"THAT'S VERY KIND. MAYBE ONE OF THESE DAYS WE'LL HAVE A COAT TO STICK IT ON?"

go unnoticed. *The Times* had its finest reporter, W. H. Russell, at the front. There was no censorship and he was not a man to mince his words. His dispatches caused an outcry in London and Florence Nightingale came to the hospital of Scutari to do legendary nursing work among the wounded. The French were better prepared than the British. Even so their losses during the winter were still considerable. Since the French authorities doctored the casualty lists, however, their public remained unaware of the extent of the losses. As for the Russians, two-thirds of their reinforcements, mainly serfs, died of starvation or of sickness before reaching their destination.

Since Sebastopol was now surrounded by the allies, Menshikov had to break their grip or the city would fall. Three times he attacked—at Balaclava, at Inkerman and at the Tchenaya river. Each time he was repulsed after confused and bitter fighting. It was during the Balaclava engagement that the most notorious blunder of the war occurred. The British were defending their naval base from a Russian attack. Raglan, viewing the fighting from the hills, wished his cavalry to prevent some Russians making off with some British guns. The order which he sent to his cavalry commander, Lord Lucan, was vague, and since Lucan could not see the guns Raglan was referring to, incomprehensible. They were also incomprehensible to Lord Cardigan, commander of the Light Brigade, who was to carry out the attack. Lucan and Cardigan however were related to each other by marriage and hated each other. Both stuck rigidly to the principle that orders were orders and were quite incapable of discussing sensibly between them what exactly Raglan meant. The one man who might have helped them, Major Nolan, who had carried the order from Raglan, was so eager for action and so contemptuous of these squabbling aristocrats that his brief comments only angered and misled them further. The result was that the Light Brigade, the finest cavalry regiment in the world, charged along the wrong valley with lances erect into the teeth of the main Russian artillery. Nearly 700 charged. Only 195 came back.

> Theirs not to make reply,
> Theirs not to reason why,
> Theirs but to do and die.
> Into the Valley of Death
> Rode the six hundred.

So wrote the poet Tennyson in a poem which glorified the action as a feat of bravery. A French officer watching the action from afar made a briefer and more appropriate comment—'*magnifique, mais ce n'est pas la guerre*' (magnificent, but it is not war).

After Tchernaya, the French managed to seize the Malakov fort

The Charge of the Light Brigade: the main Russians guns are on the left

which overlooked the city. Todleben then decided that the city was no longer defensible, and in September 1855 evacuated it.

The Crimean campaign was virtually over. A British naval expedition to the Baltic achieved next to nothing and to the east of the Black Sea, the Russians were holding their own in fighting round the fortress of Kars. The Russians were ready for peace. Nicholas had died in 1855 and was succeeded by Alexander II, an intelligent young man who was shocked by the shortcomings that the war had demonstrated in the Russian army and administration. Only the British, who wished to make up for the humiliation of the Crimea, wanted to continue, but once France showed that she was prepared to negotiate with the Russians she also came to terms. With Napoleon III acting as host in Paris, peace terms were finally agreed in 1856. The war had cost the lives of about 500,000 men.

Russia lost more than 300,000, France about 100,000 and Britain 60,000. It was the most costly European war during the period 1815 to 1914.

By the Peace of Paris Russia suffered a major defeat. She lost territory at the mouth of the Danube, abandoned all claims to protect Turkish Christians and accepted that the Black Sea should contain no warships in times of peace. Turkey was accepted as part of the Concert of Europe and it was laid down that no power had the right to intervene between the Sultan and his Christian subjects. In return, the Sultan promised reforms which would improve the position of his Christian subjects and gave greater independence to Moldavia-Wallachia (future Rumania) and to Serbia. The free navigation of the Danube river was guaranteed by the major powers.

It was an inadequate peace to end an unnecessary war. The terms were too hard on Russia. The promises of reform made by the Sultan were never kept and too little allowance was made for the increasing vigour of Balkan nationalism. Though the allies had gained most of what they fought for—prestige, Turkish independence, and the end to Russian expansion round the Black Sea—they had done nothing to make the Eastern question less dangerous. As the second half of the century would show, Tsar Nicholas had been right in his diagnosis of Turkey and Palmerston wrong. The Turkish Empire in Europe was dying. What the Crimean War decided was that Balkan nationalism rather than Russian designs on Constantinople should be the central issue of the Eastern Question from 1856 to 1914.

Chapter 8
Another Napoleon

The most important single date between 1789 and 1914 was 1848. In this year a series of revolutions convulsed Europe from Palermo to Paris, from Berlin to Belgrade. Though the events of this year in France will be dealt with in this chapter and those of the rest of Europe in another, and though the causes and consequences of these events vary considerably from one country to the next, it is worth remembering that all the revolutions are closely linked. The Sicilian rising of January 1848 set the Parisian cafés buzzing with anti-government talk. The French revolution of February 1848 inspired the Viennese students to action. Even England felt the winds of change. The Chartist movement which had languished since 1841 was roused by the example of the continent to a final effort in April 1848. It failed but was temporarily alarming enough to persuade the government to place the Duke of Wellington in command of the defence of London. For a moment, Europe seemed to sense that the long winter of political repression might be over. The natural spring of 1848 was a political springtime when a summer of constitutional and social reform appeared near at hand. Within a year, the high hopes of the reformers were dashed and by 1850 much of Europe was controlled once more by reactionaries. Nonetheless, after 1848 Europe could never be quite the same again.

The 1848 Revolution in France

Paris was the first of the great European capitals to see the street barricades going up. At the beginning of 1848, the July Monarchy (so called because Louis-Philippe first came to power in July, 1830) had been in existence nearly eighteen years—the longest period of stable government that France had experienced since the 1789 Revolution. 'France is bored', said the poet and orator, Lamartine, who was to play a central part in the political events of the months to come, and his words have often been taken as a satisfactory explanation of the lack of support for Louis-Philippe when the crisis came. But boredom alone cannot make a revolution. Many Frenchmen were embittered as well as bored by the regime of Louis-Philippe. There were a number of reasons for this bitterness. In the first place, there was a major economic crisis which affected

both the countryside and the towns. The corn harvest failed in 1846
and 1847 and, as the price of bread rose, other industries became
depressed. Most of Europe suffered in the same way but the
situation in France was made worse by over-speculation in railway
development which created a financial crisis. Consequently, there
was widespread unemployment and hunger which the government
was unable to remedy. Secondly, the government had shaken the
loyalty of the propertied middle classes, its most faithful supporters,
by its recent foreign policy. In the 1830s Louis-Philippe had
pursued a peaceful policy, the cornerstone of which was an understanding with England. It was not in the least glorious but good
for business. In 1847, however, Louis-Philippe and Guizot, his
prime minister, took a diplomatic stand on the Spanish Marriages
question which appeared to sacrifice the important friendship of
England purely in the interests of Louis-Philippe's family. Thirdly,
it was widely felt that some kind of social reform was urgently
needed. France in the 1840s was in the early stages of her industrial
revolution and conditions in some of the developing towns like Lille
or Amiens were as bad if not worse than anything England had
experienced. Yet while on the north side of the Channel men like
Shaftesbury were successful in forcing the government to take
action to improve social conditions, Guizot could not be persuaded
that social reform was the business of the government at all.
Fourthly and most significantly—for this it was that sparked off the
February revolution—Louis-Philippe's regime refused to consider

*A political banquet held in
honour of the anti-government
deputy from Soissons*

Place de la Bastille, February 24th 1848. The throne of Louis Philippe is burnt by the revolutionaries

the question of parliamentary reform. The population of France at this time was about 35,000,000. Of these only 241,000 had the vote. In 1847 Guizot had even refused to give the vote to the National Guard and, as public opinion swung against him, he relied more and more on corruption to maintain his ministry in power.

The revolution came with surprising suddenness. Political banquets had been held regularly over a period of six months to whip up support for parliamentary reform. A clumsy attempt by the government to suppress them led to demonstrations and the building of barricades by students and workers. There was widespread disorder and it soon became clear that Guizot could not count on the loyalty either of the National Guard or of the army. When Louis-Philippe finally brought himself to dismiss his prime minister, it was too late. Some troops, unnerved by the demonstrators, had fired upon them, killing more than thirty and turning a riot into a revolution. On 24 February the king abdicated and, having escaped through the gardens of the Tuileries Palace, eventually arrived in Newhaven disguised as a Mr. William Smith.

The swift collapse of the July monarchy left France in a bewildered state. The leaders of the revolution got together immediately and, acclaimed by the demonstrators, formed a Provisional Government on the day of Louis-Philippe's abdication. They were an interesting group including Albert, a worker to represent the workers, Louis Blanc, author, political thinker, and the first real Socialist to hold public office in Europe, and Lamartine, poet and historian. However, they were united only in their contempt for the July monarchy and in their determination to have no more kings in France. In February and March they managed to agree on three major policy decisions. They opened the National Guard to all classes; they set up the National Workshops in an attempt to deal with the unemployment problem, and they ordered that elections should be held immediately, in which all men sound in body and mind should have the right to vote. Thereafter, their divisions became more clearly apparent, as did the contrast between the political attitudes of Paris and those of the provinces. The new electorate, more than 9,000,000 strong, went to the polls in April and returned an Assembly far more moderate in opinion than the Provisional Government. It quickly showed its mood by excluding Blanc and Albert, the heroes of the Parisian workers, from the new ministry. Up to this point the 1848 revolution in France had contained many elements of farce. It now became a tragedy. Blanc had been the inspiration of the National Workshops which he had intended to be publicly-owned industries providing work for the unemployed and competing with private enterprise. His plan, however, was compromised from the first. Most of the Provisional Government were deeply suspicious of any threat to private industry. Moreover, the economic depression deepened further and the number of unemployed so increased that the Workshops were unable to provide genuine work and became little more than centres for distributing relief. The moderate assembly, more representative of the tax-paying middle classes and of the rural peasantry than of the urban working classes, decided that the Workshops were a luxury that the nation could ill afford. As they were closed down, many of the Parisian workers, starving and desperately disillusioned, took to the barricades once more. The 'June Days' began.

They did not turn out to be just another few days of demonstrations and rioting. Bloody civil and class war raged through the streets of Paris. Fear of a 'Red' revolution ran deep amongst the propertied classes and General Cavaignac was called in with more than 30,000 troops. He crushed the revolutionaries with efficient ferocity. It is not known how many were killed in the fighting and the fighting was not the end of the savagery. At least 1,500 were executed without trial and 6,000 sent into exile for their part in the rising. In the words of an intelligent and anxious observer: 'Something hard, ferocious and inhuman is coming into our conduct. The men of order, those that are called respectable folk, ask for shootings, nothing but shootings.' By the end of June the men of order were triumphant but the spring hopes of 1848 blighted without hope of revival.

The way was now open for the Bonapartists. Ever since the last exile of Napoleon on St. Helena, a small group of Frenchmen remained loyal to his memory and to his dynasty. They carefully fostered the legend of the military hero who was at heart a man of peace and a champion of freedom. When the Duke of Reichstadt, Napoleon's son and heir, died in 1832, Louis-Napoleon, the only surviving son of Napoleon's brother Louis, was accepted as head of the dynasty. His two attempts—the first in 1836, the second in 1840—to overthrow the July monarchy by force ended in fiasco and did nothing to improve his reputation. Bonapartism, however, flourished since Louis-Philippe vainly attempted to attach some of the glamour of the Bonaparte past to his own inglorious regime. He completed the Arc de Triomphe to commemorate the victories of the First Empire, and caused the body of the Emperor to be brought from St. Helena to be reburied with tremendous ceremony in Paris. Thus, when in the autumn of 1848 a shaken and divided France looked for a President who, untarnished by the recent past, could maintain law and order and lead the nation to a more unified and glorious future, the name Bonaparte had a magic all of its own. When the presidential elections were held on 10 December, Louis-Napoleon had been in France just seventy-five days since his return from exile. To most Frenchmen he was unknown. To the Paris politicians who heard him speak badly in the Assembly with a strong German accent, he seemed quite insignificant. Thiers, an experienced and influential politician, summed up the general feeling thus: 'He is a noodle whom anyone could twist round his finger.' For the electorate, however, the name was enough. In the December election, Louis obtained about 75 per cent (5,434,226) of the votes cast, while his nearest rival, General Cavaignac, the victor of the June Days, mustered fewer than 20 per cent (1,448,107).

Louis Napoleon

The French people imagined that they had elected as their President for the next few years a chip off the old Bonaparte block; the Parisian politicians that they would be serving a figurehead whom they could easily manipulate to their own advantage. Both were greatly mistaken. Louis-Napoleon was the third and youngest son of Louis Bonaparte and Hortense de Beauhamais—a nephew, therefore, of Napoleon I. He was born in 1808 when his father was

143

still King of Holland. The marriage of his parents was not happy. For the first fourteen years of Louis-Napoleon's life they lived apart and, though there was something of a reconciliation after 1822, his father was always a stranger, even an enemy. His early life was unsettled in other ways. Waterloo was fought when he was only seven and exile for Napoleon I meant exile for all Bonapartes. Hortense managed to remain a wealthy woman and travelled extensively in Italy, Switzerland and Germany in the first years of exile with the result that her children's education was much disrupted. Louis-Napoleon was a moody child with an affectionate nature but intellectually lazy and easily bored. It was only when he reached the age of twelve and was entrusted to the care of an excellent teacher and scholar, Philippe le Bas, that he began to make educational progress. When his family was resident in Germany, he attended the Grammar School at Augsburg and eventually reached fourth position in a class of ninety-four, his private tuition continuing out of school hours and during the holidays.

Even before his formal education ended in 1826 he was a much-travelled young man who had had more than his fair share of excitement. After leaving school, his adventures became more serious. Having journeyed south into Italy with his cousin and elder brother, he was almost immediately caught up in the 1830 revolution. Italian liberals looked back to the Napoleonic period as a golden age, so the young Bonapartes naturally supported the liberals against the Austrians. The latter, however, were too strong, the liberals too divided. Louis, having seen his elder and only surviving brother die of measles, had to make a dramatic escape from the Adriatic to Paris. The Duke of Reichstadt's death, the following year, left him head of the family. Henceforward his life was dedicated to the restoration, in his person, of the Bonaparte dynasty to France. This was the aim of both the Strasbourg plot of 1836 and the Boulogne landing of 1840. The affair at Strasbourg proved a fiasco because the soldiers who were supposed to provide the armed support in the takeover of the city were so unimpressed by Louis's appearance that they could not believe that he was really a Bonaparte. In the confusion officers loyal to the July Monarchy were able to regain control. The government, unready to take him very seriously, shipped him off to the U.S.A. without trial. The Boulogne landing was even more humiliating. Success hinged on the absence of the commanding officer of the garrison. Since the expedition arrived twenty-four hours late, the officer in question was back on duty and more than equal to the attack. Of the fifty Bonapartists who landed, only five survived, one of whom was Louis, captured half-drowned as he tried to escape to an off-shore boat. This time the government was more severe, sentencing him to life imprisonment.

Louis Napoleon in the fortress of Ham. Obviously it was not the most uncomfortable of imprisonments! Note the bust of Napoleon I brooding over his nephew

In fact, he was to be in the fortress of Ham for six years. These he put to good use, improving his reputation as an author and journalist. He had begun publishing in the 1830s. His *Political Musings*, the central argument of which was that France needed a Bonaparte again, appeared in 1832. His most important political work, *Napoleonic Ideas*, followed in 1839. His uncle, he argued in this book, wished to establish both order and freedom in France. His wars were forced upon him by his enemies. He failed because of them, and because he tried to go too far too fast. The obvious conclusion? What France and Europe needed was another Napoleon. His prison writings were more journalistic. He wrote articles about his famous uncle, about canals, sugar-beet, and the history of artillery. One more weighty work was published in 1844, *The Elimination of Poverty*, which outlined a complicated scheme for settling the poor on land paid for by the state. Whatever the merits of the scheme, it attracted attention and allowed Louis to pose in 1848 as a social reformer in whom the poor could trust.

145

The governor of Ham prison was much impressed by the studiousness and charm of his prisoner. As the years passed, he was less closely supervised. In the early summer of 1846, his quarters were being repaired. Friends smuggled in carpenter's clothes and, in this disguise, shouldering a plank, he walked out of the main entrance. A dummy placed in his bed deceived his warders for another twelve hours and he was able to make good his escape to London. Two years later he was President of the Second French Republic.

It is not easy to say what sort of man the new President was after so extraordinary a career. He puzzled his contemporaries and has puzzled historians ever since. He was not impressive in appearance. 'A short, thickish, vulgar-looking man', wrote Croker, a leading London diarist who met him in exile in England. He was not a good speaker either in public or in private. In fact he was extraordinarily taciturn, keeping his thoughts and feelings from even his closest friends. Often he appears not so much to have thought out a policy as to have felt his way towards it. In the words of McManners a modern historian, 'he lived instinctively, like a sleepwalker.'

Nonetheless it is clear that Louis-Napoleon had his own powerful if peculiar philosophy and real political qualities. His destiny as successor of the First Napoleon was his religion. His faith in this destiny had never faltered in the long years of exile, humiliation and imprisonment and was to sustain him during the twenty-two years that he was ruler of France. Though he had none of his uncle's intelligence, energy, or genius as a military commander, he had one quality that the First Napoleon did not possess—a feeling for the trends of the times, in particular the hopes and fears of ordinary people whose support was vital to the success of Bonapartism. Louis-Napoleon never preached a simple return to the good old days of 1799 to 1815. He carefully rewrote the Napoleonic legend to match the aspirations of France in the 1840s. Unlike his uncle, Louis had a genuine sympathy for suppressed nationalities like the Italians. Moreover he firmly believed that strong governments could only exist if they were based on the will of the people and looked forward with hope rather than fear to the coming of democracy. He also had an understanding of the plight of the industrial poor. His Bonapartism, therefore, was different from his uncle's original. While it revived memories of past glories, it also made sense in a radically altered present.

The Second Republic

Those Paris politicians who hoped to 'manage' the new President must have found the years 1848 to 1851 quite a shock. Louis proved firm, decisive, and skilful. If he was to fulfil his destiny and become Emperor, the Assembly, which was an essential part of the 1848 constitution and very suspicious of the presidential power, must be brought to heel. From the first, therefore, he set himself up as the champion of the unified nation against the selfish divisions of the Assembly. In 1849 he toured the French provinces. A cholera epidemic gave him the chance to display his courage and his concern for the poor and sick. He also showed real interest in industry and commerce, particularly in railway development. In the summer of 1849 he used the Italian crisis with some success to improve his reputation among French Catholics. French troops were sent to save Rome for the Pope, first from Garibaldi and the liberals who were in possession of the city, and secondly from the Austrians who were advancing on Garibaldi in overwhelming numbers. As he felt his popularity increasing, he took a stronger line with the politicians. Before the end of 1849 he dismissed the ministry of Barrot on the grounds that, through the Assembly, it was obstructing the progress of France in its own selfish interests. Another major obstacle to any further increase in Louis' powers was the fact that the control of the armed forces was in anti-Bonapartist hands. Much of this obstacle was eliminated in 1851 with the dismissal of General Changarnier, commander of the garrison of Paris and of the National Guard. Louis and Changarnier detested each other. The General was a great dandy and popular at society parties. It was he who coined a nickname for the President which society found particularly apt—'the melancholy parrot' (*le perroquet melancolique*). He was dismissed on the grounds that he had forbidden his regiment to acclaim the President in the customary manner at a public review. Men upon whom Louis could personally count were appointed to key military positions.

According to the 1848 Constitution, no President could be elected to a second term of office, so that if Louis was to retain power in 1852, decisive action was essential. By 1851 the Assembly was very unpopular. It had deprived 3,000,000 voters of the right to vote and ignored Louis' demand that this right be restored. In July 1851 it refused to give the majority necessary for the revision of the constitution to enable the President to stand for re-election. By so doing, it virtually signed its own death warrant. Secure in the knowledge of his personal popularity, Louis, in the best Bonaparte tradition, resolved on a *coup d'état*.

December 2, the anniversary of his uncle's crushing victory over the Austrians at Austerlitz, was chosen as the day. The Duc de Morny, Louis's half-brother and Maupas, the Chief of Police, were the planners and executors. They did their work well. The *coup d'état* was carried out with an efficiency and ruthlessness of which Louis-Napoleon himself was incapable. At 5 a.m. on 2 December, proclamations that the Assembly was dissolved and that the President proposed to continue in office for another ten years were already being distributed. Between 6.15 and 6.45, eighty-six leading opponents who might have organized counter-measures were individually arrested. By lunchtime another 200 deputies, who had protested to the police when they found the Assembly closed, were also in prison. At first there was little public reaction, either positive or negative. Morny, however, had always reckoned that 4 December would be the real day of decision and he was right. The barricades went up in the morning, the troops, 30,000 of them, came in during the afternoon. Six hours were enough, all resistance being crushed at an official cost of 215 lives. Morny and Maupas did not stop there. 26,884 suspected opponents were provisionally arrested, of whom 9,500 were shipped off to Algeria and 239 of the most dangerous to French Guiana. Many quite innocent people were included in the purge. When Louis realized how far his henchmen were going, he intervened, pardoning more than 3,000 of their victims. But their brutality remained on his conscience and was never forgiven or forgotten by many Frenchmen. On 21 December another plebiscite was held to test the nation's reaction to the events of the previous three weeks. The combination of past popularity and present brutality proved enormously effective. 7,500,000 Frenchmen 'desired the maintenance of Louis Bonaparte's authority and delegated to him the powers necessary to establish a constitution. . . .' Only 650,000 did not.

The Emperor

The Second Empire

The Second Empire was soon to follow. In January 1852 Louis published the new Constitution. There was to be a Senate and a Parliament to advise the President. Since the Senate, however, was entirely nominated by Louis himself and the Parliament mainly composed of 'official' candidates, he had in fact proclaimed a virtual dictatorship, all the more so since the Press was taken firmly under government control. Not all the parliamentary deputies, however, turned out to be government 'yes-men'. Though they were nominated by the Prefects, the local government officials, they were often nominated because they were local notabilities not because they were Bonapartists. As the years passed, both Parliament and Senate showed increasing independence of thought. These developments, however, lay in the future. In October 1852 the President suggested that the Second Empire was near at hand. It would mean, he said, peace and economic progress. A month later, a grateful Senate asked him to become Emperor. The country immediately reinforced this request by a 7,800,000 vote in favour 'of the re-establishment of the imperial dignity in the person of

Louis-Napoleon Bonaparte', with 2,000,000 abstentions and only 250,000 against. On 1 December, on a throne at the royal palace of St. Cloud, Louis assumed the title Napoleon III. He had proved true to his destiny.

The new Emperor was to rule France with the help of a handful of advisers—mainly relatives and old friends—of character and talent. Probably closest to him was his illegitimate half-brother Morny, until his death in 1865 the strong man of the regime. His cousin, Prince Napoleon, was a prominent if provocative adviser, and Walewski, another Bonaparte bastard, proved an able diplomat.

Outside the family, there were men like Persigny, who had followed Louis faithfully from his earliest adventures; Rouher, a cynical lawyer and administrative genius; Chevalier, an engineer and economist of vision; the Pereire brothers, Portuguese Jews, financiers of unusual flair and daring; and Haussmann, Prefect of the Seine, another administrator of tremendous drive and energy. In 1853 this group was joined by Eugénie de Montijo, whom Napoleon had married in the January of that year. She was twenty-six, beautiful, and very strong-willed. She was more in love with the Emperor's career than with the Emperor himself. 'Even as a girl', she was to write many years later, 'I had a taste for politics'. A devout Catholic, she was to become the champion of the clerical interest and of an aggressive foreign policy. From the first she dominated a brilliant court, and as the years passed her political influence grew.

During the Second Empire Paris became the most colourful and notorious centre of high society in Europe. While there was the respectable society of the Court, where the Empress Eugenie presided over an unending round of balls and ceremonies, a lively but much less respectable society of writers, artists, and the rich flourished in the fashionable boulevard cafés. Offenbach, a composer of clever comic operas, was in his prime, and this café society thronged to his productions. The most famous of these, *Orpheus in the Underworld*, was a satire on life at Court and made much of the Emperor's attachment to women other than his wife. Napoleon, not in the least put out, ordered a special performance, for which he paid the composer 22,000 francs and thanked him for an 'an unforgettable evening'. The sexual freedom of Paris appalled and fascinated the rest of the continent. The can-can dance was one sensation for foreigners, the courtesans or fashionable prostitutes another. 'Who are all these ladies?' a Russian Grand-Duke asked his friend at the Longchamp races. 'They are all "gay" ladies', replied his friend meaningfully. 'Where are all the respectable ones?' he asked. 'There are none left!' Such a society was not without its critics, who maintained that the country was going to

The Empress

the dogs. The catastrophes of 1870–1 were seen by many as a divine punishment for such wickedness!

Napoleon III had promised that the Empire would mean peace and economic progress. If he was to break his word about peace within two years, he kept it about economic progress. He and his leading advisers were strongly influenced by the writings of St. Simon, a French aristocrat, who had died in 1825. St. Simon had little influence in his own lifetime but he was one of the most original thinkers of the early nineteenth century, with an acute understanding of the revolutionary economic and social forces at work in his generation. In modern society, he argued, the army, the Church, kings, dukes, and lords, were all out of date. The men who mattered were bankers, industrialists, scientists, and engineers. In a well-run state, such men would be rewarded in proportion to their efficiency and massive progress would be made through the encouragement of their skills. This progress would lead to the end of poverty and, in time, to justice, equality and contentment for all men. Inspired by St. Simonian ideas, Napoleon believed that his State should give a clear lead in encouraging industrial and scientific progress, and actively supported men like Chevalier, the Pereire brothers and Haussmann.

France needed such encouragement. Her industrial revolution had barely begun. Not only was she far behind Britain and Belgium, but there was a danger of her losing ground to Germany as well. In 1850 she had barely 2,000 miles of railway (Britain had 6,084 miles), her coal production was limited, her iron production tiny. Barely one worker in thirty was employed in a large machine-powered factory. Moreover, the attitudes of French industry and commerce were conservative. In particular there was a deep suspicion of the type of large-scale capital investment which British experience had shown to be essential to rapid industrial progress. By the end of the Second Empire, however, major changes had occurred. The population had increased by 1,500,000. The number of factory workers had doubled. Exports and imports had increased by 400 per cent, coal and iron production by 300 per cent, and the value of company shares by 500 per cent. 12,000 miles of railway—the basic network of modern France—was completed and the whole system reorganized on a regional basis by the State. The State also took over and extended the canal system. The electric telegraph linked all major towns. The appearance of these towns was also transformed in this period. Haussmann gave the lead in the capital where he began an ambitious programme of public works. Paris not only

◄The Rebuilding of Paris: here part of the Latin Quarter is being demolished to make way for the wide boulevards which not only made Paris much more attractive as a capital city but made street barricading much harder for potential revolutionaries

gained its boulevards and Opera House, but sewers, a pure water supply, and gas-lighting into the bargain. Industrial development and public works on this scale could not have occurred without a change in French financial methods. Here the lead was given by the Pereire brothers, whose bank, the Credit Mobilier, largely financed the railway boom. More cautious but eventually more successful banking institutions, such as the Credit Foncier and the Credit Lyonnais, also contributed to large-scale industrial expansion. The government helped in other ways to break down traditional business attitudes. Both Napoleon and Chevalier, his chief economic adviser, were free-traders, and in 1860 signed a Free Trade treaty with Britain. It was very unpopular in France but brought a new competitiveness to the country's industry.

There were crises, notably in 1857 and 1863, and after 1865 the economy slowed down. Generally speaking, however, the Second Empire was a period of rapidly increasing prosperity for most classes of French society. Only those at the very bottom of the social ladder, the urban poor, benefited little or nothing.

Another important aspects of Napoleon III's home policy was the 'liberalization' of the régime in the 1860s. The term 'liberalization' refers to the attempt by the Emperor to give more power to the Senate and to the Parliament than had been allowed in the 1852 constitution and greater freedom of expression to the Press without destroying his own authority. Napoleon knew that in the last resort his power was based on the approval rather than the fear of the majority of Frenchmen. There was too much that was genuinely liberal and democratic and too little that was ruthless in his character for him ever to be the dictator of a police state. Morny and Haussmann maintained from the first that the 1852 constitution allowed too little freedom and that discontent was bound to grow if the Emperor took no action. In 1859 Napoleon marched to the aid of the Italians as they fought for their freedom against the Austrians. As many of his opponents were quick to point out, 'how could France give to others what she refused to give herself?' So liberalization was attempted. In 1860 the Senate and Parliament were given a greater say in financial affairs and were consulted more regularly. Such a minor step pleased no-one, and after 1863 opposition within Parliament grew more vigorous. On the advice of Morny, Napoleon allowed more freedom of expression and insisted on major educational reforms. By now, the best days of the regime were passed. Morny died in 1865, Napoleon's health was failing, his foreign policy was moving towards disaster and the economy was slowing down. Finally, in response to ever-increasing opposition, Napoleon undertook major constitutional reforms. In 1868 and 1869 further freedom was granted to the Press, trades unions were allowed more power, and in 1870 a new constitution was published which con-

An election meeting 1869 : this meeting held in a Parisian gymnasium shows the tremendous interest in politics following the policy of liberalization

verted France from a virtual dictatorship to a constitutional monarchy, by giving much more authority to the new Parliament. The new constitution was given an overwhelming vote of confidence by the electorate. Whether or not it would have worked, however, will never be known. Within three months of its introduction it was swept away with the rest of the Second Empire in the Franco-Prussian War.

Foreign Policy

Napoleon III made foreign policy very much his own affair—at least until the breakdown of his health after 1865. It was characteristic of the man—devious and daring, at first successful, ultimately disastrous. Despite the famous assurance of 1852 that 'l'Empire, c'est la paix', France was fighting Russia in 1854. Napoleon was not looking for war, but, as the previous chapter has shown, his support of the Catholic priests in the Holy Places dispute was to lead him remorselessly into the Crimean War. Neither the alliance with Britain nor the war itself was immediately popular in France. Only after French troops had distinguished themselves (while the British did not) at the capture of Sebastopol, and after Napoleon and Walewski had put on a brilliant display of prestige diplomacy at the Paris conference in 1856, could Napoleon claim

153

that his Crimean venture had popular backing. It did not matter that France gained nothing concrete from the war. Paris once more seemed the centre of European affairs. For both the French and their Emperor the Peace of Paris was a triumph.

His next foreign venture was no more popular to begin with. His experiences in 1830 had made him an Italian nationalist for life, yet when he became Emperor in 1852, the Austrians seemed as powerfully entrenched in Italy as ever. However, the one genuinely Italian state in N. Italy, Piedmont, round which the nationalists had rallied unsuccessfully in 1848 (see Chapter 9), had joined France and Britain against Russia in the Crimean War. Cavour, the brilliant prime minister of Piedmont, used the Paris conference to bring the Italian question to the notice of the European leaders both in public and in private. Though at the time France could not take any public action hostile to Austria, henceforward Napoleon was secretly looking for every opportunity to aid Cavour in expelling the Austrians from Italy. In January 1858 a dramatic incident occurred which spurred him on. As the Emperor and Empress drove to a gala performance of *William Tell* at the Opera, members of an Italian secret society led by Orsini attempted to assassinate Napoleon because they felt that his public coolness towards the Italian question represented a betrayal of his ideals of 1830. They bungled the job, killing eight and wounding 150 innocent bystanders without harming their chosen victim. The crime had the effect of convincing Napoleon that Destiny meant him to go quickly to the aid of Italy. He was fascinated by the handsome, black-bearded Italian, and stage-managed his trial to bring 'the Italian question' dramatically before the French people. At the end of the trial, an eloquent letter described as written by Orsini to the Emperor was read in open court. It ended 'may your Majesty not reject the last prayer of a patriot on the steps of the scaffold! Let him liberate my country and the blessings of its 25,000,000 citizens will follow him through the ages!' Orsini actually did the writing but the Prefect of Police, on Napoleon's orders, told him what to write. In the summer, Cavour was invited by the Emperor to Plombières, a secret meeting which led to an agreement that, in return for Savoy and Nice, the French army would march to the aid of Piedmont if Austria declared war on her. Chapter 10 describes how war broke out and the part played by France in the Italian Risorgimento. What concerns us here is its effect within France. No Italian policy could have the support of all Frenchmen. The French liberals wanted the end of Papal as well as Austrian influence in Italy. The French Catholics, on the other hand, saw the triumph of Italian liberals as a major threat to the Papacy. There was also general anxiety lest a strong united Italy might prove a bad neighbour to France in the future. So there was little enthusiasm for the war. However, the

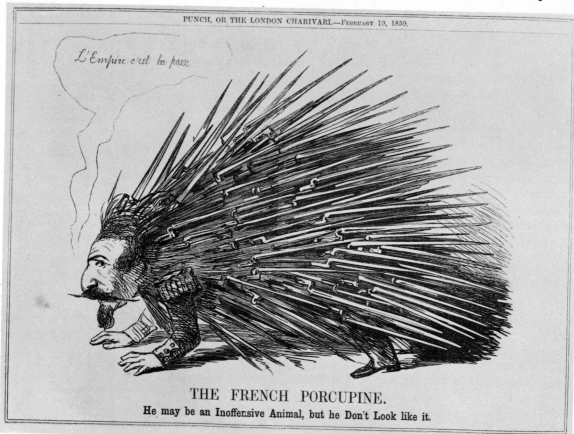

PUNCH, OR THE LONDON CHARIVARI.—FEBRUARY 19, 1859.

L'Empire c'est la paix

THE FRENCH PORCUPINE.
He may be an Inoffensive Animal, but he Don't Look like it.

The French Porcupine: Punch takes a cynical view of Napoleon's insistence that he is a man of peace

victories of Magenta and Solferino, and the acquisition of Savoy and Nice, inspired a tremendous outburst of patriotic pride in the summer of 1859. On 14 August the Emperor was rapturously acclaimed as he reviewed a victory march through the streets of Paris. It was perhaps the most triumphant moment of his career. In the long run, however, his Italian venture satisfied no-one. The French liberals were angered because Napoleon pulled out of the war when it was but half won, leaving Venice to the Austrians. The French Catholics were dismayed because French victories so encouraged the Italian nationalists that they took possession of the Papal states except for Rome itself. And so double-faced was French policy in 1859 and 1860 that no one in Europe ever trusted Napoleon again.

In foreign as well as in home policy 1860 was a turning-point. Previously, Napoleon III had been one of Fortune's favourites. Thereafter, she deserted him.

The first tragedy was Mexican. After civil war between the Catholic royalists and anti-clerical republicans, the victorious republican leader, Juarez, refused to pay the debts owed to foreign countries. Britain, France, and Spain, to whom Mexico owed most money, decided to send in troops to collect their debts, an action which was possible only because the traditional defender of the Americas from European interference, the U.S.A., was engulfed by civil war. Britain and Spain soon withdrew, but Napoleon, egged on by the Empress and the Catholics, kept his troops there with more ambitious plans in mind. A Catholic champion was found in Maximilian, brother of the Austrian Emperor, and backed by the French army he was proclaimed king of Mexico in 1864. The war against Juarez, however, was far from won. 34,000 French troops became tied down far away from home, while the rising power of Prussia became ever more menacing. Worse still, the U.S.A., united and at peace after 1865, demanded the evacuation of all European forces from Mexico. Eventually, at the end of 1866, Napoleon withdrew his troops, hoping that Maximilian would abdicate and return to Europe. Maximilian, however, was a Habsburg and obstinate. His wife, Carlotta, as ambitious for him as Eugénie was for Napoleon, urged him to stay. As the forces of Juarez closed in on her husband, Carlotta, almost out of her mind because of the dashing of their hopes, sailed to Europe in a desperate bid to obtain aid. There was nothing anyone could do. It was too late. On 19 July 1867, Maximilian, deserted by all save a handful of followers, was captured and shot. Europe, above all Catholic Europe, was horrified. The distant tragedy was the direct consequence of French bungling and treachery, and Napoleon's behaviour looked particularly base.

The Second Empire was itself moving into its final act, the climax of which was a tragedy of size and consequences far beyond anything that happened in Mexico. In the 1860s the balance of power in Europe was drastically altered by the emergence of Prussia as a first-class power (see Chapter 10). In 1864 Schleswig-Holstein had been annexed, in 1866 Austria had been decisively beaten in the Seven Weeks War and it was the clear intention of Bismarck, the Prussian Chancellor, to unite all Germany including the South German states bordering on to France. Napoleon was ageing fast and increasingly weakened by a painful bladder complaint. He was no match for Bismarck's diplomatic genius. The two men had met at Biarritz in 1865. Napoleon had then assumed that if Austria and Prussia went to war, Austria would win. Even in the unlikely event of a Prussian victory he was sure that France would be able to secure territorial gains in the Rhineland. Consequently, he assured Bismarck that France would remain neutral in such a war. So the crushing Prussian victory over the Austrians at Sadowa took him completely by surprise and his frenzied attempts to gain compensation for France along the Rhine were skilfully used by

Bismarck to increase the distrust already felt by Belgium, Luxembourg, and the South German states for French scheming. France felt humiliated, and the court party, which was in favour of an aggressive foreign policy and was led by the Empress Eugénie, increased in popularity and political influence.

The chance to put Prussia in her place seemed to come in 1870. The ruling dynasty of Prussia, the Hohenzollerns, put forward a candidate for the vacant Spanish throne. The Duc de Gramont, the hot-headed anti-Prussian foreign minister of France, took a tough line. If necessary, France would go to war in order to prevent the Hohenzollerns from gaining the Spanish throne and thus creating a potentially hostile power on France's southern border. Leopold, the candidate, had no desire to cause a European war, nor had William I, king of Prussia and head of the Hohenzollern dynasty. To Bismarck's dismay, the candidature was withdrawn. Yet such was the feverish mood of France that this striking diplomatic victory was not enough. Gramont and the Empress, backed by a patriotic press, demanded that Prussia should give a guarantee that the Hohenzollerns would never again seek the Spanish throne. Against his better judgement Napoleon ordered Benedetti, the French ambassador to Prussia, to demand these guarantees from King William. They met at Ems. It was a friendly meeting but William, who regarded the whole affair as closed, was not prepared to give the necessary guarantees. He then telegrammed an account of his meeting to Bismarck in Berlin, as was his custom. Bismarck wanted war with France. He realized that both the French and the Prussian press were very excitable and easily provoked. He therefore edited the Ems telegram so that it seemed as if the king of Prussia and the French ambassador had insulted each other, and released it to the Berlin press. For the French, the publication of the edited telegram was the last straw. 'You see before you', cried Gramont, 'a man whose face has been slapped.' 'Down with Prussia!' 'To Berlin!' roared the Parisian crowds as they demonstrated during the summer evenings. Napoleon knew that the armies were not ready, that France had no allies. He realized better than anyone the terrible risk his country was running. But he was in great physical pain. Eugénie, Gramont, and Ollivier, the new Prime Minister, were all in favour of war. He felt unable to overrule them and a war-fevered country. On 19 July 1870, France declared war on Prussia.

Three months later the Emperor was a prisoner, the Empress an exile in England. The Second Empire had disintegrated and a republican Paris was besieged by the Prussians. The French armies, outnumbered, badly led, armed and supplied, had taken the offensive only to be swept back on 6 August by the superbly efficient Prussians, generalled by the redoubtable Moltke. At the battle of Gravelotte (17 August) the French forces were divided in two. Marshal Bazaine retreated to Metz with one half where he was surrounded, while Napoleon and Marshal MacMahon, in two minds whether to defend the routes to Paris with their remaining troops or to attempt to relieve Bazaine, were attacked by greatly superior forces at Sedan. On 1 September 1870, Napoleon III surrendered with 104,000 men 'Having failed to meet death in the midst of my troops,' read his note of surrender to the Prussian king, 'nothing more remains for me but to surrender my sword into your majesty's hands'. Bonapartism could not survive such a defeat. Paris declared Napoleon deposed and set up a republican government to continue the war. After six months imprisonment in Germany, Napoleon was allowed to join his wife in England. A dying man, he lived quietly at Chislehurst in Kent until his death in January 1873.

The catastrophe of 1870 has obscured much of the achievement of Napoleon III. The man of mystery seemed exposed at last as the nonentity he really was. Later generations have echoed Bismarck's contemptuous judgement—'a sphinx without a riddle . . . a great unfathomed incapacity'. But there was more to Napoleon than this. Bismarck only came up against him when he was past his prime. Between 1848 and 1860 Napoleon ruled France with skill and outwitted most of Europe. In these years he more than fulfilled his destiny. He was a strange man but, in his own peculiar way, he had a kind of greatness.

Napoleon III surrenders to the Prussians after the Battle of Sedan

Chapter 9
Where Liberalism and Idealism Fail

First, some definitions. By liberalism is meant that political philosophy (or set of political attitudes) which, inspired by the ideas of the French Revolution, regarded freedom of thought and speech, freedom from arrest and from imprisonment without trial, as among the most important rights of man, and parliamentary government as a better form of government than absolute monarchy. By nationalism is meant the attitude that a people conscious of a common language or culture or tradition (like the Germans, the Italians, or the Poles) should weld themselves into an independent nation-state and that nation-states already independent should do their utmost to increase their power and prestige. In the mid-nineteenth century almost all liberals were nationalists but not all nationalists were liberals. As the next two chapters show, the events of the 1830s and 1840s forced liberals (especially in the German states) to decide whether their liberalism or nationalism mattered to them more. Most chose nationalism.

In 1831, only a year after the successful July Revolution in France, Victor Hugo, the great French novelist, described how 'he already heard the dull sound of revolution still deep down in the earth pushing out under every kingdom in Europe its subterranean galleries from the central shaft of the mine which is Paris.' Seventeen years later, news of the February revolution in Paris brought this subterranean revolution bubbling to the surface. The 1848 revolutions were the most considerable of the nineteenth century. They were also the last to be inspired from Paris and which could be described as liberal. When they subsided in 1849 with few of their original hopes fulfilled, an era ended. In the years that followed, nationalism replaced liberalism as the dominant political force and, while there were no significant revolutions for the rest of the century, wars between nation-states became commonplace.

The 1848 revolutions occurred on the scale they did because, in the 1840s, Europe was out of balance. Economic, social, and technological developments were transforming the continent, yet governments continued to behave as if nothing was happening, although they knew quite well that this was not the case. In the towns of Central Europe a middle class was steadily increasing in size and wealth. In major cities like Berlin, Vienna, and Milan, an industrial working class had come into existence. Metternich's

Europe had nothing to offer to these types of men since it was inspired by the spirit of a pre-industrial age.

What temporarily united the middle and working classes was the economic crisis of 1846–8. There was a major depression both in agriculture and in industry. Harvests—the potato-crop especially—failed. In certain areas—Ireland, Flanders, and Silesia, for instance—entire populations starved. As food prices rose, an industrial depression set in, bringing extensive unemployment to the cities. Some parts of the continent suffered more than others, the worst catastrophe being the Irish famine, but throughout Europe, in the cities as well as in the countryside, there was an acute sense of insecurity which led in turn to widespread political restlessness. In 1847 the American consul in Amsterdam had to deal with hundreds of Germans who were trying to emigrate to the U.S.A. 'All well-informed people', he wrote home, 'express the belief that the present crisis is so deeply interwoven in the events of the present period that "it" is but the commencement of that great Revolution which they consider sooner or later is to dissolve the present constitution of things.' So it proved.

Acute economic and social unrest was not, however, enough in itself to bring revolution. Ireland, after all, suffered the greatest economic distress, yet experienced few political disturbances. The events in Paris provoked the response they did in Austria, Germany, and Italy because in those areas not only was there great unrest but governments quite lacking in confidence. In Vienna, which for the last thirty years had been the tireless co-ordinator of conservative forces, Metternich's authority was declining. He was still nominally in power but, since the death of the Emperor Francis in 1835, his position had been steadily undermined. Francis's successor, the Emperor Ferdinand I, was a half-wit and his government was paralysed by rivalries within his court, of which the most deadly was between Metternich himself and Kolowrat, the powerful Minister of Home Affairs. In Berlin Frederick William III, who had co-operated closely with Metternich, had been succeeded by Frederick William IV, who was much less ready to fit in with Austrian schemes. Yet when the crisis broke, he was no more prepared for it than Ferdinand. As for the rulers of Italy, they depended on Austria for survival. Metternich never believed that his system could last for long. He knew that the forces of history were against it. He only hoped that it might outlive him. However, he lived too long. By 1848 there was less a political system in Central Europe than a political vacuum.

The Austrian Empire

The news of the February Revolution in Paris caused a ferment in

Vienna. On 13 March 1848 a student demonstration clashed with troops and sparked off an uprising of discontented workers in the Viennese suburbs. The government panicked. Since one of the main demands of the revolutionaries was the resignation of Metternich, who more than anyone symbolized the old order, the court united against the elderly Chancellor and forced him into an English exile. Otherwise there was no clear policy and, when on 15 May workers armed with shovels and spades flocked into the city centre to back the students, the government gave way completely to the revolutionary demands. A parliament was to be elected by universal suffrage in the western half of the Austrian Empire. Its chief function would be to draw up a constitution. In the meantime, a Committee of Public Safety was to maintain law and order in the capital and find work for the unemployed. As in France, however, the provision of work for the unemployed turned out to be a much more difficult task than the revolutionary leaders had imagined. By early summer, disillusion was spreading among the workers, and the unity of the revolutionaries, which was so vital to their success, began to crack.

Meanwhile in the Hungarian part of the Empire an even more formidable revolution had occurred. It possessed an exceptional leader in Kossuth, a lawyer and journalist from a minor Magyar noble family. He was a superb orator and writer, whose heroic and eloquent opposition to the Habsburgs was to make him the hero of European liberals until his death in 1894. Yet he was in fact less a liberal than a nationalist. Though he genuinely wanted greater freedom for Hungary, it was so that the Hungarian (or Magyar) people could control the historic lands of St. Stephen at the expense of the millions of other inhabitants of this region who were of different races (Slovaks, Ruthenians, Rumanians, Serbs, Croats, etc.). On learning of the events in Paris, he led a campaign in the Hungarian Diet for free institutions in Hungary. Students in Budapest rioted, like their counterparts in Vienna, and were supported by peasants visiting the Hungarian capital for the traditional March fair. Kossuth was able to persuade the Hungarian Diet to pass the 'March laws' which made Hungary, Transylvania, and Croatia into a single state with its own parliament and ministry. On 11 April these laws were approved by the Emperor Ferdinand.

A similar succession of events was taking place in Bohemia and Moravia, an area mainly inhabited by Czechs. Palacky, the Czech leader, backed by a rising of students and workers in Prague, pressed for the union and greater independence of Bohemia, Moravia, and Silesia. Having been promised a charter by Ferdinand, he summoned a congress to work out what position the Czechs (who were a Slav race) should hold in a new federal Austrian Empire.

161

Where Liberalism and Idealism Fail

In June 1848 the revolutionaries were at the height of their power. Then their decline was rapid. Divisions among their leaders, especially divisions inspired by racial or local differences, were the root cause of this decline. In Prague, the Bohemian capital, the Czechs and Germans began to quarrel, giving the Austrian army led by General Windischgratz the opportunity to intervene. Since his wife had been killed accidently by rioters, his intervention was forceful and thorough. After a five-day battle, the Czech revolution was over. In Hungary, Kossuth's insistence that Magyar should be the only official language of the new state and the arrogant attitude taken by the Magyar Diet towards the Slavs were fatal to the revolutionary cause. The Slav races concluded that the Habsburgs were, after all, preferable to the Magyars and when Jellacic, Croat soldier and politician, attacked Hungary from the south with Habsburg encouragement, Slovaks, Serbs, and Rumanians also rose against the Magyar masters. Kossuth's appeal to the Viennese revolutionaries brought no response. They were struggling for survival themselves and anyway distrusted him. The Austrian government, slowly recovering its confidence, sent an army to join Jellacic. It enjoyed only partial success against the Hungarians but, again under the leadership of Windischgratz, turned on Vienna and after a three-day siege in October ended the revolution there. Windischgratz's next step was to secure the appointment of his brother-in-law, Prince Felix Schwarzenberg, as Chief Minister. At last the counter-revolution had the leadership it needed. Schwarzenberg was a man of steel, with tremendous administrative ability, determination and clearheadness. One of his earliest measures was to bring about the abdication of the Emperor Ferdinand who was succeeded by his nephew, Francis Joseph I.

Hungary still held out, although threatened both by Austrians and by Slavs. In Kossuth, the Magyars had an indomitable leader, and in Gorgei a general of great skill. In the spring of 1849 Gorgei defeated both Windischgratz and Jellacic. He then recaptured Budapest. A wave of patriotic enthusiasm swept through Hungary, and a triumphant Kossuth declared the country independent. His triumph was shortlived. While Kossuth and Gorgei quarrelled bitterly about what they should do next, Francis Joseph turned to Tsar Nicholas of Russia for aid. In July 1849 three armies invaded Hungary—the Austrians under Haynau from the west, the Russians under Paskievic from the north, and the Croatians under Jellacic from the south. In August one Hungarian army had to surrender at Temesvar, and Gorgei, hopelessly outnumbered, surrendered to the Russians at Vilagos. He and his army were handed over to Haynau who took sadistic vengeance. Thirteen Hungarian generals (the so-called martyrs of Arad) were hung, and more than four hundred imprisoned. Another 100 politicians were executed and

The victors:
Top left *Windisch-Gratz;*
Top right *Schwarzenberg,*
Bottom right *Radetsky.*
The vanquished:
Bottom left *Kossuth*

terrible atrocities by the Slav troops at the expense of the Magyars were left unpunished. Kossuth fled from Hungary, burying the historic crown of St. Stephen near the border with Turkey. He spent the rest of his life in exile, the unswerving champion of an independent Hungary which he was never again to see. Thus the revolution ended in the Austrian Empire.

The German Confederation

The news from Paris in the spring of 1848 also sparked off revolutions in the German Confederation. Parts of Germany, the Rhineland provinces in particular, were more industrialized than any part of the Habsburg lands and possessed a prosperous and educated middle class from which emerged liberal leaders of real calibre. In many parts of the Confederation the conditions of the peasantry and the industrial workers were terrible, parts of Silesia for instance suffering almost as badly as Ireland. Among skilled working-class craftsmen socialist ideas were beginning to circulate and a number of German working men were driven into exile because of their extreme socialist views. One of these, Wilhelm Weitling, founded the League of the Just in Paris, which in 1847 became the Communist League. It was for this League that Marx and Engels wrote the Communist Manifesto which was published, fittingly, in February 1848. Though neither the Communists nor other extreme socialist groups played any direct part in the course of the revolution in Germany, their existence indicates the political awareness of the German working classes.

Much more immediately important in 1848 were the liberals and nationalists, who wanted both a constitutional government with a freely elected parliament and a united Germany. At this stage, both in Germany and in Italy, liberalism and nationalism went hand in hand. Only after 1848 did there emerge a large number of nationalists who were not also liberals. German national feeling had grown in strength in the 1830s and 1840s. Fear of French ambitions in the Rhineland had inspired a mass of patriotic poetry. Hegel, the political philosopher who argued that the pattern of history ordained that a new era was about to dawn with a free united and powerful Germany in a dominating position, was tremendously popular with university students and schoolteachers. A Bavarian nobleman reflected the sense of natural frustration when he wrote in 1847: 'One reason for the widespread discontent is the weakness of Germany among other states. No-one will deny that it is hard to be unable to say abroad "I am a German"—not to be able to pride himself that the German flag is flying from his vessel, to have no German consul in cases of necessity but to have to explain, "my fatherland was once a great and powerful country, now it is shattered into eight and thirty splinters." ' That they had both liberal and nationalist aims turned out to be a source of real difficulty to the 1848 revolutionaries because, as we shall see, they found it impossible to decide on their priorities.

The German Confederation was disrupted by a series of revolutions, the first of which began in the state of Baden. The most important, however, flared up in Berlin, the Prussian capital, on 18 March. The population of Berlin had increased from 180,000 to 400,000 in less than a generation. A large number of factory-workers were facing unemployment and the news from Vienna of Metternich's fall, combined with rumours of risings all over Germany, caused the street barricades to rise. Savage street-fighting between students and workers and the Berlin garrison shocked Frederick William IV into withdrawing the garrison from the city. He then appointed a liberal ministry, led by Camphausen and Hansemann, which immediately summoned a Prussian National Assembly, elected by universal suffrage, to draw up a constitution.

Almost simultaneously, revolutionary leaders from all over the Confederation met at Frankfurt and decided that a parliament representative of all Germany should meet as soon as possible to decide how the new Germany should be reconstructed. Two months later, on 15 May, nearly 600 deputies, elected from most of the states of the Confederation, assembled in the Church of St. Paul in Frankfurt. This Frankfurt Assembly was in many ways a gifted body. Some of the most outstanding university teachers of the time led its debates, and lawyers, doctors, and businessmen, as well as the nobility were well represented. Its greatest weakness was its lack of political experience. Since it included men of very varied opinions and was faced by huge problems of constitution- and nation-making, it tended to spend too much time in debate and too little in arriving at decisions and gathering the forces necessary to make its decisions effective. As Jakob Grimm, a liberal writer, remarked, 'we Germans, it must be admitted, have a great tendency to learned discussion.'

There was much optimism when the Assembly opened. Heinrich von Gagern, the President, ended his first address with these ringing phrases. 'Let us unite as far as union is possible. Let us sacrifice what must be sacrificed in order to obtain better conditions. We are the Unity of our Nation and Fatherland for which we have yearned for so long.' Tumultuous applause followed from the packed galleries of St. Paul's church. As the debates continued, the nationalist temper of the delegates became very apparent. In Posen (Prussian Poland) and in Schleswig-Holstein, duchies directly bordering Denmark, German rights seemed threatened respectively by the Poles and the Danish king. The Assembly decided that it must speak out for Germany, especially when other European powers began to show an interest in the Schleswig-Holstein affair. 'May Russia, may France, may England dare to interfere with our just cause', declared one delegate to loud applause, 'and we will reply to them with one and a half million armed men.' Such claims however, were ridiculous. The Assembly could not raise 150 men let alone 1,500,000. Prussia and Denmark came to a settlement over Schleswig-Holstein without bothering to consult the Assembly, whose essential weakness was further demonstrated when a rising of discontented Frankfurt workers, directed against the Assembly, had to be put down by Prussian and Austrian troops. These 'September Days' in Frankfurt had much in common with the 'June Days' in Paris. The violent mob action served only to strengthen the conservatives. When, in Berlin, the mob attacked the royal arsenal, and the liberal government was unable to maintain law and order, Frederick William IV dismissed the Camphausen ministry, replaced it by a conservative one, and ordered General Wrangel to occupy the city. Once this was done (November 1848), the revolution in Prussia and in most of the other German states was over.

The Frankfurt Assembly still survived and continued to discuss the future of Germany with vigour. Its progress, however, was hindered by a major difference of opinion among the delegates concerning what geographical shape the new Germany should take. While some felt that it should include all German-speaking peoples including Austria, and that Austria should be the centre of gravity of the new nation, others argued that Austria with her huge and multiracial territories could never be absorbed in Germany and that Prussia should be the centre of gravity with Austria excluded completely. When in the spring of 1849 Schwarzenberg made it clear that the Habsburgs were determined to revive the old Confederation, the Frankfurt Assembly decided to offer the Imperial crown to Frederick William IV. This was the last chance of the revolutionaries. The Assembly represented many of the emerging forces of Germany and still retained its popularity among educated Germans. What it obviously lacked was force, which still rested with the separate German states. In offering the imperial crown to the Prussian king, it hoped to secure both unity and the military resources of the Prussian state. It was also offering to Frederick William IV the chance of winning for Prussia a position in Europe which she had not held since the reign of Frederick the Great.

The Prussian king was not, however, the man for such a challenge. Though he had qualities which impressed many liberals— intelligence, eloquence, a deep interest in Germany's glorious mediaeval past, and an apparent readiness to consider reforming ideas—he was no liberal when it came to the crunch. His political thinking was muddled but one thing he never doubted was his divine right to be king of Prussia, and of the other German princes to rule their own states. He was also too indecisive and anxious to play the part that the Assembly hoped of him. When in April 1849 he heard of the offer of the imperial crown, he refused, and gave this reason: 'I was not able to submit a favourable reply ... because the German National Assembly does not have the right, without the consent of the German government (i.e. the governments of the princes) to bestow the crown that they have offered me.' In other words, he could not accept the basic liberal belief that a popularly elected assembly had more authority than any merely inherited power. As he put it in a nutshell to one of his closest advisers, the imperial crown 'would have been a dog-collar fastened round my neck by the sovereign German people'.

His refusal was the effective end of the Assembly. The representatives from Austria and Prussia withdrew, and those from other states soon followed their example. A few of the more extreme delegates moved from Frankfurt to Stuttgart where they attempted to raise revolution once again. This time, however, workers and peasants did not stir and the governments took prompt action. The scattered risings were easily suppressed by Prussian troops and the last delegates forcibly dispersed.

The Italian Peninsula

The other area of Europe to be severely shaken by revolution was the Italian peninsula. As in Germany, the revolutionaries were both liberals and nationalists. They wanted both constitutions with freely elected assemblies and the expulsion of foreign tyrants, especially the Austrians. As in Germany, the Austrian Empire, and France, there were major differences of opinion among the revolutionary leaders and a failure to agree on priorities. The fiasco of Mazzini's Savoy invasion of 1834 and subsequent ineptly organized Mazzinian conspiracies convinced many Italians that noble though Mazzini's ideals were, his practical politics were suicidal. Italy was simply not ready for revolution by conspiracy and spontaneous popular action. Widely-read authors of the 1840s were Gioberti and Balbo. Gioberti argued that unity must come through a confederation of Italian princes headed by the Pope, Balbo for a confederation headed by the king of Piedmont. Equally influential were dramatists like Pellico and Niccolini. They often wrote about heroic periods of Italian history when Italians were struggling to be free from foreign domination and their audiences were able to identify the present with the past. There is a story that when Niccolini's *Giovanni da Procida*, which tells how the French were expelled from

Sicily in the thirteenth century by a popular revolt, was performed in Milan, a senior French minister was the guest of the Austrian governor. The Frenchman was most upset by what appeared to him to be excessive anti-French feeling in the Milanese audience. 'Don't worry,' said the Austrian governor, 'the envelope is addressed to you, but the contents are for me.' It was also in the 1840s that Italy's greatest composer, Verdi, began to capture public attention. Some of his early operas like *The Lombards* or *Attila* deal, like the plays of Niccolini and Pellino, with the heroic Italian past, others, like *Nabucco* or *Joan of Arc* with a captive people struggling to be free. The magnificent chorus, in *Nabucco*, of Hebrew slaves in Babylon, longing to return to their homeland, was rapturously applauded wherever it was sung. His last opera before the revolution, *Macbeth*, contained another superb chorus, *'la patria tradita'* ('the fatherland betrayed'). It has been said that the emotion caused by the singing of this opera at La Scala opera house was a major factor in the Milanese revolution of 1848. Another way that Italians got round Austrian censorship was through conferences called theoretically to discuss such harmless subjects as science or engineering. Daniel Manin, the leader of the Venetian revolution, discussed a great deal of politics both as a member of a railway committee and as a delegate to a scientific conference, while Cavour, who did so much to unite Italy in 1859, began his political education as a member of the Piedmont Agricultural Society.

Revolution, therefore, came to Italy less suddenly than to other parts of Europe. Patriotic Italians had been waiting hopefully for some years and they had, unlike the Germans or the Austrians, a man whom they thought to be an obvious and generally acceptable leader—Charles Albert, King of Savoy. Not only was he the one Italian ruling an Italian state but he appeared genuinely determined to bring about a free and united Italy. In 1845 he had directed D'Azeglio, a Piedmontese politician with many contacts with revolutionaries throughout the peninsula, to 'tell those gentlemen to keep quiet and not move, for at present there is nothing to be done; but they may be certain that, if the opportunity comes, my life, the life of my sons, my resources, my wealth, my army, all shall be given for the cause of Italy.' His motto was *Italia farà da se* (Italy will do it herself). As later events were to prove, he had fatal weaknesses as a leader. So hesitant that his nickname became 'il Re Tentenna' (King Wobble), he was also ambitious and devious, and he trusted no-one. He was no liberal and, despite his fine words, not much of a nationalist. His main interest was to extend the power of Piedmont in northern Italy at the expense of the Austrians. Unfortunately for the revolutionary cause, these defects did not become apparent until the revolution was well under way.

In 1846 Italians had been electrified by the election of Cardinal

Pio Nono

1848 The first shots: revolution in Palermo

Mastai—Ferretti as Pius IX (Pio Nono) in succession to the sternly conservative Gregory XVI. Pio Nono was a kind-hearted man who wished to improve the conditions of his subjects in the Papal States. He was also attracted by Gioberti's ideas of an Italian federation headed by the Pope. He had no political experience, however, and little understanding of the passions lurking beneath the surface of Italian politics. Soon after his election he freed 1700 political prisoners. He then set about encouraging railways and gas-lighting. He lowered customs duties, granted greater freedom to the Roman press and finally, in October 1847, summoned an elected assembly to advise him on important matters. Hardly surprisingly he was hailed as a liberal and possibly national champion. Metternich could not believe his ears. 'I have foreseen everything,' he exclaimed, 'except a liberal pope.' As Metternich well knew and Pio Nono soon discovered, it was almost impossible for the Head of the Catholic Church to be a liberal in the mid-nineteenth century.

Nonetheless between 1846 and 1848 the Pope's apparent liberalism encouraged liberals all over the country. In Piedmont Charles Albert granted a constitution; in Tuscany the press was allowed greater freedom; in Venice Manin began a campaign for greater Venetian independence, and in Lombardy Austrian economic measures and the practice of employing Germans before Italians were bitterly criticised. By the end of 1847 the Austrians had decided that the time had come for tough measures. In January 1848 Manin was arrested in Venice, and a Milanese demonstration was so roughly handled by Austrian troops that sixty-one people died.

Open revolution began in Palermo on 18 January 1848, and Ferdinand of Naples was soon granting reforms. News from Paris as well as from Palermo brought the revolutionaries of central and northern Italy into action. After five days of bitter fighting, the Milanese drove out their Austrian garrisons. Manin, released from his Venetian prison by rioters, persuaded the Austrian authorities to leave his city peacefully. Rome and Florence were granted constitutions while on 24 March Charles Albert of Piedmont declared war on Austria.

The subsequent war, upon which the fate of the Italian revolutions hung, was disastrous. Charles Albert was no general and, quite unprepared for war in the spring of 1848, he advanced so slowly that the Austrians were able to regroup after the setbacks of the previous months. The Austrian general Radetzky, although aged eighty-two, was still one of the toughest, most energetic, and skilful generals in Europe. Since Vienna was in chaos after Metternich's fall, he was his own master and he had no intention of compromising with the revolutionaries.

For two months the Piedmontese held their own with Tuscan help. Charles Albert, however, quarrelled with the Lombards, and Pius IX, appalled by the turn of events, announced that he could not support a war against Austria. These divisions among the leaders seriously weakened the Italian cause. In July Radetzky defeated Charles Albert decisively at Custozza, forcing him to sign an armistice and to withdraw to Piedmont. The disunity of the revolutionaries then became even more apparent as each locality sought its own salvation in its own way.

In Rome the Pope's reputation had sunk drastically after his refusal to support the war against Austria. The power of the extreme revolutionaries increased throughout the summer of 1848,

The Austrians are driven from Milan

and in November Rossi, one of the chief ministers of the Papal States, was assassinated. At this, Pio Nono fled from Rome, convinced that liberalism was a menace to the Papacy and to the Catholic Church. From Gaeta he appealed to the major Catholic powers for armed intervention against 'the faction of miserable men that exercise (in Rome) the most atrocious despotism and every sort of crime." Never again did he flirt with liberalism or nationalism.

As the Austrian government reasserted itself in Vienna, more reinforcements were sent to Radetzky. Milan was reoccupied and savage treatment handed out to the defenceless inhabitants. Hearing the news from Milan, Charles Albert went to war again, but his second campaign was even more of a disaster. It lasted six days and ended in total defeat at Novara. Having surrendered to Radetzky, Charles Albert handed over power to his son, Victor Emmanuel II, and departed for a Portuguese exile. His parting words to his generals were worthy of a greater and more honest man. 'To the cause of Italy my life has been dedicated. I have not succeeded. I recognize that my person is the one obstacle to peace. Since I have failed to find death on the battlefield, I make my last sacrifice for my country. I lay down by crown and abdicate in favour of my son.' Victor Emmanuel made the best peace he could and, despite strong pressure from the Austrians, managed to retain the constitution (*Statuo*) which his father had previously granted.

The defeat at Novara was, to all intents and purposes, the end of the Italian revolution. Yet, despite overwhelming odds, a handful of men fought on in 1849 to redeem some glory after the months of disunity, defeat, and bitter recrimination. In Rome a republic was set up with the indomitable Mazzini as its leader and with Garibaldi as the commander of its defences. Garibaldi was the son of a fisherman of Nizza (Nice) and, a fervent nationalist and republican, had joined Mazzini's 'Young Italy' movement. Having been sentenced to death for conspiratorial work, he had spent many years of exile in South America where he fought in the civil war and gained a fantastic reputation as a guerrilla leader. On his return home in 1848 he had been deeply ashamed of the poor showing of the Piedmontese troops against the Austrians and was determined to set an example to his countrymen by the defence of the Roman Republic. This he did. Not only did an Austrian and a Neapolitan army move in on the city but, most formidable of all, a French one, sent by President Louis Napoleon to please French Catholics, also joined the attack. The Neapolitans were defeated and the French were so severely mauled by the Garibaldian defenders that further reinforcements had to be sent. By 1 July 1849, however, even Garibaldi had to accept that further defence was impossible. He resolved to take to the hills and to continue the struggle there. 'I offer neither pay nor quarters nor provisions', he declared in his appeal for volunteers, 'I offer hunger, thirst, forced marches, battles, and death. Let him who loves his country in his heart and not with his lips only, follow me.' 4,000 men left with him the next day. The march was as hopeless and as heroic as the defence. Austrian troops were all over Central Italy and as he struggled north-east in the hope of reaching Venice, his volunteers melted away. Garibaldi, his pregnant wife, and a few others reached the Adriatic but their small flotilla was intercepted by Austrian ships and most of his remaining supporters drowned. In the marshes near Ravenna his wife died in his arms, and virtually alone he disappeared once more into exile after a series of hair-breadth escapes.

Giuseppe Garibaldi

Now only one city held out, Venice. Her leader, Manin, a lawyer and journalist before he became involved in politics, proved to be the most sensible and resolute of the leaders of 1848. Despite the Piedmontese defeats at Custozza and Novara, the Venetians decided to continue the struggle. 'Venice will resist Austria at all costs' ran the proclamation. 'President Manin is invested for that purpose with unlimited powers.' Standing surrounded by lagoons, Venice was defended with skill and courage, but in August 1849 cholera ravaged the city and the Austrians began an indiscriminate bombardment. When Manin heard that Garibaldi could bring no relief he decided that the fighting must cease. The city surrendered on 23 August and Manin too went into exile. Unlike Mazzini and Garibaldi, the other heroes of 1849, he died before the Risorgimento of 1859–60 when so many of his dreams for Italy were fulfilled.

Why did the Revolutions Fail?

As the summer of 1849 passed into autumn, revolution was clearly at an end throughout Europe. Manin, Mazzini, Garibaldi, and Kossuth were all in exile. The Frankfurt Assembly had broken up. French troops, sent by President Louis Napoleon, had brought about the return of Pio Nono to a pacified Rome. And in Vienna the conservative Schwarzenberg ruled the Habsburg Empire with a firm hand, advised by the indestructible Metternich, who, until his death in 1859, was to hold an honoured position as 'elder statesman'. While the rulers of Central Europe stamped out the last embers of revolt and congratulated themselves on their capacity for survival, thousands of ex-revolutionaries gathered in western Europe, especially in London, shaken and embittered by the startling rise and fall in their fortunes. Obsessively they asked themselves why they had failed and too often their answers were oversimplified and over-personal. The most popular scapegoats were the French leaders like Ledru-Rollin and Lamartine. Their failure, so the

Daniele Manin

argument ran, had led to the tragedy of the 'June Days' in Paris, the fatal turning-point not only of the French, but of the whole European revolution.

In reality, the reasons for the failure of 1848 were more complex. Partly it was due to personal differences between the leaders. Kossuth and Gorgei quarrelled in Hungary and there were deep divisions within the Frankfurt Assembly. Even more serious were the divisions between the groups which, united in the spring of 1848, had been able to overthrow so many governments. The crucial differences were of class and of race. The French revolutionary movement tore itself apart when the Parisian working classes, led by a few socialists, fought to keep those social benefits which a mainly middle-class assembly seemed determined to abolish by closing down the National Workshops. A similar sequence of events followed in Germany. The Frankfurt Assembly, apparently unwilling to provide any significant improvement in industrial conditions, had to be defended from infuriated workers by Prussian and Austrian troops. The events of 1848–9 made it increasingly clear that in an industrial society middle- and working-class interests were often not merely different but contradictory. As industrialization spread through Europe, class tensions tended to increase rather than decrease and liberals came to be seen not so much as champions of the people against the princes but as defenders of middle-class interests against the mass of workers. Communism and other less extreme socialist theories had had little influence before 1848. In the second half of the century, they began to make much more sense to many more people. More serious still than class tensions as a cause of failure were racial tensions or, in Italy, the suspicions between different areas of the peninsula. In Bohemia, the revolutionary movement was sabotaged by rivalries between Czechs and Germans, in Hungary between Magyars and Slavs, in northern Italy between Lombards and Piedmontese. While the French refused to come to the aid of the Italian liberals, Tsar Nicholas did not fail to come to the aid of the Emperor Francis Joseph in 1849. There was one other cause of failure which was beyond the control of any man: the cholera plague which swept westwards through Europe in the autumn of 1848. It struck hardest at the cities, the heart of the revolution, killing hundreds each day while it lasted. Those it did not kill it exhausted, and in its train left social chaos. The population of those cities struck by cholera were seldom in a mood to continue manning the barricades.

If the revolutionary leaders were often inept or divided, and the forces at their disposal small, disorganized, and exhausted, the conservative leadership was tough and resourceful, once the first months of panic had passed. Moreover in Central Europe they never lost the loyalty of their armed forces. Bismarck, perhaps the

173

most clever politican of the nineteenth century, had watched the activities of the German liberals, especially the Frankfurt Assembly, with contempt. 'The great issues of today will be settled, not by speeches and majority votes', he told the Prussian liberals in 1862, 'that was the great error of 1848-9, but by iron and blood.' His analysis contained much truth. It was the men of iron and blood—Radetzky, Windischgratz, Haynau, Wrangel, Jellacic, and Schwarzenberg—who triumphed in 1849.

Nevertheless, convinced though both the victors and vanquished were that the 1848 revolution had failed, it would be wrong to consider that the failure was total. Notwithstanding the return of Metternich to Vienna and the thousands of liberal exiles, central Europe in 1848 was in certain ways a significantly different place from what it had been before 1848. In Italy the heroism of Manin in Venice and Garibaldi in Rome created a patriotic legend which kept alive the spirit of resistance and unity throughout the next decade. Piedmont managed to keep something more concrete, the constitution granted by Charles Albert. In Germany, many constitutions had been temporarily won by the revolutionaries and though many were considerably modified after the revolutions were suppressed, few were actually abolished. In Prussia, for instance, the constitution of 1850 allowed considerable power to the king but it also instituted an Upper Chamber and a popularly elected Lower House with a real say in financial matters. Much the greatest achievement, however, of the 1848 revolution was the abolition of serfdom in every part of Central and Eastern Europe except Russia and parts of the Balkans. This meant that for the first time millions of peasants were free to move, and to buy and sell land, if they had the means. Over the years, two immensely important developments resulted from this new freedom. First, the number emigrating from Central Europe to America rose dramatically and did something to solve the problem of rural overpopulation which had caused so much misery before 1848. Secondly, more and more land passed into the hands of peasant owners. Thus was accomplished a social change of the first magnitude which did for the mid-European peasant much of what 1789 had done for his French counterpart. For all its disappointments, therefore, the last great revolution of the French-inspired Age of Revolutions brought about a major improvement in the living conditions of millions.

Chapter 10
Realism and Nationalism Triumph

Just as men in the 1920s and 1950s used to talk of 'pre-war' days to mean the times before 1914 or 1939, the men of the 1850s talked of pre-March (or *Vormarz*, as the Germans put it) to refer to the times before the revolution of the spring of 1848. This phrase reflected the feeling that there had been an immense if vague change in the atmosphere and attitudes of European politics. To some extent, this change was a matter of personalities. If the 1830s and 1840s had been years of Metternich and Mazzini, of Manin and Charles Albert, of the Frankfurt parliamentarians and Frederick William IV, of Guizot and Lamartine, the 1850s and 1860s were those of Cavour and Victor Emmanuel, Bismarck and William I, and Napoleon III. There was also a change in political outlook. The 1830s and 1840s were years of tremendous idealism, typified by Mazzini and his 'Young Europe' movement. A marvellous world of free and peace-loving nations was near at hand. Liberal nationalists leading a united people in spontaneous revolution would bring the reactionary powers of darkness crashing down. Liberals and nationalists wrote excellent pamphlets, made moving speeches and refused to compromise their principles. Yet, as the 1848 revolution demonstrated only too clearly, their effectiveness in practical politics, especially in relation to the vital issue of German and Italian unity, was terribly limited.

'The sad events of the years 1848, 1849, and 1850 completely cured me of my idealism', wrote Pagenstenker, a former member of the Frankfurt Assembly, in his memoirs, and many other European liberals were affected in the same way. Previous revolutionaries had been too idealistic, high-minded and principled. Politics was a messy business and demanded a more ruthless and crafty approach. Political success would never be achieved if men continued to act as if the world was as they hoped that it some day would be rather than as it really was. Realism rather than idealism was the prime requirement.

It is no coincidence that the term *Realpolitik* (political realism) was invented in this period. It was first coined by a liberal who, like Pagenstenker, had come to the conclusion that his fellow liberals were so fond of theorizing about the world that they never came to terms with political realities. With the success of ruthless and often cynical politicians like Cavour and Bismarck, it soon came to mean

the use of power, unfettered by any consideration of moral principles, to increase the political power of a state. Bismarck maintained
that he learnt his *Realpolitik* from Schwarzenberg. Cavour learnt
his from the fiasco of 1848 in northern Italy. While Bismarck was
openly contemptuous of German liberals and taunted them for their
failure in 1848, Cavour quietly despised the Mazzinians and
dismissed their theories as nonsense. Though in many ways so
different from each other, these two men, by their success and by
their methods of succeeding, not only transformed the map of
Europe but inaugurated a new era of power politics.

Cavour and Italian Unification

Cavour was a Piedmontese of noble birth. After a brief spell in the
army, he devoted himself to farming and, by using machinery and
scientific methods on his family estates, made himself a small
fortune. He was also greatly interested in industrial development
and invested astutely in the growing industries of northern Italy.
Since his family was well connected with some of western Europe's
leading politicians and since he had travelled widely through the
continent, he was always fascinated by politics. His active political
career did not begin, however, until his late thirties when he became
editor of the political journal *Il Risorgimento*, first published in
Turin in 1847. In 1850 he was elected to the Piedmontese parliament and quickly became the right-hand man of D'Azeglio, who
had been appointed prime minister in 1849 after the disaster of
Novara. At various times in the next eighteen months Cavour was
responsible for finance, for naval affairs, for industry, and for
agriculture. He also proved to be an effective debater and altogether
the most capable politician of the day. D'Azeglio, who had been
wounded in the war against Austria, could not attend parliament
regularly and Cavour became leader in his absence. By forming a
loose alliance with the opposition, he manoeuvred his former chief
into such an impossible position that in 1852 King Victor
Emmanuel, who actively disliked him, had no option but to make
him prime minister. For the rest of his life he made himself
indispensable.

Camillo Cavour

Cavour is often described as a liberal, and both as editor of *Il
Risorgimento*, and also as a minister he was certainly sympathetic to
liberal attitudes. He was an expert financier and did much to
encourage commercial development and freer trade. He more than
anyone was the architect of Piedmont's 'industrial revolution'.
Roads and railways were rapidly improved. Genoa was developed
as a major port and La Spezia as a naval base. He also disliked the
power of the Catholic Church and did his utmost to reduce it in
Piedmont. Yet his liberalism had clear limits. He was keen on

parliament less as a matter of principle than because he could manage it. He often used his control of the civil service to secure the election of his own candidates. When in 1857 elections went against him, he prevented a number of opposition members from taking their seats. He used secret funds to influence the press at home and abroad, and tyrannically suppressed Mazzini's *Italia del Popolo* when its outspoken editorials seemed to be endangering his diplomatic schemes. There is no doubt that he enjoyed political power for its own sake.

He has often been described as a nationalist, indeed as a patriotic statesman whose every diplomatic manoeuvre was directed towards the unification of all Italy. This he was not. When he was in his early twenties, he recalled how he had day-dreamed 'of waking one morning as the directing minister of the Kingdom of Italy' but middle age had made him more cautious. His chief concern was to extend the power of Piedmont in northern Italy and to use nationalism and the appeal of a united Italy as a means to this limited end. In 1856 Manin, exiled in Paris, set up the National Society, the aim of which was to direct a single patriotic movement to end the divisions among Italians which had proved so fatal in 1848 and thus help to bring a united Italy into being. The society built up a large following and Cavour gave it much encouragement. He did so, however, not because he was in whole-hearted agreement with its aims. As he noted in his private correspondence. 'Manin's ideas are always a trifle far-fetched. He wants the unity of Italy and other such rubbish—nonetheless in practice all this may prove useful.' With every justification, Mazzini and Garibaldi regarded him with the gravest distrust. He was, they felt, *'piemontesissimo'*, a man who would always sacrifice Italy to Piedmont. Though Italy could never have been united without Cavour, the bitterness and confusion which immediately followed the unification was partly the consequence of his policies and methods.

The Risorgimento, or in other words those events which brought about the unification of most of Italy in 1859/60, was a chapter of accidents which Cavour brilliantly manipulated to the advantage of Piedmont. His fundamental conviction was that neither Piedmont nor Italy could alone achieve anything against Austria. Charles Albert's boast that *Italia farà da se* had been proved to be an empty one by the events of 1848. Austria could only be defeated if a major European power came to Italy's aid. From 1853, therefore, Cavour did his utmost to bring 'the Italian question' into the forefront of European politics and to persuade either the British or the French that Austrian misrule in Italy justified their intervention. For some years he had little success. Even after Victor Emmanuel had insisted that Piedmontese troops should fight an expensive and, in Cavour's opinion, entirely useless war on the side of the British and

French in the Crimea in 1855/6, neither country took much more than polite notice of Italian complaints against the Austrians. After the Paris negotiations which ended the Crimean War, Britain pointed out that 'the present state of Italy was unsatisfactory', and Napoleon III gave characteristically vague and secret assurances that, when the time was ripe, France might intervene. Otherwise Cavour returned home empty-handed and disappointed. His only hope was that somehow Napoleon III might be provoked into a more positive anti-Austrian attitude. In the meantime, he worked steadily to build up anti-Austrian feeling in the peninsula.

His break came in 1858 when Orsini tried to assassinate Napoleon. The French Emperor's mind worked in a tortuous way and the attempt of an extreme Italian nationalist to murder him for not doing enough for Italy, persuaded him to do more. Six months later, he and Cavour met in secret at Plombières and there worked out a scheme which was transformed into a formal alliance in January 1859. Piedmont was to provoke Austria into a war. The French would then march to the aid of Italy and once victory was won, northern and central Italy would be reconstructed in the following manner. Piedmont was to gain Lombardy, Venetia, Modena, Parma and the Papal States to the north of the Appennines. Tuscany, and the Papal provinces of Umbia and the Marches were to form a central Italian state ruled probably by a relative of Napoleon. The Pope was to keep a small area round Rome and become President of the new Italian Confederation. In return, France would gain Savoy and Nice from Piedmont. Both Napoleon III and Cavour were born conspirators, and at Plombières they were in their element. Cavour left a graphic description of how the two plotters settled down to solve the problem of how to provoke a war with Austria. 'The Emperor came to my aid and we put our heads together and went through the whole map of Italy looking for this cause of war which was so difficult to find. Having traversed without success almost the whole Peninsula, we arrived with virtual certitude at Massa and Carrara. . . .' Cavour's agents, they agreed, would inspire an appeal in the provinces of Massa and Carrara against the misrule of the Duke of Modena. Piedmont would demand an inquiry into the situation, and the Duke, backed by Austria, would refuse and war would quickly follow.

Things turned out rather differently. The next few months were frantic for Cavour as he struggled to provoke Austria into war, and at the same time to hold the slippery Napoleon to his bargain. Britain, alarmed by the rumours of a secret agreement between Piedmont and France and of a future war in northern Italy, set peace-keeping diplomacy moving. Trying to force the pace, Cavour persuaded Victor Emmanuel to mobilize the Piedmont army, and Lombards, fleeing from Austrian conscription schemes, readily joined Piedmontese regiments. Meanwhile Napoleon III lost his nerve under pressure from Britain and Prussia, and on 18 April, 1859, Cavour learnt that the French had joined the other Great Powers in asking Piedmont to demobilize. 'Now there's nothing for me to do', he declared, 'but to put a pistol to my head and blow my brains out', and the following day Piedmont agreed to disarm. However, in the nick of time, Austria had lost patience. The Emperor Francis Joseph decided that the belligerent Piedmontese needed to be taught a lesson. Without consulting his Chancellor, he ordered his military staff to organize a short sharp war. On 19 April Europe learnt that the Austrians had provoked a war. The Plombières plan, therefore, could be put into action. As D'Azeglio said to Cavour, the Austrian attack was 'one of those lucky turns of the lottery that arrive only once in a century.'

The French, led by Napoleon in person, were soon across the Alps and, reinforced by the Piedmontese regular army and Garibaldi's irregulars, marched eastwards against the Austrians

Map 11 Italy 1859–60

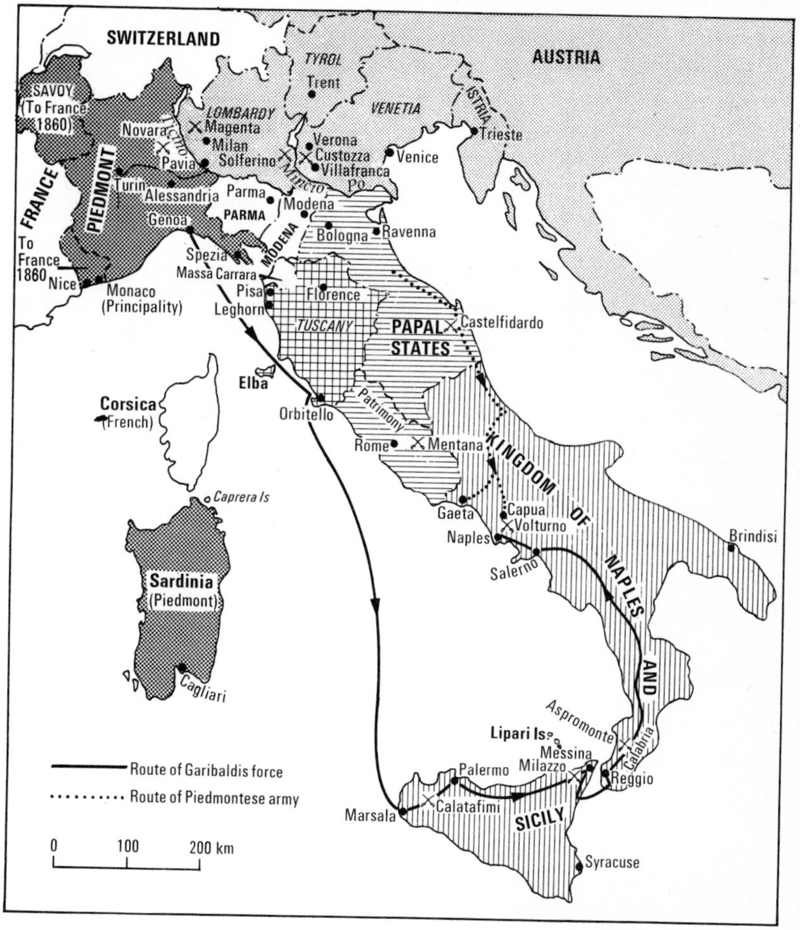

(see map 11). Having forced a crossing of the river Ticino near the main Turin-Milan road, they forced them to battle at Magenta, soundly defeated them, and entered Milan in triumph. Continuing his advance east with 174,000 men, Napoleon again fought the Austrians at Solferino in hilly country south of Lake Garda. This proved a savage battle, the Austrians losing 22,000 men and the French 17,000. Once again the Austrians retreated. By this time, however, Napoleon had had enough. The French losses at Solferino had greatly upset him and he was aware that the Prussians were massing 400,000 men along the Rhineland frontier ready to come to Austria's aid if the war continued much longer. He also suspected that Cavour might double-cross him in the reconstruction of central Italy. Without consulting the Piedmontese, he had an hour's conversation with the Austrian Emperor at Villafranca

The Battle of Solferino 1859: to the left of centre of this picture by Doré based on eyewitness reports of the battle, Napoleon III on horseback directs his troops in a chaotic affair following the chance meeting of the French and Austrian armies. The tower of Solferino and the foothills of the Alps can be seen in the background

and arranged a preliminary peace. Piedmont would gain Lombardy. Otherwise Italy would remain unchanged except that it would become a federation with Austria as a member. Cavour at first could not believe his ears. Beside himself with disappointment, he tried to persuade Victor Emmanuel to continue fighting alone. When the king refused, he resigned.

At this stage, when Cavour's schemes seemed in tatters, the National Society proved its worth. In Parma, Modena, Tuscany, and Romagna, nationalists had seized power as the French advanced against the Austrians and held on to it despite Villafranca. Two able leaders, Farini and Ricasoli, decided that their only salvation lay in union with Piedmont and made sure that resolutions to this effect were passed by the revolutionary assemblies. Plebiscites were then held which showed huge majorities in favour of annexation by Piedmont. Against such popular feeling Austria was powerless and none of the Great Powers was prepared to back an Austrian counter-attack in Italy. Cavour became prime minister again in January 1860 and found that the devious Napoleon III was ready to back a Piedmontese takeover in Central Italy if he received Savoy and Nice according to the Plombières agreement. Plebiscites were again held which seemed to show that most of the inhabitants of Savoy and Nice did wish to be united with France, but since both French and Piedmontese troops were much in evidence during the voting, it is impossible to say how accurately they reflected the genuine will of these provinces. Many Italians were shocked by Cavour's readiness to use territories so long Italian as diplomatic bargaining counters. Garibaldi, whose birthplace was in Nice, never forgave him for this particular piece of diplomacy.

In Cavour's opinion, the time had now come to stop and survey the situation. Austria might still be in Venetia, Pio Nono in Rome, and the Bourbons in Naples, but Piedmont had made considerable gains and most of northern and central Italy was now united. The immediate task ahead was to reorganize the new state so that genuine unity and progress could be achieved. But he was no longer master of events. Patriotic enthusiasm flooded the length and breath of the peninsula, and thousands of Italians were not prepared to accept that barely half their country should be liberated, however satisfactory such a situation might appear to the power politicians. In the spring of 1860 Garibaldi went into action to free the rest of his countrymen.

By now Garibaldi was a legend in his own lifetime. After the tragic death of his first wife and his flight into exile in 1849, he had lived in Tangier, the U.S.A., and Peru. He had sailed round the world, and in 1854 had received a hero's welcome in London. He had then returned to Caprera, a tiny windswept island off the coast

181

of Sardinia, where he lived the life of a peasant farmer. In 1859 he had hastened to Piedmont to make himself available to Victor Emmanuel but found himself cold-shouldered. The king and Cavour felt that he was too much of the guerrilla and popular revolutionary to be given a responsible military position. During the war against Austria he led a band of irregular volunteers with great success, often operating behind the enemy's lines, and after Villafranca went south to help the nationalists in Central Italy. Finding that even now he could gain no major position in the regular army, he became convinced that Cavour was using him and the ideal of Italian unity for his own limited purposes. In November 1859 he publicly attacked 'the miserable fox-like policy that, for the moment, is holding up the triumphant progress of the Italian movement', and when he learnt of the handover of Nice and Savoy he stormed into the Piedmont parliament and accused a white-faced Cavour of making a mockery of nationalism, liberalism, and democracy.

In May 1860 he sailed from Genoa in two paddle-steamers with 1,089 volunteers whose average age was twenty and whose only uniform consisted of shirts of red flannel. These were to become the famous 'Thousand' or 'Red Shirts' and their destination was Sicily. To all observers it looked a crazy expedition. The Bourbons

Garibaldi, having triumphed in Sicily and Southern Italy meets Victor Emmanuel near Naples

had 20,000 troops defending Palermo, the capital of Sicily, another 16,000 in Calabria (the toe of Italy) and another 40,000 defending Naples. Cavour, convinced that it was just another hopeless Mazzinian gesture, did his best to prevent the expedition leaving Genoa but such was Garbaldi's fame that he dared not take too open a stand against him. The Thousand landed at Marsala and at once advanced towards Palermo (see map 11, p. 179). Most Sicilians watched and waited. At Calatafimi a Bourbon force of 3,000 in a strong position barred the way. 'Here we either make Italy or die', declared Garibaldi and drove the enemy off with a suicidally courageous frontal attack. Many Sicilians were now convinced that Garibaldi was invincible. When he attacked Palermo, the population rose in revolt against the Bourbon troops. They soon surrendered the city to Garibaldi who was proclaimed dictator. Less than two months later he had conquered the whole island, and on 15 August crossed the straits of Messina to the mainland with 3,000 men. There was hardly any fighting as he marched north towards Naples. The news of his approach caused popular rejoicing everywhere and the totally demoralized Bourbon troops deserted, sometimes murdering their officers before they did so. On 7 September he and six companions who had taken the train from Salerno entered Naples to the tumultuous applause of a huge crowd. Before long he was planning his advance on Rome.

Cavour, however, had other ideas. The news of Garibaldi's phenomenal success had filled him with dismay. Not only were Sicily and Southern Italy backward areas which might well prove a burden to the more prosperous north but Garibaldi and his Mazzinian followers had dangerous democratic and republican ideas. Moreover, an attack on Rome might upset the settlement of northern Italy, since it was unlikely that the rest of Europe, Catholic France in particular, would stand by and allow an assault on Papal territory. He, therefore, acted fast to forestall the Garibaldians. When his own attempt to promote a revolution in Naples before Garibaldi arrived failed, he persuaded Victor Emmanuel to march south with the main Piedmontese army. While Garibaldi was winning his biggest and most closely fought battle against the Bourbon troops in the valley of the river Volturno, the Piedmontese swept the Papal army aside at Castelfidardo. (Cavour explained to the French that the Piedmontese had to go through Papal territory if Rome was to be saved from the Garibaldians.) Much was at stake when the two victorious Italian armies met. Though Garibaldi loathed Cavour, he had great respect for Victor Emmanuel. He, therefore, surrendered all his conquests personally to the king and made his way quietly and with dignity to his island home. A plebiscite in the conquered territories voted overwhelmingly in favour of unity with Piedmont and, by the end of 1860, all Italy with the exception of Rome and Venice was united. It was, as Gladstone the British statesman put it, 'one of the greatest marvels of our time', and a triumph for Cavour's brand of politics.

The years that immediately followed unification were a sad disappointment. For most Piedmontese, unification meant Piedmontisation and, especially in the south, lands confiscated from the Church and from the Bourbons passed into the hands of northern Italian businessmen who exploited them more ruthlessly than their predecessors. Within a year of Garibaldi's triumphant entry into Naples, civil war had broken out in the south with thousands of peasantry rallying to the Bourbon cause. Eventually the Piedmontese were victorious, but only after many atrocities on both sides. Since then, southern Italy and Sicily have never taken easily to what they regard as northern rule. Another major setback to the steady development of unified Italy was Cavour's death in 1861 when he was still only 50. His death was quite unexpected and, since he carried so much policy around in his head, very disruptive. The young country could ill afford the loss of a man of his calibre, especially since his successors Ricasoli and Ratazzi had none of his skill either as financiers, diplomats, or managers of parliament. Ministry followed ministry in quick succession, and without a stable government directing policy, economic difficulties piled up. There were, moreover, many Italians who could never accept that Rome, still ruled by the Pope, and Venetia, still ruled by Austria, need remain outside the new nation. The reluctance of their government to challenge the French (who defended the Pope) and the Austrians, filled them with contempt. They found their leader in Garibaldi who quickly became an embarrassment to the government which was determined to remain on good terms with the other major European powers. In 1862 he was arrested as he was planning an attack on Venice. Later he was shot at and wounded by government forces at Aspromonte as he was leading another band of volunteers on Rome. Finally in 1867 his last expedition, without any official support, was met and defeated at Mentana outside Rome by a joint Franco-Papal force. The failures of these expeditions and the attitude of the Italian government to their greatest national hero further increased the sense of disappointment.

Nonetheless by 1870 the whole peninsula was united—less it must be said through the efforts of the Italians than of the Prussians. In 1866 Prussia and Austria went to war and Italy allied herself with Prussia. This proved a sensible move for, although the Austrians defeated the Italian army at Custozza and the Italian navy at Lissa, the Prussians were so completely victorious in Germany that in the peace that followed they were able to force Austria to hand over Venetia to Italy. In 1870 Prussia and France went to war and the French troops defending Rome were immediately brought home.

The Eternal City was occupied by the Italian troops and declared the capital of the kingdom of Italy. Pope Pius IX shut himself up in the Vatican declared himself a prisoner and refused to negotiate in any way with the Italian government. His action meant that many Italian Catholics found it very difficult to support the government. Thus, though by 1870 all the peninsula was Italian, the internal problems of the unified state were considerable.

Bismarck and German Unification

The example of the Italian Risorgimento revitalized German politics which had stagnated since the 1848 revolution. In the late summer of 1859, as the National Society of Italy was organizing revolts in Central Italy against Austrian rule, a German National Association was founded which, three years later, had a membership of 25,000. Its members were influential, including princes and nobles as well as professors and businessmen. More important still, it had clear-cut aims which were both liberal and nationalist. United Germany must be ruled by a parliamentary government and it should be united round Prussia, rather than Austria.

The fact that it was pro-Prussian was very significant. Austria and Prussia had struggled for political dominance in Germany since the time of Frederick the Great but throughout the nineteenth century Austria had held the upper hand. In economic matters, however, Prussia had forged ahead since the formation of the *Zollverein*, and in the 1850s and 1860s was developing rapidly as an industrial power. During the 1848 revolution the Frankfurt parliamentarians had been bitterly divided, between those wanting a great Germany including Austria and those wanting a lesser Germany excluding Austria and therefore dominated by Prussia. Eventually the lesser Germans won but were let down by Frederick William IV who refused their offer of the imperial crown. The Prussian king and his advisers then flirted with a scheme of unifying the German princes under Prussian leadership. Schwarzenberg, the Austrian Prime Minister, made it clear however that he strongly opposed such a scheme and in 1850 mobilized 200,000 troops to crush disturbances in Hesse-Cassel and to prevent Prussia extending her influence any further. Though some of his ministers were ready for war, Frederick William lost his nerve. At Olmutz, Schwarzenberg virtually dictated a settlement which re-established the old Confederation under Austrian presidency. For Prussia, it was a major humilitiation which was not quickly forgotten. Before long it was inevitable that Austria and Prussia would again come into conflict and the readiness of the National Association to look to Prussia rather than Austria strengthened Prussia's position.

The National Association was, however, in a difficult situation since it was as liberal as it was nationalist. But Prussia was not famous for its liberalism, nor for the respect that its government had for parliaments and assemblies. The German liberals who led the National Association hoped both to unify Germany round Prussia and to liberalize Prussia simultaneously, but in the prevailing mood of realism they were prepared to compromise and to put national unity first and liberalism second. As one of them put it, 'better the stiffest Prussian military rule than the wretchedness of the small states'. What happened in fact was that only half of the liberal nationalist ideal was achieved. Germany was unified round Prussia but, in the process, German liberalism was fatally weakened.

The man most responsible for this turn of events was Otto von Bismarck, Chancellor of Prussia from 1862 and the outstanding politician of the nineteenth century. He was born in 1815 in Brandenburg-Prussia. His father was a Junker, a member of the Prussian landlord class, with estates on the banks of the river Elbe; his mother came from a family of well-known scholars and civil servants. She made sure that her son received the best possible education, first in Berlin and then at Gottingen. At the University of Gottingen he did just enough work to obtain the qualifications necessary for becoming a civil servant, but spent much more time drinking and duelling. In 1836 he tried to become a civil servant but found the bureaucratic life intolerable. He was very bad at taking orders. 'My pride', he wrote at the time, 'bids me command rather than obey.' After a few months he resigned and went to live on his

Bismarck with his monarch and constant ally the Emperor William I. Bismarck is on the right

country estates where his style of life—incessant and dangerous riding, drinking, and hunting—gained him a reputation as the 'wild' and 'crazy' Bismarck. He was a big man in every way, more than six feet tall with the strength and agility to match. He was endowed with considerable intelligence and nervous energy. An aggressive and passionate man, he also possessed, for all his cynicism in political affairs, a deep personal religious faith which, among other things, usually convinced him that God was on his and Prussia's side. The eight years that he spent as a country squire cultivating his estates were years of deep frustration for him, and when in 1847 he joined the Prussian Diet in place of a neighbouring member who had fallen ill, he at last discovered the life which suited him.

He at once commanded attention because of his extremely conservative views. 'I am a Junker', he wrote, 'and must profit by it.' He therefore championed the old landed aristocracy and the Divine Right monarchy against the rising tide of liberalism. The 1848/9 revolutions filled him first with consternation, then with contempt. The scheme for German unification eventually put forward by the Frankfurt Assembly he rejected with scorn. This is how he ended a speech to the Prussian Diet. 'Our army harbours no revolutionary enthusiasm. You will not find in the army, any more than in the rest of the Prussian people, any need for a national rebirth. They are satisfied with and proud of the name Prussia. Prussian we are and Prussian we wish to remain.' Through his mother's family connections and through his own obvious ability, he gained greater political responsibilities. In 1851 he was sent as one of the Prussian representatives to the Diet of the German Confederation which Schwarzenberg had revived. Here he discovered the extent of Austrian influence in German affairs and became convinced that a major war between the two powers was but a matter of time. He made himself famous by his insistence that in no matter, however trivial, should Prussia seem to lose face to Austria in the Federal Diet. Between 1859 and 1861 he was Prussian ambassador to the Russian court, and in 1862, high in the government's favour, he was appointed to be a special envoy to Paris.

It was in 1862 that Prussia entered a momentous constitutional crisis. In 1857 Frederick William IV had had a nervous breakdown and his brother and heir William had become regent. William was less intelligent but a good deal tougher than Frederick, a soldier by training and a conservative by instinct. Since 1859, however, within the House of Deputies set up by the constitution of 1850, the liberals were increasingly powerful. Believing that William's coming to power marked the beginning of a new era, they were determined that he should take them fully into partnership in the government of the country. In 1860 the test came. William and von

187

Roon, his Minister of War, were convinced that the Prussian army was neither big nor efficient enough. They proposed to abolish a citizen militia which had been in existence since 1814 on the grounds that it was too poorly trained for modern warfare, and to raise a much larger and up-to-date force by extending conscription. These proposals the liberals in the House of Deputies firmly opposed since they approved of the citizen militia and disapproved of the greatly increased costs which Roon's reforms would cause. They also resented the attempts of the government to bypass the House of Deputies altogether. General elections in 1861 and 1862 increased the liberal majority and hardened its opposition to the army reforms. William, however, was not a man of compromise and was prepared to abdicate when he could find no minister who was ready to ignore the House of Deputies. Roon's last suggestion was to try Bismarck. 'He is not here and he wouldn't do it', said the king. 'He is here and he will do it', answered Roon. Roon was right. On 22 September 1862 Bismarck was appointed Minister-President with the specific task of making the army reforms effective.

He was now forty-seven and had worked out his fundamental political views. His main interest was foreign affairs and his intention was to extend the power of the Prussian state as far and as fast as possible. Like Cavour, he understood the popular appeal of nationalism and used it for his own ends. Like Cavour, he was quite ready to tolerate parliaments if he could use them. Only when they opposed him did he turn on them. Like Cavour, politics was a game at which he enjoyed winning and in which any manoeuvre, however devious, was justifiable if it seemed in the interests of Prussia or of his own position. To an even greater extent than Cavour he had an uncanny knack of turning every diplomatic crisis to his own advantage.

When he compared himself with his contemporaries, his chief quality, he concluded, was his realism. 'Because they have yet scarcely outgrown the political nursery,' he wrote, 'the Germans cannot accustom themselves to regard politics as a study of the possible.' His study of the possible showed clearly that the strong overpowered the weak. A successful politician, therefore, would always make sure that the balance of forces was in his favour before he acted. In one of his first speeches after taking office he told the liberals that 'Germany does not look to the liberalism but to the power of Prussia', and to increase and exercise that power he bent his very considerable energies.

His immediate problem, of course, was the House of Deputies, whose opposition remained as firm as ever. Bismarck's solution was extremely simple. He got round the opposition by ignoring it and by ordering the collection of taxes to pay for the army reforms as if the House of Deputies had no constitutional rights whatever. So docile was the Prussian population that the tax-collection proved no problem despite liberal protests. Bismarck knew, however, that he was playing a dangerous game and that such high-handed action could not be permanent. He tried, therefore, to distract the opposition and gain popularity for the government by an active and 'German' foreign policy (see map 12).

His first success came in 1864 when he intervened in the highly complicated Schleswig-Holstein affair. The Duchies of Schleswig and Holstein, about which the German liberals had been so excited in 1848/9 once again became a crisis centre in 1863. The new king of Denmark was trying to make the mainly German-speaking duchies more completely part of Denmark, while at the same time his own claim to the Danish throne was disputed by one Frederick of Augustenberg. The Diet of the German Confederation decided

Map 12 Germany 1864–71

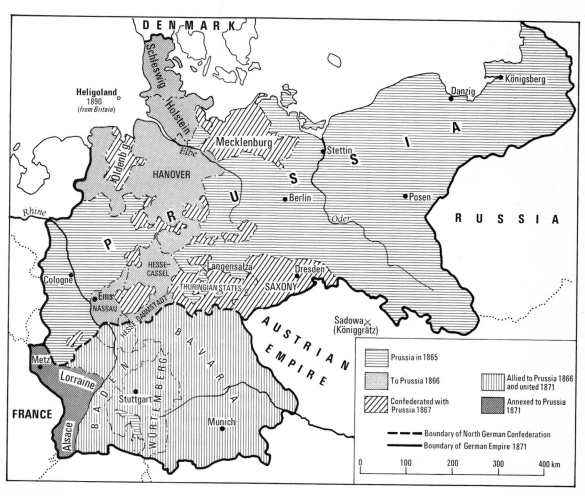

189

that it must champion the rights of the Germans in the duchies, and eventually Bismarck was able to persuade the Austrians to march with the Prussians as representatives of the Confederation and force the Danes to hand over Schleswig-Holstein. In fact he did not care an iota about the rights of the Germans within the duchies or about the claims of the Confederation. 'It is no concern of ours', he admitted privately, 'whether the Germans of Holstein are happy.' He took action because the crisis seemed to offer a splendid opportunity of strengthening Prussian power in Northern Germany and of embarrassing Austria.

The war was soon won though not as easily as Bismarck had expected. Prussia took over the administration of Schleswig, Austria that of Holstein. The Confederation was ignored. Bismarck then set about provoking Austria with an apparent recklessness which shocked many Prussians as well as the rest of Europe. He had been assured, however, by Roon and Moltke, the Prussian Chief of Staff, that the Prussian army was more than ready for a major war with Austria, so he pressed on with complete confidence. After frequent disputes over the administration of Schleswig-Holstein and over Prussian schemes for the reform of the German Confederation, war broke out on 14 June 1866. Nine of the fifteen German states backed Austria and most European rulers assumed that, after quite a long struggle, Austria would win.

On 15 and 16 June Prussia attacked both Austria and Hanover. Seven weeks later the war was over and Prussia completely victorious. Moltke's methods of warfare were much the most advanced in Europe and the Prussian armies the best trained and armed. By skilful use of railways, Prussian troops were concentrated quickly and in crushing force. On 28 June the Hanoverians were defeated at Langensalza, and on 3 July the main Austrian army overwhelmed at Koniggratz (Sadowa). Vienna lay at Prussia's mercy. In the following few months Bismarck's diplomatic genius became apparent. While most Prussians, including the king, were intoxicated with victory and wished to demand major acquisitions of territory from the defeated Austrians, Bismarck insisted on a moderate peace. He feared France might come to Austria's aid. Moreover, a humiliated Austria would be a bad and dangerous neighbour. The important thing was to end Austria's chances of remaining a serious rival to Prussia in Germany. By the Treaty of Prague, Prussia gained much territory from those German states which had allied with Austria but none from Austria herself. The Habsburgs, however, were pushed out of Germany by the abolition of the old German Confederation, which was replaced by a North German Confederation dominated by Prussia, and four independent states in the south—Wurttemberg, Bavaria, Baden and Hesse-Darmstadt.

Bismarck then used this military triumph to deal with the liberal opposition. Before the war he was not popular. His Schleswig-Holstein policies, and his provocation of Austria in 1865 and 1866, had shocked responsible opinion, and the Lower House had become so critical that at one stage he was driven to suspend its sittings. However, as the French ambassador Benedetti observed in 1866, 'every Prussian has something of Frederick the Great in him, whatever his views on liberty', and the news of the Prussian victories aroused tremendous patriotism throughout the country. In the general elections held in June and July 1866, the liberals were trounced by the conservatives. Yet once again Bismarck was no more ready to humiliate the liberals than the Austrians. Instead he held out an olive branch and asked the Lower House to approve his unconstitutional money-raising activities of the previous four years. At the same time, he made it clear that he and the king might feel bound to behave in exactly the same way if similar disputes arose in the future. In the atmosphere of patriotic pride and unity, the liberals gave their approval and in effect accepted a minor part in the political life of the state. The power of the Prussian king and his Chancellor remained much stronger in Prussia and in the new North German Confederation than the liberals of 1848 or of 1859–62 had intended. There was a parliamentary assembly (*Reichstag*) elected by universal suffrage in the new Confederation, but it was subordinate to a Federal Assembly (*Bundesrat*) made up of nominees of the governments of the various states of the Confederation and to the king and Chancellor. That Germany had no real experience of parliamentary government before 1918 followed directly from Bismarck's success in persuading German liberals to put their national ideals before their liberal ones.

Sadowa had obviously transformed the balance of power in Central Europe and had particularly upset the French who found themselves with an unprecedentedly powerful neighbour on their Rhineland frontier. For the next four years, from 1866 to 1870, Bismarck and Napoleon III waged diplomatic war. As Chapter 8 shows, the sick and ageing French Emperor was no match for Bismarck. France received a series of rebuffs from Prussia, and French patriotic indignation, fanned by a fiercely nationalistic press, ran high. Finally, the Hohenzollern candidature and the 'Ems telegram' incident led to war and another decisive Prussian victory. The affair of the Ems telegram showed Bismarck at his most characteristic. Before he received William's telegram describing the interview at Ems with Benedetti, the French ambassador, he was acutely depressed. He had done his utmost to encourage the Hohenzollern candidature for the Spanish throne, in the hope of provoking a quarrel with France (see page 157). For once, William and his Hohenzollern family had refused to co-operate, the candidature had been withdrawn and, in Bismarck's opinion, Prussia had suffered a diplomatic humiliation 'worse than Olmutz'. All his schemes had gone awry and he even thought of resigning. Once he read William's telegram, he was a changed man. Well aware of the excited state of public opinion in both Berlin and Paris he realized that a carefully edited version of the telegram could give the impression of an unfriendly meeting and cause another major crisis. The edited version which he published in Berlin read as follows: 'The French ambassador at Ems requested His Majesty the King to authorize him that he may wire to Paris that his Majesty the King had pledged himself at all future times nevermore to give his consent if the Hohenzollern should revert to their candidature. At that His Majesty the King has refused to receive the French ambassador again and has told him through the adjutant on duty that His Majesty has nothing further to convey to the ambassador.' The result was just as he had wished. It was the French who clamoured for and then declared war. Bismarck was thus able to address the Federal Assembly of the North German Confederation and maintain that 'France had left Germany no honourable choice but war and had committed a grievous sin against humanity!'

Though the war (see Chapter 8) dragged on rather longer than he had expected, his use of the Prussian victories for political purposes was masterly. As soon as war was declared, he persuaded the independent South German states to fight with the Prussians against the French. In the excitement after the triumphs of Sedan and Metz he further persuaded them to become part of a united Germany. Just as victory against Austria had brought about the unification of northern Germany, so the victory against France brought about the unification of the whole nation.

By November 1870 the constitutional basis of the new Germany had been thrashed out by the representatives of the south German states and Bismarck. It inherited much from the North German Confederation. The new Germany had a federal structure within which the old states retained their kings and princes and some of their old individuality. There was a parliament (*Reichstag*) elected by universal manhood suffrage and a federal Council or Bundesrat made up of delegates from the different states in proportion to their size. Since Prussia was much the largest state, she had much the most delegates. The new Germany was also to be an Empire (*Reich*), and its Emperor the king of Prussia. Like the North German Confederation before it, the new German Empire seemed quite liberal and democratic. Its appearance, however, was deceptive. The Emperor controlled both the imperial army and the civil service, both of which came to be staffed mainly by Prussians. Prussia also had firm control of the Federal Council. The Emperor

William I is declared Emperor of Germany at Versailles at the end of the Franco-Prussian War

appointed and dismissed his ministers, who were directly responsible to him rather than to the assemblies. Bismarck became the new imperial chancellor as well as remaining Minister-President of Prussia. As long as he retained the backing of the Emperor, he, and not the assemblies, was the real master of Germany.

The Empire was formally proclaimed on 18 January 1871. The setting was the Hall of Mirrors in the immense palace of Versailles near Paris. The pomp and ceremony were magnificent, and for millions of Germans it was a dream of thirty years or more come true. But even at this moment, one last stroke of Bismarckian *Realpolitik* was needed. William would only accept the imperial crown if it was offered to him by all the German princes. However, Louis of Bavaria, who was exceptionally proud of his family's long tradition of independence, was reluctant to co-operate. Bismarck only got round him by secretly bribing him with a pension of £20,000 per year, the money coming from funds confiscated from King George of Hanover, defeated in 1866. In the Hall of Mirrors, after a hurried and irritable consultation between William and Bismarck, who could not agree on the precise title of the new Emperor, the Grand Duke of Baden cried out before the assembled dignitaries, 'Long live his imperial and royal majesty, Kaiser Wilhelm!' That unity which liberalism and idealism had so signally failed to achieve twenty-two years before had come about through the force of nationalism manipulated by the realist of the century in the interests of the Prussian state.

Chapter 11
Europe in an Uneasy Balance

After the Prussian victory in the Franco-Prussian war and the triumphant unification of Germany in 1871, there was no major war between the great powers of Europe until 1914. The ensuing years of peace were, however, uneasy. The emergence of a strong Germany destroyed the previous European balance of power and eventually led the nations of Europe to seek new alliances to safeguard their interests. By 1907 the continent was divided into two hostile camps armed to the teeth yet arming still further for fear that they might be outgunned by the enemy. Simultaneously, the Industrial Revolution spread to every country. The German 'take-off' occurred between 1860 and 1880. With foreign, mainly French, investment assisting, the Russian economy followed suit in the 1890s. As in Western Europe, industrialization meant urbanization and a shift of population from the country to the town. Thus in the later decades of the nineteenth century many Europeans found themselves in a new urban world, facing new situations both at home and at work. They were often rootless and sometimes starving. With the spread of elementary education, however, they were usually literate and open to new political ideas. The misery of industrial and urban conditions made many men socialists. The rapid growth of the power of the modern state, and the oppression which often stemmed from this growth, made some men anarchists. Much the most popular, powerful, and disruptive political feeling of this period, however, was nationalism.

Nationalism

Nationalism was an attitude of mind which regarded the maintenance and improvement of the nation's strength as the chief object of government. If the nation was already free and unified, like France or Germany or Russia, it must at all costs secure and strengthen its position in Europe and in the world. If, however, the nation was still unfree, though conscious of its national unity through common race or language, like Poland, Ireland, or Bulgaria, it must win complete independence. Nationalism had a long history and was powerful in Europe throughout the nineteenth century. It had inspired the unification of Italy and Germany and a series of revolts elsewhere. As the century progressed, it captured the popular imagination and grew more feverish and emotional. A fiercely nationalistic public opinion had forced a reluctant British government into the Crimean war. Bismarck manipulated the hysterical nationalistic press of Paris and Berlin to bring about the Franco-Prussian war in 1870. It seems that the citizens of the rapidly growing industrial areas of Europe, recently uprooted from a secure if backward rural and traditional existence, had an emotional need to feel part of a larger group—a need which was often satisfied by a fervent national pride.

The most energetic and most confident nation in Europe was Germany. The military and political achievements of the years from 1848 to 1871 were followed by an economic advance which enabled the Germans to rival the British as the foremost industrial nation of Europe. A number of writers proceeded to glorify these achievements and to suggest that the German race possessed certain virtues which destined it to dominate Europe. In his *History of Germany in the Nineteenth Century* (first published in 1879) and in his *Politics* (published in the 1890s) von Treitschke argued that Germans possessed a nobility of character plus industry, energy, and military strength far in advance of other European races. Only the English could begin to rival them but they were too involved in commerce to be taken seriously. 'The highest moral duty of the nation-state', he maintained, 'is to increase its power. Feebleness is the political sin against the Holy Ghost.' Through national strength would come national unity. 'An army organized on a really national foundation is the sole political institution which binds citizen to citizen . . . it is not the German parliament which has become the real and effective bond of national union but the Germany army.' War was both natural and glorious, and through war Germany would achieve her deserved supremacy. Similar ideas, flavoured with anti-semitism—the Jews were an alien race who sullied the purity of Teutonic Germany—were put forward by Stocker, an army chaplain, and by Hasse, an army doctor. They reached a receptive audience. Conscious of the strength of their army and of their economy, the fast-increasing German population began restlessly to look for further conquests, at first overseas, then nearer home. Only as long as Bismarck remained Chancellor was this restlessness controlled.

French nationalism, though never so confident or so popularly based as German nationalism, had plenty of vigour. Its driving force was the desire to avenge the bitter humiliation of 1870–1 and to recover the lost provinces of Alsace and Lorraine. 'Think of it always, speak of it never' had been the advice of Gambetta in the 1870s, but in the 1880s and 1890s men like Maurice Barrès and Paul Déroulède openly clamoured for a war of revenge. Barrès was only eight years old when his Lorraine home fell to the Germans, but it was an event he never forgot. 'We who look back to the dark years in the vague mist of our childhood', he wrote in 1884, 'feel that the honour of the Fatherland is embodied in the marching regiments; the military trumpets remind us of our conquered soil; the waving flags seem to be our signal to the distant exiles; our fists clench; we have only to make ourselves ready to provoke war.' Déroulède was the most active French nationalist. He founded 'the League of Patriots' in 1882, penned hundreds of soldiers' songs and organized fêtes in honour of such national heroes as Joan of Arc. The determined peacefulness of the French government eventually filled him with such despair that in 1899 he vainly attempted to set up a military dictatorship by a *coup d'état*.

Italian nationalism would have been comic if it had not been so wasteful in men and resources. Encouraged by writers like Carducci who demanded that the new Italian nation should think like its Roman ancestors, and Corradini who looked forward to a modern Julius Caesar, the Italian public expected to be able to match the other major powers both in Europe and overseas. Such unrealistic expectations persuaded successive governments to indulge in an aggressive foreign and colonial policy which led eventually to disastrous and humiliating defeat. At Adowa, in 1896, the Italian army, scrambling greedily for a part of Africa, managed to become the only European army to be decisively defeated by an African, Menelek of Abyssinia.

Within the Austrian Empire nationalism had a disruptive rather than a unifying effect. The different races within the Empire came to think of themselves as separate nations and to demand greater independence. In Austria itself, many of the German-speaking population looked forward to the time when they would be part of a greater Germany. The young Adolf Hitler, born an Austrian in 1889, was punished at school for singing the German rather than the imperial Austrian anthem. At the same time Hungarians, Czechs, Serbs and Croats demanded more and more independence.

The Czechs, Serbs and Croats were Slavs and looked to other Slav races for support against the Habsburgs. The Pan-Slavist movement, encouraged by the Russian scientists Danilevski, strengthened Slav unity and quickened the desire for national independence among the subject Slav races. Despite her own chronic internal problems, Russia also pursued a belligerent nationalist policy in this period. She used the Pan-Slavist movement to increase her influence in the Balkans and to weaken Austria, while her rapid expansion eastwards into Asia led to a ferocious and catastrophic war with Japan in 1904. Tsar Nicholas and his advisers, however, learnt nothing. After defeat in the east, they began to fish once again in troubled Balkan waters. Their readiness to support Serbia against Austria led Russia into the First World War, the disasters of which helped to end the Russian monarchy.

Nationalism flourished in small as well as in large powers. The new Balkan nations—Bulgaria, Greece, Rumania, Serbia—proved as ready to fight each other for local supremacy as they had been to fight their Turkish oppressors. In Poland a significant number of citizens not only planned for their freedom from Russian over-lordship but for the subjection of the neighbouring Lithuanians, Letts, and Ukrainians to Polish rule. At the opposite end of the continent, the Irish struggled to persuade the English to grant them Home Rule. It was Parnell, the Irish leader, who best expressed the spirit of this late nineteenth-century nationalism during a speech at Cork in 1885. 'No man', he said, 'has the right to fix the boundary to the march of a nation; no man has the right to say to his country—thus far shalt thou go and no further.' The nation-state must expand its power to its fullest possible extent and should expect the unquestioning loyalty of all its citizens. 'Our country, right or wrong' was a fitting slogan for the times. Such aggressive and unprincipled nationalism was pernicious. Its eventual consequences were devastatingly destructive.

Socialism

While the growth of nationalism increased unease between the nations of Europe, the growth of socialism caused unease within them. With the development of trades unions, co-operative move-ments, and friendly societies among the working classes all over the continent, political parties whose chief aim was to improve the conditions of the working classes also came into existence.

Since much of the suffering in industrial areas seemed to stem from the power which property-owners enjoyed through the ownership of private property—factories, banks, land, transport, fuel—distrust of all private property was a central feature of these new parties. 'Whereas it has long been known and declared that the poor have no right to the property of the rich,' wrote John Ruskin, English art critic and socialist in 1860, 'I wish it also to be known and declared that the rich have no right to the property of the poor.' His French contemporary, Proudhon, having asked himself the question 'what is property?' in 1840 provided the brief answer, 'property is theft'. In a socialist state all the most important 'means of production'—the big factories, the railways, the fuel supplies, the banks and so on—should be controlled by the state. In other words they would be public rather than private property. Such ideas obviously ran completely counter to the accepted beliefs about property of the ruling classes in Europe. They seemed to under-mine the whole order of society. Hardly surprisingly they caused

widespread unease, especially when they were combined, in the doctrines of extreme socialists like the Marxists, with the conviction that a genuinely socialist society could only be brought about by violent revolution.

Socialism developed in different ways in different countries. In Great Britain, where an urban working class had been longest in existence, the trades union movement proved to be very suspicious of socialist, especially Marxist, theories. Though a number of socialist political organizations were formed in the 1880s, they only managed to attract a small number of followers. In the last ten years of the nineteenth century, however, when economic conditions were poor and the employers, with the help of the law-courts, seemed to be set on reducing trades union rights, backing grew for a new party to represent the labouring classes. In 1893 the Independent Labour Party was founded at Bradford, and in 1900 the trades unions, the I.L.P. and some of the socialist groups founded during the 1880s combined to form the Labour Representation Committee (L.R.C.) to fight the next parliamentary election. In the 1906 election L.R.C. candidates won twenty-nine parliamentary seats, and from then on the parliamentary Labour party was firmly established. It remained suspicious of continental, especially Marxist, socialism.

Marx was a German, and German socialism was deeply in-

Industrial unrest : ten men die after a May Day clash between miners and police at Fourmies in northern France 1891

fluenced by his ideas, especially after 1864 when Lassalle, a gifted non-Marxist socialist leader, had been killed in a duel. In 1869 Leibknecht and Bebel, both followers of Marx, created the Social Democratic Workers Party which, enlarged and reorganized as the Social Democratic Party (S.P.D.), was able to win the support of many of the German trades unions. The 500,000 votes which it polled in the 1877 election made it a political group of real significance. In 1898 it polled 3,000,000 votes and won fifty-six seats in the Reichstag. By 1912 it was the largest single party, with 112 seats.

A Marxist Socialist party also appeared in France when the French Labour party was founded in 1882. By 1893 it was strong enough to secure the election of Guesde, one of its leaders, to the Chamber of Deputies and, by 1898, the total socialist vote (which included many non-Marxists) reached 700,000. The following year a socialist, Millerand, became Minister of Commerce in a new coalition government, and from then on the socialists were a powerful group in the Chamber of Deputies. Unlike their counterparts in Britain and Germany, however, trades unions and socialists in France kept apart. The French trades unions, or *syndicats*, as they were known, never matched the British or German unions in numbers, but, organized in the Confédération Generale de Travail (C.G.T.), they made up in militancy for what they lacked in numbers. The C.G.T. had little time for the policy of gaining reforms through parliamentary means. From 1895 onwards it concentrated on advance through strike action and was influenced more by anarchist than by socialist ideas.

Italian socialism developed rather similarly to the French. In 1882 the first Italian Socialist gained a seat in parliament and in the next twenty years a comparatively powerful group of socialists in parliament was built up. At the same time Italian trades unions proved increasingly ready to use strike action and, on the eve of the First World War, were attracted by anarchist as well as by socialist ideas.

Within the Habsburg Empire socialism was weakened by national rivalries, though in the major industrial areas local socialists groups built up a considerable following. The most famous and most popular Austrian socialist leader before World War I was Karl Lueger who led the Christian Socialist party in Vienna. He was a man of considerable charm and ability. Mayor of the capital in the 1890s he set new standards of administrative efficiency and brought the privately owned gas, water and transport systems under municipal control. He also discovered the political appeal of anti-semitism and made his party firmly anti-semitic. The young Adolf Hitler spent six years in Vienna just before the First World War and learnt a great deal.

Of all European socialists, the Russians were the most extra-ordinary and, in the long run, the most significant. In the 1860s and 1870s a non-Marxist form of Socialism, known as Populism, was taken up with enthusiasm by many young Russian students. Believing that the country's salvation lay in the creation of socialist village communes, many of them moved into the countryside to convert the peasantry to their views. The government, much the most reactionary in Europe, stamped out this movement in 1874 and 1875 by many arrests and trials. Opposition groups were driven underground or into exile and they became convinced that only violent revolution could bring political change to Russia. Not surprisingly Marxism, with its emphasis on the inevitability of a violent working class revolution, greatly appealed to some Russian socialists when it was introduced to them by Plekhanov in the 1880s. A Social Democratic party was founded in exile in 1883, and in the 1890s, led by Plekhanov and Vladimir Ulianov whom the world was later to know as Lenin, it began vigorously to plan how Marxist ideas might be put into practice in Russian con-ditions. Ulianov and Plekhanov first met at Geneva in 1895 and, to begin with, Plekhanov found the younger man rather uninterest-ing. However, as soon as the conversation turned to politics he noted that Ulianov 'became a changed man, thoroughly aroused, and revealing a mind of great brilliance and power. Every remark showed deep reflection. One felt that his opinions were backed by life experience and while his life experience was quite simple and not extensive, it was sufficient to make him an expert in revolutionary work.' This meeting began a vital partnership. Plekhanov was the writer and theoretician, Ulianov the organizer and man of action. In 1900 they began producing the newspaper *Iskra* (the Spark) which, having been secretly printed in Leipzig and stored in Berlin in the cellars of the offices of the main German Social Democratic newspaper, was then smuggled into Russia by an underground chain of sympathizers. The movement grew in numbers and in confidence. In 1903, however, it ran into a severe crisis. A major difference of opinion arose over whether the party should consist of a relatively small number of completely committed, highly trained 'professional revolutionaries' or should be opened to a wider, less disciplined, and less professional membership. Lenin, backed by Plekhanov, insisted that the party should remain small and disciplined. He won the day but broke the party in two. He and his majority were henceforward known as the Bolsheviks (the majority), his opponents as the Mensheviks (the minority). It was a severe blow to the Social Democrats and they took many years to recover. Until 1917 their political influence within Russia was small.

The socialist group which gave the Tsar's secret police the most difficult time before World War I was the Socialist Revolutionary party, founded in 1900. It was terrorist in the best Russian tradition without being Marxist and between 1901 and 1904 carried out a campaign of political assassination which greatly sapped the confidence of an already harassed government. As Russian industrialization accelerated after 1890 and large factories appeared in St. Petersburg and Moscow, trades union activity increased. Strike action became frequent, the most massive and the most famous being the General Strike of 1905.

Very different though the socialist parties in the different countries of Europe turned out to be, European socialists before World War I were always conscious that they were part of an international movement. Their cause was the cause of the working classes the world over. 'The proletarians have nothing to lose but their chains. They have a world to win. Workers of the world unite' were the words with which Marx had concluded the Communist Manifesto, and in 1864 he tried to bring this unity into existence by founding in London the First International Working Men's Association. The First International (as it is usually known) had a tumultuous history. Marx himself was no great organizer nor an easy man to work with. A number of conferences were held but they proved more remarkable for their conflicts than for their unity. The Franco-Prussian war split the French and German delegates and a bitter dispute developed between the anarchists led by Bakunin

who wished to work for the destruction of all systems of government and the orthodox Marxist socialists who wished to concentrate
on the destruction of capitalist governments. By 1872 Marx had
managed to expel the anarchists, but at such a cost to the First
International that it was dissolved four years later.

The Second International which lasted from 1889 until World
War I was an altogether more impressive organization. Through its
efforts an International Socialist Bureau was set up in Brussels to
co-ordinate the efforts of socialists everywhere and an Inter-
parliamentary Socialist Commission was organized in 1905 to co-
ordinate the socialist parliamentary parties in Western Europe.
1907 saw the creation of the International Bureau of Socialist
Women, and between 1907 and 1910 four conferences of socialist
journalists were held.

Deep divisions, however, existed behind the facade of unity.
Anarchists still came to disrupt the conferences by jumping on
tables and shouting. More serious were the differences of opinion
about tactics. On 1 May 1890 French and Austrian socialists
declared a general strike, while the British and Germans contented
themselves with mass demonstrations. This difference of opinion
about the correct way to use strike action was followed by an even
more serious difference about the correct policies to be followed by
parliamentary socialist parties. This dispute came to a head in 1899,
the year in which the French socialist Millerand agreed to join a
coalition and mainly non-socialist government and in which
Bernstein, a well-known German Marxist, published a book called
The Pre-conditions of Socialism and the Tasks of Social Democracy.
Bernstein argued that Social Democrats should drop their talk of
revolution and work for reform through the existing institutions of
society, a course of action Millerand was following in France by
joining a coalition government. For the next five years the argument
raged between the traditional 'no-compromise with capitalism'
Marxists and the 'revisionists' who agreed with Bernstein. Eventually, at Amsterdam in 1904, the Second International gave its
ruling. By 25 votes to 4, with 12 absentions, the leaders of European
socialism laid down that 'Social Democracy cannot aim at participat-
ing in governmental power within capitalist society', and condemned 'any attempt to disguise existing class conflicts in order to
facilitate support of bourgeois parties'. In other words, Millerand's
action and Bernstein's ideas were unacceptable. Between the
Amsterdam Congress and the outbreak of World War I, the
International devoted much of its attention to the menace of war.
It hoped that a general strike of European workers might be
enough to prevent a major war breaking out. In fact, the events of
1914 merely demonstrated the powerlessness of the Second
International and showed how weak was the hold of socialism in

Anarchism in action: the assassination of the Austrian Empress, 1898

comparison to nationalism on the minds of men, even of working men. The war came so fast in 1914 that the socialist leaders were taken by surprise. Hurried attempts to work out a common policy failed because of national suspicions. The one man who might have inspired a common policy, the Frenchman Jaurès, was assassinated by a patriotic fanatic the day before France and Germany mobilized. The French socialist leaders joined the government. The German trades unions, in a fervour of patriotism, ended their strikes to help the war effort, and the S.P.D., forgetting its Marxist heritage, voted in the Reichstag for war. When Lenin read this news in a Berlin newspaper, he could not believe it. 'It is impossible', he first insisted, and when eventually convinced, he declared 'the Second International is dead.' Only the Russian and the Serbian socialist parties condemned the war as a war of capitalist governments fought at the expense of the common people. Lenin's advice to the ordinary soldier—'take your rifles and turn them on your officers and capitalists'—was universally ignored. The Second International *was* dead to all intents and purposes.

Anarchism

There was one other political group which spread even more fear and consternation than the Marxists among the respectable classes in Europe at the end of the nineteenth century—the anarchists. In 1892 an anarchist bomb killed a Parisian café-owner and four policemen, in 1893 another one killed twenty Spanish theatre-goers. The same year, another exploded in the French Chamber of Deputies without killing anyone. Between 1893 and 1901 anarchists assassinated Presidents Carnot of France, Canovas of Spain and McKinley of the U.S.A., the Empress Elizabeth of Austria and King Umberto of Italy. The British journal *Blackwood's Magazine* accurately reflected the general reaction of the time when it commented 'the mad dog is the closest parallel in nature to the anarchist.' Only the lunatic or the totally depraved, it was felt, could carry out such senseless acts of destruction. In its origins, however, anarchism was an intellectually powerful and optimistic creed. Drawing on the writings of Chinese philosophers as well as more recent thinkers like Proudhon and Tolstoy, men like Bakunin and Kropotkin argued that all governments, by their very existence, interfered with the freedom of the ordinary man. Proper freedom could only be obtained if men returned to a much more natural life in small communities. The new industrial state had grown so large, so powerful, and interfered so greatly in men's lives, that it must be overthrown, as Kropotkin put it, 'through permanent revolt by word of mouth, in writing, by the dagger, the rifle, by dynamite'. In France, Sorel, an engineer turned political philosopher, concluded that violence had a virtue of its own in the political situation of the time and encouraged French unions to use violent methods in their struggle for better conditions. In Spain, Italy, and France, anarchism flourished among working men as much as socialism. Anarchists played an important part in the 'Semana Tragica' of 1909 when the workers of Barcelona in Spain rose in revolt and were only repressed after the Spanish army had bombarded the city with artillery. They were also active in the week of strikes which paralysed Italy in June 1914.

Though the First World War did not come until 1914, there was plenty of violence in the years that preceded it. Terrorism, strikes, lock-outs, bomb-throwing, street-brawls, militant suffragettes, and an increasing readiness to accept violence as a justified way for both nations and individuals to behave were much in evidence in the years after 1890. Anarchism was a symptom of a fevered society.

The major powers in the nineteenth century: Imperial Germany

Despite the strength and restlessness of the new German nation, Bismarck was convinced that Germany should rest content with her new boundaries. As he put it to the Reichstag in 1887, 'we belong to what old Prince Metternich called "the satiated states".' His main worry was that a revived France, determined to recover Alsace and Lorraine, might unite with Russia and force Germany to fight a war on two fronts. To prevent this, he worked to create a system of alliances which would isolate France and bind Russia to Germany. In 1873 a first step was taken with the formation of the Dreikaiserbund or League of the Three Emperors (of Germany, Austria, and Russia). Impressive though it sounded, this league did not amount to very much. Austria and Russia disagreed too deeply about the Balkans. Two years later Bismarck seriously considered another war with France, whose rapid recovery was filling him with dismay. Joint pressure from Britain and Russia dissuaded him. That same year (1875) a major Balkan crisis occurred, eventually causing Russia to go to war with Turkey, and Britain and Austria to threaten war against Russia. Bismarck took the opportunity to set himself up as an 'honest broker' and called a Congress of the major powers at Berlin in 1878 which managed to bring about a peaceful, if not very lasting, settlement in the Balkans. During these negotiations, he decided that Germany must come to a closer understanding with Austria to balance Russian hostility to Germany which had increased significantly in the 1875–8 crisis. The result was the Dual Alliance of 1879 which bound Germany and Austria-Hungary much more tightly than the Dreikaiserbund. At the same time, so as to prevent Russia joining up with France—the obvious counter-move to the Dual Alliance—he strengthened the Dreikaiserbund by promising Russia German help against the Turks. He also bound Russia further by the secret Reinsurance treaty of 1887. On top of all this, he succeeded in enlarging the Dual to the Triple Alliance in 1882 by persuading Italy to come in with Germany and Austria-Hungary. This was a display of diplomatic juggling of enormous skill, isolating France completely from the rest of Europe. But it could only be temporary, as Bismarck well knew. In his last speech to the Reichstag in 1888 he stressed that Germany's only real security was her own strength. 'The pike in the European pond', he declared, 'prevent us from becoming carp. . . . We Germans fear God and nothing else in the world.' His successors had neither his skill nor his conviction that it was in Germany's interest to maintain a peaceful Europe. Consequently Germany came to be the most dangerous pike in a European pond full of pike and his system of alliances eventually had the effect of dividing them into two hostile shoals.

Within Germany, Bismarck's position was secure as long as the Emperor William I lived. His power was immense. He knew it and revelled in it. Modesty was never one of his sterling qualities. 'Louis XIV of France', he once observed, 'had said "L'état, c'est moi". I say "Moi, je suis l'état".' As he grew older, he grew vainer, more obstinate, less tolerant of criticism and more irritable. But he lost little of his political skill. His first major problem after the unification was the place of the Roman Catholic Church within the new Empire. Prussian Poland included many Catholics, and the addition of the mainly Catholic states of southern Germany to the Empire strengthened the Catholics as a political group. The treatment of Pope Pius IX by the Italian government had scandalized Catholics all over Europe and there were demands in Germany for intervention on the Pope's behalf. Bismarck reacted strongly. Like many German Protestants, he was deeply suspicious of Catholicism. The trouble with Catholics was their loyalty to the Papacy, which though mainly a spiritual power was also a political power outside their own nation. 'The issue', he explained to the Prussian House of Deputies in 1873, 'is essentially a political one, concerned with the age-old struggle between king and priest, the struggle which dominated German history through the Middle Ages down to the fall of the Medieval Empire, when the last Emperor perished on the scaffold, with a French conqueror allied to the Pope.' He therefore let loose what came to be called the *Kulturkampf*—or civilization struggle. The Jesuits, the most powerful Catholic teaching order, were expelled from the Empire. All religious orders in Prussia were abolished and Catholic education was everywhere brought under close state supervision. Resistance, however, was firm and, with the exception of an attempt to assassinate Bismarck, passive. Many bishops went into exile. Thus, when Leo XIII, moderate and approachable, succeeded the uncompromising Pius IX in 1878, Bismarck was prepared to negotiate. Slowly and skilfully he gave ground so that by 1887 Leo could announce that the *Kulturkampf* was over. The exiled bishops and priests were able to return. So were all the orders except the Jesuits. Bismarck's main achievement was to bring Catholic education more closely under the supervision of the state.

During the struggle against the Catholics he had depended on liberal support to secure the necessary parliamentary support. After 1879, however, he turned to the conservatives. The issue that really caused the break with the liberals was 'protection'. In the 1870s and 1880s Germany, like every European country, faced the challenge to home agriculture caused by the flood of cheap food-stuffs from overseas. While the liberals stood for free trade and cheap food, the conservatives, who were mainly landowners, demanded protective tariffs. True to his Junker upbringing, Bismarck introduced the necessary tariffs against the bitter opposition of the liberals. It was the end of an unnatural alliance and of liberalism as an effective political force in Germany.

If German liberalism declined, German socialism flourished. Bismarck's attitude to socialism was one of sustained hostility. What he had seen of the Paris Commune in 1870 had convinced him that socialism and anarchy were much the same. In 1878 he described the followers of the S.P.D. as 'the menacing band of robbers with whom we share our largest towns', and hurried through the Reichstag a set of anti-socialist laws which prevented workers' associations from publishing or even meeting for political purposes. Yet though the police enforced the laws with harshness, socialism continued to thrive. Bismarck then decided to kill it with kindness. In the 1880s he carried through the most far-reaching programme of social reform in Europe. In 1882 all working men were compulsorily insured against sickness; in 1884 against accidents. In 1889 these insurance schemes were extended to cover old age and permanent ill-health. As far as the Chancellor was concerned, this 'state socialism' was created solely to weaken the German socialists. 'Whoever has a pension for his old age', he pointed out, 'is far more content and easier to manage than one who had no such prospect.' Politically, his social reforms were hardly a success since support for the S.P.D. continued to grow. From every other viewpoint, however, they were thoroughly successful. The German worker had greater security than ever before and German industry showed no sign of faltering. Other European countries quickly copied this German 'state socialism'.

At the beginning of 1890 Bismarck was contemplating another direct attack on socialism like the anti-socialist laws of 1878, but before the end of March he had been forced to resign. The man who forced his resignation was the young emperor, William II. Bismarck's firm ally, the Emperor William I, had died in 1888 at the age of ninety. His son, the Emperor Frederick III, already mortally ill with cancer when he came to the throne, died three months later and was succeeded by his son, William II. Between the old Chancellor and the young Emperor there was immediate friction, since both were wilful and tactless individuals. Within the Prussian court there was much hostility to Bismarck who was trying to make sure that his son, Herbert, would succeed him as Chancellor. 'It was a question', said the Emperor William II, 'whether the Hohenzollern or Bismarck dynasty would rule.' The Emperor wished to take a softer line than Bismarck with the socialists and this difference proved to be the last straw. Bismarck offered his resignation which was gratefully accepted.

The old Chancellor had enjoyed power too long to let go of it gracefully. He hated the boredom of retirement and diverted himself by maintaining a constant stream of criticism against the policies of the new government, particularly over its handling of foreign affairs. He never forgave William II. After his death in July 1898 a tombstone was erected on his grave, which, on his instructions, bore these words 'A true German servant of Emperor William I.'

On Bismarck's resignation in 1890 William II announced that 'the office of watch on the ship of state has fallen to me. The course remains as before. Full steam ahead.' The German ship of state certainly steamed on at full power but, as Bismarck was quick to note, the course was not as before. Neither the Emperor, nor his Chancellors (Caprivi, Hohenlohe, Bulow, and Bethmann-Hollweg) had Bismarck's skill and caution, and they were increasingly unable

DROPPING THE PILOT.

'The Dropping of the Pilot'; Bismarck's resignation as pictured in one of Punch's most famous cartoons

to control their admirals and generals. During his retirement Bismarck was visited by Admiral von Tirpitz, then busy planning the fleet that would challenge the British command of the high seas. 'Germany must keep within her frontiers', Bismarck warned him. In 1897 the Emperor paid his last visit. 'Jena came twenty years after the death of Frederick the Great', Bismarck remarked after his departure. 'The crash will come twenty years after mine if things go on like this.' He was right almost to the month.

'The Rat Queue': during the siege of Paris by the Prussians rats became quite a delicacy!

The Third Republic of France

Defeat by the Prussians in 1870 left France fiercely divided. While Paris was still being besieged by the Prussians, an assembly met at Bordeaux and elected the veteran politician Thiers to make peace. (The Emperor Napoleon III, having been taken prisoner after the battle of Sedan, abdicated and retired to an English exile where he was joined by the Empress Eugénie.) The Germans demanded Alsace-Lorraine, five billion francs and the maintenance of an army of occupation in France until the money was paid as the price of peace. Thiers was in no position to bargain. He accepted the terms and the Bordeaux Assembly confirmed his acceptance by 546 votes to 107. Paris, however, was in an ugly mood. It was the Parisians who had first declared themselves against the Emperor Napoleon and who alone had resisted the Prussians with any sustained courage. Among them were many republicans and socialists who hoped to create a radically better society out of the ruins of defeat. They distrusted Thiers and the Bordeaux Assembly which, they feared, would try to restore some kind of monarchy as soon as it could.

Thiers' government moved to Versailles and there passed a number of measures which were intended to bring the country back to normal. Two of these—the removal of cannon from Paris and the ending of payments to the National Guard—were interpreted by the Parisians as attempts to weaken their position. The capital openly rebelled. On 15 March 1871, the Paris Commune was established and the red flag flew above the Town Hall. The demands of the 'communards' were potentially revolutionary. They wished to see a radical reduction in the power of the central government and a compensating increase in local government. Paris and other major cities should become virtually self-governing. Thiers, however, had no intention of bargaining. He waited until enough of the French regular army had been released from German prisons and then struck. While the German troops watched from a distance with a mixture of horror and contempt, the French regular army attacked the French capital which was armed to the teeth. It was the most terrible episode in modern French history and made

Parisian troops, having mutinied and joined the Commune execute their former officers, General Lecomte and General Thomas. (This photograph is a reconstruction of the scene for anti-Communard propaganda purposes.)

the Prussian siege of the previous year look like child's play. The army eventually gained a foothold inside the city on 21 May. For the next six days, vicious street-fighting forced the communards to withdraw from barricade after barricade. Before the last surviving resisters were cornered for execution in the Père Lachaise cemetery, they had murdered their hostages (including the archbishop of Paris) and set fire to the city. More than 20,000 people died in the fighting and the government ordered the shooting of thousands of Parisians captured during the struggle. Thousands more were imprisoned or exiled. It was the June Days of 1848 all over again but a hundred times worse.

From this awful baptism (of the Paris Commune) emerged the Third Republic which proved to be the longest lasting system of government France has known since 1789, only ending with Hitler's 1940 'blitzkrieg'. Its first years, however, were very uncertain. There was no great enthusiasm for a republican form of government and if the Count of Chambord, the head of the Bourbon family, could have brought himself to recognize the tricolour as the flag of France, a monarchy might well have been established. However, he could not, and in the years that followed the idea of a monarchy gradually lost its appeal.

Nonetheless, the Third Republic continued to look fragile. Government succeeded government with bewildering speed and roused little popular enthusiasm. The fragility, however, was more apparent than real. Behind the constantly changing governments, there existed a strong, stable and efficient civil service. Socially and economically, France was changing less fast than her neighbours and her extensive peasantry and prosperous middle class were more interested in stability than change. Moreover, so divided were French politicians that their main aim was less to do what they wanted than to hinder their opponents. The Third Republic, therefore, went on.

Some major crises, however, shook it seriously between 1871 and 1914. In 1886 a General Boulanger became Minister of War. He was a handsome man, who rode a black horse with skill. Though not specially intelligent, he learnt to play the part of the strong silent man. His arrival at the War Ministry coincided with an international crisis and a political scandal. The Germans arrested a French customs official and the President of the French Republic having discovered that his son-in-law had been selling political honours, had to resign. Boulanger became the man of the hour, the hero-figure who would stand up to the Germans and save France from the sordid intrigues of the politicians. He won a series of by-elections in the provinces and in January 1889 a Parisian by-election

General Boulanger on his black horse

with a huge majority. With the mobs shouting him on, he seemed to have the Republic at his mercy. Boulanger, however, was no Bonaparte. On the crucial night his mistress attracted him more than the prospect of power. 'Caesar', sneered a disillusioned supporter, 'was only a garrison Romeo.' His chance was gone. The government recovered its nerve and began to arrest his leading supporters. Boulanger himself fled into exile and eventually committed suicide on the grave of his mistress.

An even more serious crisis occurred between 1896 and 1900. In 1894 a Captain Dreyfus, a French army officer from a Jewish family in Alsace, was sentenced to life imprisonment on Devil's Island in the French West Indies, having been found guilty of spying for Germany. Anti-semitic prejudice played a large part in his condemnation since the evidence against him was extremely flimsy. Furthermore, a secret file which purported to prove his guilt was not made available to his lawyers—which was quite illegal. By 1896 a Colonel Picquart had done enough research to

January 13th, 1895. The cover of Le Petit Journal shows the disgrace of the 'traitor' Dreyfus in front of his regiment

The 'Aurora' headline

suggest that Dreyfus was in fact innocent, and, though the army
quickly transferred him to Tunis, Picquart was able to pass on his
evidence to a member of the French Senate before his transfer took
effect. The storm really broke when the government, with extraordinary clumsiness, tried to pretend that justice had been done
and no inquiry was necessary. The man Picquart reckoned was
really guilty, one Esterhazy, was put through a mockery of a court-
martial and hurriedly acquitted. At this point, the famous novelist
Zola picked up his pen and wrote an open letter to the President of
the Republic which the Newspaper *L'Aurore* published on its
front page under the huge headline 'J'Accuse'. 'I accuse', wrote
Zola, 'the first court-martial of having broken the law in con-
victing an accused person on the evidence of a document which
had remained secret and I accuse the second court-martial of
having covered up this illegality by committing in its turn the
judicial crime of knowingly acquitting a guilty person.' The results
of this letter were sensational. Zola himself was brought to trial and
the country was split into two bitterly hostile groups. The anti-
Dreyfusards regarded themselves as patriots upholding the honour
of the country, the army, and the Church against foreigners, Jews,
Radicals and other such subversives; the Dreyfusards saw themselves as the lovers of justice upholding the rights of the innocent
individual against a powerful conspiracy of generals, priests and
politicians. The nationalist Déroulède made himself a leading anti-
Dreyfusard and tried unsuccessfully to use the crisis to organize a
coup d'état. Street-fighting between the different factions became
commonplace. Before long, however, the case against Dreyfus
collapsed. Colonel Henri, who had forged the vital piece of evidence

against Dreyfus, admitted his guilt and committed suicide. The real spy, Esterhazy, fled to London where he told his story to the world. Yet still the army authorities blundered on. Dreyfus was re-tried. Incredibly, he was found 'guilty with extenuating circumstances' and sentenced to ten years imprisonment. Although the President of the Republic felt bound to intervene and cancel the ten years sentence, it was not until 1906 that Dreyfus was completely cleared. The affair had cost him twelve years of his life and left him a broken man.

Its consequences for France were far-reaching. The Catholic Church had ranged itself on the side of the anti-Dreyfusards and the dispute had become one of republicans and anti-clericals against monarchists and churchmen. The collapse of the army's case greatly discredited the latter and led to tough anti-clerical laws being passed between 1902 and 1905. The wounds inflicted by this crisis went deep and were slow to heal.

The public reputation of the politicians of the Third Republic was further damaged by a number of political scandals of which the most serious was the Panama scandal of 1893. A company set up to cut the Panama Canal in Central America was at first enthusiastically backed by many politicians whose lead was followed by the French public. However the company seriously underestimated the difficulties of the project, its finances were incompetently and corruptly handled and eventually it failed. Many small investors (but few of the politicians) lost a lot of money. There was a huge outcry and many of the politicians involved went into temporary retirement. Scandals of this type indicated to Frenchmen that too many of their republican politicians were mere adventurers out to feather their own nests. As a result, the early years of the twentieth century were marked by the growing readiness of nationalists at one extreme and anarchists at the other to work against rather than through the parliamentary institutions of the Third Republic.

Italy

The years after unification brought disillusion to many patriotic Italians. The new Italy might look a major power but she was without the military, economic, and diplomatic strength to behave like one. Internally, moreover, the country faced greater problems than any of her rivals, with the possible exception of Austria-Hungary. The chief problem was the south. Bad enough in 1860, it was far worse in 1900. While the population expanded rapidly, competition from the more advanced north wiped out industry south of Rome and the mainly peasant population grew poorer and poorer. Brigandage was frequent. The Mafia controlled much of Sicily. The illiteracy rate of some of the southern provinces was five

times greater than that of Piedmont. Since only the literate possessed the franchise, the south was hopelessly under-represented.

In fact, the constitution adapted from the Piedmontese *Statuto* of
1848 was inadequate for the new nation. A key section of the
Italian population, the Catholics loyal to the Pope, would have
nothing to do with it after Pius IX insisted that he was a prisoner in
the Vatican and roundly condemned the new state which he
regarded as impossibly liberal and anti-clerical.

The new Kingdom of Italy, therefore, appeared too often to be
run by the few for the benefit of the few who were generally
northern, rich, and middle-class. Governments were made up of
loose coalitions and elections could be 'managed' by the sixty-nine
provincial prefects. The deputies elected to parliament possessed
extensive powers of patronage. Graft and corruption were commonplace. By 1900 there was a cynical distrust of parliamentary
institutions throughout the peninsula. Opposition, especially from
the working classes, tended to be extra-parliamentary.

Italian history between 1870 and 1914 can be divided into three
distinct periods. In the first, which lasted until 1896, parliamentary
governments failed to tackle the main problems of the country.
Between 1896 and 1900 anarchy and revolution were very close.
Finally from 1900 to 1914 there was a period of stability and
industrial progress which, by 1914, was threatened from a number
of directions.

The first period was dominated by Depretis, a radical in his
youth who, in his maturity, successfully juggled coalitions to keep
his government in power. The chief achievements of these years was
the increase of the electorate from 600,000 to about 2,000,000 in
1882 and the signing of the Triple Alliance with Germany and
Austria-Hungary in 1882. At the same time, Depretis felt bound to
follow an active imperial policy. With the French occupying
Tunisia and the general scramble for Africa under way, Italy could
not stand idly by. Between 1882 and 1885 the Italian army gained a
foothold on the Eritrean coast.

Crispi, Depretis' successor as prime minister, followed similar
policies, though he was less skilful a manager of parliament and
more aggressive an imperialist. Since Italy gained nothing from the
Berlin Conference of 1884 which had redrawn the boundaries of
Central Africa, there were many demands that national honour
must be redeemed by the seizure of some considerable part of the
African continent. Crispi first declared Eritrea a colony and Abyssinia a protectorate. In 1896 he ordered the conquest of Abyssinia.
The result was the defeat at Adowa and Crispi resigned.

He left the country in chaos. The colonial policy had been

expensive as well as disastrous. His anti-socialist policies had irritated the main socialist parties, the P.S.I. and the P.R.I., without weakening them. Near famine conditions existed in many parts of the peninsula and riots and brigandage were frequently reported. The worst explosion came in 1898. Striking workers threw up barricades in the streets of Milan. The city authorities proclaimed a state of siege and more than a hundred citizens lost their lives in the street fighting that followed. In 1900 King Umberto was murdered by an anarchist to avenge the dead of Milan. Led by a new prime minister, Giolitti, and a new king, Victor Emmanuel III, the government was able to come to terms with the socialists, most of whom were ready at this time to work with rather than against parliament. Revolution was avoided and there was a gradual return to law and order.

In the next ten years industrial production nearly doubled and there was a general increase in prosperity. With this happier economic climate to help him, Giolitti managed to win the confidence of the socialist leaders far more successfully than his predecessors. As Turati, the socialist leader, acknowledged, 'on the other side (of the House of Deputies) there is a man who understands us.' While he was prime minister, the franchise was extended to all men over the age of thirty. He also managed to lessen the antagonism of the Catholic church towards the Italian state. Immediately before World War I, however, internal tensions were growing again. Giolitti had been able to do little for the south and a war to seize Tripolitania from Turkey in 1911 had proved more difficult and expensive than expected. Furthermore Italian socialists had become exicted by syndicalists ideas of the French type. 'Italian socialism', wrote the young Mussolini in the Milan paper *Avanti*, 'needs to live a heroic and historical day. It needs to clash as a bloc against the bourgeois bloc'. The heroic days came in the Red Week of June 1914. A two-day general strike was followed by a revolt in the Ravenna area, where 18,000 workers on bicycles were joined by the peasantry of the surrounding countryside. It soon petered out since the socialist leaders were unready to provoke a bloody conflict with the army. It showed, however, after half a century of unification, how deeply divided Italy still remained.

The young Mussolini

The Austrian Empire

The swift and complete defeat of the Austrians by the Prussians in 1866 had been a terrible shock to the Habsburg dynasty and caused a radical re-organization within the Empire. In the weakness of defeat the Emperor Franz Joseph was in no position to resist Hungarian demands for greater independence, and in 1867 the so-called Dual Monarchy was brought into being. While defence, foreign, and financial policy throughout the Empire were to remain the Emperor's responsibility, Hungary was to have virtual home rule with its own parliament and a separate set of laws. At the time Franz Joseph saw the arrangement as a temporary measure, a way out of a tight corner. It was, however, to last till the end of the Empire in 1918. Though there were many representative assemblies in the Dual Monarchy—parliaments, provincial diets, and delegations—these assemblies were less powerful than their British, French, or Italian equivalents. In the Austrian part of the Empire the essence of power was retained by the Emperor through his council of ministers and civil service; in Hungary, by the Magyar aristocracy. The Empire remained a ramshackle affair—'a despotism tempered by slovenliness' was how one critic described it—more suited to the eighteenth than to the nineteenth century.

In 1867 the Emperor Franz Joseph was thirty-seven and had another forty-nine years of his reign before him. Granted the extent of his powers, his personality was vital to the development of his Empire. In many ways he was an impressive man. He worked extremely hard at the business of government and, though he had many able ministers, was always master in his own house. He bore his many public and private griefs—his son committed suicide and his wife was murdered by an anarchist—with dignity and courage. There is no doubt that he was universally respected. His major shortcoming as a ruler was that, in a period of unprecedentedly rapid economic and social change, his view of his duties was out of date and quite inflexible. His only real interest was to maintain intact the Habsburg Empire. He honestly believed in divine right, that the Empire had been entrusted to the Habsburgs by the grace of God to rule as he and his successors saw fit. Changes came when the dynasty seemed threatened, seldom otherwise.

With traditional Habsburg dignity, the Emperor Franz Joseph receives a German deputation

The nationality question was the Habsburgs' greatest problem. In the Austrian part of the Empire the main racial groups were the Germans, the Poles, and the Czechs, and rivalry between Germans and Czechs was strong especially in Bohemia. In Hungary the Magyars, though less than half the total population, were completely dominant and ignored the claims of the other main racial groups, the Ruthenians, Rumanians, Slovaks, Serbs, and Croats. The policy of the dynasty was to accept the Magyar position in Hungary and play off the other racial groups against each other. This 'divide and rule' approach worked satisfactorily for many years, but the more potent a political force nationalism became, the more dangerous it grew. In 1918 it backfired with a vengeance.

The nationality issue strongly influenced Austrian foreign policy in this period. Defeat in 1866 made the Empire much more an Eastern than a Central European power and the Black Sea and the Balkans became correspondingly more vital to her security. The policy of accepting Magyar dominance over the South Slavs (the Serbs and Croats) in Hungary forced the South Slavs to look more and more to their Slav brothers, especially to Serbia and to Russia, for aid. Russian ambition in the Balkans after 1905 caused great anxiety in Vienna, as did the growing belligerence of Serbia. By 1914 many senior members of the government were convinced that a short sharp war against Serbia was vital if the unity of the Dual Monarchy was to be maintained.

The Russian Empire

The death of Tsar Nicholas in 1855, which was soon followed by the Treaty of Paris indicating the defeat of Russia in the Crimean War, ended an epoch when Russia, by the size of her army and by the determination of her rulers to destroy revolution in Europe, had been the major continental power. The Crimean defeats had indicated serious social and economic as well as military weaknesses in the Russian state and the new Tsar, Alexander II, was more ready than his father to consider major reforms. One of his earliest and most important reforms was the emancipation of the serfs in 1861. In order to gain the co-operation of the nobility, to whom most serfs belonged, he represented the move as essential if a social revolution was to be avoided. 'Better that the reform should come from above than wait until serfdom is abolished from below' is how he put it. Legally, of course, the former serfs were instantly better off but only a small number gained any obvious economic advantages from their change in status. Heavy compensation had to be paid to their former owners and heavy taxation kept them close to poverty. Since the rural population of Russia was growing as fast as any in Europe there was a terrible land hunger. Desperate peasant

Above *Forced labour in Siberia, political prisoners at work*

Right *Tzar Nicholas II and the Tzarina in their coronation robes*

revolts had been a feature of Russian life throughout the eighteenth and nineteenth centuries. They did not obviously diminish after 1861. Other reforms were happier. The legal codes of Russia were improved and local assemblies (*zemstvos*) were set up in Russian towns. Alexander's reign, however, ended in tragedy. The atmosphere of reform in the early years of his reign which followed the stern repression of the reign of Nicholas naturally caused plenty of political discussion and encouraged demands for more radical reform. Alexander, however, was no radical and, after a desperate revolt of the Polish nobility in 1863 and an attempt on his life in 1866, he yielded to advisers and became more repressive. The extraordinary gulf between the government and the peasants and workers, and between the government and the intelligentsia, became ever more clear. The opposition turned to terrorist tactics in the 1870s and 1880s. One notorious group, known as 'the People's Freedom', came to the conclusion that assassination was the only effective political weapon. Target number one was the Tsar. Having managed to blow up two storeys of the Winter Palace in St. Petersburg without harming Alexander (though killing sixty soldiers), they finally got him with bombs in the open street on 13 March 1881.

This assassination convinced the last two Romanov Tsars, Alexander III and Nicholas II, that the only way to rule Russia was by repression. Alexander III was a powerful and determined man. With Pobedonostsev, a fanatical churchman, as his chief adviser, he resisted every demand for constitutional and social reform. Liberalism was, in Pobedonostsev's opinion, 'the greatest lie of our time'. When Alexander III died in 1894, Pobedonostsev kept his influence. Tsar Nicholas had none of his father's strength of character but his attitude to change was much the same. A timid suggestion about constitutional reform put forward by the *zemstvos* was described by him as 'senseless dreams about participation in the affairs of imperial government'. Yet Russia was, at this moment, changing faster than ever before, and in a way which was bound to increase the need and the demand for major political and social reform. Between 1880 and 1914 the population rose from 97,000,000 to 165,000,000, a rate of increase faster than that of most of Europe. Between 1890 and 1914 there was an astonishing industrial revolution. In the 1890s the Russian economy grew faster even than the German and between 1906 and 1914 it was still growing at 6 per cent each year. Between 1890 and 1914 there was an eightfold increase in iron and steel production, a fourfold increase in coal production. The man behind this economic expansion was the Minister of Finance, Count Witte, who used the powers of the state to develop key sections of industry and encouraged massive foreign investment. Though the greatest investment came from France, much British capital went into the Russian oil industry.

'Bloody Sunday' St Petersburg 1905. Troops in the foreground guarding the Winter Palace open fire on the unarmed demonstrators

Yet even this remarkable advance was made at the expense of, rather than for the benefit of, the mass of Russian people. Between 1894 and 1902, two-thirds of government expenditure went into the industrial development which, in the main, would directly increase Russian military power. To pay for this 'investment' heavier and heavier taxes were demanded from the hard-pressed peasantry, while in the towns the growing number of industrial workers lived in conditions typical of the early industrial revolution in Western

221

Europe. Nor surprisingly, Social Democrats and Social Revolutionaries as well as the more moderate liberals found ready ears for their schemes of revolution or reform.

Revolution finally came after the humiliating defeats of the Russo-Japanese war. By the end of 1904, peasant riots, industrial strikes and terrorist outrages reduced the country to near-anarchy. On 22 January 1905 about 200,000 people gathered in the centre of St. Petersburg to present a petition to the Tsar. 'We have been made beggars', read the petition signed by more than 135,000 people; 'the moment has come when death would be better than the continuation of our sufferings.' The Tsar, however, had left for his country residence and in order to disperse the crowd the city authorities allowed the troops to open fire (see p. 221). At the end of 'Bloody Sunday', 130 lay dead in the streets and more than 3,000 were wounded. The country was then paralyzed by a wave of strikes, and on the battleship *Potemkin* the crew mutinied. Tsar Nicholas bowed unhappily before the storm, agreed to summon a Duma or consultative assembly and replaced the hated Pobedonostsev by Count Witte. The meeting of the Duma satisfied most middle-class liberals and, with the return of the army from the Far East, Nicholas and the old guard began to recover their nerve. The advice offered by the first Duma was contemptuously rejected and when it grew restive it was dismissed. Four Dumas met between 1905 and 1914 and none were better treated. Furthermore Witte was soon replaced by a tough conservative, Stolypin, who at once launched a ruthless campaign against the terrorists. In 1906 and 1907 1,500 political prisoners were executed. In the same period about 4,000 state officials were killed or wounded. Stolypin however, was no mere reactionary. While he was minister, he cancelled the debts still owed by former serfs and gave financial aid to any peasants who wished to buy their own land. In this way he helped to bring about a major revolution in peasant land-holding which did much to solve the agricultural problem which had caused such distress in previous years. His talents were hardly appreciated. In 1911 he was himself assassinated at the opera. 'He is gone', said the Tsarina, who loathed him, when she heard the news, 'Let us hear no more of him.' Such a comment vividly illustrates the total failure of the Tsar and Tsarina to understand their situation. Stolypin's death was in fact a catastrophe for the dynasty. The men who succeeded him were usually nobodies or rogues who hastened the Tsar and his family towards war, revolution, and ultimately their own tragic destruction.

Chapter 12
The Development of the Modern State

First, some definitions. A state is an association of persons of a limited geographical area, the authority of whose government is accepted, willingly or unwillingly by the population as a whole and which does not recognize the right of any other political institution, except international law, to give it orders. Since the inhabitants of most modern states share a sense of common nationality, most modern states are known as nation-states. In the past, however, there have been states which have been much smaller than nation-states, such as the city states of ancient Greece or mediaeval Italy; and states which have been made up of many nationalities, such as the ancient Roman Empire or the Habsburg Empire of the eighteenth and nineteenth centuries. A government is the supreme law-making and law-enforcing body within the state, whose laws must be obeyed by all citizens. A civil service is the state department or departments whose job it is to put into action the policies decided by the government.

What powers a state should have over its citizens or, more particularly, to what extent a government has the right to interfere in the lives of individual citizens has been the subject of discussion and controversy ever since men became aware that they lived in groups and that these groups possessed codes of conduct which each member of the group was expected to obey. The controversy was vigorously continued in the nineteenth century. Compare these two attitudes. Lord Melbourne, British Liberal Prime Minister from 1835 to 1841: 'The whole (only) duty of government is to prevent crime and preserve contracts.' Louis Blanc, French socialist author and member of the French Provisional government of 1848: 'The government should be regarded as the supreme director of production and be invested with great strength to accomplish its task.' In Lord Melbourne's view, the powers of the state and of the government within the state were very limited. The more laws that were passed the greater the interference in the life of the individual. Such interference was tiresome and could only be justified to preserve law and order, safeguard property and protect the country from foreign attack. Melbourne was in fact stating the view which eighteenth-century French philosophers and British political theorists and economists had made thoroughly respectable. It was dominant among educated Europeans well into the second half of the nineteenth century, especially in those political groups which called themselves liberal. It is often known by its French name—*laissez-faire* or leave well alone—which neatly captures its principle of non-interference. It is sometimes referred to as an individualist philosophy of state since it stresses the right of the individual to do as he pleases. As the French revolutionaries put it in the Declaration of the Rights of Man and Citizen: 'Liberty consists of the power to do whatever is not harmful to others; thus the enjoyment of the natural rights of every man has no limits except those which assure other members of society those same rights.' *Laissez-faire* beliefs were held particularly strongly in economic matters. Government interference in the trade between nations and in the relations between employers and workmen in industry were considered especially dangerous.

Louis Blanc held the opposite opinion. Because of the nature of industrial society, he argued, the state could and must use its powers to improve the quality of life of all its citizens, especially the poorer classes. Lack of government interference had allowed employers to inflict terrible factory conditions and miserable rates of pay upon their work-people. Only state action could put these matters right. In the words of F. Lassalle, leader of the German workers, and, like Blanc, a socialist, 'the true improvement of the conditions of labour and of the working class as such, which it demands with justice, can be achieved only with the assistance of the state. Such a view of the improving, interfering function of the state came to be widely held in Europe after 1870, by non-socialists as well as socialists. Since, in contrast to the individualism of the early nineteenth century, it stressed the duty of the state to act in the interests of the community or collection of individuals rather than merely defend the right of the individual to do as he pleased, it is often known as 'collectivism'.

At the end of the eighteenth century, the duties of the state were few. Most European rulers felt that their chief duty was to defend their subjects from foreign attack, though, if they were a Louis XIV of France or a Frederick II of Prussia, that they should also bring glory to their country by attacking and defeating their neighbours. All rulers agreed that they must maintain law and order throughout their state; most believed that they should protect a particular Christian sect—Catholicism in France, Spain, and Italy; Anglicanism in England; Orthodoxy in Russia. And some, though by no means all, felt that they had the special responsibility of encouraging trade, industry, and education. Most of the money that they collected to pay for the expenses of the state was spent on fighting wars, administering justice, and maintaining a court which would impress their neighbours. The only state officials whom most Europeans would meet in the normal course of events were judges, army recruiters and tax collectors. State activity for the benefit of the community was very limited.

For much of the nineteenth century *laissez-faire* attitudes kept governments reluctant to increase their responsibilities. Changing circumstances, however, slowly overcame this reluctance. Populations, towns and businesses grew greatly in size. Trades unions, co-operative and friendly societies, employers' federations and international cartels came into existence. As these groups grew larger and more numerous, political and social problems multiplied. Increasingly men turned to governments as the only organizations powerful enough to solve these problems. Simultaneously, Europe became more democratic. All Frenchmen of twenty-one and over had the vote from 1870; all men in Germany from 1871, in Belgium from 1893, in Holland from 1896 and in Norway from 1898. Universal male suffrage was introduced in Sweden and Austria in 1907, Turkey in 1908 and Italy in 1912. In Finland and Norway, some women gained the vote though it was not until after World War I that female suffrage spread generally through Europe. These new electorates came both to demand and to obtain government action to improve the quality of their communal life.

So government activity greatly increased after 1870. It was most marked in six areas—public health, elementary education, factory conditions, public utilities (gas, electricity, road, and rail services for instance), compulsory insurance, and military conscription (see Chapter 18).

Public Health

As Chapter 5 has shown, sanitation in early industrial Europe was deplorable, partly from ignorance and partly from the reluctance of local and national authorities to take any action. The absence of any adequate drainage or sewage systems caused polluted water supplies. Cholera, diphtheria, typhoid and typhus fever—all water-borne diseases—took their terrible toll. Chadwick, the first great campaigner for better sanitation in Britain, estimated that 'the annual loss of life from filth is greater than the loss from death or wounds in any of the wars in which the country has been engaged in modern times.' His efforts led to a Board of Health being set up in London in 1848, but after six unhappy years it was abolished. Such was the strength of *laissez-faire* attitudes in mid-Victorian Britain that the Board was regarded, in the words of *The Times*, as 'a reckless invasion of property and liberty'! Not until 1875 did the Public Health Act create an effective system of control which not only laid down basic standards of public sanitation but appointed medical officers of health and sanitary inspectors to make sure that these standards were maintained.

By this time medical science was bringing about a much deeper understanding of the causes of disease. The Frenchman Louis Pasteur (see Chapter 14) had demonstrated that many dangerous diseases in animals and men were caused by tiny living organisms (germs) which were carried in the air, in water, and in milk, and were also closely connected with dirt, pollution, and decay. Working from Pasteur's 'germ' theory, Rudolf Virchow, a Prussian professor and doctor, carefully investigated the breeding of germs in sewage, polluted water and milk, and proved the connection between pollution and disease. Virchow was a member of the German Reichstag and used his prestige to bring a scientific sewage and water supply system to the city of Berlin. By 1883 another German doctors, Robert Koch, isolated the germs that caused tuberculosis and cholera, and linked them both with dirt and pollution. Clearly dirt was dangerous and could not be left as the responsibility of the individual. The pollution of a water supply by one careless person might cause the death of thousands, while poor sanitation in one town might lead to a country-wide epidemic. Other European states began to follow the example set by Britain and by Germany. A mass of laws passed between 1875 and 1914 enforced cleaner water supplies, efficient refuse collections and disposal, and new standards of purity in food and drink. By 1914 medical science, backed by state intervention, had made the killer epidemics of Chadwick's day things of the past.

Education

In 1750 a young priest became curate of a remote parish of north-western France. Soon after he arrived, he paid a visit to the house in the village which was called the parish school. There he found an old man lying in a bed surrounded by a crowd of noisy and uncontrollable children. 'Are you the schoolmaster, my good friend?' the curate asked. 'Yes, Sir' was the reply. 'And what do you teach the children?' 'Nothing, Sir.' 'Nothing!—how is that?' 'Because', replied the old man, 'I know nothing myself.' 'Why then are you made the schoolmaster?' 'Why sir, I have been taking care of the village pigs for many years and when I got too old and infirm for that work, they sent me to take care of the children.' In the late eighteenth century, there were many schools like this all over Europe. In Prussia, although educational standards were higher than anywhere else on the continent, discharged soldiers often became schoolteachers, in Holland domestic servants too old to serve their masters well, and in Switzerland unemployed workers. Many children received no education at all. The best schools were those run by religious institutions—the Brothers of the Christian schools in France and the Methodist schools in England were outstanding—but on the whole the education provided by the Christian churches only reached a minority of Europeans. It was, moreover, a limited education since its chief aim was the production of pious Christians. Even the old-established schools where the rich were accustomed to send their children—the Jesuit schools of Catholic Europe and the gymnasia and grammar schools of Protestant Europe—were in a bad way. 'Empty walls without scholars and everything neglected but the receipt of salaries and endowments', was the verdict of a Lord Chief Justice on the grammar schools of England in 1795. The best educated Europeans were usually those whose fathers could afford a private tutor.

Nonetheless, few responsible Europeans doubted the importance of education. Progress, the French philosophers had insisted, could only continue if society was well educated. The greatest happiness, for the greatest number, the English Utilitarians taught, can only come about if the whole population is properly educated. Furthermore, many governments at the end of the eighteenth century accepted that it was their responsibility to enforce some minimum standard of education upon its citizens. Frederick William I of Prussia had ordered all parents to send their children to elementary school; Joseph II of Austria had tried to create a system of popular education in 1774; and Catherine II of Russia, after experimenting with boarding schools for the aristocracy, turned to popular education in 1782. By 1800 there were 315 state schools in Russia with about 20,000 pupils. Though these reforms proved much less effective than the rulers had intended, they were a start. Even Adam Smith, the Scottish political economist and firm enemy of state intervention in most matters, argued that the state must provide education, not so much for the upper and middle classes who could be expected to look after their children, but for the common people.

Education, however, was slow to develop in nineteenth-century Europe. A major obstacle to progress was 'the religious difficulty'. Bitter controversies arose as to what should be the place of the Christian churches in education, especially if the state interfered to provide education for all its citizens. Since the Middle Ages almost all European education had been in the hands of the various churches. Though in the eighteenth century they had not carried out their responsibilities particularly well and though they were unable to meet fully the nineteenth-century demand for education, they were most unready to hand over these responsibilities either to the state or to a rival Christian group. In a way, their attitude was understandable. One was a Catholic or an Anglican or a Calvinist because one was sure that one's particular Christian group had the right approach to Christianity, which was much the most important thing in one's life. To have one's children suffer an education which had no religious aspect or which, worse still, presented a rival approach to Christianity was intolerable for millions of Christian parents. In France there was a lengthy and bitter conflict over education between the Catholics and the anti-clericals, in Germany a shorter but equally bitter one between Bismarck's government and the Catholics. In Britain an inter-Protestant quarrel between Anglicans and Nonconformists delayed effective state intervention in education for a quarter of a century.

The best educated nations of Europe in the nineteenth century were France and Germany. Napoleon gave the French a good start. Though his plans for elementary education had not advanced far when he abdicated in 1815, secondary and university education directly supervised by the state were well established. Elementary education remained the responsibility of the Catholic Church whose educational influence was increased by the Bourbons between 1815 and 1830. After the 1830 revolution Guizot became Minister of Public Instruction and important reforms were carried out. By an Act of 1833, rich communes (local authorities) had to provide free education for all boys in their area. The poorer communes were subsidized by the state. Between 1834 and 1847 the number of schools increased by a third, and by 1849 3,500,000 were going to French elementary schools. One effect of these reforms was to loosen the hold of the Catholic Church on elementary education. In 1850, however, the pendulum swung back. Louis Napoleon, President of the Republic, being in need of Catholic support, appointed a staunch Catholic, the Vicomte de Falloux, as his Minister of Public Instruction. An Act soon followed (usually known as the Falloux Law) which restored the control of many state schools to the Catholic Church. The Falloux Law gave rise to much controversy and for the next forty years popular education was an explosive political issue. In 1863 Louis Napoleon (now Napoleon III) appointed a new Minister of Public Instruction, Victor Duruy. He was unusually able. He made elementary education compulsory and took care to see that money was available not only for the increased numbers but also to raise the salaries of teachers in order that men of real calibre would enter the profession. A cautious and tactful man, he did his best to play down the religious difficulty, though by increasing the number of state schools he effectively lessened Catholic influence. Duruy was as interested in the quality as in the quantity of schools. One of his greatest achievements was to alter the traditional, mainly classical, curriculum of the secondary schools. 'What I saw in schools and colleges', he wrote, 'during my two years as Inspector-General of Schools, confirms my belief that while it is excellent to give classical studies to our future scholars, doctors and lawyers, it is no less important to give our future industrialists, businessmen and farmers those special studies that their careers demand.' When the British government sent Matthew Arnold to report on the effects of the reforms of Guizot and Duruy on French education he concluded that they 'had given to the lower classes, to the body of the common people, a self-respect, an enlargement of spirit, a consciousness of counting for something in their country's action which has raised them in the scale of humanity.'

During the Third Republic the struggle between the anti-clericals and Catholics became still more ferocious. Many politicians were convinced that further improvements in French education were impossible until Catholic influence was destroyed. A major crisis followed the appointment of Jules Ferry as Minister of Education in 1879. He was a passionate educational reformer. In a famous speech in 1870 he had declared, 'I take this oath; of all the problems of the present time, I choose one to which I will give all that I possess of intelligence, of spirit, of courage, of moral and physical strength—the education of the people.' He was also an uncompromising anti-clerical. Churchmen were expelled from his advisory council on education and religious instruction abolished in state schools. When he became Prime Minister he went further and tried to prevent Catholic teaching orders, especially the Jesuits, from teaching at all. These measures aroused tremendous hostility and were only temporarily effective. What Ferry and his advisers were aiming to do was to use the state schools to produce a new type of French citizen, patriotic, devoted to duty, loyal to the government, and indifferent to religion. In rural areas the school-master and parish priest became bitter enemies, and the school-master often found himself in an impossible position. 'The parents won't come to him', Clemenceau observed in 1894, 'the country squires are his opponents. With the priest there is hidden hostility; with the Catholic schools, there is open war. They steal his pupils. They crush him in a hundred ways, sometimes with the connivance of the mayor, usually with the co-operation of the big influences of the commune.' Nonetheless French popular education managed to advance rapidly. All tuition fees in state schools were abolished in 1886. In 1870 only 60 per cent of the population had been literate; in 1900, 95 per cent were. In the same period there were major improvements in female education.

State education had been comparatively strong in eighteenth-century Prussia, and though churchmen played an important part in education, they never challenged the ultimate authority of the state. This tradition was continued. Throughout the nineteenth century the Prussian system of education was, like the Prussian army, the envy of Europe. 'The classical land of schools and barracks' was how a French visitor in 1831 summed up his impressions. By 1857 a well-organized system which linked schools with factories made elementary education free and compulsory for all Prussian children. James Kay, a great English educational reformer, travelled in Prussia and was impressed by what he saw. 'Education now is perfectly free' he wrote home enthusiastically. 'The poorest man can send his children free of all expense to the best public schools in his district.' In other parts of Germany education tended to copy the Prussian pattern. At the secondary level German schools followed a broad curriculum to the highest academic standards in Europe, while German universities in the mid-nineteenth century enjoyed a golden age. After unification the Prussian system was extended throughout the German Empire. In Southern Germany the Catholic Church was much more influential than in the former Prussian areas, in education as in other spheres. When Bismarck and the German Catholics quarrelled in the 1880s during the so-called *Kulturkampf*, educational policy was one of the points of disagreement. When the complex and bitter dispute finally ended in a compromise the Catholic influence in German education was less than it had been.

Parts of the Austrian Empire also enjoyed a good standard of popular education in 1870. Building on eighteenth century foundations, Leopold von Hasner, the Minister of Education, was able to enforce a system of universal, compulsory education for all children between the ages of six and fourteen. The effectiveness of Hasner's reforms varied, however, from one province of the Empire to another. In Austria they were thoroughly successful, in Hungary less so. As late as 1900 a third of the imperial population was illiterate. The further south and east one went in Europe the more primitive education remained. In 1900 50 per cent of all Italians were illiterate, 66 per cent of the Spanish and Portuguese and over 90 per cent of the Russians and Balkan inhabitants.

Compared with France and Germany, Britain was educationally backward. While the upper classes enjoyed an excellent education at the 'public' schools and universities of Oxford and Cambridge, all thoroughly reformed in the course of the century, the rest of the population remained neglected. The British government was most reluctant to intervene and provide elementary education. In 1833 it grudgingly granted £20,000 per annum to be spent on education by two church societies. Though this grant rose hugely with the passing of years, the church societies were unable to meet the needs of the industrial towns. In the 1860s it became clear that many English schoolchildren were still not going to school at all and Britain's educational standards were falling well behind those of her continental competitors. Eventually, in 1870, W. E. Forster, the minister responsible for education in Gladstone's Liberal government, persuaded Parliament to pass an Education Act which allowed the government to set up state schools (board schools) where there were no adequate church schools. Forster's Education Act was the beginning of effective popular education in this country, but a beginning only. School attendance was not made compulsory until 1880, nor was school instruction quite free of charge until 1891. Secondary education still lagged behind. Not until the 1902 Education Act was state secondary education properly established. By the end of the century responsible Englishmen were concerned about the shortcomings of the national education system, particularly in the technical and scientific fields. In 1884 the Samuelson Committee noted that 'the education of a certain proportion of persons employed in industry abroad is superior to that of the English working man; first as regards the systematic instruction of drawing given to adult artisans, more especially in Belgium, France and Italy; and secondly to the general diffusion of elementary education in Switzerland and Germany.' In 1875 the Devonshire Committee had investigated the state of science-teaching in English 'public' schools. Its conclusion was brief: 'We are compelled to record our opinion that the present state of Scientific Instruction in our schools is extremely unsatisfactory.' These reports, combined with the fear of French, German, and American technical superiority, had some effect on public opinion and led to major improvements in scientific education in schools and universities between 1890 and 1914. Generally speaking, however, Britain remained unduly complacent about her educational standards.

Factory Conditions

In contrast to education, Britain led the way in factory reform. Two acts had been passed as early as 1802 and 1819 to restrict the hours worked by children in textile mills, but since there was no way of checking whether they were enforced, they were not effective. An act of 1833 was more important because it created an inspectorate to check that textile manufacturers were observing the regulations which forbade the employment of any child under nine years of age and which restricted the hours worked by children aged 13–18 to 69 hours per week. A campaign was then launched by Lord Shaftesbury to obtain a ten-hour day for all working men. Shaftesbury's oft-quoted words at the end of his parliamentary speech in favour of the ten-hour principle are worth repeating. 'We ask', he said, 'but for a slight relaxation of toil, a time to live and a time to die.' Despite the formidable opposition of uncompromising *laissez-faire* politicians like Cobden and Bright, the British parliament agreed to the ten-hour principle in 1847 and for the rest of the century intervened periodically to further regulate hours of work and industrial conditions. After 1870 other European governments followed Britain's example. The most important French factory acts were passed in 1874 and 1892, the German in 1874, 1891, and 1914, the Austrian in 1883, the Italian in 1886. By 1914 every European country apart from Russia and the Balkan states had factory regulations, enforced by the State.

Public Utilities

When it came to the control of such things as gas, electricity, and water supplies, national governments usually encouraged the initiative of local authorities. Between 1870 and 1914 the major cities of Europe were transformed by energetic mayors and city councils, who, reacting strongly against the public squalor which had resulted from uncontrolled expansion of the early industrial revolution, rivalled each other to build the proudest town hall and the best serviced city. Birmingham, inspired by Joseph Chamberlain, mayor from 1873 to 1875, was the pace-setter of Europe. During his term of office the city was, in Chamberlain's own words 'parked, paved, assized, marketed gas-and-watered and improved' (see fig. 121). Other English cities followed Birmingham's example and the national government gave them further local powers by a series of Local Government Acts of 1882, 1888, and 1894. Local authorities in France were granted greater powers in 1884 and those in Germany a few years later. Other countries followed the same trend. Italian cities, with their centuries-old tradition of inter-city rivalries, were very active in this period. In Austria Karl Lueger, mayor of Vienna, transformed the capital. Like Chamberlain, though on a larger scale, Lueger replaced the private gas, water, and transport companies by publicly owned municipal ones. He also forbade private building in the countryside immediately bordering on the city and kept a zone of forest and meadow round the outskirts of the city (see fig. 122). Through his efforts Vienna was, in 1900, the best administered city in Europe.

Compulsory Insurance

The most direct interference by the state in the individual lives of its citizens and in their freedom to do as they pleased was compulsory insurance. Germany was the originator. Bismarck saw compulsory insurance as a way of lessening the appeal of socialism to the working man. 'There must', he wrote in 1878, 'be a positive advancement of the welfare of the working classes', and insurance seemed to be the best advance. By 1882 the German workers were compulsorily insured against sickness and against accidents. In 1889 they were granted old age pensions. The money for the scheme came from employers and employees with a state subsidy on top. Between 1885 and 1890 about 50,000,000 individual payments were made of social insurance worth about 200,000,000 dollars. The idea was soon taken up by other governments. Compulsory insurance came to Austria in the 1880s, Belgium, Denmark, Italy and Switzerland in the 1890s, and to Britain in 1911. However much old fashioned *laissez-faire* thinkers might criticize such compulsory interfering schemes, they proved popular and successful.

There was, therefore an immense enlargement of state activity between 1789 and 1914. It is often referred to as the 'nineteenth-century revolution in government'. From it followed two important consequences. The first was a huge growth in the size of European civil services. Between 1881 and 1911, for instance, the German civil service increased from 450,000 to 1,180,000, the British from 81,000 to 644,000. The second was the creation of new taxes to cover the immense cost of the new government activity. In 1874 only Britain had the income-tax, which was merely 3d in the pound. By 1914 only France of the advanced industrial countries had not. Customs duties or tariffs were another useful source of income but by the end of the century most governments were also having to use inheritance-taxes or death duties to cover their expenditure. Both income-tax and inheritance-taxes were usually graded; i.e. the more you had, the higher proportion you paid in tax. Graded taxation had the effect of redistributing some of the national income from the richer to the poorer. From this financial foundation the social security systems of modern Europe were to develop.

Chapter 13
Living and Leisure

Historians are only just beginning to investigate systematically how ordinary Europeans lived, what clothes they wore, what food they ate, what kind of houses they inhabited, how much spare time they had and how they chose to spend it. There are few history books to which we can turn in order to find out about European living and leisure. However, there is a source of information more vivid than any history book and in many ways just as valuable, the novels of the period. Nineteenth-century Europe was particularly rich in novelists: indeed it has been called the golden age of the European novel. A down-to-earth, straightforward century, its atmosphere encouraged the creation and enjoyment of novels more than any other art form. While the poets, painters, and architects of the nineteenth century do not compare with the greatest of other periods, and the composers are at least equalled by those of earlier centuries, the novelists are indisputably the best that the world has so far known. For the historian they are a delight not only for their style, but also for their information. Outstanding writers like Tolstoy and Dostoevsky in Russia, Balzac and Flaubert in France, and Dickens in Britain believed that they must place their fictional characters in settings of complete realism and as often as not chose contemporary or near contemporary settings which they could describe with the accuracy of an eyewitness. Tolstoy's *War and Peace* portrays the Russian aristocracy during the Napoleonic Wars, his *Anna Karenina* the official and aristocratic world of St. Petersburg in the 1850s. In contrast, Raskolnikov the hero-villain of Dostoevsky's *Crime and Punishment* lives in the dangerous and poverty-stricken world of the revolutionary Russian student. Balzac's immense *Human Comedy* is set in middle-class Paris of the 1830s and 1840s, Flaubert's *Madame Bovary* in French provincial life in the 1850s. Dickens' *Oliver Twist* inhabits a London workhouse in the 1830s. Obviously the novelists only give us those scenes of European life which suit the purposes of their stories. They give as little in the way of precise dates or addresses, and nothing in the way of statistics. Nonetheless these fragments of European life in the nineteenth century have an atmosphere and accuracy of detail which make them historical records of the first importance.

Every level of European society is described somewhere in the page of the novels. In Turgenev's *Fathers and Sons** (1861), the way of life of a minor Russian landowner in the middle of the century is marvellously concentrated into a single paragraph.

In the meantime, while his parents were still alive and to their great chagrin Nikolai Petrovich Kirsanov had contrived to fall in love with the daughter of his former landlord, a petty official by the name of Pepolovensky. She was a comely girl and, as they say, an 'intellectual' who read the serious articles in the science columns of the periodicals. He married her as soon as the term of mourning for his parents was over and, abandoning the Ministry of Land Distribution, in which his father's influence had obtained him a post, was blissfully happy with his Masha. At first they lived in a country villa near the Institute of Forestry, then in town, in a pretty little apartment with a spotless staircase and a chilly drawing room and finally in the country where before long his son Arkady was born. Husband and wife lived very comfortably and quietly; they were hardly ever apart—they read together, sang and played duets together at the piano; she grew flowers and looked after chickens while he went hunting now and again and busied himself with the estate and Arkady grew and grew comfortably and quietly like his parents. Ten years passed like a dream. In 1847, Kirsanov's wife died. The blow nearly killed him and, in a few weeks, his hair turned grey. In the hope of somewhat distracting his thoughts, he decided to go abroad . . . but then came the year 1848. Reluctantly he returned to the country and, after a fairly prolonged period of inactivity, he set about improving the management of his estate. In 1855, Nikolai Petrovich brought his son to University. He spent three years with him in Petersburg, seldom going out anywhere and trying to make friends with Arkady's youthful fellow students. But this last winter, he was not able to go to Petersburg and so we meet him, quite grey now and a trifle bent, in the month of May 1859, waiting the arrival of his son who has just taken his degree as he himself had done.

In Tolstoy's *Anna Karenina** part of the courtship of Levin and Kitty (which was closely modelled on Tolstoy's own courtship) takes place at the Moscow ice-rink where the Moscow aristocracy met in winter to enjoy themselves.

At four o'clock that afternoon, Levin stepped out of a hired sleigh at the Zoological Gardens and, with a beating heart, turned along the path to the ice-hills and the skating ground, sure of finding Kitty there as he had seen the Schubatsky's carriage at the entrance. It was a bright frosty day. At the gates there were rows of carriages, sleighs, drivers and policemen. Well-dressed people, their hats shining in the sunlight, crowded about the entrance and along the well-swept paths between the little old-fashioned Russian chalets with their carved eaves. The old curly beech trees in the gardens, their branches all laden with snow, looked as though they had been freshly decked with sacred vestments. . . . He went towards the ice-hills, which resounded with the rattle of chains on sledges being dragged up and sliding down, the rumble of toboggans and the ring of merry

* Trans. Rosemary Edmonds, Penguin Classics.

voices. A few steps further and he saw the skating-rink and, amid the many skaters, at once recognized her. On that day of the week and at that hour people belonging to the same set and all acquainted with one another used to meet on the ice. There were crack skaters, parading their skill, and beginners clinging to chairs and making timid awkward movements, boys and elderly people skating for their health; and they all seemed to Levin fortune's favourites because they were near her. All these skaters, it appeared, with complete unconcern would skate up to her, skate past her, speak to her even and were enjoying themselves quite independently of her, delighting in the excellent surface and the fine weather.

Middle-class life was also frequently and carefully described. Take for example a Parisian couple, the Marneffes, as Balzac describes them in *Cousin Bette* *.

The lovely Madame Marneffe, natural daughter of the Comte Montcomet, one of Napoleon's most famous lieutenants, had been married with the aid of a twenty-thousand franc dowry to a junior official in the Ministry of War. Through the influence of the illustrious Lieutenant-General Marshal of France for the last six months of his life, this pen-pusher had reached the unlooked-for position of senior book-keeper in his office, but just as he was about to be appointed head clerk, the Marshal's death cut off Marneffe's and his wife's expectations at the root. Monsieur Marneffe's means were small for Mademoiselle Valerie Fortin's dowry had slipped through his fingers and melted away in paying his debts, buying all the things needed by a young man setting up house, and above all in satisfying the demands of a pretty wife accustomed in her mother's house to luxuries which she had no mind to give up; so the couple had been obliged to economize in house rent. The situation in the Rue du Doyenné, not far from the Ministry of War and the centre of Paris, suited Monsieur and Madame Marneffe. . . .

The apartment occupied by this couple presented the flashy display of meretricious luxury all too often met with in Parisian homes, in establishments like theirs. In the drawing-room, the furniture covered in faded cotton velvet, the plaster statuettes masquerading as Florentine bronzes, the clumsily carved painted chandelier with its candle rings of moulded glass, the carpet, a bargain in whose price was explained too late by the quantity of cotton in it—everything in the room to the very curtains (which would have taught you that the handsome appearance of wool damask lasts only three years), everything cried poverty like a ragged beggar at a church door.

The dining-room, looked after incompetently by a single servant, had the nauseating atmosphere of a provincial hotel dining-room; everything in it was greasy and ill kept.

Thus a middle class French family living beyond their means in the Paris of the July Monarchy. Now a middle-class household of considerable wealth in the Hamburg of Imperial Germany at the end of the century, as described by Thomas Mann (born himself the son of a German merchant in 1875) in *The Magic Mountain*.

* Trans. Ayton Crawford, Penguin Classics.

Top left *An officer and gentleman: Prince Augustus of Prussia*

Top right *The prosperous middle classes: the French Stamaty family*

Bottom *A working class group in London 1909*

The hero of the story, Hans Castorp, loses both his parents while he is still very young and goes to live with a guardian, Consul Tienappel.*

Certainly . . . he (Hans) wanted for nothing where his bodily needs were concerned and not less in the sense of safeguarding his interests—about which he was too young to know anything at all. For Consul Tienappel, an uncle of Hans' deceased mother, was administrator of the Castorp estate; he put up the property for sale, took in hand the business of liquidating the firm of Castorp and Sons, Importers and Exporters, and realized from the whole nearly 400,000 marks, the inheritance of young Hans. This sum Consul Tienappel invested in trust funds and took unto himself two per cent of the interest, without impairment of his kinsmanly feelings.

The Tienappel house lay at the foot of a garden in Harvester Linden-strasse; the windows looked out on a plot of lawn in which not the tiniest weed was suffered to flourish, and then on public rose bushes and then upon the river. The Consul went on foot every morning to his business in the Old Town—though he possessed more than one fine equipage—in order to get a little exercise, for he sometimes suffered from cerebral congestion. He returned the same way at five in the afternoon, at which time the Tienappels dined, with due and fitting ceremony. He was a weighty man, whose suits were always of the best English cloth. His eyes were watery-blue and prominent behind his gold-rimmed glasses; his nose was ruddy and his square-cut beard was grey; he wore a flashing brilliant on the stubby little finger of his left hand. His wife was long-since dead. He had two sons, Peter and James of whom one was in the navy and seldom at home, the other occupied in the paternal wine trade and destined heir to the business. The housekeeping for many years had been the care of an Allina goldsmith's daughter named Schalleen who wore starched white ruffles at her plump round wrists. Hers it was to see to it that the table, morning and evening, was richly laden with cold meats, with crabs and salmon, eel and smoked breast of goose, with tomato ketchup and roast beef. She kept a watchful eye on the hired waiters when Consul Tienappel gave a gentleman's dinner and she it was who, so far as it in her lay, took the place of a mother to little Hans Castorp.

Nor was working class life ignored. Indeed, the novels of Dickens in Britain and Zola in France did much to make the educated public aware how terrible the conditions of working-class life often were. Here is early morning in a northern French mining village during the period of the Second Empire as described by Zola in *Germinal*, first published in 1885.†

The cuckoo clock downstairs struck 4 and still nothing could be heard but the gentle sound of light breathing, accompanied by two deeper snores. And then, suddenly, Catherine got up. In her sleep, she had instinctively counted the four strokes through the floor but had not found the strength to wake up properly. She dragged her legs out of bed, felt for a match,

* Trans. H. T. Lowe-Porter, Penguin Modern Classics.
† Trans. L. W. Tancock, Penguin Classics.

struck it and lit a candle. The candle lit up the square room with its two windows. It was almost filled by three beds, but there was a cupboard, a table and two walnut chairs which stood out against a cream-painted wall. That was all; clothes hanging on pegs, a jug on the floor beside a red earthenware basin to wash in. In the bed on the left, the eldest son Zacharie, a fellow of twenty-one, was sleeping with his brother Jeanlin who was nearly eleven, in the right hand one two children, Lénore and Henri, and one six, the other four, were asleep in each other's arms; whilst Catherine shared the third bed with her sister Alzire, who was so puny for nine years that she would not even have noticed her by her side, had not the poor deformed creature's hump-back stuck in her ribs. Through the open glass door was a sort of cubby hole where the parents slept in a fourth bed, against which they had had to put the cradle of their last born Estelle, scarcely three months old.

Catherine's first job downstairs had been to see to the fire. A coal fire burned night and day in the cast iron kitchen range with its grate in the middle and ovens on either side. Eight hectolitres of escaillage—hard coal picked up off the roads—were issued to each family per month. The stuff was not hard to light and Catherine, whose job it was to cover the fire at night, had only to poke it up in the morning and add a few bits of specially selected soft coal. Then she put the kettle on the grate and stooped down to look in the cupboard. . . . All that was left was a bit of bread, plenty of cream cheese but only the merest shave of butter. And sandwiches had to be made for the four of them. At length she made up her mind, cut slices of bread, spread one with cheese, scraped a little butter on the other and clapped them together. This was the 'briquet', the sandwiches taken every morning down the mine. The four briquets were soon set out on the table in a row graded with strict justice from the biggest one, which was father's, to the smallest for Jeanlin.

Housing

As these extracts show, there was an enormous variation in the style of life of Europeans in the nineteenth century. Then, as in any other period of human history, an important part of any individual's style of life was the house in which he lived. In the Russian countryside, a serf often lived in a single-roomed wooden hut with his animals as well as his family. There would be no glass in the windows, only dried bladders to keep out the wind. In the centre of the room usually stood a large brick stove, which, during the long winter months, was kept alight night and day. In the depths of the winter, the only way the family kept warm was by sleeping together on the stove's brick top. Such conditions were not confined to Eastern Europe. In 1841 an Irish census graded housing into four classes. The Census Commissioners reported that 'nearly half of the families of the rural population are living in the fourth and lowest state'—in windowless mud cabins of a single room. In Ireland furniture was often a luxury. In 1837 the village of Tullahobaghy in County Donegal had 9,000 inhabitants with just 10 beds, 93

Lancaster House

The East End of London in the 1870's as seen by G. Doré

chairs and 243 stools between them. At the other end of the social scale were the aristocratic parkland palaces like that of the Duke of Westminster at Eaton Hall in Cheshire (completed in 1870). In the town the variations were as marked. In its East End London contained some of the worst slums of nineteenth-century Europe. Yet it also possessed the marvellous elegance of Nash's Regent Street and the detached splendour of Lancaster House, the luxuriousness of which provoked the comment from Queen Victoria as she came into a reception there from Buckingham Palace: 'I have come from my house to your palace!'.

Different floors for different classes : a cartoon plan of a typical Parisian apartment of the 1860's

Housing developments in north-west Europe differed significantly from those in the rest of the continent. While Britain, Belgium, and Holland tended to build small single family houses, other countries built multi-family tenement blocks. In 1900 the average number of occupants per house in Manchester was 4.8, the corresponding figure for Paris was 38.0, for Vienna 50.7 and for Berlin 75.9. A cartoon of the standard Parisian apartment block during the Second Empire contained eight separate apartments and thirty-two people, ranging from the obviously rich on the first floor to the desperately poor in the attic (see above).

241

Living and Leisure

Britain's reluctance to build upwards rather than sideways caused her to pioneer another characteristic of modern living, the suburb. The first suburbs were an escape from the dirty congestion of the new industrial cities. 'Nothing', remarked a journalist in the *Quarterly Review* of 1850, 'has so much contributed to drive away the opulent from the dwellings of the poor as the dread of unwholesomeness and dirt.' Before 1800 the prosperous merchants of Leeds in Yorkshire lived close to the town centre, the western half of which was a pleasant residential area. In 1792, however, one of the earliest successful steam-driven textile mills was built further to the west on the banks of the River Aire and the prevailing winds carried its fumes across the town. By 1840 the prosperous had for the most part moved from the centre to the more healthy high ground well to the north of the town, establishing their suburban villas in the Headingley and Roundhay areas. In the first half of the century, suburban living was only for the really wealthy who could afford to keep a horse and carriage and had the time for the leisurely journeys to and from their work. In the second half of the century, first the railways and then the tramcar made suburban living possible for a much greater proportion of the European population. As more tried to escape from the congested city centres, so the cities themselves ate up the countryside and congestion moved into the suburbs themselves.

Food

Where food was concerned, the French were regarded as the best cooks and the most civilised eaters, so the upper and middle classes of Europe followed what they considered to be the French fashion. For most of the nineteenth century a heavy breakfast was usual, although it had been unfashionable the century before. Porridge might well be followed by a fish course and bacon and eggs, to be completed by toast and jam. At mid-day a light lunch was taken and the main meal would be dinner some time between 5 and 7 p.m. Before retiring for the night, cakes would be served between 9.30 and 10 p.m. with tea or coffee for the women and wine for the men. Dinner was a massive affair. 'It is a bad dinner', an English nobleman noted in 1824, 'when there are not at least five varieties—a substantial dish of fish, one of meat, one of game, one of poultry and above all a ragout with truffles . . . they form the absolute minimum.' In the same period most Irishmen ate little besides potatoes. In Eastern Europe there were similar contrasts. Tolstoy's *War and Peace* contains this description of an aristocratic dinner party in Moscow in 1812.

The footmen bustled about, chairs scraped, the orchestra in the gallery struck up and the guests took their places. The strains of the Count's band were succeeded by the clatter of knives and forks, the voices of the company and the subdued tread of waiters. . . . Pierre spoke little, examined the new faces and ate with a will. Of the two soups, he chose à la tortue and from the savoury patties to the game, he did not let a single dish pass or refuse any of the wines which the butler offered him, mysteriously poking a bottle wrapped in a knapkin over his neighbour's shoulder and murmuring 'dry Madeira—Hungarian—Rhine wine'. Pierre held up a wine glass at random out of the four crystal glasses with the count's monogram that stood before each guest and drank with relish, gazing with increasing amiability at the company. Before the ices, champagne was served. The orchestra struck up again, the count kissed his 'little Countess' and the guests rose to drink her health . . . then in the same order as they had entered but with faces a little more flushed, the company returned to the drawing room.

The basic diet of many Russian peasants at that time was black bread and cabbage, improved every now and then by some fish, cucumber or garlic.

As these examples show, neither the rich nor the poor in Europe had a balanced diet at the beginning of the century, but thanks to the work of scientists like Liebig the importance to health of a sound diet became much better understood with the passing of the years. The marked increase in life expectancy of all sections of European society in this period was to some extent the result of better eating habits.

Fashion

The clothes worn by most Europeans around 1800 did not differ greatly from those worn by their parents or grandparents. In rural districts traditional local costume was usual, and often survived virtually unchanged throughout the century. In industrial districts poverty and factory conditions demanded that working people wore the simplest clothes—cotton dresses and bodices with shawls for the women, and loose-fitting cotton jackets and trousers for the men. With increasing prosperity, however, the working classes were able to spend more money on clothes and they tended to follow the fashions of the upper and middle classes. In 1853 Surtees, a minor English novelist, complained that 'the housemaid now dresses better—finer at all events—than her mistress did twenty years ago and it is almost impossible to recognize working people when they are in their Sunday dresses.'

For those who could afford to buy good clothes regularly, London was the centre of male fashion, Paris of female. In the last years of the eighteenth century, the clothing of the English country gentleman—top-hat, neckcloth, medium length coat cut away at the front, waistcoat, breeches and riding-boots—had become

the fashion of all Europe (see above) and the superiority of English male wear was not seriously challenged before World War I. To begin with, naturalness was the keynote. Hairpowder, wigs, and pigtails did not fit the 'rural' style and were abandoned, hair and sideburns being allowed to grow rather long. During the period of the Directory in France and of the Regency in Britain male costume became more extravagant and the young 'dandy' frequently appeared in cartoons of the time. In contrast, the 1830s and 1840s were much more sober. The colourful waistcoats, frilled shirts and large cravats of previous years disappeared. Cutaway coats gave way to frock coats or jackets and boots and breeches to tight trousers strapped beneath the instep. Black became the accepted colour for evening dress. A man who wore anything more striking was regarded as a bit of a cad. For the rest of the century formal dress altered very slowly, though the growth of sport caused many changes in informal wear, the 'Norfolk' jacket and gaily coloured blazer gaining favour in the 1880s and 1890s. Viscount Lewisham caused a sensation in 1893 when he was the first man to appear in Parliament with turn-ups on his trousers, and just before the war the lounge-suit and homburg hat was often to be seen alongside the traditional frock coat and top hat.

Female fashion in the nineteenth century changed much more. In 1800 the Paris line was extremely simple. Daydresses were rather like high-waisted nightdresses with a hemline round the ankles and a low-cut neck. Shawls were the answer to cold and draughts. In the 1820s it grew less simple. The waist dropped, tight corsets returned after an absence of thirty years, skirts were flounced and sleeves and hats became enormous. In the 1840s modesty was the keynote. Dark green and browns replaced bright colours,

little bonnets extravagant hats. Skirts supported by masses of petticoats reached the ground and for a lady to expose even her ankles in public was regarded as indecent. Not surprisingly a few, mainly French, women rebelled. Christened *lionnes* (lionesses) by the journalists, they were described in a French newspaper as 'rich, married women, pretty and flirtatious, who can handle the whip and the pistol as well as their husbands, ride like lancers, smoke like dragoons and drink any quantity of iced champagne.' In the 1850s the masses of petticoat, which had become a severe restriction on a woman's ability to move, were replaced by the hooped petticoat or crinoline (see below). The Empress Eugénie, wife of Napoleon III, made the crinoline particularly her style. The obvious risks presented by a high wind were met by wearing long linen pantaloons. So large did crinolines become that it became impossible for more than one woman to sit on a sofa. In 1851 the world of European fashion was shaken by the redoubtable Mrs. Bloomer who sailed in from the U.S.A. determined to bring European women back to sanity by converting them to her 'bloomers'—an early form of trouser-suit. She was met with ridicule and had little influence though much publicity. In the 1870s the crinoline gave way to the bustle, first made of horsehair, then of wire. Skirts grew longer and trailed in the dust. As the twentieth century approached, a much greater freedom appeared. There was a rage for lace

The Crinoline Age: Paris fashions 1859

A French lady at a fashionable reception in 1886. The painting is by Tissot

and ostrich feathers, for more colour and more obvious display. 1910 was a dramatic year in female fashion. The Russian ballet came to Paris and inspired a completely new Asiatic trend. Colours became even more striking, stiff skirts and bodices were replaced by softer draperies. Skirts sometimes became so narrow that the wearers could only take steps of two or three inches. Just before the war, Paris abolished the collar on daydresses and replaced it by the V-neck. As Europe prepared for war, the priesthood was denouncing the new style as a danger to morals, the medical profession as a danger to health (the pneumonia blouse)! Between 1910 and 1914 the general impression given by fashionable women was that they were trying to look as much like slaves from an eastern harem as possible.

Female Emancipation

This slave trend was rather surprising since the feminist campaign to reduce female subjection to man was reaching new heights between 1910 and 1914. It is hard nowadays to imagine the complete male dominance of European society for most of the nineteenth century. Even the comparatively enlightened French revolutionaries had not allowed women to play any part in politics, and Napoleon's laws made the wife and daughter of the French family little better than household serfs. Throughout the continent the rights of a married woman to property of her own or to divorce were very limited, and secondary or university education for women was almost unheard of before 1870. The main function of women was to marry, then bear and raise children. This, it was held, was so demanding an occupation that any woman with energy to spare for other things was unusual. Religious opinions and the customs of centuries combined to discourage women from pursuing careers and from claiming equality with their husbands. Those individuals who spoke out against female subjection—like Mary Wolstonecraft and J. S. Mill in Britain, Ferdinand Lassalle and August Bebel in Germany—were regarded as cranks.

By the end of the century, however, women were asserting themselves. One reason why they did so was because they had more time to spare. They were living longer and spending less time on child-bearing and child rearing. The average British family of 1870 had about five children, in 1900 between 3 and 4 and in 1920 between 2 and 3. Other industrialized countries showed a corresponding decline in family size which was due less to infertility than to the more extensive use of birth control methods. France was the pioneer here, despite the strong opposition of the Catholic Church to any form of artificial birth control. In 1842 the Bishop of le Mans wrote an anxious letter to the Pope. The use of contraceptives was so widespread in his diocese that its classification by the Catholic Church as among the seven deadly sins was causing his priests great difficulty at confession time. Nonetheless religious opinion and 'respectable' opinion in general strongly opposed birth control, at least in public. Many middle-class Englishmen believed that sexual abstinence was good for the health. In 1877 Bradlaugh and Mrs. Besant were put on trial in England for distributing an American pamphlet on contraceptives. In private, however, the practice spread, beginning among the urban middle classes and then moving slowly among the workers. Birth control propaganda leagues appeared in Holland in 1885, in Germany in 1889, in Spain in 1904, in Sweden in 1911, and in Italy in 1913.

Social and economic changes created new careers which women could fill better than men. The growth of large business enterprises

with international markets which made use of new office equipment like typewriters and telephones demanded armies of secretaries and telephonists. The new elementary schools needed female teachers, the new hospitals female nurses. In Britain before 1870 there was a handful of teachers and nurses and virtually no secretaries. In 1900 there were 40,000 nurses, 45,000 teachers and 90,000 secretaries. Linked with these social and economic demands went a massive improvement in female education. The first university to admit women was Zurich in Switzerland in 1867. Paris quickly followed. So did the universities of Sweden and Finland in 1870. The first French *Lycée* (grammar school) for girls was opened at Montpellier in 1884, and state secondary education for German girls began in 1894. Fully qualified professional women then began to make their appearance. Holland's first female doctor began practising in 1870, France's first female lawyer in 1903. And certain outstanding professional women like Florence Nightingale in nursing, Mme. Montessori in education, and Mme. Curie in scientific research became world-famous.

Europeans of 1914 had much more leisure than their ancestors of 1789, particularly if they were city-dwellers. Many activities filled

New employment opportunities for women: telephonists of the late nineteenth century

this leisure time. Of these, two—the mass reading of newspapers and the playing or watching of organized sport—deserve special attention.

The Press

In 1789 newspapers were in their infancy. Heavy taxes made them expensive and therefore kept the readership small. Government censorship restricted their freedom. For most of the period, the British press was the freest and most influential in Europe. By 1800 a number of daily papers had established themselves in London, the most outstanding of which were the *Morning Chronicle* and *The Times*. By 1830 *The Times* was the most famous newspaper in the world. Two gifted editors, Barnes and Delane, made it the mouthpiece of the rising and confident middle classes. It was perfectly ready to criticise governments both at home and abroad and did so with such vigour that it won for itself the nickname 'the Thunderer'. It created its own international reporting system which was both swift and efficient. In the middle of the century it seemed to have

The censored press : a French cartoon caricatures the censorship of the July Monarchy in 1833

the power to make and break governments. The Crimean dispatches of one of its most gifted correspondents, W. H. Russell, certainly helped to cause the fall of Aberdeen's government in 1855.

In France the revolutionaries gave complete freedom to the press. This did not last long. First the Jacobins, then Napoleon, severely restricted it. Napoleon feared a free press. 'Four hostile newspapers did more harm to the Directory', he once said, 'than 100,000 men in the field.' When he came to power, he turned the *Journal des Debats* (the Journal of Debates), previously an intelligent, balanced, and independent political newspaper, into the official government mouthpiece and called it the *Journal de L'Empire* (The Empire Journal). After Napoleon's downfall it regained some of its former independence, but Bourbon censorship still gave the French press generally a difficult time. Elsewhere, the press was even less free. The best known and most influential German paper, the *Allgemeine Zeitung*, was directly controlled by Metternich, the Austrian Chancellor.

Cheaper newspapers became possible because governments reduced newspaper taxes and more people were prepared to pay newspapers to carry their advertisements. In 1836 the *Siècle* (Century) and the *Presse* (Press) were launched in France at half the price of existing papers. By publishing novels in serial form, they were able to attract a wider readership. Yet cheap though they were compared with the older, more serious papers, they were still too expensive to be bought by the working classes. The first genuinely popular paper was the *Petit Journal* (Little Journal), first published in 1863 at the price of one sou. By 1866 it was selling 250,000 copies.

Censorship remained a problem for French and other continental editors. Karl Marx's career as editor of the *Rheinische Zeitung* was quickly ended by the Prussian authorities and, except for a few months during the revolution of 1848, the European press had to be extremely careful until late in the century. Louis Napoleon, who was helped to power by the free press of France in 1848, suppressed nine-tenths of it until the last years of his regime.

Despite censorship there was a steady improvement in news coverage. Three great agencies for the rapid collection of news items came into existence, Havas in Paris, Wolff in Berlin, and Reuter's in London. Havas ran a pigeon service between London, Paris, and Brussels but it could never match Reuter's greatest scoop which was to report the assassination of the American President Lincoln two days earlier than anyone else.

The growing efficiency of news coverage reflected a growing interest in news among all sections of the European population. By 1870 there were at least 6,000 newspapers in Europe, by 1900 there were more than 12,000. While in 1870 most newspapers were still serious and directed towards a middle-class readership, by 1900 newspapers which aimed to entertain the newly educated working classes had really arrived. Technological improvements made this change possible. Automatic type-setting machines became available in the 1880s and new paper-making methods made newsprint cheaper. The telephone made possible swifter and more vivid reporting, photography more attractive layouts. An early and sober form of the new journalism in Britain was the *Daily Telegraph*. Its founder J. M. Levy cut its price to a penny, attracted advertisements, and by 1870 was selling 190,000 copies per day against *The Times's* 70,000. Much more colourful was the *Daily Mail* of the 1890s (owned by Lord Northcliffe) which cost a halfpenny and sold well over 1,000,000 copies. The *Mail* made good use of methods which had already proved successful in the United States. Its headlines were striking. It stressed 'human interest' stories—love, crime, adventure, for instance—and it included many sporting and patriotic features. It presented politics in a shorter, simpler way than its rivals. 'Produced by office boys for office boys', was the verdict of Lord Salisbury on the *Mail* when he was Prime Minister, but it went from strength to strength. Using the same approach, the *Petit Journal* pushed its circulation by 1914 to over 2,000,000. In Berlin the *Lokal-Anzeiger* topped 1,000,000. Many contemporaries, like Lord Salisbury, criticized what they regarded as the poor taste and superficial approach of these papers. Their owners had a simple reply. We give the people what they want, they said, and their circulation figures seemed to prove that this is what in fact they did.

Sport

Sport organized on a national and international level was another development of the late nineteenth century. In earlier centuries sports and pastimes had flourished, especially those connected with war like boxing, wrestling, archery, and horse-racing. Their rules and organization, however, were locally based and varied greatly from area to area. Modern sport is a British invention. In the eighteenth century the British were famous for their unusual interest in sporting matters and they were the first to work out nationally acceptable rules. Boxing, for example, which was one of the oldest and most popular sports was thoroughly reorganized between 1790 and 1870. In 1795 the British champion Jackson defeated his challenger Mendoza by seizing his long hair in one hand and pummelling him unconscious with the other. The first step in improving the rules was the setting up of the London Prize Ring in 1838. Another was the 'Queensbury' rules, drawn up in 1867. These rules which introduced padded gloves among other things are the basis of modern boxing. By the end of the nineteenth century the sport was extremely popular in Britain and the U.S.A. and was spreading slowly but surely throughout the world.

Here is a description of football as played in England in 1801. 'An equal number of competitors take the field and stand between two goals placed at a distance of 80 to 100 yards the one from the other. The goal is usually driven into the ground about two or three feet apart. The ball, which is commonly made of a blown bladder and cased with leather, is delivered into the midst of the ground and the object of each party is to drive it through the goal of their antagonists, which being achieved, the game is over.' Obviously this game had something in common with modern football, though it was

A football match: Cup Final 1891, Blackburn Rovers v. Notts. County

rougher. 'When the exercise becomes exceedingly violent,' the 1801 description continues, 'the players kick each other's shins without the least ceremony and some of them are overthrown at the hazard of their limbs.' In Britain football developed in two distinct ways. In 1823 William Webb Ellis, a pupil at Rugby School, picked the ball up during a game and ran with it. Rugby School then developed its own type of football in which passing the ball from hand to hand was a central part. This game spread to other public schools and to the universities of Oxford and Cambridge. In 1871 the Rugby Football Union was formed to lay down the rules and organize the game on a national basis. Meanwhile pure football, or soccer, in which no handling of the ball was allowed also flourished in English schools and universities. In 1863 the London Football Association was founded, which later became simply the Football Association of the whole country. Outside the British Empire the only country to which Rugby spread was France. Parisian clubs were formed in the 1870s and in 1906 the first international between France and England took place. In contrast, soccer proved very popular and spread quickly first in Europe and then all over the world. F.I.F.A., the organization supervizing soccer internationally, was founded in 1904.

Simultaneously other major sports were regulated by bands of enthusiasts. The British Amateur Athletic Association was founded in 1880, its equivalent in Belgium in 1889, in Sweden in 1895, in Czechoslovakia, Greece, and Hungary in 1897, and in Italy and Germany in 1898. The international athletic organization, the I.A.A.F., was founded in 1913.

Major Walter Wingfield patented his idea of lawn tennis in 1874. His original game was played on a court the shape of an hour glass but by the time the first lawn tennis championship was played at Wimbledon in 1877 the familiar rectangular court had become usual. The British Lawn Tennis Association (L.T.A.) was founded in 1886 and, since the game quickly gained popularity both in Europe and in the States, the International Lawn Tennis Federation (I.L.T.F.) was set up in 1912.

The new passion both of playing and for watching organized sport was best symbolized by the revival of the Olympic Games in 1896. The original games of classical Greece had been part of a religious festival which had been held at Olympia for more than a thousand years before coming to an end in 393 A.D. The man who inspired their revival was a Frenchman, Baron Coubertin. He was convinced that much of the glory of classical Greece was due to its passion for sport, which created healthy minds in healthy bodies. His revived games, he hoped, would encourage individual competition and sportsmanship and help to overcome the national rivalries

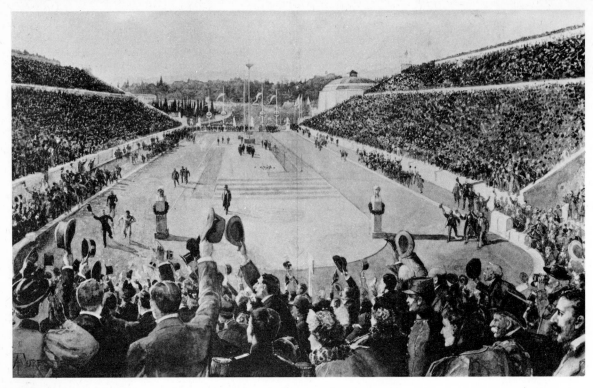

The First Olympic Games

which were so distressing a feature of the world in the late nineteenth century. The games were first held in Athens in 1896, then in Paris (1900), in St. Louis (1904), in London (1908) and in Stockholm (1912). Thirteen different nations took part in 1896, twenty-eight in 1912. The first four were completely dominated by Britain and the U.S.A., but at Stockholm, other European nations made their presence felt—the Finns, for instance, winning six gold medals. For all Baron Coubertin's hopes that individual sportsmanship might overcome national rivalries, the Games quickly came to be regarded as yet another arena in which national prestige was at stake, and by 1912 medal-counting was becoming a national pastime.

This development was perhaps inevitable. It may be no coincidence that the period which saw the rapid development of organized sport and of a vast and fervent popular following for sports teams was also a period of intense nationalism. The emotional feeling that the sports fan felt for his local and national team was much the same as that of the patriot for his country in times of international crisis.

Chapter 14
Confident Science

In this chapter the term 'science' will be used to mean systematic knowledge of natural or physical phenomena discovered by observation and experiment, 'technology' the systematic study of industrial and mechanical methods with the aim of improving them. Nowadays science and technology are closely linked. Few 'technological breakthroughs' occur which do not owe much to the careful experimental work of research scientists. But this has not always been the case. As this chapter will show, one of the most important technological advances of all time, the harnessing of steam power to factory machinery, was achieved with little direct aid from scientists. Only in the second half of the nineteenth century did science begin to aid industry in the way that we now take for granted.

1789 and 1914 are dates without meaning in the history of science. Modern science had its origins in the sixteenth century. Thanks to Newton and Descartes, the late seventeenth century was a period of remarkable scientific advance. Then followed a period of comparative stagnation between 1700 and 1760. In the late eighteenth century the pace of scientific inquiry quickened and has been in continuous acceleration ever since. The achievements of scientists between approximately 1760 and 1895 will be the subject of this chapter. They were so immense that by the end of the nineteenth century it was popularly felt that there were few problems which scientists would not soon solve. As Carl Snyder, an American popularizer of science, wrote about 1900, the universe was 'simply a machine so orderly and compact, so simple in construction that we can reckon its past and gauge something of its future with almost as much certainty as that of a dynamo or a waterwheel. In its motions, there is no uncertainty, no mystery'.

Scientific advance between 1760 and 1895 is best treated under four main headings: heat and energy; electricity and magnetism; chemistry; and biology.

Heat and Energy

Scientific study of the relationship between heat and energy was a consequence rather than the cause of the appearance of a successful steam engine. It was not until 1824 that the brilliant young French scientist Sadi Carnot provided a satisfactory explanation of how steam engines worked, and by that time they had been working in factories for nearly forty years and driving locomotives for nearly twenty. As an Englishman, R. S. Meiklejohn, remarked with pardonable exaggeration soon after the publication of Carnot's explanation: 'there is no machine nor mechanism in which what the theorists have done is more useless. It (the steam-engine) arose, was improved and perfected by working mechanics—and by them only.' If Carnot's theories had no immediate practical application they were extremely important in the development of the science of thermodynamics. He established that the work done by an engine was directly related to the transfer of heat between different temperatures and that high pressure machines were more efficient than low pressure ones because, in the process of condensation, the steam at the higher pressure experiences a greater fall in temperature. Carnot's life was tragically cut short by cholera when he was only thirty-six and it was left to others to follow up the implications of his discoveries. In 1843 two Englishmen, J. P. Joule and J. R. Mayer, working independently arrived almost simultaneously at the principle of 'the conservation of energy'. Joule devised an ingenious apparatus and conducted the experiments which enabled him to measure the mechanical equivalent of heat. In a public lecture in 1847 he described his discovery thus: 'the general rule is that whenever living force [what nowadays is called kinetic energy] is apparently destroyed, whether by percussion, friction or any similar means, an exact equivalent of heat is restored. The converse of the proposition is also true, namely that heat cannot be lessened or absorbed without the production of living force.' Joule went on to point out that the principle ought to have many practical uses. 'The knowledge of the equivalency of heat to mechanical power is of great value in solving a great number of interesting and important questions. In the case of the steam engine, by ascertaining the quantity of heat produced by the combustion of coal, we can find out how much of it is converted into mechanical power and thus come to the conclusion how far the steam engine is susceptible of further improvements.' Through the work of Lord Kelvin and von Helmholtz the principle of the conservation of energy was applied to other forms of mechanics and given a sound mathematical basis. Thermodynamics became the most flourishing branch of physics in the second half of the nineteenth century. Though it did not do much to improve the efficiency of the steam engine, despite Joule's hopes, it led to the discovery of three revolutionary methods of harnessing energy—the steam turbine, the internal combustion engine, and the refrigerator—all of which were being developed commercially before 1900.

Electricity and Magnetism

Another source of energy, electricity, was the subject of intense research in the nineteenth century. For much of the previous century, electricity produced by friction was regarded as a freak of nature. A Dutch instrument maker, Musschenbroek, managed to store electric charges in jars made of sheet metal on the inside and glass outside, the so-called Leyden jars. These became the playthings of the European aristocracy. Louis XV of France, who was easily bored, entertained his court by making a whole brigade of guards jump in unison by electrifying them from an immense battery of these jars. The investigation of an American, Franklin, a Frenchman, Coulomb, and two Italians, Galvani and Volta, led to a much better understanding of the nature of electricity in the second half of the eighteenth century. Franklin argued that there must be one type of electricity, the nature of which was best understood if it was regarded as either positively or negatively charged. This explanation is still the basis of the modern theory of electrical charges. Franklin also became known all over the world by his experiment of flying kites in thunderstorms which demonstrated that lightning was a form of electricity. He was then able to invent effective lightning conductors. Coulomb, who became interested in electricity through his efforts to improve the accuracy of the mariners' compass, showed that the forces between magnetic poles and those between electrical charges obeyed the same laws as those of gravity. This discovery enabled electricity to be linked with the laws of Newtonian physics. It was no longer a freak phenomenon.

The electric battery, a vital step forward if electric power was to be harnessed for practical use, was the invention of Volta, using discoveries of his fellow Italian Galvani. The latter, a professor of anatomy at Bologna, was carrying out electrical experiments in a laboratory which also contained pieces of animal for anatomical research. He noticed that pairs of frogs' legs twitched whenever he made an electric spark and later discovered that he could cause this twitching effect if he placed two different metals together to the nerve and muscle of the frogs' legs. What Galvani had in fact discovered was current electricity. He did not realize it but Volta did. In 1795 the latter showed that electricity could be produced without any animal parts at all, simply by placing two different pieces of metal together with a damp cloth in between. This arrangement was the original electric battery.

Other scientists swiftly built on these discoveries. It was found that the passing of an electric current through some chemical solutions isolated the elements of these solutions. Using this process of electrolysis and the batteries of the Royal Society—the largest in the world—Humphrey Davy discovered two new metals, sodium and potassium. In Denmark Oersted, having accidentally found in 1820 that an electric current deflected the needle of a compass, established that magnetism was a form of electricity. The electro-

magnet and the electric telegraph were the most important technological consequences of this discovery. Oersted's work inspired
other scientists, notably Ampère, Gauss, and Ohm, to further
research at the end of which they were able to explain how electric
current flowed through conductors and to measure its force
mathematically. The final discoveries of this fertile period of
electrical science were due to the inspired experimental work of the
Englishman Faraday. By a number of ingenious experiments in the
1830s he first discovered the principle of electromagnetic induction.
From there he moved on to invent the first dynamo, thus showing
how electric current could be used as a source of power.

The only way Faraday could explain the electrical phenomena
that he had observed was to assume that electricity, magnetism,
light, heat, and chemical combinations were all different aspects of
atomic behaviour, that in fact there was a unity of all natural forces.
Further experiments in the 1840s caused him to conclude that the
real energy of a magnet was not in the iron bar but, in the field of
space round about it, and that to understand electro-magnetic
behaviour, one had to think in terms of fields of force. His contemporaries were not immediately convinced, partly because Faraday
did not have the command of mathematics to express his ideas in
precise mathematical formulae. In 1864, however, Clerk Maxwell
redefined his 'field of force' theories in a way acceptable to the
mathematical physicists of his day, and by 1867, extending Faraday's ideas, he demonstrated that electromagnetic action travelled
through space in waves at the speed of light. The technological
impact of Faraday's discoveries were not immediate. There was in
fact to be a time lag of nearly fifty years before an efficient electrical
technology developed. A dynamo capable of supplying electricity
on a large scale was only perfected by Siemens and Wilde in 1867.
In the next two decades Lodygin in Russia, Swan in England, and
Edison in the U.S.A. developed reliable electric lighting and power
systems which made electricity available at a reasonable price for
public and domestic use.

Chemistry

Chemistry was another science firmly established during the
nineteenth century. It first grew out of the study of combustion.
During the eighteenth century progress was delayed by the widely
held notion that combustion was due to a substance, phlogiston,
which must exist in anything that burnt. Bodies that burnt well, it
was believed, held much phlogiston, those which did not were
described as dephlogisticated.

The first step towards a better understanding of combustion was
taken in the 1770s when Priestley in England and Scheele in

Sweden isolated oxygen and showed that bodies burnt better in it than in air. When Lavoisier, the greatest French scientist of the eighteenth century, heard of the discovery of oxygen he put forward a new explanation for combustion which really makes him the founder of modern chemistry. What he correctly realized was that oxygen alone was responsible for combustion and the notion of phlogiston could be abandoned. He then went on to argue that if one accepted the oxygen rather than the phlogiston principle, all the natural substances of the world could be classified into a combination of elements and named according to the way that they combined. In 1789 he wrote his *Elementary Treatise on Chemistry* which described his method of classification and suggested how compounds should be named. 'It may be seen', he wrote, 'that the language we have adopted is both copious and expressive. The first and lowest degree of oxygenation in bodies, converts them into oxides; a second degree of oxygenation constitutes the class of acids, of which specific names, drawn from their particular bases, terminate in -ous as the nitrous and sulphurous acids; the third degree of oxygenation changes these into species of acids distinguished by the termination in -ic as in nitric and sulphuric acids.' His suggestions have proved lasting.

Then followed great activity all over Europe to identify chemical elements and to measure the proportions in which they combined to form chemical compounds. Some of this work had technological consequences. Chlorine, which had been isolated as early as 1774, was soon used on a large scale for bleaching in the linen industry of Glasgow, while in France a process developed by Leblanc for manufacturing soda from salt was widely used in the textile industries.

The analysis of chemical compounds showed that they tended to combine in certain fixed proportions. To explain this, John Dalton (1766–1844) put forward his atomic theory. In his *New System of Chemical Philosophy*, first published in 1808, he argued that the fixed proportions reflected the way atoms combined within the compound, an atom being the smallest possible particle of a chemical element. To make up compounds the atoms of the various elements combined in a simple numerical form. For instance, to make up the compound nitrous oxide, two atoms of nitrogen combined with one atom of oxygen, which Dalton wrote as N_2O; to make up nitric oxide, one of nitrogen with one of oxygen (NO); and nitrogen peroxide, one atom of nitrogen with two of oxygen (NO_2); Dalton's theory provided a satisfactory explanation of the composition of most inorganic chemical compounds. With the aid of electrolysis, chemists, of whom the most outstanding was the Swede, Berzelius, were able to identify the elements of almost all the earth's and mineral deposits of the world's surface. Obviously these advances in chemistry were of great importance to the developing mining and metal industries. Dalton's theory also caused chemists to concentrate their attention on atoms to discover whether in fact they were the basic units of matter.

In 1837 Jean Dumas and Justin von Liebig lectured to the French Academy of Science. 'Scarcely sixty years have elapsed', they declared, 'since the memorable epoch when there appeared . . . the first fertile attempts at chemical theory which we owe to the genius of Lavoisier. This short space of time has been long enough for the most profound problems of *inorganic* chemistry to be basically considered and we are convinced that this branch of our knowledge possesses nearly all the fundamental ideas required to deal with the means of observation at its command. . . . But how can we apply, with a like success, such ideas to *organic* chemistry?' Dumas and Liebig used the rest of their lecture to provide an answer to their question. The chemistry of all living organisms, they maintained, was founded on a base of carbon, hydrogen, oxygen, and nitrogen. 'In fact,' they ended, 'to produce with three or four elements combinations as varied, perhaps more varied than those which compose the whole organic realm, nature has taken a course as simple as unexpected; for with all the elements she has made compounds which possess all the properties of the elements themselves. There lies the whole secret of organic chemistry, we are convinced.'

Dumas and Liebig were the leading organic chemists of Europe of their generation. Between them, they proved that organic compounds combined in a more complex way than inorganic ones, and they suggested that the clue to explaining how they combined lay in the molecular structure of the compound (i.e. in the way the atoms of the combining elements actually bound together). As a result of the independent work of the Italians Canizzaro and Avogadro, of the Frenchman Pasteur, and of the German Kekulé, it became clear that no longer was it enough to think of the molecules of an organic compound merely as a number of atoms combined in certain proportions. The shape of their combination was important too. In 1854 Kekulé was travelling in a London omnibus when he saw in his mind's eye what he called the dance of the atoms. The dance showed him, he recalled, how 'frequently two smaller atoms united to form a pair; how a large one embraced the two smaller ones; how still larger ones kept hold of three or even four of the smaller whilst the whole kept whirling in a giddy dance'. This image haunted him until 1865 when, working on benzene (C_6H_6), he became convinced that this compound must contain a ring of six carbon atoms and that the atoms of different elements must vary in their power to link with other atoms. While carbon had four links or valencies, nitrogen had three, oxygen two and hydrogen one. By the end of the century it was realized that the molecular structure of organic compounds must be thought of in three dimensions which could be measured by geometric methods. Organic chemists came to be able not only to analyse very complex organic compounds but to synthethize them.

The synthesis (putting together) of organic compounds had important technological consequences. For instance, it revolutionized the dyeing industry. In 1856 an English chemist Perkin discovered magenta, the first artificial aniline dye, when he was trying to make a substitute for quinine. This breakthrough was ignored by the British but immediately exploited by the more scientifically aware Germans. They made rapid profits from synthetic dyes, and by 1900 their chemical industry dominated the whole of Europe. Artificial manures were another useful product. The chemical industry also found a very profitable market for nitric acid, without which the explosives of World War I could not have been made.

Biology

The last major branch of the natural sciences to be developed in the nineteenth century was biology. Here the two chief advances were first the theory of evolution, secondly the germ theory of disease. The eighteenth century had been a great age of zoological and botanical collectors, the most energetic of whom was a Swede, Carl Linnaeus (1707–78). He devoted his life to a singlehanded classification of all the animals, plants, and minerals in the world. His classifications caused other naturalists like Buffon and Lamarck in France and Erasmus Darwin in England to consider how the differences and similarities of plant and animal life could be explained. Of these the boldest thinker was Lamarck (1744–1829). He argued that many present-day animal species must originally have had a common ancestor. Their modern differences were due to a process of adapting to their surroundings over a long period of time. The giraffe's long neck, for instance, was the result of continually stretching for leaves. Lamarck was a lively thinker, so too was Erasmus Darwin, but they did not possess the evidence to make their theories convincing. Between 1790 and 1840, however, geologists like Hutton and Lyell began to provide, by their unearthing of fossil remains of animals long extinct, some of the evidence that biologists were lacking. Lyell's investigations into the process of rock stratification indicated that the pattern of the earth's crust had been formed slowly and uniformly over millions of years, not by a series of catastrophes as had formerly been thought. The positioning of fossils in the stratifications proved that certain animal

Darwin

261

species had also been in existence for millions of years, that some species still surviving were older than others (reptiles for instance were older than mammals) and that other species had become extinct.

Before long, the findings of biologists and geologists were blended to provide a satisfactory explanation of how natural species had come to take their present form. The man responsible for this crucial step forward in man's understanding of himself and his past was Charles Darwin, grandson of Erasmus Darwin. In the *Origin of Species*, published in 1859, Darwin drew on the extensive field-work he had done in the 1830s during a round-the-world trip as naturalist on board H.M.S. Beagle and on the geological writings of Lyell and others. 'When on board H.M.S. Beagle', he wrote in the Introduction, 'I was much struck with certain facts in the distribution of the organic beings inhabiting South America and in the geological relations of the present to the past inhabitants of the continent. These facts seemed to throw some light on the origin of species, that mystery of mysteries as it has been called by one of our greatest philosophers.'

Darwin's theory of evolution had two more parts. The first was the argument that different forms of life were descended from a common ancestor as a result of a process which had lasted millions of years. The second was an explanation of how the evolutionary process had occurred.

The form modern species take, he suggested, was due to 'natural selection', to the struggle for survival which is part of the natural order of things. The lions which survive are those which are strongest and the best hunters, the deer which survive are the swiftest runners. They hand on these characteristics which, with the passing of time, become more concentrated in the species, which thus becomes as a species more fit to survive. 'As buds give rise by growth to fresh buds', Darwin wrote, 'and these if vigorous branch out and overtop on all sides many a feeble branch, so by generation, I believe, it has been with the great Tree of Life which fills with its dead and broken branches the crust of the earth and covers the surface with its ever-branching and beautiful ramifications.' In 1871 he published *The Descent of Man*, which included man in the evolutionary scheme. The human species obviously had much in common with the ape and shared the same ancestral line. The differences between men and apes was due to a process of adaptation in the struggle for survival over millions of years. Chapter 15 shows how the theory of evolution led to an immediate and bitter conflict between Darwinists and Christians which raged for the rest of the century. Most scientists, however, came to accept that the case for the *fact* of evolution was proved. There was,

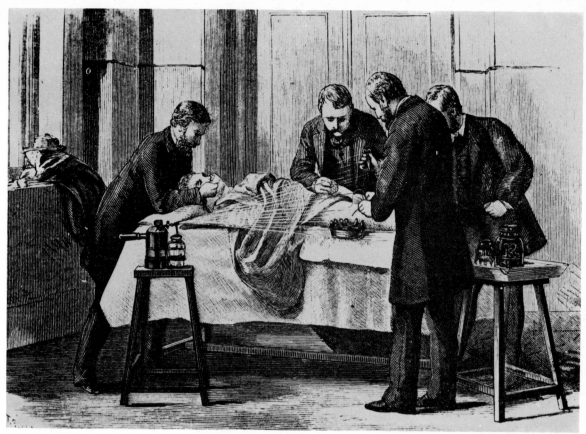

An operation making use of the carbolic spray developed by Lister

however, much less agreement about Darwin's *explanation* of evolution through natural selection. The genetic research of Mendel (1822–84) and later geneticists suggest that it was rather too simple.

There were other major advances in biology besides evolution. In 1855 Pasteur, who had already made himself an international reputation as a chemist, began investigating the fermentation of liquids like beer and vinegar. He became convinced that the cause of this phenomenon was tiny living organisms, invisible to the naked eye. Further studies of a silkworm disease in the Lyons district— which he cured—led him to the 'germ' theory of disease. Disease in men and animals as well as in insects was caused like fermentation, he argued, by tiny living organisms or germs. Other doctors and biologists were arriving at the same conclusion. In Germany Koch isolated the germs, first of anthrax, then of tuberculosis and of cholera. In Scotland Lister, a practising surgeon, worked out methods, based on the germ theory, of reducing the risk of infection in hospitals. 'In 1864', he later recalled, 'I was struck with an account of the remarkable effects produced by carbolic acid upon the sewage of the town of Carlisle, the admixture of a very small proportion not only preventing all odour from the lands irrigated with the refuse material, but destroying the entozoa which usually infest cattle fed upon such pastures.' He developed a carbolic antiseptic which he first used in 1865. It proved immediately successful, and Lister's antiseptic techniques began to be used throughout the world. In combination with the use of anaesthetics (perfected in the 1840s) antiseptics drastically reduced the horrors and risks of surgery, and of hospital treatment in general. Thus the nineteenth century saw the beginnings of scientific medicine.

Four Leading Scientists of the Period: Lavoisier (1743–94)

Antoine Laurent Lavoisier was the son of a wealthy Parisian lawyer who made sure that his child obtained an excellent education at the College Mazarin. From an early age he showed a flair for maths and the natural sciences. When he was only twenty-three he wrote an essay on the best means of lighting a large town which won him the gold medal of the Academy of Sciences. He joined the Academy in 1768 and towards the end of his life became first one of its directors and then, in 1791, its treasurer. His father had purchased a noble title for him in 1772 and in the 1770s and 1780s he was very active in public affairs. In 1775 he was placed in charge of the manufacture of gunpowder throughout the country and made many improvements. Having created a successful farm of his own, he was asked to act as secretary of a committee which was set up in 1785 to report on the condition of French agriculture. During the years of crisis leading up to the 1789 revolution he was attached to the royal treasury. In 1789 he was elected a member of the noble estate. Nonetheless he managed to co-operate with the new revolutionary government between 1789 and 1792. He acted as both secretary and chairman of the committee which advised the adoption of the metric system of weights and measures in France. However, Lavoisier had not only been a distinguished scientist and public servant: from 1768 he had also been a farmer-general, one of the hated groups of tax-collectors in the Paris area. This was to cost him his life during the Reign of Terror. First denounced by Marat in 1792, he was imprisoned and eventually guillotined in May 1794 during one of the last Jacobin purges. 'It required only a moment to sever that head', remarked an eyewitness of the execution, 'and perhaps a century will not be long enough to produce another like it.'

Lavoisier was a scientist whose talents covered an extraordinary range. His most famous work in chemistry has already been described but he was very active in other fields. His first interest was geology and he helped to prepare one of the earliest mineralogical

Lavoisier with his wife

maps of France. He also gave careful attention to the problems of heat and energy, and at the time of his death seemed to be working towards the kind of answers that Joule was to reach. He was also fascinated by the chemistry of fermentation, of animal heat, and of respiration. His papers, published years after his death, indicate that he may have been on the verge of further important discoveries. His death was, to say the least, untimely.

Faraday (1791–1867)

Michael Faraday was the son of a Yorkshire blacksmith who had travelled south in search of work. At the age of 14 he was apprenticed to a bookseller and bookbinder of North London. In his spare moments he read any book on the natural sciences which came into the shop. Having learnt of the work of Davy at the Royal Institution, he went to hear him lecture. This proved the turning point of his life. Davy inspired him, as he put it, 'to enter the service of science'. He wrote to Davy asking for a job, and enclosed the notes he had made on Davy's lecture as evidence of his keenness. After some hesitation, Davy appointed the young man of twenty-one as his assistant and soon took him on a tour of Europe, visiting some of the greatest scientists of his generation.

Faraday proved to be an experimental scientist of genius, the greatest the world has ever known in the opinion of some historians of science. 'He smells the truth' was how one authority put it, and once having got the smell, he was able to devise brilliant experiments to test the truth of his theories. His first major discoveries were in chemistry. In 1820 he isolated two new chlorides of carbon and a compound of carbon, iodine and hydrogen. In 1823 he liquefied chlorine. Simultaneously, he was experimenting with electricity. Oersted's 1820 research fascinated him and before long he made his first great electrical discovery, the principle of electromagnetic rotation.

Davy found the brilliance of his assistant hard to bear and, believing that Faraday had taken too much credit for himself for the joint work that they had done on chlorine, opposed his election to the Royal Society and managed to delay it until 1824. However, Faraday's career was not seriously affected. In 1825 he was made Director of the Laboratories of the Royal Society. Not only was he able to carry out much more elaborate experiments, but he also began to give regular lectures to both adults and children which proved very popular.

A second period of fertile research began in 1831. Ten days of constant experiment established the principle of electro-magnetic

Faraday demonstrates some of his discoveries at a Christmas lecture for children at the Royal Institution, in 1856

induction. He built the first dynamo. Then, investigating static electricity, he worked out his theory of electric lines of force.

This intensive research work on electricity caused him a nervous breakdown, and he only resumed serious research again after prolonged convalescence in Switzerland. In the later years of his life he concentrated on the relationship of electricity to light, which enabled him to develop further his theories of lines and fields of force. From 1833 he was a professor of the Royal Society, and when he retired in 1858 the government gave him a house at Hampton Court where he spent the last years of his life. His discoveries made him internationally famous and his brilliant popular lectures made him a much-loved public figure. A very retiring person, his chief interests were his work and his wife. Unusually for a scientist of his generation, he was very religious, being a member from childhood of an obscure Christian group called the Sandemanites.

Liebig (1803–73)

Justin von Liebig was born in the German town of Darmstadt, the son of a dealer in chemicals. He studied pharmacy for a short time but then decided to become a chemist. Such was his brilliance that he obtained his doctorate when he was still only nineteen. He then moved to Paris to work in the private laboratory of a leading French scientist Gay-Lussac. His reputation grew swiftly and in 1826, when he was barely twenty-three, he was appointed Professor of Chemistry at the University of Giessen. Here he established a laboratory which not only was a centre of important research, but

Liebig's famous research laboratory at Giessen

specialized in teaching research methods to young scientists. So successful was Liebig as a teacher that this laboratory became world-famous and attracted some of the best students in Europe. It was also an important factor in making Germany much the best scientifically educated nation in Europe. He became bored with practical teaching, however, and when he moved to Munich University, he restricted himself to lecturing and writing.

In the 1820s and 1830s he directed his own and his students' energies towards the analysis of organic compounds. Their results were very fruitful. In collaboration with his close friend Wöhler he discovered the 'benzoyl radical' and greatly increased the understanding of the chemistry of radicals and halogens. In his middle age he became interested in fermentation and in agricultural chemistry. He was always an arrogant and provocative man. As he grew older, he often jumped to conclusions from limited evidence. As a result he was involved in bitter controversy with other scientists and proved wrong as often as right. In a famous dispute over fermentation with Pasteur, for instance, he was the loser. Nonetheless his influence in Germany and in Europe was immense. He was made a baron in 1845 and was constantly consulted by governments and industry. Despite his shortcomings he was the greatest chemist of his generation and an effective popularizer of the chemical discoveries of the time.

Pasteur (1822–95)

Louis Pasteur was the son of a Burgundian tanner. While he was at school in Arbois he did so well that at the age of sixteen he was sent to Paris to continue his studies. Poor health and homesickness brought him back to Burgundy where he continued his education. His teachers were impressed by his mathematics but not by his chemistry, which they summed up as 'mediocre'. He only became interested in chemistry on his return to Paris in 1843 where, working as a laboratory assistant, he finally obtained his doctorate in 1847. In the following year, he completed the research which first made him internationally famous. He had become interested in crystallography and his studies of racemic acid showed that it possessed two types of crystal with different qualities of refracting light. He concluded rightly that this difference must indicate a difference in molecular structure.

The next productive period of his life began when he became head of the new science faculty at the University of Lille. Here he began his great research work into fermentation. A useful by-product of this work was the process for purifying milk which to this day is known as 'pasteurization'. In 1865 his old teacher Dumas persuaded him to join the government mission which hoped to solve the mystery of the terrible silkworm disease which was ruining the French silk industry. Within three years he had isolated the bacilli (germs) which were causing the disease and developed a successful means of preventing its further outbreak.

He then suffered a severe stroke which left him semi-paralysed. Nonetheless he continued to work. In fact his most important discoveries were still to come. In the 1870s he mastered anthrax and in the 1880s chicken cholera which was then ravaging French farms. Finally he turned his attention to one of the most dreaded diseases of man and animals, rabies. To master chicken cholera, he had worked out a successful method of inoculation against the disease. Using dogs alone, he obtained a weakened form of the rabies virus which might be used for inoculation. On 6 July 1885 a nine year old Joseph Meister was bitten by a rabid dog and his mother asked Pasteur to use the inoculation in the hope of saving the child. 'The death of the child seeming inevitable', Pasteur wrote later, 'I decided, not without lively and sore anxiety, to try on Joseph Meister the method which had constantly succeeded with dogs.' The treatment was successful. In October 1885 Pasteur could note in his Journal: 'after a lapse of three months and three weeks since his accident, his health leaves nothing to be desired.'

In the following years money poured in from all over the world to finance further research with rabies. He was able to found the Pasteur Institute which he headed until his death in 1895. Though few have done more to improve life for their fellow men he remained quite unaffected by the fame his genius had brought him. His work was his life. When he was on his deathbed, his chief interest was the

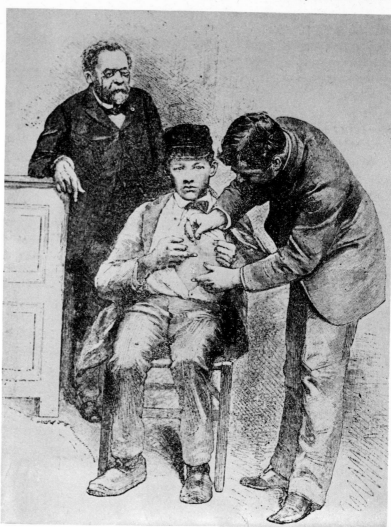

Pasteur supervising the inoculation of Joseph Meister

research work of his pupils. 'Where are you with it? What are you doing?' he would ask them. His last reported words were, it is said, 'you have to work'.

The End of the Century

In 1870 the natural sciences appeared to be unifying. The kinetic theory of gases, summed up by Clerk Maxwell in 1862 as 'the theory of gases being little bodies flying about', was another strong argument in favour of the atomic basis of matter. The advances in organic and inorganic chemistry, in thermodynamics, in electro-magnetism and even in biology seemed to indicate, as Faraday had believed, that there was a unity to natural phenomena. Most scientists thought that the world about us whether living or non-living was made up of chemical elements. These elements it was assumed, consisted of eternal and indestructible atoms. Energy could be explained in terms of the movement of these atoms according to fixed and measurable laws. The universe, therefore, could be regarded as a vast mechanism, the essential framework of which was already well known. The function of scientists in the future would be to fit in the missing girders—to discover more chemical elements, establish further thermodynamic laws—but it was not expected that any fundamental rethinking of the nature of matter or of energy would be required. For the next twenty years, until the 1890's, scientific research seemed to confirm this view. Further elements were discovered, as had been predicted, and the principles of thermodynamics were found to be applicable to gas pressures.

It is not surprising, therefore, that the confidence of scientists was great and the confidence of the public in scientists boundless. Public interest in scientific matters increased dramatically during the century. Many scientists, of whom Faraday and Liebig are the most famous, went to great trouble to explain the latest advances in language the layman could understand. An American in Paris in 1865 noted in his diary how 'in all the principal towns of France and even the smaller villages men distinguished either by great scientific or literary achievement have come to lend earnest aid to the cause of social progress by the diffusion of knowledge.' Throughout the continent there was a rapid improvement in scientific and technical education and, especially after 1870, a widespread realization of how much scientific discoveries applied through industry were doing to improve the lot of mankind.

With this confidence in the power of science went a new appreciation of the importance of scientists. Just before 1900, A. J. Balfour, an able philosopher as well as a British Cabinet Minister, remarked that 'they (the scientists) are the men who are changing the world and they do not know it. Politicians are but the fly on the wheel—the men of science are the motive power'. At the end of the century there were few Europeans who doubted that the rise of science marked a change for the better, that thanks to science man had achieved a new level of civilization and would surely and speedily mount higher still. The previous hundred years had demonstrated clearly the certainties of science and its power to improve the human condition. Its uncertainties and destructive power had barely been glimpsed.

Chapter 15
The Challenge to Religion

There is much that is contradictory about the religion of nineteenth century Europe. From one point of view, held by many churchmen of the time, the century was one of tremendous religious vitality. Almost all the churches of Europe, particularly the Catholics of France and the Anglicans of England, thoroughly reformed themselves after the corruption and decay of the eighteenth century. Regular church attendance and public support for Christian principles remained an important sign of respectability throughout the century. Missionary activity which spread the Christian gospel to the pagan parts of the world was undertaken on a scale quite unparallelled since the early days of Christianity. From another point of view, however, it was an age of uncertainty and failure. At the end of the eighteenth century many Christian churches needed reforming but they still held the hearts and minds of the vast majority of Europeans. Europe was a Christian continent and had been so for a thousand years. The dominant churches— roughly speaking the Roman Catholics in the south, the Protestants in the north and the Orthodox in the East—were rich and influential. Particular churches in particular areas were protected by the state and were usually the only providers of education. In rural areas, the parish priest was often the only educated member of the community. The Bible was the continent's best seller and, as interpreted by the parish priest, the chief guide to good or bad behaviour for most Europeans. A handful of intellectuals in France and Britain might scoff at Christianity but they were a small, unpopular minority. A Scots mob tore open the grave of the distinguished philosopher David Hume after his death in 1776 because he had argued that to believe in miracles such as those described in the Bible was absurd.

By the end of the nineteenth century the situation was different. Europe might still appear a Christian continent but the hold of Christianity on the hearts and minds of educated men—and more and more men were educated—was weaker. At Christmas time in 1886 the Bishop of Cremona in Italy wrote to the Pope that 'intellectual youth, which one day will be the mainstay of society, is steadily detaching itself from the Church', while at much the same time the scientist T. H. Huxley, a firm opponent of religion but not a man much given to rash prophecies, could write: 'that this Christianity is doomed to fall is, to my mind, beyond a doubt'.

The Challenge to Religion

Between 1789 and 1914 the Christian religion, in Europe, suffered a series of blows from which it has never properly recovered.

These blows came from three directions. In the first place, European states became less ready to protect a particular church. Instead they tended to become referees between the various Christian and non-Christian groups as they disputed amongst themselves, especially over education. This development was most marked in Western Europe. Secondly, advances in historical and scientific thinking brought into question the truth of some of the central beliefs of Christianity. Thirdly, the process of urbanization created new centres of population to which the organization of the churches (which had originally developed to meet the needs of a rural society) was not always able to adapt.

Church and State

As Chapter II showed, serious conflicts developed between church and state during the French Revolution, and by 1815, most Catholic leaders both in France and elsewhere, had come to condemn everything the Revolution stood for and to support absolutist monarchies against liberal revolutionaries. In France the Bourbon kings, Louis XVIII and Charles X, did their best to restore the Catholic Church, which they regarded as an important defence of their own authority, to the position it had held before 1789. Consequently most Frenchmen who were liberal and republican tended also to be anti-clerical. The successful liberal revolution of 1830, therefore, led to the curbing of the power of the Catholic Church. In the uncertain days of his Presidency of the Republic (1848–51) and in his first years as Emperor (1852–60) Louis Napoleon needed the support of Catholics and the Church was able to recover some influence, especially in education. In the last years of the Second Empire (1863–70) and in the 1870s and 1880s the pendulum swung the other way. One of the most striking character-istics of the republican governments of the 1880s was their fierce anti-clericalism, and Catholic educational institutions suffered severely, especially when Ferry was in power. In the 1890s the Catholic Church became deeply involved in the Dreyfus affair, siding against Dreyfus who was backed by liberals and republicans. When his innocence was finally proved, the embarrassment of the Church was considerable, and the republican government took the opportunity of passing another set of anti-clerical laws. Catholic orders and schools were closely supervized by the state, and in 1905 the Concordat which Napoleon I had signed with the Pope in 1804 was ended. The Catholic Church became in the eyes of the law just one of the various Christian churches in France, though in practice its influence remained much greater than that of any other church.

In other mainly Catholic countries, similar struggles occurred. In Belgium the liberal revolution of 1830 against the Dutch had been supported by almost all sections of the population and the first government to hold power after the revolution was both Liberal and Catholic. However, it soon became divided over education. The Catholics revived the university at Louvain and in 1834 the liberals founded a rival to it in Brussels. Eventually the differences became so serious that, despite the efforts of King Leopold, who hated the idea of a split for religious reasons, a separate Catholic party was formed in 1847. In the election held that year the Liberals won, and remained in power until 1884. They pursued a generally anti-clerical policy, especially in educational matters. In 1884 the Catholic party won a majority and governed Belgium for the next twenty years. It immediately restored religious instruction in state schools, and from 1895 insisted that this instruction should be in the Roman Catholic faith.

The bitterest and most disastrous conflict between church and state occurred in Italy. In the first half of the nineteenth century, Italian Catholic leaders were usually prepared to co-operate with Metternich and with rulers of the Italian states to prevent revolution. Between 1846 and 1848, however, Pius IX, carried away by the dream of a unified Italy, flirted with the idea of becoming the head of a new Italian federation and temporarily became a hero of the liberal revolutionaries. His experiences during the revolution of 1848 completely altered his views. Rossi, whom he appointed Prime Minister of the Papal States, was murdered by an extreme revolutionary and Pius fled from Rome condemning the revolutionaries and all that they stood for. For the rest of his long life (he died in 1878) he refused to co-operate with the Italian liberals even after their successes in 1859–60. He tried to prevent Victor Emmanuel from entering the Papal States in 1860 and when the Papal army had been defeated at Castelfidardo, he called in the French to defend Rome. When Venice was handed over to Italy by the Austrians in 1866, Rome was the only city still outside the unified country. Pius was determined to keep it that way. His French army fought off Garibaldi in 1867 and only after it had been recalled to fight the Prussians in 1870 did the Italian government attack Rome. Pius still would not give in. He ordered what troops he had to fight on and the city only fell after bitter street fighting. He then refused to negotiate with the Italian government which nonetheless granted him complete control of the Vatican area, his own postal service, and a state pension. Obstinately Pius declared himself 'a prisoner of the Vatican', refused to accept that Rome and the Papal States were lost for ever and forbade Italian Catholics to co-operate in any way with the Italian government. His successor, Leo XIII (1878–1903), continued this policy. Many Catholics followed Papal

273

instructions. There were massive abstentions in general elections and some of the most talented Italians were unable to hold office in the young state because their conscience prevented them. Not surprisingly, Italian governments after 1861 were anti-clerical. In 1866 many monasteries and seminaries for the training of priest-teachers were dissolved. It was not until 1905 that there was any compromise. In that year, Pope Pius X allowed bishops to decide whether their flock might take part in local politics, and liberals and Catholics began uneasily to work together against the socialists.

In Germany the conflict between church and state was sharp but short. Soon after unification, Bismarck decided that the Catholics of Germany showed too much independence and readiness to listen to a non-German Pope. He therefore let loose the so-called *Kulturkampf* (civilization struggle). The Jesuits were expelled from Germany, in 1872, and in 1875 all religious orders, with the exception of the nursing ones, were expelled from Prussia. After some complicated diplomatic manoeuvring Bismarck was eventually ready to compromise with Pope Leo XIII, but as a result of the *Kulturkampf* Catholic education in Germany came under closer state control.

In Britain the Protestant church, protected by the state, was the Anglican Church or the Church of England. It also lost authority and influence in the course of the century. In 1800 it was much the largest and the most powerful of the many different churches in the British Isles but it was widely criticized for its lack of energy and enthusiasm. More lively and considerably more successful in bringing the Christian religion to the working classes were those Protestant sects like the Methodists, Presbyterians, or Baptists, which were not protected by the state and were often known as the Nonconformists. In the 1820s and 1830s, demands that the Anglican church should be reformed were widely heard. *The Black Book*, listing the evils of the church, was published and sold in vast numbers. Its sequel *The Extraordinary Black Book*, published in 1831, had a similar success. 'Nothing is heard', wrote an anxious and conservative clergyman of the time, 'but dissatisfaction with the Church, with her abuses, her corruption, her errors. In fact there is not a single stone of the sacred edifice of the Church which is not examined, shaken and undermined by a meddling and an ignorant curiosity.' The privileged position of Anglicans was significantly weakened in 1829 when the government repealed the laws which prevented non-Anglicans like the Catholics and Non-conformists from holding public office. In the 1830's the power of the Anglican church in mainly Catholic Ireland was reduced. Between 1836 and 1841 the whole structure of the church was investigated and reorganized by the newly created Ecclesiastical Commissioners. Between 1833 and 1870 the government granted money to church schools to improve national education, but since in many areas church schools were not being built nearly fast enough to meet the educational need, the 1870 Education Act created state schools (board schools) independent of church control. Though there had to be religious instruction in these schools, it could not be recognizably Anglican or Catholic or Nonconformist. So successful were these board schools that the older church schools found them extremely difficult to compete with. Further education acts helped the church schools to survive, but in the course of the century the influence of the Anglican church, and indeed of the Christian churches in general, in British schools, was lessened. The same was true at university level. In 1800 the three English universities of Oxford, Cambridge, and Durham were only open to Anglicans. In 1828 University College, London ('the godless institution of Gower Street') was set up to end this Anglican monopoly. Entry to it was open to anyone whatever his religious or irreligious opinions. In 1871 Oxford and Cambridge were forced by law to end their discrimination in favour of Anglicans.

Thus relations between church and state, between religious institutions and national governments, were often difficult in Central and Western Europe and by the beginning of the twentieth century the political power of the Christian churches in these parts of Europe was greatly reduced. In contrast, relations between church and state in Eastern Europe were much more friendly. If anything, the political power of the Eastern churches increased rather than declined during the nineteenth century. The main reason for this was the conviction of the Habsburg Emperors of Austria and the Romanov Tsars of Russia that a powerful church protected by the state was necessary for the defence of the state and of the royal dynasty against revolution and disorder. Shaken by the revolutions of 1848, Franz Joseph of Austria signed a Concordat with the Catholic Church in 1855 which gave to the Pope greater freedom to discuss matters with Austrian Catholics and to Catholic bishops more say in education. In Russia the Orthodox Church became almost a government department. Between 1880 and 1905, when Pobedonostsev was Procurator of the Holy Synod, the church was used to combat all forms of political and social unrest. It produced a steady stream of propaganda, the chief message of which was how dangerous were any reforming ideas and how important was complete obedience to the Tsar. Such a close association with the Tsarist state meant that the Russian Church was poorly placed to weather the revolutionary storms of 1917.

As churchmen tried to face up to the problems of church and state, they found that some of the beliefs which they regarded as central to their Christian faith were challenged by scientists and by historians. In the previous century there had been no obvious conflict between science and christianity. Descartes, the French mathematician, and Newton, the English physicist—seventeenth century scientists to whom the eighteenth century owed much—were both men of deep religious faith. Newton wrote as much theology as he did science. He felt that his scientific discoveries merely displayed the glory of God since they indicated a universe of quite extraordinary size designed with such skill and so harmoniously that the Creator must have been, as the Bible said, both benevolent and omnipotent. The literal truth of the Bible was not questioned. In contrast, the geological and biological discoveries of the nineteenth century set science firmly against religion. Both geologists, who were investigating the age of the earth, uncovering stratifications and fossils, and biologists, who were classifying animals and plant species, began to ask themselves the same question—when and how did living organisms, including man, take their present form and for what reasons. Building on the work of the Swedish naturalist, Linnaeus, Erasmus Darwin in England in 1794 and Lamarck in France in 1802 suggested that animal species might have evolved from a common ancestor over a very long period of time. Their explanation of how evolution could occur was so lacking in evidence that their ideas won few supporters. Between 1830 and 1833, however, Sir Charles Lyell, England's leading geologist, published his *Principles of Geology*. This carefully researched work showed, from the evidence of fossil remains, that the earth was at least 100,000,000 years old. It therefore made nonsense of the conventional Christian belief of the time, based on calculations made by Archbishop Ussher, using figures in the Old Testament, that the world had been created in 4004 B.C., and threw doubt on to the whole Creation story as told in the book of Genesis. Lyell himself was a respectable man with no desire to cause controversy, and he was able to distract attention from the controversial parts of his theory by attacking those biologists who, like Lamarck, were using fossil evidence to question another Christian belief based on Genesis—that each animal had been created by God as it is today, and that in fact there had been no evolutionary process. A few Christians who read Lyell's book carefully and realized the force of his arguments worked out the theory that God must have placed misleading fossils in the rocks to test man's faith more thoroughly!

After some rumblings in the 1840s the storm finally broke when Charles Darwin, the grandson of Erasmus Darwin, published *The

Origin of Species in 1859. In this book, which must rival Marx and Engels Communist Manifesto as the most influential publication of the nineteenth century, Darwin explained his theory of evolution (see Chapter 14). For Christians, Darwin's theory was obnoxious for three main reasons. First, by emphasizing that evolution was a process lasting millions of years and that animal species were not created independently in their present shape, he implied that the book of Genesis, including the much loved story of Adam and Eve, could not be literally true. Secondly, by portraying the world of nature as a vicious struggle for survival in which the fitter destroyed the less fit, he contradicted Newton's view of a harmonious universe, the masterpiece of a wise and benevolent creator. Thirdly he presented man as a sophisticated descendant of the ape rather than of the angels. *The Origin of Species* and its successor, *The Descent of Man*, caused an immediate uproar in Britain and were quickly translated into many languages. They convinced much of the scientific world and their main ideas were energetically spread to non-scientists by gifted popularizers like T. H. Huxley in Britain and Ernst Haeckel in Germany. The conflict between science and religion was open and fierce. Haeckel wrote towards the end of his life in 1899:

> One of the most distinctive features of the expiring century is the increasing vehemence of the opposition between science and Christianity. That is both natural and inevitable. In the same proportion in which the victorious progress of modern science has surpassed all the scientific achievements of earlier ages has the unsoundness been proved of those mystic views which would subdue reason under the yoke of an alleged revelation; and the Christian religion belongs to that group.

More and more Europeans agreed with him.

Further telling criticisms of nineteenth-century Christian beliefs came from historians. There had been an upsurge of interest in the study of history in the early years of the century and a more disciplined approach had led historians to subject the original documents on which their descriptions and explanations of past events were based to more thorough and critical investigations. The best historical scholars were German, and at the University of Tübingen a number of historians began to give to the books of the Bible the same kind of critical investigation as they gave to other historical documents, in order to discover how much of it could be regarded as accurate, how much exaggeration, and how much mere fancy. It soon became clear that much of the Old Testament was legend, with a little truth hidden somewhere among a great deal of fancy. Moreover, parts of the New Testament were shown to be inconsistent and to have been written some years, perhaps more than a generation, after the events that they described. In 1835–6 D. F. Strauss, who had studied for a while at Tübingen, published his *Life of Jesus* (*Leben Jesu*), which portrayed Jesus as a mortal man whose life was transformed into the legend that could be read in the New Testament by the communal imagination of his followers. So powerful was Jesus' personality, Strauss argued, that his disciples, 'a recently established community, revering its founder with all the more enthusiasm on account of his unexpected and tragic end', made up for his death by adding a series of miracles, including the Resurrection, to the otherwise historically accurate story of his life. In 1863 a French professor, Renan, wrote another biography of Jesus which portrayed the founder of Christianity as a simple-minded man with 'no knowledge of the general state of the world . . . the charming impossibility with which his parables abound when he brings kings and the mighty men upon the stage, prove that he never thought of aristocratic society except through the prism of his own simplicity.' Both Strauss and Renan were translated into English and widely read. They demonstrated to educated Europeans that it was possible and intellectually acceptable to approach the Bible as a collection of interesting historical documents rather than the Word of God, every part of which must be regarded as literally true.

Against the combined assault of biology, geology, and history, Christian leaders were at a loss for some time, as we shall see. The result was a sharp increase in the number of Europeans who would no longer call themselves Christian. In 1911 the English Free Church Yearbook noted, with alarm: 'the truth is—and we must face its startling reality—that the educated middle classes, especially the young people, are losing touch with the House of God.'

Urbanization

The third challenge which nineteenth century churchmen had to face was that of urbanization. The city of Birmingham in 1851 possessed church places for less than 30 per cent of its population. In 1880 Berlin, a city of more than 1,500,000, had places for just 25,000. The attitude of many workers to the churches, especially the old established ones, was indifference or hostility. An English Chartist wrote that in the 1840s 'we had . . . a feeling of contempt towards them [the clergy] because we thought them so uncommonly like hypocrites. The same with regard to religion generally. There was little real enmity against it as far as I could see among working men. We only thought it a humbug and not worth a sensible man's troubling his head with.' For Marxist socialists religion was a drug—'the opium of the people'—or as Marx elsewhere described it 'the sigh of a creature overwhelmed by misfortune, the soul of a heartless world'. Traditional Christianity, many socialists believed, was a myth, used by the ruling bourgeoisie to distract the workers from the misery of their present conditions by visions of a non-existent Paradise. In the most purely socialist revolution of nineteenth century Europe—the Paris Commune—the revolutionary leaders seized churchmen as hostages and eventually put many of them, including the Archbishop of Paris, to death.

The Response of the Churches

The reaction of Christian leaders to these fundamental challenges took two general forms. The first, which lasted for the first three-quarters of the century, was a determination to maintain their traditional beliefs and practices, come what may. In the last quarter of the century they became more flexible, more ready to reinterpret their religious faith in terms which made sense in the rapidly changing society of which they were part.

The readiness of European states to disentangle themselves from particular churches which traditionally they had protected at first dismayed these churches. When the British government lessened the power of the Anglican Church in Ireland in 1837, it was abused in extravagant terms by a number of gifted young clergymen from Oxford University, who then began a movement to fight off the forces of reform and liberalism and to restore the Anglican Church to its former honoured position as the most vital spiritual force in English society. 'Our aim was wholly conservative', wrote William Palmer, a member of the Oxford Movement, 'it was to maintain things that we believed and had been taught, not to introduce innovations in doctrine and discipline.' The more, however, the members of the Movement studied the history of the Anglican Church, the more close appeared its links to be with the Roman Catholic Church. Newman, the leader of the Movement, eventually became a Catholic in 1845, and those who remained within the Church of England introduced more colour, ritual and ceremony into their churches. These developments horrified most Anglicans and the chief effect of the Oxford Movement was to divide and demoralize the Anglican Church at a time when it needed all the strength of unity.

In France the Catholic Church reacted in a similar conservative way to reforming liberal governments and those Catholics who tried to remain faithful to their church, yet were sympathetic to the political ideals of liberalism, were placed in an impossible position. In 1830 Lamennais, a Breton abbot and a gifted writer, founded a newspaper, *L'Avenir* (the Future), in the hope of persuading the Catholic Church to come to terms with liberal as well as conservative regimes. The French Catholic bishops thoroughly disapproved of *L'Avenir*, so in 1831 Lamennais visited Rome in the hope of winning the support of Pope Gregory XVI. He failed. In 1832 the Pope declared that the main liberal principles of freedom of conscience and freedom of the press were wrong. Lamennais was appalled. He eventually left the Church, and after the 1848 revolution became a liberal deputy in the French Assembly. When he died in 1851, he refused to accept the last rites of the Church. Other gifted liberal Catholics like the German scholar Dollinger and the English Lord Aston found themselves in difficulties either with their local bishops or with the Papacy, which took a resolutely conservative line until the death of Pius IX in 1878. Pius himself became more conservative the longer he lived. In December 1864 he issued his *Syllabus of Errors*, a list of those characteristics of modern society which a good Catholic should condemn. Among the errors were socialism, communism, rationalism, liberty of the press, and liberty of conscience. It was also an error to think 'that the Roman pontiff (the Pope) can and ought to reconcile himself and adjust himself to progress, liberalism and modern civilization.' The syllabus was greeted with disbelief in many parts of Europe. It was as if the Pope had placed himself, as the British representative in Rome put it, 'at the head of a vast ecclesiastical conspiracy against the principles which govern modern society'. In 1870 Pius further demonstrated his refusal to compromise with the spirit of the times by decreeing that the Pope, when speaking officially as the Head of the Catholic Church on matters of faith and morals, was 'infallible' (i.e. he could never be wrong). *The Syllabus of Errors* and the declaration of Papal infallibility caused serious splits among Catholics and lessened the appeal of Catholicism to educated Europeans.

The challenge of science and history was met with a similar combination of dismay and uncompromising hostility. In Britain, Darwin and his popularizer, Huxley, were violently criticized. In 1860 the British Association held a meeting at Oxford to debate publicly the value of Darwin's theory and its meaning for religion. Huxley was speaking for the Darwinists and Wilberforce, the most eloquent bishop of his generation, for the Church. It was quite a meeting. The atmosphere was electric. An eminent society lady fainted with excitement. Captain Fitzroy, a fervent Christian in whose ship, the *Beagle*, Darwin had sailed round the world and carried out the research on which his theories of evolution were based, was on his feet waving a Bible and shouting that here was the truth and how greatly he regretted that unknowingly he had harboured such a viper on board his ship. *MacMillan's Magazine* which reported the meeting described how 'looks of bitter hatred were directed at those who were on Darwin's side.' In the debate itself Wilberforce, who was no scientist and had little understanding of the strength of Darwin's case, was reduced to cheap sneers like asking Huxley whether it was through his grandfather or grandmother that he claimed descent from the apes. For many years Christians were unable to discuss Darwinism at a serious level. 'Absurd facts to prop up his utterly rotten fabric of guess and speculation' is how the *Quarterly Review* dismissed *The Origin of Species*. In Germany Haeckel was faced with the same kind of reaction.

The historians fared no better. In France Renan lost his professorship. In England a group of young Anglican teachers, who in a joint work, *Essays and Reviews*, suggested in 1860 that Anglicans should take note of the historical study of the Bible which had been proceeding in Germany and should look at the Bible as a historical document in need of scholarly interpretation, stirred up a hornet's nest. Two of the writers were brought to trial in church courts, the English bishops as one body condemned the book, and 11,000 clergymen and 137,000 laymen signed a declaration that the whole Bible 'not only contained but was the Word of God'. Such reactions, which verged on the hysterical, did the churches no good.

In the last years of the nineteenth century there was a significant change in the attitude of Christian leaders and a real improvement in the fortunes of the Christian churches, particularly of Catholicism. This was partly due to Pope Leo XIII, who succeeded Pius IX in 1878 and lived until 1903. It was also due to the growth of socialism which made liberals more ready to co-operate with Catholic conservatives.

Leo XIII was a brilliant diplomat who realized that some compromise with modern civilization was necessary if Catholicism was to survive at all. He encouraged the French Catholics to co-operate with the Third Republic; skilfully negotiated with Bismarck to bring the *Kulturkampf* to an end; and gave his backing to Catholic thinkers who were trying to find a way of blending the discoveries of modern science with traditional Catholic teaching. He also suggested that Catholic working men should form their own trades unions. On many issues, however, he was as conservative, if not so publicly, as Pius IX. He would never admit that Papal control of Rome had gone for ever nor would he co-operate with the Italian government. The *Syllabus of Errors* and the doctrine of Papal Infallibility were both maintained. When Alfred Loisy, a leading French Catholic scholar, began to teach the Bible in the light of modern historical criticism he, like Renan, was deprived of his professorship. When he abandoned his priesthood and began to work out a new justification of Catholicism in terms of its historical development, he was excommunicated.

Nonetheless, so different was the atmosphere within the Catholic Church during Leo's pontificate that there was a much greater readiness to put forward new ideas, and between 1890 and 1908 the so-called 'modernist' movement did its best to meet the challenge of science and history. Leo, however, died in 1903, and his successor, Pius X, found the freedom of thought within the church disturbing. In 1910 all Catholic priests had to swear that they would have nothing to do with 'modernist' ideas, and councils of vigilance were appointed in every diocese to keep a check on them. As a dismayed Italian nobleman complained, 'since the death of Pope Leo, the Roman Curia has assumed towards world thought a reactionary attitude reminiscent of the days of Pius IX, when the Church was at war with everything and everybody.'

Towards the end of the century, energetic attempts were made by churchmen to meet the challenge of urbanization. In England, as early as 1848, a Christian Socialist movement had been founded by Anglican churchmen like Ludlow, Maurice, and Kingsley, who had been gravely disturbed by Chartism. Frowned upon by the Anglican leaders who did not accept that the social problems of the working classes were their direct concern, it had petered out by 1854. More effective were the Guild of St. Matthew (founded in 1877) and the Christian Social Union (founded in 1889). Both groups insisted that Christianity was concerned with all aspects of human society and that the Anglican Church must take an active interest in social problems. Throughout the century, however, the Anglicans never won the same trust among the working men as the Nonconformists, especially the Methodists.

In France, there was a prompt response to Pope Leo's suggestion that Catholics might form their own trades unions. Though employers were often suspicious and the powerful Marxist C.G.T. openly hostile, Catholic unions were firmly established by 1900. Among the many Frenchmen who were trying to blend Catholic and Socialist ideas, the most outstanding was the writer Peguy. He belonged to a group which from 1904 met regularly to discuss as Catholics the problems of an industrial society. 'The horror of Jesus', he once wrote, 'is terrifying for the rich. He loves only poverty and the poor.' Though Peguy and his friends were in trouble during Pope Pius' purge of modernism, their 'Catholic Socialism' did much to strengthen Catholicism in urban France. Another Christian Socialist party developed in Austria led by Karl Lueger. Its anti-semitism, however, was more obvious than either its Christianity or its socialism.

Whatever their problems in Europe, the achievement of the Christian churches overseas was spectacular. Wherever European adventurers and traders penetrated, there Christian missionaries followed them (and sometimes preceded them), to convert the native inhabitants from paganism. Some of the earliest missionary enterprises of the nineteenth century were British. The period between 1792 and 1813 was a great age for founding missionary societies—the Baptist, the London, the Church, and the Methodist Missionary Societies, and the British and Foreign Bible Society all appearing in these years. After 1815 Roman Catholic missionaries, led by the Jesuits, spread throughout the world. France might be the most anti-clerical country in Europe but she supplied more Catholic missionaries and more funds for their missions than all other countries combined. Inspired by such powerful personalities as the Scotsman Livingstone and the Frenchman Lavigerie, missionary activity increased as the years passed. By 1900 there were more than 61,000 Christian missionaries in Africa, Asia and Oceania, of whom 41,000 were Catholics, 18,000 Protestants, and 7,000 Orthodox. More than 41,000,000 non-Europeans called themselves Christians, the majority of whom had been converted between 1870 and 1900. This missionary enterprise, to which every Christian sect contributed, showed what vitality the Christian religion could still inspire.

Chapter 16
The Arts in an Industrial Age

The nineteenth century is a bewildering period in the development of European art. Style followed upon style, experiment upon experiment. There was much controversy about the merits of rival styles and fundamental debate concerning the nature of art itself. Furthermore, the relation of the artist to society significantly altered. In the years immediately after the French Revolution, artists like the painter, David, and the composer, Beethoven, were inspired by revolutionary ideals and felt themselves to be an integral part of a new and improving society. Most of their work was appreciated by the public as soon as it appeared. Half a century later, however, there had developed, in the words of Sir Kenneth Clark, 'a chasm in the European mind as great as had split Christendom in the sixteenth century and even more dangerous. On the one hand were the new middle classes, nourished by the Industrial Revolution. It was hopeful and energetic but without a scale of values. . . . On the other side of the chasm were the finer spirits—poets, painters, novelists. They mocked the respectable middle classes . . . and called them philistines and barbarians.' In return, much of their work was met with public ridicule when it first appeared. Most artists reacted to the Industrial Revolution with horror. When Robert Burns, the Scots poet, visited the famous Carron ironworks in 1787, he left these lines scratched upon a window pane.

> We cam no here to view your works
> In hopes to be mair wise
> But only lest we gang to Hell
> It mae be no surprise.

A deep nostalgia was felt for the pre-industrial past, as expressed by William Morris (1834–96) in his poem 'Earthly Paradise'.

> Forget six counties overhung with smoke
> Forget the snorting team and piston stroke
> Forget the spreading of the hideous town
> Think rather of the packhorse on the down.
> And dream of London, small and white and clean.
> The clear Thames bordered by its gardens green.

By the end of the century, many artists were isolated from and antagonistic to the society round about them.

At the risk of some oversimplification, it is possible to detect three main phases in the course of European art between 1789 and 1914 when music, painting, sculpture, and architecture were all affected by a similar prevailing mood. The first, or Classical, phase was drawing to a close in 1789. Its chief characteristics were its respect for the achievements of the ancient Greeks and Romans and its confidence in the powers of reason. Artists were ready to express themselves through certain accepted forms and according to certain rules, many of which had been laid down in classical times. The second, or Romantic, phase succeeded Classicism between 1800 and 1830. Romanticism stressed feeling rather than reason, while Classicism had always subordinated feeling to reason. 'The artist's feeling', wrote the German Romantic painter C. D. Friedrich (1774–1840), 'is his law.' 'Rules and models', declared the English literary critic, William Hazlitt (1778–1830), 'destroy genius and art.' With this stress on the feelings of the artist and its rejection of accepted rules, the Romantic era was inevitably one of great individuality and experimentation. Towards the end of the nineteenth century a new mood began to prevail. The emphasis was no longer on the expression of the individual artist's feelings but on the best way to express the essential nature of the particular art form— painting, sculpture, music, or architecture. 'Art', wrote Oscar Wilde in 1891, 'never expresses anything but itself.' When the Russian composer Stravinsky was asked just before World War I what was his principle aim as a composer he replied, 'I produce music itself. When music itself is not the aim, music suffers.' This third phase is represented in architecture by the work of the American, Sullivan, in the 1880s and 1890s, and of the Germans Behrens and Gropius between 1900 and 1914, in painting by the Cubist period of Picasso and Braque in Paris between 1906 and 1914, and in music by Bartok in Hungary after 1907, and by Stravinsky in Paris after 1910. It is often termed 'Modernism' since some of the most important trends in the contemporary arts are inspired by the innovations of the years from 1880 to 1914.

Music

In 1789 Joseph Haydn was 57 and W. A. Mozart 33. Thus two of the greatest composers the world has known were at the height of their powers. Between them they had brought the classical form in music to maturity. They wrote sonatas and symphonies in which both the pattern of the movements and that of the harmonies within the movements were governed by rules which musicians of the time found no difficulty in accepting. Using this classical framework, Haydn and Mozart were able to produce music of great individuality, and Mozart in particular of emotional power.

Mozart died in 1791, aged only 35, Haydn in 1809. The outstanding composer of the next generation was Ludwig van Beethoven (1770–1827). He was born in Bonn in Germany, the son of a musician employed by the Elector of Cologne. His father, realizing his son's exceptional gifts as a pianist, quickly developed them as a source of family income. When he was barely seven, Beethoven was appearing in public as a child prodigy. Fortunately his musical education was taken in hand by Neefe, the court organist at Cologne and an excellent teacher. He had no doubt about his pupil's potential. 'If he goes on as he has begun', Neefe noted when Beethoven was still only 12, 'he will certainly become a second Mozart.' When he was 17, Beethoven did in fact have a meeting with Mozart in Vienna. Mozart listened to him playing for a while, then gave him a tune and asked him to improvize around it. So impressed was he by Beethoven's response to this challenge that he exclaimed to some of his friends waiting in an adjoining room, 'keep an eye on this fellow, one day he'll give the world something to talk about.'

By now Beethoven was showing comparable talent both as a composer and as a pianist, and some of the Viennese aristocracy put up the money for him to continue his musical studies and to develop as a composer. Nonetheless, in his twenties he remained best known as a pianist. When he was thirty, however, he was overtaken by one of the worst tragedies than can happen to a musician, he began to go deaf and was forced to concentrate on composing. Eventually he became so deaf that he could hear nothing of the works that he had written. But there was no lessening of his skill as a composer. His last compositions, especially those he wrote for string quartet, are now regarded as among the most impressive music ever written.

Beethoven was a difficult man, even before the tragedy of his deafness. Moody, suspicious, and extremely proud, he often treated his patrons with astonishing rudeness. He never married and tended to live in squalor without noticing it. 'In society', a contemporary wrote, 'he gives the impression of a very able man, reared on a desert island and suddenly introduced into the civilized world.' With the onset of deafness, his moodiness and suspicions increased and his behaviour became quite eccentric.

Unlike Haydn and Mozart who composed with ease and fluency, Beethoven's compositions emerged only after much thought and effort. He began thinking about his Ninth Symphony for instance in 1812 and did not complete it until 1823. Nonetheless his output was large—nine symphonies, seventeen string quartets, thirty-two piano sonatas and many other instrumental and choral works including an opera. Beethoven was also a genuinely liberal composer. The revolutionary ideals of freedom, equality, and brotherhood actively inspired him. The best way of understanding the emotional power of liberal ideas in the early nineteenth century is to go to a performance of his opera *Fidelio*, which is the story of the triumph of freedom and virtue over tyranny. In one scene political prisoners, unjustly held by the tyrannous governor, are allowed out into the open air for a few moments. As they emerge, they sing a hymn to freedom, the words of which run—'O happiness to see the light, to feel the air and be alive once more. Our prison is a tomb. O freedom, freedom come to us again.' The accompanying music is of quite exceptional beauty.

Like Haydn and Mozart, Beethoven usually composed within the sonata/symphonic form. He wrote, however, on a grander scale. His symphonies are longer. They demand larger and more varied orchestras which include the piccolo and trombone for the first time. They have a new vigour and appear more openly emotional. For this reason Beethoven, though firmly in the classical tradition, may be regarded as pointing the way towards Romanticism.

The first indisputably Romantic composer was C. M. von Weber (1786–1826) for whom Beethoven had a great respect although Weber was sixteen years his junior. They met in Vienna when Weber was supervizing the production of his opera *Euryanthe*. He was greeted by Beethoven, who was dressed in a shabby green dressing-gown, with 'so there you are, my boy; you're a devil of a fellow! God bless you!' Weber's compositions are more loosely organized than Beethoven's. He aimed to represent moods and feelings more directly. He was fascinated by the relationship of literature with music and his works which have proved most lastingly popular are his operas like *Oberon* and *Der Freischütz* (the Marksmen) in which he was able to represent human emotion in musical terms much more directly than was possible in the sonata/symphonic form.

In the years after Weber's death, various composers explored further the connection between literature and music. Inspired by a poem or a novel or a play, they composed music to reflect the mood of the story or even of particular incidents within it. For instance, Franz Liszt (1811–86) composed a symphony inspired by the *Divine Comedy* of the mediaeval Italian poet Dante and piano music inspired by his contemporary, the French poet, Lamartine. The composer who went furthest in this direction was the Frenchman, Hector Berlioz (1803–69). English writers—Shakespeare, Sir Walter Scott, and Byron for instance—were for him a constant source of inspiration. So too was the German Goethe. Some of his music virtually tells a story. One of his most popular works nowadays is the 'Fantastic' Symphony, completed in 1830. According to an 'Introduction, which Berlioz supplied with the music, the symphony 'develops, in such a way as they may be musical, different situations in the life of an artist'. In each situation, the artist is in a different mood towards the woman with whom he has

287

fallen head over heels in love. He starts in delirious joy and ends in total horror when he realizes that she is quite untrustworthy. The loved one is represented by a musical theme which appears in each of the five movements and which Berlioz termed the *idée fixe* (fixed idea). Each movement conveys in musical form the changing moods of the story. Berlioz thought and acted on a grand scale. He wrote a Requiem to be staged by an orchestra of 155 (including 16 kettle-drums), four brass bands, and a choir of 700–800 voices. Clearly there had been a change from the elegance and restraint of the classical tradition.

The dominant figure of the Romantic period in music was a friend of Berlioz, the German Richard Wagner (1813–83). Wagner was the son of a minor Saxon civil servant. Though his family was deeply interested in music, he did not begin a serious study of music until he was seventeen. A turning point of his life, he later main-tained, was when he first heard a performance of Beethoven's *Fidelio*. This fired his ambition and before long he was making his living as an operatic conductor and composing his own operas. He had a tempestuous life. At first his operas had mixed receptions and, since he was very extravagant, he was constantly in debt. He was often in political difficulties. Openly sympathetic towards the 1848 revolutions, he was banished from Germany from 1849 to 1861. From 1864 to 1865 he lived in Munich where the eighteen-year-old King of Bavaria, Albert, who greatly admired his music, gave him a home and a pension. Before long, however, his favoured position with the king and his readiness to meddle in political matters upset the king's older advisers and caused his banishment from Munich. Eventually he established his family at the small Bavarian town of Bayreuth where he spent his last years building a theatre to be devoted to the performance of his operas. After considerable financial difficulties, the Bayreuth theatre was com-pleted and continues to this day as the home of Wagnerian opera. Wagner was exceptionally arrogant, promiscuous, and irresponsible in matters of finance. He was also a musical genius whose operas, or music dramas as he preferred to call them, are among the outstand-ing artistic achievements of the nineteenth century.

The stories of most of his operas are drawn from old German legends and their language is German though hitherto most operas had been in Italian. By writing his own texts (or libretti as they are usually known) he was able to blend more closely the drama and the music. He also developed a technique which he called the *leit-motiv* (or leading motive). In a way similar to Berlioz' introduction of his *idée fixe* into each movement of the Fantastic Symphony, Wagner had special musical themes to reflect the main ideas of the opera and repeated them in varied forms as the drama unfolded. His orchestra-tion was both subtle and rich. Again like Berlioz, he demanded

Detail from one of J-L David's best-known works: Napoleon, with Josephine kneeling at his feet, and with the Pope sitting a trifle unhappily behind him, crowns himself Emperor— Notre Dame

larger orchestras with powerful brass sections including tubas and bass trombones. He also made extensive use of harp and percussion. His operas are very long, a typical performance lasting from four to five hours. Many of them were nationalistic, grandiose hymns of praise to Germany's heroic past. When he was not composing music, Wagner was writing political pamphlets. He was strongly anti-semitic and, as he grew older, a fervent nationalist and anti-democrat. It is perhaps no coincidence that he was Hitler's favourite composer.

In the second half of the nineteenth century, composers explored so many different avenues that it is impossible to give them a common label. National pride led many to investigate the musical past of their country and to build compositions round the folk-music tunes which they discovered. Others, like Debussy and Ravel in France, reacted sharply against Beethoven and Wagner and aimed to compose music which combined the clarity and balance of eighteenth century music with a new colour and vividness. Another group, which included Bruckner, Mahler and Richard Strauss, extended the Romantic tradition writing symphonies and operas of great complexity and intensity of feeling.

The most complete rejection of Romanticism came in the first year of the twentieth century and was most clearly expressed by the Russian, Igor Stravinsky (1882–1971). He was born in St. Petersburg and, though his family was very musical, his father being an opera singer, he trained to become a lawyer. At the age of twenty, however, he met the gifted composer, Rimsky-Korsakov, and decided to become a musician. His first teacher was Rimsky-Korsakov whose daughter he married in 1908. When he was twenty-five, he met Diaghilev, director of the famous Russian ballet who was experimenting with new and controversial dance sequences. Diaghilev gave him a chance to show his ability by commissioning three ballet scores—*Firebird* (1910), *Petrouchka* (1912) and *The Rite of Spring* (1913). The first two, which were gay, tuneful, and influenced by folk-music, caused no great stir. *The Rite of Spring*, however, was a different matter. Soon after the curtain rose on the first performance, there was pandemonium in the audience. The majority were jeering or hissing, the minority demanding that the new masterpiece be properly heard. So great was the din that neither the audience nor the dancers could hear the orchestra. As the uproar continued, one of the audience recalled how 'a young man seated behind me in a box stood up during the course of the ballet to enable him to see more clearly. The intense excitement under which he was labouring betrayed itself when he began to beat frantically on the top of my head with his fists.' What seemed so shocking about the music was that it had neither tunes nor conventional harmonies. Instead it had fragments of melodic

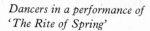

phrases, nerve-racking rhythms and discords. Stravinsky's state-
ments about his intentions were as uncompromising as his music.
He denied that music could and should reflect a non-musical idea
or action. As he wrote in 1921, 'I have never tried in my stage
works to make music illustrate the action or the action the music . . .
I have never made 'applied music' of any kind. Even in the early
days, I was concerned with a purely musical construction. The only
forms which are worth anything are those which flow from the
musical material itself.' The Romantic tradition in music could
hardly have been more firmly rejected.

Painting

In 1785 the Frenchman, J-L David, completed his *Oath of the
Horatii*, a painting which was immediately regarded by contemporaries as marking a new renaissance. Both in subject matter and in
form, it is severely classical (see page 292). David was influenced by
the sculptures of ancient Rome and by the recently discovered
frescoes of Pompeii and Herculaneum. The strength of the painting
lies in the simplicity and balance of the composition. The colours
are sombre and the eye is not distracted from the central figures by
any ornament or piece of landscape.

David soon became the most influential artist in France and built
up a school of painters who adopted a style similar to his own. He
welcomed the French Revolution, first becoming a deputy in the
National Assembly and then chairman of the Convention. The
revolutionary leaders thought highly of him and commissioned
him to record some of the heroic events of the period. In 1790, for
instance, the Jacobin Club commissioned a commemorative

painting of the Tennis Court Oath. The great respect he had for the Jacobin leaders helped him to create what many now regard as his masterpiece *the Death of Marat*. After Robespierre's fall, he turned to Napoleon as the only possible saviour of France and once Napoleon seized power, he became the best patronized painter in France. He idolized the Emperor and produced a stream of portraits and set-pieces, of which the huge *Coronation* is the best-known, which glorified the Bonaparte dynasty. Stylistically, he did not greatly change. There is the same sense of balance and restraint in *Coronation* as in *Oath of the Horatii*. The composition is essentially simple, and the bright colours come more from an accurate rendering of the ceremonial dress than from the artist's imagination (see colour plate facing p. 188).

Napoleon, however, encouraged other painters whose style was very different from David's. Take for instance, Girodet's *Ossian receiving the Generals of the Republic* painted in 1802 (see below). 'I don't understand that painting. No, my good friend, I don't understand it at all', said David to Girodet and to an acquaintance he later

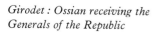

Girodet : Ossian receiving the Generals of the Republic

David: The Oath of the Horatii

commented: 'Either Girodet is mad or I no longer know anything about the art of painting.' David's puzzlement is understandable. The qualities of his paintings were those of the Classical tradition, Girodet in contrast looks forward to the Romantic age. His subject matter is wreathed in fantasy and mystery. The composition is swirling and complicated by a thousand eye-catching details. There is little restraint and no balance. The aim of the picture is above all to convey a feeling of glory and heroism.

The best representative of the Romantic period in painting is another Frenchman, Delacroix (1798–1863). His personality was as striking as his style. Almost certainly he was the illegitimate son of Talleyrand, the ex-bishop who survived the Revolution and Napoleon to end up as Foreign Minister of the restored Bourbons. He had a good education and so much talent that he could have been as good a poet or musician as he proved to be a painter. Though his health was poor, he had an arresting appearance. The writer Gautier recalled 'his ferocious beauty, strange, exotic, almost disturbing'. He travelled widely. England had a great impact on him, especially the plays and poems of Shakespeare and Byron and the landscape paintings of Constable. So too did Spain and Morocco with their hot colourful primitiveness. Animals, particularly wild animals, fascinated him and he was often at Paris Zoo during feeding time.

Unlike David, who painted with meticulous care, Delacroix painted in a fury. Only thus, he believed, could the full force of artistic imagination be expressed. One of his early and most famous works is *The Massacre of Chios* (see below). Though the composition is carefully thought out, what immediately claims attention is the overwhelming mood of violence and desolation. For Delacroix intensity of emotion counted for more than perfection of form. One of the best ways of appreciating the difference between Classicism and Romanticism is to compare *The Massacre at Chios* with *The Oath of the Horatii* (left).

Delacroix : The Massacre at Chios

In painting, as in music, so many developments occurred in the middle of the nineteenth century that to label them all Romantic does not mean very much. One important development was landscape painting which became popular throughout Europe. Germany produced C. D. Friedrich, France the Barbizon school, but the artists who took landscape painting to its highest point were the Englishmen Constable (1776–1837) and Turner (1775–1851). Of Constable, Leslie, his biographer, wrote: 'I have seen him admire a fine tree with an ecstasy like that with which he could catch up a beautiful child in his arms.' He devoted his life to capturing the spirit of nature as he found it in the English landscape. Both he and Turner realized that a natural atmosphere could never be captured on canvas by mere imitation. It could only be conveyed through an imaginative use of colour, line and light. The more traditional painters and critics found many of their pictures distasteful. When Constable presented his *Willows by a Stream* for exhibition at the Royal Academy, he was told to 'take away that nasty green thing'. Similarly, Turner's *Rain, Steam and Speed* (see colour plate facing p. 189) in which the steam engine is barely recognizable but the impression of rain, steam, and speed is exceptionally vivid was dismissed as 'one of Mr. Turner's little jokes'.

In the second half of the century, an attempt in France to solve the problem with which Turner and Constable had grappled—how best to capture the essence of landscape on a two-dimensional canvas—led to the formation of one of the most famous groups in the history of painting, the Impressionists. The group really dates from 1869 when Monet (1840–1926) and Renoir (1841–1919) used to meet at the riverside café of La Grenouillère just outside Paris to work out how best to paint the ripples and reflections of the river. Also attached to the group were Manet (1832–1883), Sisley (1840–99), Pissarro (1830–1903) and others. Their conclusion was, in Monet's words, that 'light is the principal person in the picture'. As the light changes, so the object being painted in that light will alter in appearance. Since light is always changing out of doors the landscape artist can only hope to capture a fleeting impression which will be primarily a blend of light and colour. The Impressionists produced pictures, therefore, which concentrated upon atmosphere and colour. Sunlight, steam, fog, or water was suggested by patches of colour, and objects were seldom clearly outlined (see colour plate facing p. 312). Few artists have been so ridiculed. At their first exhibition in 1874, the public could hardly believe its eyes. An art critic of the time described his feelings as follows, 'I have seen people rock with laughter in front of these pictures but my heart bled when I saw them. These would-be artists call themselves revolutionaries, Impressionists. They take a piece of canvas, colour and brush, draw a few pieces of colour on them at random and sign the whole thing with their name. It is a delusion of the same kind as if the inhabitants of Bedlam picked up stones from the wayside and imagined that they had found diamonds.' Not until the end of the century did the public come to realize that the Impressionists' way of looking at the world was in fact a valid one and that they had brought a brilliance of colour to painting such as the world had never before seen.

Their impact on their fellow painters was revolutionary. By emphasizing light and colour, impression rather than imitation, they undermined the age-old idea that the painter's chief function was to imitate as accurately as he could what he saw. Simultaneously, the perfection of photographic techniques further reduced the need of the painter to be an accurate imitator since the camera was inevitably so much more accurate. The next generation of painters were forced to re-think their aims from first principles.

The most significant of the next generation was Paul Cézanne (1839–1906). His father was first a hat maker and then a successful banker of Aix-en-Provence in Southern France. While at school, Cézanne showed a talent for drawing and decided that he wished to become a painter. Though his father hoped that he would become a lawyer, he allowed him to go to Paris in 1861 to try his luck as an art student. He became acquainted with the leading Impressionists and showed some of his paintings at their exhibition of 1874. For many years, however, he had little success either in selling his paintings or in winning a reputation. Dividing his time between Paris and Provence, he lived off the allowance granted him by his reluctant father and worked away developing his style.

Cézanne was a solitary, anti-social man with a reputation for obstinacy and, despite his private means, miserliness. Though his genius went unrecognized for most of his life, he never doubted his own powers and worked away comparatively careless of the opinions of any but his few close friends.

He felt that the Impressionists were too concerned with the superficial appearance of things. His aim, he said, was 'to unite Impressionism with something more solid and enduring like the art of museums'. Beneath the fleeting impressions which is all our eyes can retain there is a lasting reality which it is the function of the artist to discover. In all Cézanne's paintings, whether they are landscapes or still-lifes or portraits, colour is subordinate to the shapes which make up the composition. One has only to compare Cézanne's landscapes with Monet's to appreciate his emphasis on structure (see colour plate facing p. 313). As he grew older, he concentrated on organizing his compositions on the basis of certain basic geometrical shapes. 'Everything in nature', he wrote, 'models itself according to the sphere, the cone or the cylinder.'

His last most geometrical work had a deep influence on the young Braque (1882–1963) and Picasso (1881–   ) working together in Paris between 1907 and 1914. By emphasizing still further the underlying structure of objects and by presenting these objects as if seen from different viewpoints in the same picture, they produced striking compositions which at first sight look little more than complex geometric patterns. On close viewing hints of faces, or figures, or objects can be traced. In these works the cube is the recurring shape so the style is known as 'Cubism'. From Cubism to completely abstract art was only a short step, the first completely abstract painting appearing in Paris in 1910. So in painting as in music, artists in the early twentieth century totally rejected the aims and the methods of the past.

Architecture

Since the Italian Renaissance, the architecture of Greece and Rome had strongly influenced European architects and still did so at the end of the eighteenth century. David's counterpart in architecture was C. N. Ledoux (1736–1806). Between 1760 and 1806 he designed many buildings in the Paris area of which the most striking were the toll-houses on the edge of the capital. These, like David's paintings, give the impression of great solidity, strength and balance. Though Ledoux made use of classical details, his style is very individual. He had no time for those architects who aimed only to imitate the buildings of ancient Rome. Classical details should be used only when and where they suited the architect's purpose which would depend on the function of the building that he was designing. The Englishman Sir John Soane (1753–1837) had much in common with Ledoux. His buildings have a similar sombre solidity and classical details are always used in an individual way. Perhaps the most original architect of this period was the Prussian Friedrick Gilly (1772–1800). So short was his life that few of his designs got beyond the drawing-board. The plan he drew up for a National Theatre in Berlin (1798) shows a remarkably modern looking building. The classical details are there but they are subordinate to a simple solid structure which reflects clearly its function as a theatre and makes no effort to pretend that it is a Greek temple. Indeed, in 1800 it looked as if a new style of architecture was emerging which would shake itself free from the styles of history to design buildings which, because they met the needs of a new industrializing society, would look quite different from the buildings of the past.

However, things turned out differently. Another century had to pass before architects stopped looking over their shoulders to the styles of the past. The period of Ledoux, Soane, and Gilly (usually known as neo-Classicism) gave way instead to the Romantic phase, of which the chief characteristic was a revival of historic styles and a concentration on detail which had to be as accurate an imitation as possible. In the opinion of Sir Giles Gilbert Scott, an extremely successful Victorian architect, the chief function of architecture was 'to decorate construction'. The good architect was the one who got the decoration right.

During the nineteenth century almost every style devised by man was revived somewhere in Europe. The English were particularly keen on Gothic Revival (i.e. reviving medieval styles). As early as 1750, Horace Walpole had enlarged his house at Strawberry Hill just outside London in a light-hearted Gothic style. From 1796 onwards, the country house of the mad millionaire William Beckford at Fonthill in Wiltshire was being built to look like a mediaeval monastry. As the nineteenth century got into its stride, Gothic Revival became less fantastic, more serious and virtuous. Influential in bringing about this change of mood was A. W. Pugin (1812–52). Pugin was the son of a refugee from the French revolution who settled in London in 1793. He began his career as a theatrical designer but in the 1830s was converted to Roman Catholicism and devoted the rest of his life to designing Gothic buildings and to writing about architecture. Pugin was the fiery champion of the Gothic style. For him it was the only right style since it was the only one which was genuinely Christian. He loathed the new industrial cities, over-populated and dominated by factories. He contrasted them with the cities of the middle ages—airy, spacious, and dominated by Gothic churches. He also loathed the classical style. It was, he wrote 'a Pagan monster which has ruled for so long and with such powerful sway over the intellects of mankind'.

His most famous work was done as assistant to Sir Charles Barry, architect responsible for the Houses of Parliament which had to be

Barry and Pugin : The Palace of Westminster begun 1836

I. K. Brunel : The Clifton Suspension Bridge

The interior of the Paris Opera House

rebuilt after the disastrous fire of 1834. The basic plan was by Barry, the interior and exterior detail in the Gothic style by Pugin. It was an interesting partnership since Barry was happiest in the classical style. In fact the ground plan and composition of the facades of the Palace of Westminster are in the best classical tradition and Pugin is said to have described the famous river front which overlooks the Thames with disapproval as 'all Greek'. In the 1840s and 1850s, British architects fought the Battle of Styles, on one side the Gothicists, on the other the Classicists. For the rest of the century, the Gothicists held the upper hand though the Classicists won some famous victories. When Giles Gilbert Scott offered a Gothic design for the new Foreign Office, it was rejected out of hand by Lord Palmerston who would only have classical (which Scott duly provided). His Gothic designs reappeared in London in 1868 at St. Pancras Station.

The rest of Europe was never so keen on Gothic as the English though the French and Germans erected some Gothic churches. Neo-Renaissance and neo-Baroque (i.e. reviving the styles of the fifteenth to the seventeenth centuries) was more to the continental taste. The first neo-Renaissance building was the Beauharnais Palace in Munich (1816). Another good example is the Town Hall of Paris, immensely enlarged in an 'improved' version of its original sixteenth century style between 1837 and 1849. Later the more extravagant neo-Baroque became fashionable, the Paris Opera House by Charles Garnier in 1861 being an early and famous example of the style (left below). A good example of neo-Baroque is the huge Palace of Justice in Brussels, designed by Poelaert and built between 1866 and 1883.

Many nineteenth century buildings were designed, however, not by architects but by engineers and it was the latter who pioneered the new building materials like sheet glass, iron, and steel, and reinforced concrete which the Industrial Revolution made available.

The achievements of the nineteenth century engineers were remarkable. They built magnificent bridges, such as I. K. Brunel's suspension bridge across the Avon Gorge at Clifton with its span of 700 feet (left above). They also erected exhibition halls of a vastness undreamt of even by Roman emperors. The Crystal Palace, built in Hyde Park to house the Great Exhibition of 1851, had an area of 770,000 square feet. Joseph Paxton, its designer, was a man of little formal education who had made his reputation as head gardener of the Duke of Devonshire. For his employer's house at Chatsworth in Derbyshire he had designed great conservatories of glass on a wooden framework. For the Crystal Palace he modified this design, replacing the wooden framework with iron. The whole building was prefabricated and its erection took only nine months.

Some of the most original work with iron and steel as building materials was done in France and one of the most original and influential of all nineteenth century engineers was the Frenchman, Gustave Eiffel (1832–1923). Eiffel first intended to become a chemist and only by chance became an engineer. Realizing the strength and flexibility of the new types of iron and steel being produced by European industry, he pioneered new construction methods and quickly made a reputation as a bridge builder. His Maria Pia bridge across the Douro in Portugal (1877–8) and his Truyère bridge near Garabit in Central France (1880–4) attracted widespread interest because of their advanced design. Eiffel showed that the techniques that he used for his bridges could be adapted for roofing and for supporting walls, and the company he founded in 1867 to market his designs won contracts all over Europe. He was also an effective propagandist both for himself and for iron and steel. In 1887, he won permission to build the 984-foot tower which to this day bears his name on the south bank of the River Seine in Paris. When it was built it was the highest building in the world. It aptly symbolizes the confidence of a nineteenth century engineering and anticipates how important iron and steel were to become in the buildings of the future.

The Eiffel Tower

The engineers were bitterly criticised by the art critics of the time. None of them had a good word for the Eiffel Tower. Paxton's Crystal Palace was dismissed by Pugin as 'a glass monster' and by Ruskin, the most influential critic of the day, as 'a cucumber frame'. Ruskin could not accept that iron and steel might inspire a new and impressive style of architecture. 'We want no new style of architecture', he wrote in 1849. 'The forms of architecture already known to us are good enough for us and far better than any of us.' By the end of the century, however, many young architects were thinking quite differently. In their opinion, it was the engineers rather than the architects of the previous generation who had produced the better buildings. When Paxton designed the Crystal Palace and Eiffel his bridges, both concentrated on producing structures which fulfilled their functions as economically as possible. The beauty and power of their designs appeared to follow because they were severely functional. In contrast the architects had tried to conceal the function of their buildings behind 'historic' decoration, with results that the rising generation of architects regarded as disastrous.

Between 1900 and 1914 there was a dramatic reaction against revivalism. Germany led the way. In 1907 the *Deutscher Werkbund* (German Work League) was founded to bring about a drastic improvement in industrial design and to show that factories and machines could be designed as attractively as palaces and furniture. In the same year Peter Behrens (1868–1940) was appointed design consultant of A.E.G., the huge electrical combine. Behrens had trained as a painter and was head of the Dusseldorf School of Art

before he joined A.E.G. He had already designed a number of private houses which were uncompromisingly functional. At A.E.G. he designed everything from factories to note-paper (above). Behrens's influence is hard to exaggerate. He may not have been an architect of the first rank but he demonstrated how architects and industry could work together and how modern technology demanded a modern architecture. Three of the most famous architects of the twentieth century—Walter Gropius (1883–1969), Mies van der Rohe (1886–1969) and Le Corbusier (1887–1965) worked in his office before World War I. In 1914, the Deutscher Werkbund organized an exhibition in Cologne to which Gropius, in collaboration with Adolf Meyer, contributed a model factory. This is a twentieth-century building even more than Behrens' factories (below). The roof is flat and the stress is on the horizontal. The staircases spiral round in glass and steel frames so that their inner structure is quite exposed. There is no ornamentation. The form of the building follows directly from its function.

Gropius and Mayer: Model Factory for the Cologne Exhibition, 1914

Chapter 17
Europe and the Wider World

At the end of the eighteenth century, the great days of European empires seemed past (see map 13). The famous empires of Spain and Portugal were shadows of their former glory; the Dutch were facing great difficulties in the East Indies; the French empire had been swallowed up by the British during the Seven Years War (1756–63) and the British had themselves lost the most prized part of their empire when the American colonists won their independence in 1783. Nor was there much desire to rebuild these empires. Even Britain, whose possession of Canada, India, and the West Indian islands made her much the most powerful imperial nation, was interested less in the conquest of new lands than in the extension of her world-wide trade by peaceful means. However, as a glance at map 14 shows, the situation at the end of the nineteenth century was quite different. In 1914 the only continents not directly ruled by Europe were the Americas, though of course most of the population of the U.S.A. was of European stock. Most of Africa and all Australasia was controlled by Europeans. Even the

Map 13 The World in 1789 showing European possessions

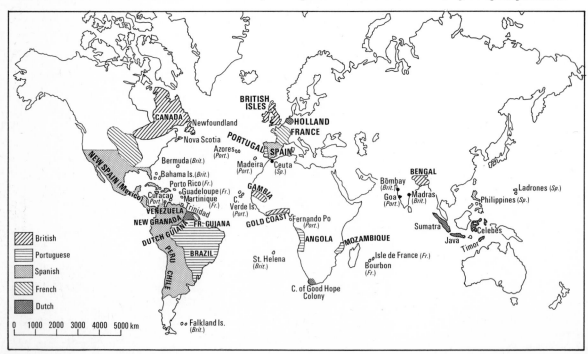

vast continent of Asia was dominated by Europe. Russia had expanded across the north and centre. Britain had tightened her hold on India and had conquered Burma and Malaya. Between them Britain and Russia controlled Persia and Afghanistan. In South-East Asia the Dutch held on to some of the East Indian islands while Britain controlled the rest. The French were masters of Indo-China. If the proud Chinese empire still maintained an appearance of independence, its vital ports and trade routes were in European hands. In fact the only non-European power of any significance in 1914 was Japan which owed its strength to its swift imitation of European economic and technical know-how.

The population explosion and the industrial revolution played an important part in bringing about this European dominance. In 1800 there were probably about 910,000,000 people in the world, of whom about 1 in 5 were European, 2 in 3 Asiatic and 1 in 10 African. The rest were American or Australasian. By 1914, the world population had almost doubled to 1,800,000,000 of which 1 in 3 were of European stock. Thus, though the population of the world had been increasing fast, that of Europe had been increasing even faster. One result of this increase, the rapid growth of industrial towns, we have already seen in Chapter 5; another was emigration. In the mid-nineteenth century 370,000 Europeans on average were emigrating each year. Between 1890 and 1914 the average had risen to 900,000. Between 1846 and 1914, 30–40,000,000

Map 14 The World in 1914 showing European possessions

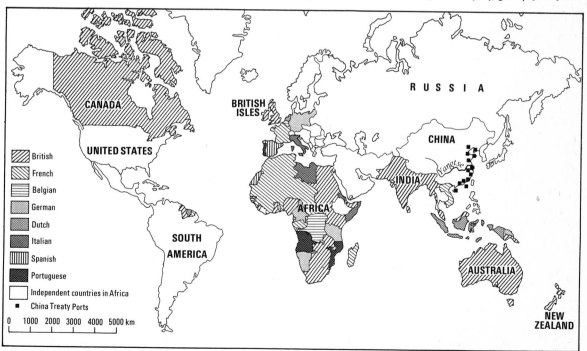

Europeans must have sought a new life in a different continent. The majority went to America but millions went elsewhere. It was an extraordinary movement of human beings. This 'great exodus from Europe', noted a United Nations report in 1953, 'has been the most important migratory movement of the modern era and perhaps the largest in all human history.'

A movement of peoples, however, is not in itself enough to conquer the world. What enabled the nations of Europe to partition the other continents between them without lengthy campaigns of conquest was the exceptional superiority that they enjoyed in the techniques of warfare as a result of the industrial revolution. One effective weapon was the steamship with its accurate guns. A bemused Chinese general, attempting to defend the capital, Peking, from an Anglo-French fleet, sent back the message to the Manchu Emperor that his job was quite impossible because 'the ships of the enemy can fly across the water without wind or tide, with the current or against it.' On land, the Martini-Henry rifle and the Maxim machine gun gave the same kind of advantages. Hilaire Belloc summed up Britain's success in her colonial wars as follows: 'We have the Maxim gun and they have not.' In the Matabele War of 1893 which won modern Rhodesia for European settlement, the victorious settler army captured Bulawayo, the Matabele capital, at the cost of five dead and twelve wounded. The African losses were a thousand times greater.

The Industrial Revolution not only gave Europeans military superiority it also gave new encouragement to European business-men and traders to look for new markets overseas. Throughout the nineteenth century, the search for commercial profit was a major reason for the European penetration of other continents. Lord Elgin, Viceroy of India from 1862 to 1863, described how English traders swarmed into the Far East, hoping for 'a new world open to their trade so vast that all the mills of Lancashire could not make stocking stuff sufficient for one of its provinces'. Similarly rubber lured the Belgians in the Congo jungle, diamonds the Germans into the deserts of South-West Africa. However, profit was by no means the only aim nor traders the only travellers. Explorers, missionaries, scientists, adventurers, soldiers, civil servants, farmers, and industrial workers all went overseas and all contributed in their own way to the increasing control of the world by Europeans. In comparison with other civilizations, European civilization was unusually vigorous in the nineteenth century and this vigour expressed itself in a multitude of ways.

There were three phases in the expansion of Europe in the nineteenth century—from 1789 to 1830, from 1830 to 1875, and from 1875 to 1914. In the first, the only active country was Britain whose main interests were the discovery of new markets for her manufactured goods and the suppression of the slave trade. In the second, emigration increased and a number of nations, notably France and Russia, interested themselves more in other continents. In the last phase, which began with the purchase of a controlling interest in the Suez Canal Company by the British government, all the great powers of Europe, with the exception of Austria-Hungary, indulged in a frenzied scramble for colonies the world over.

Phase 1 1789–1830

The Napoleonic Wars exhausted Europe and Britain alone emerged from them with the energy and the strength to pursue a policy of overseas expansion. Her strength in 1815 was enormous. Her navy was as large as all the other navies of Europe combined and by the Vienna Settlement she had secured a number of coastal settlements and islands which allowed her to take a firm grip on the trade-routes of the world.

In the Indian sub-continent, British political power was extended by wars against the local rulers and her economic power by the aggressive selling of her manufactured goods, of which Lancashire textiles were the most important. Between 1815 and 1832 there was a sixteenfold increase in the imports of British cottons into India. Consequently the previously quite flourishing Indian textile industry collapsed. Its annual value in the same period shrank from £1,300,000 to £100,000. Further east, British influence was extended by adventurers such as Stamford Raffles and James Brooke. In 1819 Raffles persuaded a hesitant British government to buy the uninhabited island of Singapore from the Sultan of Johore. 'What Malta is in the West', he declared, 'that may Singapore be in the East.' Brooke, without any official British assistance, managed to establish himself as the hereditary and absolute ruler of Sarawak!

British power was also used in a less selfish way. The horrors of the eighteenth-century slave-trade out of which Britain had made a great deal of money eventually led to an international campaign for the abolition of slavery. In this campaign the British government played an active part. In 1807 the slave-trade was abolished within the British empire. In 1815 Britain persuaded the Congress of Vienna to condemn the trade and agree at least 'to the wish of putting an end to a scourge which has so long desolated Africa, degraded Europe and affected humanity'. These proved pious words with little practical effect, so in 1833 the British government went a step further and abolished the institution of slavery within the British Empire. In the next forty years British diplomats and the British fleet worked energetically to suppress the slave-trade wherever they could.

It was a long and difficult job. The U.S.A. did not abolish slavery until 1865, nor Brazil until 1871, so there were still big profits to be made by slave-traders who were prepared to take risks. Danger made them more skilful and ruthless. Fearing interception by British naval patrols, slaving captains hid their live human cargoes under casks and coils of rope. Some, it was reputed, even threw their cargoes overboard if a search seemed likely. Despite the co-operation of the French, the Portuguese, the Austrians, Prussians, and Russians, British commissioners investigating the trade in West Africa in 1844 had to report that 'it is increasing and is conducted perhaps more systematically than ever'. One of the most systematic traders of the period was a Spaniard, Dom Pedro Blanco. He had a personal empire in the impenetrable islands at the mouth of the River Gallinas. He lived with a harem in the depths of a swamp and, as an Italian associate later described, had 'the horizon constantly swept by telescopes to announce the arrival of anti-slavery cruisers'. A full-scale naval blockade by the British navy was required to end the Gallinas trade and it was not until the American market finally dried up in the 1870s that the terrible traffic of human beings across the Atlantic finally came to an end.

Phase 2 1830–1875

The second phase of European expansion began in 1830 when the French invaded Algeria. The cause of the attack was an incident when the Dey of Algeria (an ex-pirate) struck the French consul (who was involved in a crooked financial deal) with his fan. The government of Charles X decided that the French army needed some action and the French people distraction from home affairs. It proved a much tougher war than expected. A brilliant guerrilla leader—Abd el Kader—rallied the Algerians and, though unable to prevent the French from capturing Algiers, held onto the mountainous inland regions. The fighting was vicious. In 1841 a French officer returning from an expedition against the guerrillas described how 'the soldiers were themselves ashamed. About 18,000 trees were cut down; houses have been burnt; women, children and old men slaughtered.' Not until 1879 was the country settled enough to be handed over from military to civilian rule.

In the same period other parts of Africa became better known. Mungo Park had explored most of the Niger river before his death on the Bresa rapids in 1805. Between 1849 and 1853 the German Barth made a remarkable journey from the Mediterranean to the Niger, and between 1840 and 1856 David Livingstone, the greatest explorer of the period, travelled widely in Central Africa waging a one man war against Arab slave-trading and charting

Livingstone and Stanley going from Ujiji to the Rusizi River in central Africa, in 1872

the course of the River Zambezi as he did so. Apart from Algeria, however, the only part of the continent where Europeans conquered more land was in the extreme south. Britain had gained Cape Town during the Napoleonic wars and in 1823 took possession of Durban, the only other good harbour on the South African coast. The British, however, were not the first colonists in South Africa. The Dutch (or Boers, as they were known) had been in the Cape area since the seventeenth century and they disliked British rule, especially when in 1833 it meant the end of African slavery without adequate compensation for the owners. Between 1835 and 1837 many Boers left Cape Colony for good. Taking part in the Great Trek they journeyed north-west across first the Orange and then the Vaal rivers and eventually established two new states, the Orange Free State and the Transvaal. Both the British and Boers fought bloody wars with the Bantu peoples who at this time were moving south from Central Africa. One of the greatest Bantu leaders was the Zulu king Shaka. Mortally wounded in 1828 by his two half-brothers, he said to his murderers as he lay dying before them, 'You think that you will become chiefs when I am dead. But it will not be so, for the white man is coming and you will be his slaves.' In 1879 the British destroyed Zulu power for ever at the battle of Ulundi.

Between 1830 and 1875 the white man took control of the Australian continent. In the early nineteenth century, about 70,000 British convicts were transported to Australia and to this number were added thousands of free emigrants. These settlers were soon in conflict with the natives of Australia, the aborigines, who were a nomadic people and found themselves driven from their traditional hunting grounds to make way for the farms established by the Europeans. When they tried to return, they were massacred, particularly bloody slaughters occurring at Pinjarra in 1833 and at Myall's Creek in 1838. After 1843 the British government took responsibility for the continent and tried to protect the aborigines. From a distance, however, they could do little. It is estimated that when the British first arrived in Australia there were between 100,000 and 200,000 aborigine inhabitants. After one hundred years of European settlement, they had been terribly reduced.

Asia also suffered from European aggression between 1830 and 1875. Russia acquired the most territory, firstly at the expense of the tribes of Central Asia and later of the Chinese Empire. Muraviev, Governor of Eastern Siberia, aided by Count Ignatiev, took Russian power as far as the Pacific. In 1860 the port of Vladivostock was founded. The ancient empire of China fell victim to other European powers besides Russia. In many ways the Chinese could claim to be as civilized as Europeans. The Manchu dynasty had maintained peace, law, and order for centuries and possessed a well informed and efficient civil service run by the mandarin class of scholar nobles. But it suffered from serious weaknesses. The army was no longer reliable. The system of local government prevented the Emperor from acting quickly in times of emergency. Perhaps the most serious weakness of all was the contemptuous ignorance of almost all Chinese officials of the world outside China. The foreigner was, by definition, a barbarian. As a sign of humility foreign diplomats had to kow-tow (prostrate themselves) in the Emperor's presence. Chinese port officials tended to treat foreign traders with a similar high-handedness. Consequently the Chinese were neither militarily nor mentally prepared to meet the European challenge when it came.

Trouble first came from Britain, whose diplomats, Lord Macartney in 1793 and Lord Amherst in 1816, refused to kow-tow to the Emperor. Open war eventually occurred in 1840 over the drug opium, which the British were shipping from India. The Chinese, alarmed by the social demoralization caused by the drug and the currency problem caused by its import, tried to ban the trade. There had been friction for years between the Canton port officials and the British merchants and after some incidents in 1839 during which British citizens were roughly handled, Britain declared war on China. The British fleet threatened Peking, captured

The Opium War: the British steamboat 'Nemesis' causes havoc among the Chinese junks in Anson's Bay, January 7th 1841

Nanking and there forced the helpless Emperor to come to terms. By the Treaty of Nanking which ended the Opium War in 1842 the British received 20,000,000 dollars, the island of Hong Kong, and free entry to five Chinese ports. British diplomats moreover were to be treated as equals. Almost simultaneously, the French extracted trading rights for themselves from China by the Treaty of Whampoa.

The Opium War was the first of many humiliations which the Chinese had to suffer in the nineteenth century. Between 1850 and 1864, when the Emperor was weakened by the Taiping rebellion, Britain, France and Russia made further gains. In 1857 an Anglo-French force seized Canton. In 1860 it entered Peking, burnt down the Summer Palace and secured the Treaty of Peking which gave European traders the free navigation of the Yangtze river (the major trade route of Central China) and opened further seaports to European traders. The Russians pushing westwards and southwards occupied the region between the Amur and Ussuri rivers. Despite these setbacks, many Chinese still managed to remain contemptuous of the foreigner. 'In my opinion, wrote Prince Kung, one of the Emperor's advisers, 'all the barbarians have the nature of brute beasts. The British are the most unruly but the Russians are the most cunning.' Some of the more thoughtful, however, began to ask openly whether something was not seriously wrong with Chinese society. In 1864 Li-Hung Chang, a senior civil servant, noted in a memorandum to his superiors, 'our civilian officials are plunged in the elucidation of classical texts and in the refinements of calligraphy while our military men are, for the most part, ignorant dullards. Our education seems quite divorced from utility. When we are at peace we despise foreign invention while if trouble comes our way, we explain that it is impossible for us to learn how to employ such contrivances.' Such realism remained rare in China for many years to come.

Neighbouring Japan was opened to Europeans even more suddenly. At the beginning of the nineteenth century, though there was a Japanese Emperor, real power, including the control of foreign policy, lay in the hand of the Tokugawa family. The head of the Tokugawas had the title Shogun. Since 1637 the Shogun's policy had been complete isolation from Europe. In the nineteenth century, however, the power of the Shogunate was in decline. It had developed in a society of warriors and peasants, and by 1850 the cities of Japan were growing, and a prosperous merchant class had come into existence. In 1854 Commodore Perry of the U.S. navy sailed into Tokyo Bay and demanded the opening of Japanese ports to foreign trade. As helpless as the Emperor of China against western naval power, the Shogunate did as Perry directed. The Treaty of Kanagawa (1854) opened two ports to American ships, and trading rights were soon granted to Britain, Russia, France, and Holland also.

Westernization in Japan (men only!)

The Japanese reacted much more energetically than the Chinese to the European challenge. Li-Hung Chang continued his 1864 memorandum by pointing out how much the Chinese could learn from the Japanese. 'In the past', he wrote, 'Britain and France thought that they could do what they liked in Japan but the people of that country took courage from their indignation and sent their brightest youths to study in workshops and in arsenals. They also brought machinery for making arms so that they could manufacture equipment at home. They are now capable of navigating steamships and of making artillery.' In fact a political and social revolution occurred in Japan. In 1868 the Tokugawa Shogunate was overthrown, and behind the apparent restoration to power of the Meiji Emperor a group of clever politicians began modernizing Japan on western lines. They were so successful that in some ways Japan became more European than Europe. In 1907 a Japanese guidebook told its readers 'Japanese officials now attend their offices in frock or morning coats and European visitors attending them should be similarly attired. At garden parties and special social functions, frock coats and tall hats are expected.' The modernization programme made sure that Japan kept her independence and it also caused her, again in the best nineteenth-century European fashion, to become very aggressive. In 1894 she too attacked the unfortunate Chinese, gaining Formosa and the Pescadores Islands, and in 1904–5 fought and defeated Russia.

Another part of the Far East to pass under European control in this period was Indo-China (modern Vietnam, Laos, and Cambodia). The first French colony which included Saigon was established in 1862. Further land was added in 1867 and in 1874, and in 1882 Hanoi was occupied. French engineering also divided Asia from Africa. Ferdinand de Lesseps, backed by British and French capital, completed the Suez canal in 1869, thus shortening the voyage from Western Europe to India and the Far East by four thousand miles or more.

Phase 3. The Scramble for Colonies 1875–1914

Between 1830 and 1875, therefore, there was a considerable extension of European influence in non-European areas. Sometimes this took the form of conquest and colonization, as in Algeria or in Australia, but more often of increased trading activity (as in South America and the Far East). In the 1860s European governments showed little enthusiasm for further colonization. 'Those wretched colonies', said Disraeli, referring to Australasia, 'are a millstone round our necks.' In 1871 the French government offered Bismarck all the French colonies if only he would spare Alsace-Lorraine. The offer was rejected with scorn. Colonies for Germany, said Bismarck, 'would be just like the silken sables of Polish noble families who have no shirts.' In the 1870s and 1880s, however, there was a complete change of attitude. Imperialism, or the building of colonial empires overseas, caught the imagination of the peoples of Europe. First explorers and travellers, then journalists and professors led the popular demand for overseas expansion. Imperialist societies came into existence, in Germany the Colonial Society and the Society for German Colonization, in Britain the Imperial Federation League for example. Rising politicans like Ferry in France and Joseph Chamberlain in Britain were ardent imperialists. Even the older politicians could not remain unaffected by the popular mood. Between 1874 and 1880 Disraeli encouraged frankly imperialist policies. So did Bismarck after 1885.

Just why this change of mood happened and why the nations of Europe decided between 1875 and 1914 to conquer as well as trade with as much of the world as possible is hard to explain. Lenin, leader of the successful Communist revolution in Russia in 1917, put forward a neat explanation which most communists still regard as correct. Capitalism, he argued, had so developed in the U.S.A. and in Western Europe that in the late nineteenth century it had to find new areas overseas for investment or die. Imperialism was the final phase of capitalism. If new markets had not been found, then the collapse of capitalism in Western Europe, which Marx, the founder of Communism, had predicted, would have come about. Thus, according to Lenin, economic necessity forced Europe to conquer the world. This theory, however, is too neat. The economic statistics do not support it. Nor does it explain why countries like Russia and Portugal, which were economically backward, were as imperialist as Britain, France, or Germany. Important though the desire to make money undoubtedly was, there were many other reasons why Europeans suddenly scrambled for colonies after 1875.

One significant reason was the uneasy balance of power within Europe. After 1871 the fierce nationalism of the time which could find no outlet in Europe without threatening a major war could express itself much less dangerously in a competition for colonies. 'Every virile people has established colonial power', von Treitschke, the Berlin professor, told his university audiences, and the news that one of their countrymen had planted their flag on yet another distant exotic landmark, watched in fear and wonder by the indigenous inhabitants, made the peoples of Europe feel very manly. Imperial expansion often seemed little more than a huge competitive game with profits, power, and prestige as the victors' prize.

Some empire-builders acted or claimed to act for better motives. Many felt that they had the duty to bring civilization where

Monet: Lavacourt? *Winter*

Cézanne: Rocky Landscape

barbarism reigned or that they must help Christianity to triumph over paganism. When the Frenchman Ferry was attacked in the Chamber of Deputies for his expansionist policies in Indo-China, he emphasized the duty of the French government to spread the benefits of French civilization throughout the Far East. The British more than anyone insisted that imperialism was a moral duty. As Gladstone put it in 1884 when Germany began colonization; 'If Germany is to become a colonizing power all I say is "God speed her!" She becomes our ally and partner in the execution of the great purposes of Providence for the advantage of mankind!' A British poet of the period, Rudyard Kipling, invented the phrase 'the White Man's Burden' to stress the tremendous moral responsibility that imperial conquest brought with it. Speaking in the Town Hall, Birmingham, in 1907, an ex-Viceroy of India, Lord Curzon, declared that 'Empire can only be achieved with satisfaction and maintained with advantage provided it has a moral basis. . . . I think that it must be because in the heart of a British endeavour there has burnt this spark of heavenly flame that Providence has so richly blessed our undertakings.' It must be said, however, that there was a powerful streak of hypocrisy in this European presentation of imperialism as a moral duty and the British were the most hypocritical of all. The Irishman, G. B. Shaw, commented just before World War I: 'The Englishman is never at a loss for a moral attitude. As the great champion of freedom and independence, he conquers half the world and calls it Colonization. When he wants a new market for his adulterated Manchester goods, he sends a missionary to teach the gospel of peace. The natives kill the missionary; he flies to arms in defence of Christianity; fights for it; conquers for it; and claims the market as a reward from Heaven!'

Whatever their motives, the energy of European colonizers in the period 1875–1914 was exceptional. In 1875 Disraeli, now Britain's Prime Minister, bought, with the help of Rothschilds banking house, the controlling interest of the Suez Canal Company for the British government. The following year King Leopold II of Belgium summoned an international conference to discuss the development of Central Africa. These two events led to the scramble first for Africa and then for any other part of the world which seemed ripe for conquest.

Disraeli's action, which was taken in order to protect the sea-route to India, the lifeline of the British Empire, at once caused complications. The Khedive of Egypt, from whom Disraeli bought the shares, was hopelessly in debt to British and French businessmen, and in 1878 Britain and France jointly took over the administration of the Egyptian economy. This co-operation did not last long. Faced with an Egyptian nationalist revolt, the French pulled out only to see the British take control first of Egypt and then, in 1898, of the Sudan. To balance the position in North Africa, France conquered Tunisia in 1881 and by 1914 was in control of most of Morocco.

The explorations of Livingstone and Stanley in Central Africa had fired the imagination of Leopold of Belgium. 'There are no small nations', he believed, 'only small minds.' He was determined that empires should not be the monopoly of the major powers. 'All the non-appointed lands on the surface of the globe', he argued, 'can become the field of our operations and of our success.' He gave financial backing to the International African Association which, led by Stanley, opened up the Congo Basin. Leopold's schemes soon worried both the British and the Portuguese whose territories in South Africa, Angola, and Mozambique had no clear boundaries. The Belgian king then held an international conference at which he played off the major powers against each other. By the end of it he was recognized as the king of the Congo Independent State and it was agreed that any African territory could be acquired by a European state simply by an act of occupation!

The race for colonies now began in earnest. After 1884 the German government gave active support to their explorer Dr. Peters in East Africa; in 1885 the Italians gained a foothold in Eritrea. In the same year the French took possession of the north bank of the Congo, which became French Equatorial Africa. Britain moved swiftly to counter these moves which she regarded as a threat to the strong trading position that she had already built up in Africa. She annexed Bechuanaland in 1885, Rhodesia in 1889, Nyasaland in 1893. The driving force of this expansion was Cecil Rhodes, Prime Minister of Cape Colony. He was the son of a Bishops Stortford vicar and had made himself a multi-millionaire out of South African diamonds and gold. He dreamed of a railway from which would run all the way from the Cape to Cairo through British territory. Fear of Germany, Rhodes' ambition and greed for the gold round Johannesburg led Britain to fight the Boer republics of the Orange Free State and the Transvaal in 1899. After a bitter three-year struggle (the Anglo-Boer War) these republics were swallowed up in the Union of South Africa. Fear of Dr. Peters' successes in East Africa (modern Tanzania) caused the British government to take control of British East Africa (modern Kenya and Uganda). French successes in West Africa also caused British activity in that part of the continent. All Nigeria was conquered and Gambia, Sierra Leone, and the Gold Coast more closely controlled.

Between 1889 and 1900 the French also acquired a huge empire mainly in West Africa. Much of it was desert, however, and when they tried to establish themselves in the Sudan, they were immedi-

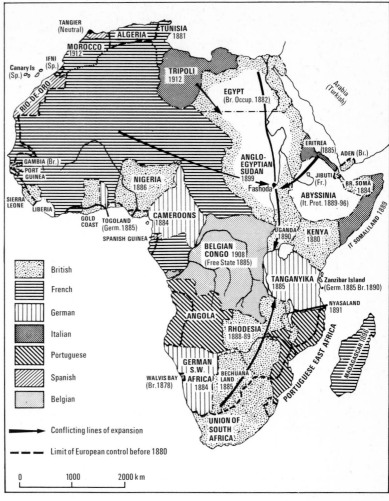

Map 15 Partition of Africa

ately driven out by the British general, Kitchener. This incident,
which took place at Fashoda in the Upper Nile valley in 1898, was
the nearest that Europe came to war during this hectic period of
colonization. In much the same period the Germans took possession
of four largish colonies—South-West Africa, German East Africa,
and Cameroons, and Togoland—while the Italians added Italian
Somaliland to their possessions in East Africa. Despite this success,
Italy felt that she was falling behind in the race. She rashly attempted to double her African empire by conquering the mountainous kingdom of Abyssinia. At Adowa in 1896 the Italian army was
completely defeated by the Abyssinian general Menelek. The
humiliation of being the only European power defeated in this
period by non-Europeans was to some extent forgotten when in
1911 Italy took Tripoli in North Africa from the decaying Turkish
Empire.

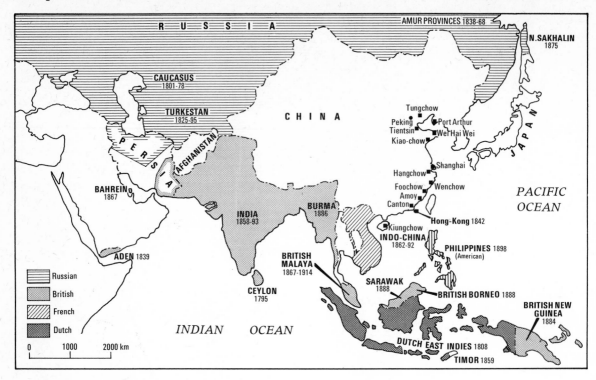

Map 16 Partition of Asia

Before 1875 less than one-tenth of Africa was controlled by Europeans. In 1914 only Liberia and Abyssinia, less than one-tenth of the continent, was not controlled by Europeans (see map, p. 315).

A similar if less thorough partition of Asia also took place in the same period (see map 16). Here France and Russia set the pace. France seized the island of Tahiti in 1881 and extended her Indo-Chinese territories in the year which followed. In 1875 Russia acquired the island of Sakhalin from Japan and in the 1870s and 1880s extended her power southwards towards Persia and Afghanistan. As in Africa, Britain acted to counter these moves, which she regarded as threats to the empire which she already possessed. In 1886 Burma was conquered. In 1904 a military expedition was sent into Tibet. In 1907 Persia was divided into three zones, British, Russian, and neutral. In 1900 a joint German-French and British force invaded China to crush the anti-European Boxer rising and added various Chinese ports to their possessions. With the U.S.A., the European powers also divided between them the islands of the Pacific. When the scramble was over, the British Empire covered 20 per cent of the world's land surface (10,500,000 square miles) and included 400,000,000 inhabitants, the French 4,500,000 square miles with 52,000,000 inhabitants, and the Germans 1,000,000 square miles with 14,000,000 inhabitants.

In the vast areas conquered, European rule brought on the one hand great benefits, on the other terrible suffering. It brought peace, stability, law, and order to areas which previously had been haunted by tribal warfare, tyranny, and barbarism. It also led to rapid industrial and agricultural improvements. The French, for instance, introduced the rubber industry to Indo-China and doubled the area of rice cultivation. In Morocco, Marshall Lyautey carried out an impressive number of public works in the years before World War I. The British in India built an extensive railway network and a vast irrigation scheme in the valley of the Ganges. Moreover, wherever Europeans settled, they introduced the major social advances of nineteenth-century Europe—medicine, sanitation, education, electricity, and so on. For the majority of non-Europeans, European conquest meant greater security and prosperity.

On the other hand, colonization too often meant frightful non-European suffering and humiliation. The British slaughtered the Australian aborigines, the French the Algerians and Indo-Chinese, and the Dutch the Indonesians. Even worse atrocities were committed by the Belgians in the Congo and by the Germans in South-West Africa. King Leopold's main interest in the Congo was the profitable rubber industry. His white officials and their African subordinates used terror to get as much rubber as cheaply as possible. In 1903 the British consul in the Congo, Roger

A victim of the regime of King Leopold in the Congo

Casement, sent home hair-raising reports, one of which quoted an African eye-witness as follows: 'We lived [searching for rubber] always going farther and farther into the forest and when we failed and our rubber was short, the soldiers came to our towns and killed us. Many were shot, some had their ears cut off, others were tied up with ropes around their bodies and taken away.' Eventually the Congo became such an international scandal that in 1908 the Belgian government took over its administration from the king, whose personal responsibility it had previously been. There was then some improvement. In South-West Africa the Herero tribe rebelled in 1904 against the Germans who were taking over their traditional tribal lands. The German government sent out 15,000 troops under General Trotha, whose stated policy was to use 'streams of blood and streams of money to annihilate the rebellious tribes'. Between 60,000 and 80,000 Hereros were killed and thousands more were transported from their homes to work as labourers on European farms.

There was also economic exploitation. Though European investment in overseas industry brought some improvement in the living standards of the area, the bulk of the profits passed into European pockets. South African gold, Congolese rubber and Indo-

Atop an elephant, the British Viceroy of India makes his state entry into his capital, Delhi

Chinese salt for instance were developed not to benefit the native population, whose poverty was desperate and whose cheap labour allowed big profits to be made, but for the shareholders in London, Brussels, and Paris, who were usually extremely wealthy.

Finally there was the constant and needless humiliation of non-Europeans. On account of their unquestionable technological superiority and the racial theories which were then commonplace in Europe, almost all Europeans took it for granted that they, the Whites, were a superior people who automatically deserved the respect and service of the inferior coloured races whom they ruled. The British in India were the most insufferable. In 1883 the British Viceroy provoked a tremendous outcry among British residents when he suggested that Indian magistrates should be allowed to try Europeans. It was a scheme, said Mrs. Beveridge, leader of the opposition, 'to subject civilized women to the jurisdiction . . . of men whose social ideas are still on the verge of outer civilization.' An officers' club in India in the late nineteenth century had to display this notice: 'Gentlemen are requested to refrain from beating the natives.'

The British, however, had no monopoly of racial arrogance. 'The Chinaman', wrote a French Jesuit priest, 'hates foreigners because our excellence is conspicuous. He is not particularly clean in his person, habit or surroundings. He has no lofty ideals, sense of duty, trustworthiness or active courage and is deficient especially in the higher moral qualities.' As for the Dutch in South Africa, they often regarded Africans as sub-human. In 1798 an English visitor to Cape Colony reported the anguish of a Boer farmer whom the British authorities had flogged and imprisoned for ill-treating a native. 'His, however, were not the agonies of bodily pain but bursts of rage and resentment for being put on a level with the Zwarte Natie (Black Native) between whom and themselves the Boers conceive the differences to be fully as great as between themselves and cattle.'

With this firmly held sense of superiority, the European nations were seldom ready to give political responsibilities to their non-white subjects. Only at the very end of our period did the British in India and the French in Indo-China begin to think seriously of sharing their power with their subjects, and not until after World War I was the granting of independence to colonial territories considered at all. Consequently, there was much hatred for the powerful and arrogant European throughout the world and European ideas of nationalism and democracy began to inspire non-European peoples to resist their masters.

Some of the first murmurings of this nationalist feeling were heard in the British Empire. The Indian Mutiny of 1857 was in

some ways a nationalist rising against the foreign master, who was interfering too much in traditional religious customs. In Egypt the revolt in 1882 led by Colonel Arabi was directed against the hated foreigner and may be regarded as the first African nationalist rising. At the end of the nineteenth century, Indian opposition to British rule, led first by Gokhale and then by Tilak, grew more formidable. Tilak, convinced that the British could only be shifted by force, launched a campaign of terrorism from 1905 to 1909 which only petered out when he was imprisoned. In Indo-China determined resistance to French rule began in 1883. Its aim was complete independence. In 1885 the young Emperor Ham-Nghi asked 'from the rich their goods, from the powerful their strength, from the poor their hands to recapture the country from the invaders'. Despite his betrayal to the French, guerrilla resistance continued until 1913 (see fig. 120). Further east in China, anti-European feeling took a violent and horrible form when 'the Boxers', a secret and fanatically anti-Christian society, began exterminating Christian missionaries and their converts in 1900. Though a European army entered Peking and took its own violent and horrible vengeance, Chinese nationalism had come to stay.

One event more than any other shook the prestige of the white man in the eyes of the world before 1914—the defeat of Russia by Japan in 1905. The European was not invincible after all. In 1906 an Englishman in Persia noticed the difference; 'It almost seems', he wrote, 'that the East is waking from its slumber and we are about to witness the rising of these patient millions against the exploitation of an unscrupulous West.' (See map 14, p. 303.)

A Tibetan swordsman dies from the machine gun bullets of Colonel Younghusband's expedition of 1904

Chapter 18
The Art of War

The nineteenth century was one of the most peaceful centuries in European history. Previously the chief families or states of Europe had fought each other frequently for many years at a time. In these wars—for example the War of Spanish Succession (1702–13), the War of Austrian Succession (1740–48)—a number of European states were usually involved. In contrast, once the Napoleonic Wars were over, the only armed conflict of the nineteenth century which involved more than two major powers and which lasted more than a few months was the Crimean War and it was fought over a limited geographical area on the very edge of Europe. Other important wars like the Risorgimento campaigns of 1859–60 and the Prussian triumphs of 1864, 1866 and 1870–1 involved only two major powers at a time and were short and localized. The next genuinely continental war after the Napoleonic Wars was in fact World War I. Nonetheless no century transformed the 'art' or business of war more than the nineteenth century. A typical eighteenth-century army would be numbered in tens of thousands. Marshal Saxe, a successful French general during the War of Austrian Succession (1740–8), argued that any army greater than 46,000 was too large for effective command. In August 1914 the German armies which attacked France through Belgium numbered 840,000. While the eighteenth-century army was officered by aristocratic amateurs and manned by vagabonds and criminals, with the result that desertion seriously reduced its fighting efficiency, the armies of 1914 were led by highly trained professionals and manned by conscripts who were themselves well-trained, well-disciplined and of high morale. The eighteenth-century infantryman would be armed with a flintlock muzzle-loading musket with a maximum range (at which accuracy was impossible) of 200 yards. His 1914 counterpart had a breech-loading rifle with a magazine whose maximum range was 2000 yards which was capable of accurate fire at 600 yards and his regiment would be supplied with machine guns. Mid-eighteenth-century artillery was made of bronze, so heavy that it could only be moved slowly on ox-drawn carriages. It fired cannon-balls a few hundred yards. Artillery in 1914 was made of steel and could be moved comparatively speedily by horse. It fired high explosive shells with considerable accuracy over distances which could often be measured in miles. At sea, a good example of an eighteenth-century warship

was the *Victory* first launched in England in 1765. Made of wood, she displaced 3,500 tons. She had four decks, three masts and one hundred guns which were made of bronze and designed for broadside pounding at a close range. By 1914 the Dreadnought type of battleship was made of steel and displaced 25,000 tons. Her oil-fired turbines made possible a speed of twenty-five knots and her ten 12-inch guns were designed for accurate shelling over thousands of yards (see page 336).

H.M.S. Victory

Tragically, almost no-one predicted correctly the horrors which these improvements in armies and armaments would cause in the event of a continental war. It was left to the twentieth century to find out.

Significant improvements in weapons and in military thinking occurred just before the French Revolution. French and British craftsmen managed to devise lighter iron guns with better firepower than the traditional bronze cannon. They were light enough to be moved by horses. Thus artillery became more mobile. Three French officers, Du Teil, Gribeauval and Guibert, were the first to work out strategy and tactics suitable for this new mobile artillery, and many of their ideas found their way into the French army drill book of 1791. While training as an army officer, Napoleon made a thorough study of military theory and was particularly influenced by Guibert. His Italian campaign of 1796–7 with its rapid marches and counter-marches to catch the enemy off-balance, its novel use of artillery and massed columns and its readiness to attack again and again, is an inspired example of the new method in action.

Left *Early nineteenth-century artillery*

Right *Early nineteenth-century rifle*

The French introduced another vital element in modern warfare —the nation in arms. Carnot of the Committee of Public Safety began a system of conscription in 1793. In less than a year he increased the size of the French army from 300,000 to 750,000. After 1798 all Frenchmen between the ages of twenty and twenty-five had to do National Service. In order to meet the French challenge, the major powers, except Britain, had to adopt some kind of conscription during the Napoleonic Wars, and almost 1,000,000 men fought at the Battle of Leipzig in 1813.

At sea there was no important advance in naval design before 1815. The British, however, developed some new and effective tactics. In the 1780s Admirals Kempenfelt and Howe devised a method of signalling messages between ships by means of flags. Such signalling made possible much more co-ordinated naval tactics as Howe showed on 'the Glorious First of June', 1794, when he broke through the French lines from a windward position and won a famous victory. Such a manoeuvre would have been suicidal without the co-ordination of the fleet which signalling made possible. Between 1794 and 1805 the British won six decisive victories over the French. The last and most decisive of all was that of Nelson at Trafalgar in 1805. Nelson was a commander of genius with an extraordinary ability to inspire his captains and his men. At Trafalgar he brought the tactic of breaking the line from windward to perfection. His double column attack cut the Franco-Spanish fleet in three and led to the capture of eighteen out of the thirty ships. Trafalgar made the British navy mistress of the oceans of the world for the next century.

The impact of the Industrial Revolution on the technology of war was not really felt until after 1815. Then came a stream of inventions which not only increased immensely the destructive capacity of weapons but demanded a quite new strategic approach. By 1842 the percussion cap, which made the firing mechanism on the musket weatherproof, had replaced the flintlock. Barrels were rifled to improve accuracy, and, by 1850, Captain Minié of the French army had perfected a bullet which expanded on firing to make a gas-tight fit with the barrel, thus greatly increasing the range and accuracy of the rifle. Meanwhile in 1839 Johannes Dreyse had designed a breech-loading mechanism which the Prussian army adopted in 1842 (the so-called 'needle gun'). Not only could breech-loaders be fired more quickly than muzzle-loaders but they could be both fired and loaded from a lying position. Magazines, first developed in the U.S.A., were attached to breech-loading rifles by the French in 1866 and the British in 1871. Reliable breech-loading mechanisms were harder to develop for artillery. William Armstrong in England had some success by 1859 and breech-loading Krupp artillery was used in the Seven Weeks War of 1866. However, they were not very reliable and it was not until the final years of the century that muzzle-loading artillery was phased out.

At sea the technological pioneers were France and the U.S.A. Britain, with her huge wooden sailing fleet, had no desire to see it rapidly made obsolete and showed a cautious attitude to new ideas. The Admiralty turned down the designs by the Swedish engineer Ericsson for a screw propeller driven by a steam engine, only to see it taken up by the U.S.A. which launched the first propeller driven warship, the *Princeton*, in 1843. By 1850 both France and Britain had followed America's lead and from then on sail was doomed. Between 1850 and 1870 ironclads—wooden steamships with their hulls reinforced by iron armour five inches thick—made their appearance driven by increasingly powerful and efficient engines. In 1870 the British navy gave up sail altogether.

In the 1820s an ingenious French artillery man, Colonel Paixhans, had designed a shell which could be fired instead of solid shot from naval cannon. This shell was like a bomb, filled with gunpowder, the explosion of which was controlled by a time fuse. Such a shell would plainly cause havoc inside a wooden ship. In 1837 the French introduced shell guns and their example was quickly followed by the British and the Americans. Metal armour seemed the best defence against shell fire and the French began building a seagoing fleet of ironclads in 1857. Ironcladding provoked ever more powerful guns which in turn provoked thicker armour. Some warships in the 1870s had armour 24 inches thick. A good example of an 1870s warship was the British 'H.M.S. Devastation', completed in 1875. She displaced 9,330 tons of which 27 per cent was armour. Her top speed was 15 knots and she carried a powerful ram as well as four 35-ton guns in two separate turrets. At the time of her launching she was described as 'an impregnable piece of Vauban fortification with bastions mounted on a floating coalmine'!.

Besides these particular inventions, two other developments—railways and the electric telegraph—began to influence military thinking. Between 1830 and 1860 the railway network of Europe was established with the telegraph beside it. Troops could now be moved on a scale and with a rapidity hitherto impossible.

However, the military leaders of Europe were slow to re-organize their forces to make the best use of these changes. The Crimean War (1854–6), in which fought the armies of France, Britain, Russia, Piedmont, and Turkey, was so remarkable for the incompetence of the generals that few lessons about the nature of modern war were learnt beyond the importance of having well-trained professionals in command rather than privileged amateurs. Much the same was true of the campaigns in Northern Italy in 1859 between France and Austria. Though the French army was moved rapidly by train to the Italian border, its supply system soon broke down. The bloodiest battle, Solferino, happened by chance (see p. 180). The armies blundered into each other when neither side was expecting the other.

There was one European state, however, which was systematic-ally modernizing its army in the light of recent developments—Prussia. Since the reign of Frederick William I (1713–40) the Prussian army had been among the best in Europe. It was much the largest in proportion to the size of its population and each Prussian province was responsible for recruiting its quota of men. 'War', wrote the French statesman Mirabeau at the end of the eighteenth century, 'is the national industry of Prussia.' The country reacted strongly to its crushing defeats by Napoleon in 1806. National service on the French model was introduced and from 1813 all men between seventeen and forty had to do some form of military service. Unlike most other European countries, Prussia did not end this compulsory military service in 1815. In 1858 the Regent, William, and his Minister of War, Roon, decided on major reforms. They were fortunate in having two exceptional men to assist them. As Chancellor from 1862, Bismarck fought and won the political battles with the Prussian assembly which made the army reforms possible. As army Chief of Staff from 1857 Moltke put the reforms into effect.

Helmuth von Moltke (1800–91) is the most important single figure in the history of modern warfare. A man of brilliant intelligence and of great capacity for work, he realized that if large modern armies were to function effectively and make full use of railway networks and of fire-power, their central organization must be first class. He therefore spent much of his time building up the Prussian general staff. Each year he supervized personally the twelve best graduates from the Prussian War Academy. Those who did not meet his high standards were rejected without hesitation. By 1870, not only had he created the largest and most professional general staff in Europe but most of the brigade and divisional commanders of the Prussian army had trained under him. Thus the Prussian army came to possess a unique knowledge of modern strategy and unity of command.

Moltke was a meticulous planner who made sure that his army was prepared for any eventuality. Prussia had three possible enemies— France, Austria, and Russia—for each of which he had a plan ready by 1866. A key factor in any Moltkean strategy was rapid mobilization by railway. The Prussian military staff had realized the importance of railways in times of war at an early stage and part of the Prussian railway network was constructed with military needs in mind. Moltke's contribution was to work out how the speediest possible mobilization could be achieved and how the mobilized troops could be best concentrated to make a successful attack on the enemy. He was only partially satisfied with the mobilization of 1866 against Austria despite the overwhelming success of the Prussian army. He therefore reformed the mobilization procedure in time for the war against France in 1870. This time they ran more smoothly and played a key part in bringing about another swift and crushing victory.

The reforms which Bismarck and Roon pushed through the Prussian assembly provided Moltke with an army of more than 1,000,000 trained men by 1870. These Moltke armed with the Dreyse needle-gun and with Krupp breech-loading artillery. A new era in warfare began when this formidable war-machine destroyed the Austrian army in seven weeks in 1866 and the French army in eight weeks in 1870.

As a result of these Prussian victories a united Germany came into existence which was militarily the most powerful nation in Europe. Between 1870 and 1914 no European power, not even Germany, felt secure from attack by its neighbours, and all worked frenziedly to strengthen their military forces. Every major power except Britain introduced conscription on the German model. By 1898 Russia had 4,000,000 men under arms, France and Germany 3,000,000 apiece and Austria-Hungary more than 2,000,000. Every nation built up its own well-trained general staff and officers became much more professional. Between 1874 and 1896 arms expenditure by the major powers increased by 50 per cent. Rifles

Machine guns in action in the Balkans 1912

and pistols were further improved and machine guns were generally adopted (see above). The story goes that when the American, Hiram S. Maxim, was in Paris in 1881, a friend advised him: 'If you want to make a pile of money, invent something that will enable these Europeans to cut each other's throats with greater facility.' The result was the Maxim machine-gun, patented in the U.S.A. in 1883 and adopted in a modified form by the British army in 1891. The British model, known as the Vickers gun, weighed only 40 lbs and fired 650 rounds per minute. Moreover, by 1900, breech-loading artillery had been perfected which fired high explosive shells.

At sea, the arms race was even more intense. Tough light steel replaced the heavy ironcladding of the 1870s so that warships, though no less strong, were speedier. Naval guns grew even more powerful. A typical battleship of 1900 was the British *Royal Sovereign* displacing 15,000 tons with a speed of 18 knots and 12-inch guns. Six years later she was made obsolete by the *Dreadnought* (see p. 336), heavier and faster, with even bigger guns. Torpedoes were first used effectively in 1877 by the Russians against the Turks. In 1899 the French produced a submarine, the *Gustave Zédé*, which could sail at 8 knots, 60 feet below the surface, and two years later had 23 submarines built or under construction. That same year the British Admiralty ordered 5 to be built, though it noted cautiously 'what the future value of these boats may be is a subject for conjecture'. By 1904, however, Admiral Sir John Fisher was completely convinced of their value. There could be no doubt at all, he wrote, 'how vast was the impending revolution in naval warfare

The first British submarine

and naval strategy that the submarine would bring'. By 1914 every major navy was well equipped with submarines.

Strategic thinking failed to keep pace with these developments in armaments. So dazzling had been Moltke's successes between 1864 and 1870 that almost every military planner between 1870 and 1914 assumed that the next major war would be won by Moltkean methods. 'The first care of a nation which has to organize the defence of its frontiers', wrote the French general Derrécagaix in 1890, 'will not be to envelop its frontiers with a girdle of fortresses but to cover its territories with a net work of railways which will ensure rapid concentration.' Once concentration had been achieved by rapid, railway-based mobilization, the victorious offensive would be launched. 'Whatever the circumstances', wrote another French general, Foch, 'it is the intention to advance with all forces to the attack.' Major wars would be swift, sharp, and decisive. Comparatively little thought was given to defensive strategy.

If military planners had analyzed closely recent wars other than the Franco-Prussian War, they might have reached different conclusions. The American Civil War (1861–5) showed that wars of large armies with modern weapons need not be short and that rifle-power could be as effective in defence as in attack. It also showed that railways, if vital to supplies, could lessen as well as increase mobility. Nearer home, the Russians fought the Turks from 1877 to 1878. The Turkish commander, Osman Pasha, decided to hold the town of Plevna against the Russian advance. He strengthened his position with field fortifications and had his troops dig trenches. The heavily outnumbered Turkish defence, armed with the most modern rifles and artillery, held off wave after wave of Russian attacks for nearly six months. Plevna demonstrated that modern firepower could be used defensively with great effect.

In 1898 Ivan S. Bloch, a Polish businessman, wrote a book which was published with the title *The Future of War*. Modern weapons, Bloch argued, were giving ever increasing strength to defensive methods of warfare. In any future conflict soldiers would have to stay in trenches or suffer frightful casualties. On the battlefields there would be no breakthrough, only stalemate. If nations were determined to break this stalemate, they would have to face a long struggle and be ready to use all their economic as well as their military strength. First hardship then famine would follow for the civilian population. Eventually the organization of the state would collapse under the strain.

Though Tsar Nicholas of Russia was worried enough by reading *The Future of War* to call an international peace conference at the Hague to discuss the reduction of armaments, Bloch had little practical influence. He was a civilian, an amateur whom professional soldiers and politicians could safely ignore. The lessons of the American Civil War were ignored too and for the same kind of reason. The Americans were amateur soldiers, it was said. No European army would get so bogged down and suffer such enormous casualties. The confidence of the professional strategists in the short offensive and decisive war was strengthened by their analysis of the Russo-Japanese War of 1904–5. On land, the Japanese won the decisive battle of Mukden by an offensive strategy using 310,000 men along a forty-mile front. At sea, Admiral Togo annihilated the Russian fleet at Tsushima Straits by the offensive tactic of 'crossing the T'. Consequently the German plan for a future war against France, drawn up in 1905 (the Schlieffen Plan) and put into operation in 1914, assumed a complete victory in six weeks, while in Britain an influential section of the army tried to build up the cavalry as an important part of a general offensive!

As it happened, Bloch was right, the professional soldiers wrong. When a continental war broke out in 1914, the result was stalemate not swift decisive victory. In the four years that were needed to break the stalemate, 10,000,000 people lost their lives and the social fabric of most of Central and Eastern Europe disintegrated.

Chapter 19
Conflagration

In the last year of the nineteenth century, representatives of the major European powers met at the Hague to discuss whether the arms race which had developed between them might be halted. Their conference failed. So did a similar one in 1907 because suspicions among these powers were so great that they were convinced that their rivals were only calling a halt because they had achieved a lead in the race which they were afraid of losing. As the years passed, the suspicions only deepened. By 1911 European diplomats were generally assuming that a war would come sooner or later. In August 1914 it came, and proved to be incredibly larger, longer, bloodier, and more catastrophic than anyone had previously dared to imagine.

There were many reasons why a war should break out in 1914. One of the most important was the fact that few Europeans had any real horror of war itself. The wars that the generation of 1914 remembered most vividly were the Risorgimento campaign of 1859, the Austro-Prussian war of 1866 and the Franco-Prussian war of 1870. They had been short wars of rapid movement and conclusive victories. Only professional soldiers had died and there was little sustained civilian suffering. Their consequences, moreover, had been glorious. They had made nations. Most people assumed that the next war would be much the same—swift and conclusive with the domination of Europe as the tempting prize. Influential political theories of the time not only encouraged national pride but also the attitude that war was the natural form of rivalry between nation-states. The biological ideas of Charles Darwin were readily applied to human society. Animal species, Darwin had argued in the 1850s and 1860s, evolved by natural selection, a savage process in which animal preyed upon animal and only the fittest survived. Modern society, the Social Darwinists argued, is evolving in the same way. The strong nations prey upon the weak and only the fittest survive. Such a process is part of the natural order of things. The well-ordered state is one which ensures that, in the unending international struggle, it survives. Another rather older political theory, that of the philosopher Hegel, suggested a similar conclusion. He argued that the study of history demonstrated that progress occurred through the unceasing conflict of opposing forces. In international affairs progress came through the

331

conflict of nation-states, and ultimately one nation—in his view Germany (he was a professor at the University of Berlin)—must dominate the world. The central idea that violent struggle was natural, indeed central, to the existence of the nation state became part of popular consciousness. As a German cigarette advertisement put it just before the outbreak of war, 'War is an element in God's natural order of things.'

At the same time that nationalistic fervour was reaching a new pitch from Belfast to Belgrade and the popular feeling was that war might be as good a way of solving international disputes as any other, the European continent had become divided by a system of alliances into two hostile camps. Bismarck's extraordinary mixture of alliances, some open, others secret, which had completely isolated France from 1871 to 1890, was too complicated for his successors to maintain. On his resignation, the Kaiser seemed to take control of foreign policy. 'There is only one man who is Master in this Empire, and I am not going to tolerate any other', he announced. 'I am the balance of power in Europe since the German constitution leaves decisions about foreign policy to me.' William II was not, however, a really masterful man. Born with a withered arm of which he was acutely aware, he had a difficult childhood and reacted violently against his English mother. He grew up into an intelligent but restless man, conscious of his dignity, given to rash and grandiose gestures but always lacking in inner self-confidence. Consequently, he allowed many men to have a hand in foreign policy—chancellors, ministers, generals, and admirals. The resulting policy, though it usually looked belligerent, was often vague and sometimes contradictory. The lack of firm control in the German capital became only too evident in the diplomatic frenzy in the last days of peace in 1914. The influence of generals and admirals, always strong, grew stronger as war seemed to loom nearer and that of the professional diplomats and politicians correspondingly declined. Eventually the historic and anguished question was wrung from Berchtold, the Austrian Chancellor: 'Who gives orders in Berlin, Moltke (the army Chief of Staff) or Bethmann-Hollweg (the German Chancellor)?'

Lacking strong direction, German foreign policy after 1890 came to reflect more and more the aggressive nationalism of German public opinion. The Germans were conscious that they were the most powerful military nation in Europe and they intended to play a part in world affairs properly proportionate to their strength. They were very keen to build up a colonial empire since the size and wealth of a nation's colonial territories was popularly felt to be a good indication of a nation's power and prestige on a world scale. Though by 1914 their overseas empire was nearly 1,000,000 square miles in area and included 14,000,000 inhabitants, the Germans felt thwarted. The French Empire spread over 4,500,000 square miles and included 52,000,000 inhabitants, while the British controlled 10,500,000 square miles and more than 400,000,000 inhabitants. The Germans were inclined to detect a conspiracy of other European nations, led by Britain, to prevent them taking their rightful 'place in the sun'. They also came to feel that there was a move to encircle them in Europe and to threaten the powerful position they had already achieved. This fear of encirclement had some basis in reality. In 1891 Bismarck's Reinsurance Treaty with Russia was allowed to lapse by the Kaiser and three years later, in 1894, the alliance which Bismarck had most dreaded, that of France and Russia, was signed. It was a defensive alliance by which the two allies promised to come to each other's aid if attacked by a third power. It was no secret that the third power, though unnamed, was Germany.

Yet in many ways the Germans had no one to blame but themselves for this development. Their nationalism was already aggressive enough to send shivers down their neighbours' spines. In a notorious speech to a German contingent going to fight in China in 1900 the Kaiser declared, 'Give no quarter, take no prisoners. Just as a thousand years ago Attila's Huns made a reputation for ruthless violence that still resounds through the ages, so let the name of Germans acquire a similar reputation which will last a thousand years.' German society, moreover, took an extraordinary pride in the army and the power that it represented. As a Prussian historian who lived through these years later recalled, 'the Prussian lieutenant stalked through the land like a young god, the bourgeois lieutenant of the reserve like a demi-god. One had to be a reserve officer to carry full weight in the upper middle-class, especially in the civil service. Militarism permeated the whole of middle-class life, together with a conventional Prussianism and a naive and conceited admiration for the Prussian way of life. The result was a disastrous narrowing of mental and political outlook.' Since the German army was the biggest (1,300,000 in 1880) and the best in Europe, it is hardly surprising that France and Russia drew together for security.

In 1900, therefore, Germany, Austria-Hungary, and Italy were allies and set against them were France and Russia. In the years that immediately followed, Britain, the one major power still uncommitted, began to move hesitantly but decisively away from her former position of 'splendid isolation'. This she did because isolation, however splendid it might look, had become distinctly uncomfortable. In 1898 Britain found herself nearly at war with France without an ally in sight. Between 1899 and 1902 she had to fight the Boers in South Africa in the teeth of European hostility. Though she emerged victorious from both encounters, she began to look round for allies. Two agreements soon followed. In 1902 a formal alliance was signed with Japan which secured British imperial interests in the Far East. In 1904, much more significantly, Britain and France came to an *entente* (understanding). At first this *entente* merely concerned spheres of interest in Africa but fear of Germany soon transformed it into a virtual alliance to defend Western Europe against German aggression.

Britain had come to distrust Germany on a number of counts. Her powerful and expanding economy which was rapidly overtaking the British was one factor. Another was recent German interference in the Near East, an area which the British regarded as especially their own. In Constantinople, for instance, German military and economic advisers seemed to threaten British interests in 1899. Sultan Abdul Hamid II granted to German industrialists the right to extend the Berlin-Constantinople railway to Baghdad. The most powerful source of bitterness between the two nations, however, was the growing German navy.

This navy was built as a direct challenge to Britain's naval supremacy, yet the Germans never felt that they were being particularly provocative. In the 1890s a new navy was a vital indication of national progress. A best-seller of the decade was the classic work of the American admiral Mahan, *The Influence of Seapower upon History*, which demonstrated that imperial and commercial greatness was seldom achieved without naval power. Mahan's work was read all over Europe but few can have read it more carefully than Admiral von Tirpitz in Germany. 'Without seapower', he concluded, 'Germany's position in the world represents that of a mollusc without a shell.' As he saw it Britain, with five major ironclads to every one in Germany, with naval expenditure running at four times the German level since 1888, and with the stated aim of keeping a fleet as large as the next two European fleets put together, was consciously determined to prevent Germany becoming the world power that her unification and economic progress so clearly entitled her to be. Tirpitz was a brilliant propagandist. By 1892 he had converted the Kaiser to his view that a navy should be built to challenge directly the British fleet in European waters. With the help of the Navy League, he set about converting the rest of his countrymen who traditionally were only interested in the army. 'Tirpitz took up the awesome task', the Kaiser recalled, 'of orientating an entire people, 50,000,000 truculent, short-sighted and foul-tempered Germans and of bringing them round to the opposite view. He achieved this seemingly impossible task in eight months. Truly a powerful man!' In 1897 a naval bill was passed by the Reichstag which made funds available for a six-year naval building programme which would include six battleships. Three years later, this programme was much enlarged, and the aim to rival Britain's building programme was openly stated.

What the German government never fully realized was how sensitive Britain was when it came to her navy. The British army was quite efficient but it was tiny by European standards, being intended for colonial duties rather than for a European war. The British navy, therefore, was not only a useful aid to British colonies and commerce but the only real defence that the nation possessed. Tirpitz's schemes, therefore, touched Britain on a raw nerve and she reacted strongly. The Germans then misinterpreted this reaction. They saw it as a sure sign that Britain was aggressively working to complete the encirclement and suffocation of Germany.

The British reaction began in 1902. In August *The Times* declared: 'we cannot allow them [the Germans] to gain upon us without imperilling our all.' The Admiralty accelerated its own building plans and set about improving the technical standards of its designs. In 1904 Britain's answer to Tirpitz, Sir John Fisher, was appointed First Lord of the Admiralty. A dynamo who believed that all best work was done in a hurry and who shocked the Royal Navy by his refusal to be bound by custom and routine, he managed to transform the service despite strong opposition from many quarters. He had no doubt that Germany was the main enemy and a very serious one. Once, typically, he suggested to King Edward VII that the best solution to the German problem was to catch the German fleet by surprise and, without declaring war, destroy it as Nelson had destroyed the Danish fleet at Copenhagen. 'My God, Fisher, you must be mad' was the king's reply and henceforward Fisher concentrated on ensuring that in the event of an official war the Navy would be more than adequate for its responsibilities. His first act was to scrap many of the technically out-of-date ships still in service. He then reorganized the fleets, formerly scattered the world over on imperial patrols, into three main divisions—the Channel fleet based on Dover, the Atlantic fleet based on Gibraltar and the Mediterranean fleet based on Malta. Such a concentration of ships in European waters was specially designed to meet the new German challenge. Not content with this, Fisher got his designers to develop a revolutionary new type of battleship. Since naval guns were becoming more powerful, longer in range and more accurate, Fisher argued that the most effective battleship would be the one with the biggest guns and fastest speed. Such a ship could find and sink its opponent while remaining out of range. The result was the *Dreadnought*, launched in 1906, which made all existing battleships obsolete (see p. 336). It did nothing, however, to discourage the Germans. They simply regarded it as a challenge to their technical and engineering skills and were soon building ships of the *Dreadnought* type themselves. The naval race continued.

H.M.S. Dreadnought

In 1905, however, a liberal government had come to power in Britain. It was a very pacific government which wished to carry out costly schemes of social reform. In the hope of reducing its military expenses, and of persuading the Germans to end the arms race which was rapidly getting out of hand, the government cut back its naval expenditure in 1907 and 1908, and at the 1907 Hague disarmament conference suggested that Germany might do the same. The Germans, however, were convinced that the British proposal was hypocritical, that it was made in the hope of making their temporary advantage permanent. They even feared a sudden naval attack, and continued to build ships as fast as ever. By the end of 1908 British public opinion had turned fiercely anti-German. Fears that the naval race was in danger of being lost were widely expressed. 'We want eight [new battleships] and we won't wait' was the popular cry, and from 1909 onwards British naval expenditure sharply increased. On the eve of war in 1914 Britain retained a significant superiority in numbers though the German ships were technically slightly more advanced. The diplomatic consequences of the naval race were disastrous. In 1897 Britain and Germany had tended to think of each other as possible allies with many ties of friendship and interest. The naval race first bred distrust, then fear, and, especially on the British side, hatred.

Following the Anglo-French *entente* of 1904, the rival alliances of Europe were these. In the centre were Germany, Austria, and Italy; on the circumference France and Russia, with Britain informally attached. In the next ten years a series of diplomatic crises bound these alliances more closely together, deepened the hostility between them, gave rise to immense expenditure on armaments and eventually led to war itself (see map 17).

There were two main trouble spots which defied satisfactory solution. The first was Morocco. At the beginning of the twentieth century, this North African state was still independent but rebellious subjects gave its Sultan constant trouble. Since 1899 the French, who controlled neighbouring Algeria, had been pressing to establish French authority over Morocco too. It was to clear the way into Morocco that Delcassé, the French Foreign Minister, had sought the *entente* with Britain. If Britain would allow France a free hand in Morocco, France would do the same for Britain over Egypt. Germany, however, was not going to stand idly by as her two main rivals carved up yet another part of Africa. Her economic interests and her national honour would both be flouted. 'Germany must object to the proposed take-over of Morocco not only on economic grounds but far more to maintain her prestige', noted Holstein, an influential adviser of the Kaiser in diplomatic matters. The Kaiser, therefore, called in at Tangier in 1905 while cruising in the

Map 17 Europe in 1914 showing the hostile alliances

Mediterranean and made a fiery speech. He hoped that an independent Morocco under the Sultan's rule would be open to the free trade of all nations and he made it clear that he would take care of Germany's interests in the area. His speech led to an immediate diplomatic crisis and then in 1906 to an international conference at Algeciras on the south coast of Spain. Although German belligerence had persuaded an anxious French government to sack Delcassé before the conference began, the German representatives were unable to make much headway at Algeciras against the united and skilful diplomacy of the French and the British. While the independence of Morocco and equal trading opportunities there for the major powers were guaranteed, it was accepted that France should have police powers over the trouble-torn area, which of course made her the dominant power. Algeciras was therefore a major setback for Germany and also marked an important development in the Anglo-French *Entente*. In 1904 this had been a very general understanding between the two powers over colonial spheres of influence. German action over Morocco in 1905 and 1906 appeared so threatening however that it became much more binding and more consciously anti-German. Not only did French and British diplomats tend to take a common diplomatic stand against the Germans as at Algeciras but, from 1905, French and British military experts began meeting in secret to work out joint plans to meet the attack of a common enemy. There was no possible enemy other than Germany. These meetings continued until 1914 when the joint plans were put into effect. Another result of this First Moroccan crisis of 1905–6 was to link Britain more closely with Russia. At Algeciras Russia backed Britain and France against Germany. Common fears about the increase of German influence in the Middle East, especially as a result of the extension of the Berlin-Baghdad railway, led Britain and Russia in 1907 to another *entente* to defend their common interests. Thus from 1907 the Triple Alliance of Germany, Austria-Italy, was matched by the Triple Entente of France, Russia, and Britain. The *Ententes* might look much less formal and precise than the Alliances but, when it came to the crunch, they proved just as binding.

The Moroccan situation caused a second and even more dangerous crisis in 1911. Since 1906 the Sultan's power had continued to weaken and the French had been able to use their police powers to increase their hold on the area. Rumours were rife that Southern Morocco contained exceptional mineral wealth and German engineers and businessmen were doing their utmost to gain a stronger economic position. In 1911 Berber tribesmen rebelled yet again and besieged the Sultan in his capital of Fez. He appealed to the French who promptly sent 20,000 troops to his aid. This action led to immediate protests from the German and Spanish governments (the latter also being interested in the area) and the German government, calculating that the time had come to cut the French down to size and to aid their businessmen, sent the gunboat, *Panther*, to the southern Moroccan port of Agadir.

This belligerent move proved to be a miscalculation. It swung the British, especially sensitive about naval movements, behind the French. It was widely held in Britain that the Germans were seeking to establish a permanent naval base at Agadir. Reacting to the excited mood of the public, Lloyd George, the Chancellor of the Exchequer, made a famous speech at the Mansion House in London. 'If Britain were treated as if she were of no account in the cabinet of nations', he declared, 'then I say emphatically that peace at that price would be humiliation intolerable for a great country like ours to endure.' Throughout August 1911 peace seemed to hang by a thread but, at the beginning of September, Germany's nerve failed. A bargain was struck whereby Morocco became virtually a French protectorate while Germany was given 107,270 square miles of the French Congo in compensation. Since most of this area was either jungle or swamp, the Germans concluded, with justification, that they had made a bad bargain, that the second Moroccan crisis had brought a second diplomatic humiliation, and that once again the British and French had conspired to prevent them gaining their rightful 'place in the sun'. Such a blow to German prestige must never be allowed to happen again. On their part, France and Britain were convinced that Germany was dangerously aggressive and that further rearmament was essential if she was to be held in check. In 1912 the British naval building programme was increased and in 1913, despite tough socialist opposition, the French parliament approved a new army bill which, over a period of three years, would enlarge and modernize the French army in Europe.

The other major trouble-spot which defied peaceful solution was the Balkans (see maps 9 and 18). The Balkan question in the second half of the nineteenth century was the famous Eastern Question under another name. As Chapter 7 indicated, European statesmen could find no solution to the Eastern Question in the first half of the century. Their successors in the second half of the century were no more effective. In some ways, the problem became harder. While the Turkish government grew more feeble yet remained as unco-operative as ever, the rivalries of the European powers were complicated by the emergence of Germany as yet another major nation with interests in the Near East. The area was further inflamed by the excited nationalism of the Slav races. At first their energies were directed against the Turks, but then, as the Turks grew weaker, against each other. Such was the extraordinary patchwork of racial and religious settlement that the sources of rivalry between Serb, Bulgar, Rumanian, Greek, Albanian, Croat, and Ruthenian were innumerable. Squabbles between the Balkan races involved the major European powers. Russia was a Slav nation and tended to back the Balkan Slavs against both the Turks and the Austrians. Serbia especially came to look to Russia for support. Austria, in contrast, regarded the emergence of the Balkan Slav nations, of Serbia especially, as a menace to her multi-national empire. By the end of the nineteenth century, therefore, Balkan rivalries were combined with Great Power rivalries to make the area 'the powder-keg of Europe'.

Between the end of the Crimean War and the beginning of the First World War, the Balkans and the Eastern Mediterranean caused frequent and dangerous international crises. The Treaty of Paris, which in 1856 ended the Crimean War, settled nothing and did not begin to face up to the problems posed by the demands of the Balkan races for complete independence from Turkish rule. This independence became more and more of a reality. After 1856 Serbia was virtually independent. The only right that the Turks still maintained was to fly their flag next to the Serbian one on the ramparts of Belgrade. In the 1860s the Rumanians ignored the Treaty of Paris, which had allowed them only partial independence from the Turks and kept them divided in the principalities of Moldavia and Wallachia. They declared themselves united in 1861 and citizens of the independent Principality of Rumania in 1866. As some Slav groups successfully won their freedom, Pan-Slavism, a cultural and political movement which stressed the unity of all the Slav races of Europe and the marvellous future that their unity would bring, gained many followers. 'Scattered Slavs', wrote the Slovak poet Jan Kollar, 'let us be united whole and no longer in fragments; then all Europe should kneel before this idol whose head would tower above the clouds and whose feet would shake the earth.' Slavs in Poland and in the Austrian empire came to look to their fellow Slavs for support as never before. At the second Pan-Slavic Congress, Russians like the scientist Danilevsky and the historian Pogodin argued that Russia, the one major Slav power, should act as the champion of those millions of Slavs who were still ruled by alien governments. This was a role which Russian governments were only too happy to play.

A serious crisis occurred in 1875: Bosnians and Bulgarians rose against their Turkish masters. Serbia and Montenegro decided that the rising provided a good opportunity to make war on Turkey. The Bulgarian rebels assassinated some Turkish officials and, as a reprisal, the Turks razed a number of villages to the ground, killing many women and children as they did so. These 'Bulgarian atrocities', coupled with the news of the murder of the French and German consuls in Salonika by a crazed Turkish mob, horrified all

Map 18 The Balkans in 1881

Europe. Russia then declared war on Turkey, won some quick victories and seemed on the verge of capturing Constantinople. These Russian successes brought the British fleet close to the Turkish capital and another Crimean war seemed near. However, the major powers decided instead to negotiate and, under the chairmanship of Bismarck, the Congress of Berlin worked out a peaceful settlement. By the Treaty of Berlin (1878) Montenegro, Rumania, and Serbia were recognized as independent states. A Bulgaria—which still excluded many Bulgars—was created under Turkish suzerainty. Bosnia and Herzegovina, while still remaining part of the Ottoman Empire in name, were occupied by Austrian troops. The rest of the Balkans—Albania, Macedonia, Eastern Rumelia—remained Turkish. The major powers were pleased with their handiwork. A 'peace with honour' was how Disraeli rather

341

smugly described the settlement when he returned to London. (During the bargaining Britain had obtained Cyprus). It was, however, no settlement at all. The Balkan races were, without exception, furious. The Rumanians had to watch thousands of their countrymen pass under Russian rule in Bessarabia (Russia's part of the Berlin bargain). The Bosnians and Herzegovinans found that they had rid themselves of one lot of foreign masters (the Turks) only to gain another (the Austrians). The Serbs who had fought to liberate the Bosnians found instead an Austria extending her power dangerously southwards. The Bulgarians, who had revolted, suffered, and apparently won their independence from the Turks in 1877, found themselves a year later neither completely free nor united. And many Greeks, Bulgars, Albanians, Serbs, and Croats still remained subject to Turkish rule. There could be no peace in the Balkans on these terms.

Turkish rule grew weaker and worse. The Sultan from 1876 was Abdul Hamid II, an alert, avaricious and devious man so nervous of plots against his life that he spent most of his reign hidden away in a huge palace full of subterranean passages and hidden fortifications. All opposition was stifled, all criticism suppressed by a network of informers and secret agents. His motto was a saying attributed to the prophet Muhammad—'Every novelty is an innovation, every innovation is an error and every error leads to hell-fire.' Under his rule, the Ottoman Empire stagnated when only radical reforms could bring new strength.

Turkish weakness was once again demonstrated in 1885 when

Abdul Hamid II : the 'Old Spider' driving through Constantinople soon after the Young Turk revolution of 1908 which had deprived him of much of his power

the Bulgars of Eastern Rumelia expelled their Turkish governor and declared themselves united with Bulgaria. The traditional alliances were then turned topsy-turvy. Serbia, looking for easy conquests, attacked the new Bulgarian state, only to be utterly defeated and saved from territorial losses by Austria which was attempting to counter Russian influence in the Balkans by a policy of friendliness towards her Slav neighbours. It was fear of Russia in the Balkans which drove Austria into the Dual Alliance of 1879 with Germany, and fear of Austria in the Balkans and of German influence in Constantinople which drove Russia into the Dual Alliance of 1893 with France. Thus a Balkan brigand squabble might threaten a European war.

Explosive though the Balkans were by 1900, the first years of the twentieth century were comparatively quiet. Between 1897 and 1905 Russian energies were concentrated on Asia and on war with Japan; it was not until after the defeat by Japan that they turned once more to the Balkans. Before long there was another major crisis. In 1908 the 'Young Turks'—a group dedicated to the reform and westernization of Turkish institutions—inspired a revolution which first forced Abdul Hamid II to grant a constitution and then, a year later, deposed him. Three months after the revolution Austria, taking advantage of the Sultan's problems, annexed the provinces of Bosnia and Herzegovina which she had been occupying since 1878. The diplomacy before the annexation was very complicated. The Austrian foreign minister either failed to make himself clear to the Russian foreign minister or double-crossed him. The result was that Russia was outraged by the annexation. So were the Serbs, who hoped for the unification of all South Slavs—including Bosnians as well as the Slavs of the Austrian Empire—in one great kingdom whose capital would be Belgrade. There was no war since Russia was not ready. However, like Germany after Agadir, she resolved that when the next crisis broke she would not be caught unawares again.

The independent Balkan states then set about dividing up what was left of Turkey in Europe. Both Serbia and Bulgaria were anxious to get an outlet to the sea—Serbia to the Adriatic and Bulgaria to the Aegean. Together they formed the Balkan League with Greece and Montenegro; in October 1912 the League declared war on the unfortunate Turks, who already had their hands full in Tripolitania (North Africa) where they had been attacked by the Italians. The League was everywhere victorious and the Bulgarians advanced rapidly to within twenty-five miles of Constantinople. Once again the Big Powers intervened. Austria had no more desire for a Serbian foothold on the Adriatic shore than had the Russians for a Bulgarian army in Constantinople. A conference was held in London and another settlement devised which was signed by all the nations involved in the previous war. The only parts of Europe left to the Turks were the city of Contantinople itself and its approaches. The rest was divided among the members of the victorious Balkan League.

Yet scarcely before the ink was dry, the victors were fighting among themselves over the spoils. The Bulgars quarrelled first with the Serbs, then with the Greeks. In June 1913 they began the Second Balkan War by attacking their former allies. They were, however, badly outnumbered, especially when the Rumanians and even the Turks joined the Serbs and Greeks. They were soon defeated, and by the Treaty of Bucharest were forced to sign away most of the gains that they had won the year before in the First Balkan War. The results of these two wars were of enormous consequence to the rest of Europe. A bitter, defeated Bulgaria turned to Austria and Germany for help against the hated Serbs. Serbia, who emerged from the second war the strongest of the Balkan nations, was bursting with confidence. At the same time, she was indignant with Austria who had prevented her gaining the Adriatic shore she so much wanted. 'The first round is won', proclaimed Pasic, the Serbian Prime Minister. 'Now we must prepare for the second, against Austria.' In Vienna, the Austrian capital, the diplomats and generals watched and waited. Serbia was plainly dangerous and must grow more dangerous still. If Austria was to act against her, it would be best to act sooner rather than later.

Thus when Europe reached the year 1914, there were many reasons why a major war might break out at any time. As we have seen, the continent was now divided into two clearly hostile camps arming ever faster as time passed. In two areas—Morocco and the Balkans—differences remained between major European states which peaceful means seemed unable to resolve. The Moroccan crises had left Germany feeling that no further humiliations by France and Britain could be tolerated. The Balkan crises had left Austria convinced that Serbia could not be allowed to grow stronger and Russia determined that Serbia should not be bullied by Austria. Statesman all over Europe began to assume that war must come, so they asked their generals, 'If it is to come, when would it suit us best?' To this question the British, the French, and the Russians answered, 'the later the better'. The German and Austrian answer was, however, the opposite. As early as 1912, General von Moltke had told Kaiser Wilhelm 'War is inevitable, and the sooner the better.' The new French army law of 1913 which would bring the French army to full effectiveness by 1916 encouraged the Germans to think in terms of an early war. Similarly, the Austrians saw the Serbian threat as a bud to be nipped as quickly as possible.

This is not to say, however, that war in 1914 was inevitable. The spring of 1914 was diplomatically calmer than in many previous years. Though the twentieth century had already seen many nasty crises, they had all been settled without a large war. Even the savage and complex Balkan conflicts of 1912 and 1913 had been held in check by the major European powers acting in concert. There seemed no obvious reason why similar crises in the future should not be settled in the same way, and when, at the end of June, 1914, yet another incident set the Balkans aflame, few European statesmen were particularly alarmed. This time, however, less than six weeks later, most of the continent was at war, not so much because European statesmen wanted it so but because, to a quite remarkable degree, they lost control of events. In a sense, the weapons of war went off by themselves. To understand how this happened and could happen, we must look carefully at the sequence of events from June to September, 1914.

June 28th, St. Vitus Day, was a solemn date in the Serbian calendar. It commemorated the Battle of Kossovo in 1389 when a Serbian army, fighting heroically to the last man, was overwhelmed by the Ottoman Turks and Serbian independence ended for centuries. The announcement that the Archduke Ferdinand, heir to the Austrian throne, would pay a state visit to the Bosnian capital of Sarajevo on St. Vitus Day 1914 was regarded by many Bosnian and Serbian Serbs as a studied insult to the Serbian people and they were roused to fury. Members of a secret society, Young Bosnia, led by Gavrilo Princip, decided to assassinate the Archduke and, thanks to the negligence of the authorities—there were just a hundred and twenty policemen manning a route of four miles—they were successful (see p. 346).

This murder convinced the Austrian government that the time for a showdown with Serbia had come. Having made sure of German backing (8 July), Austria used the flimsy pretext that Princip and his fellow assassins could never have been successful without Serbian aid and presented Serbia with an ultimatum on 23 July. It was so excessive in its demands that most European statesmen interpreted it as just the first step in yet another serious, but not too serious, crisis. As had happened so often before, the time would come for a conference of the major powers. Then would come the bargains, the compromises and eventually a settlement.

Things, however, went badly wrong this time—quickly and irremediably—mainly because the politicians were no longer masters of their generals and their railway timetables. As Chapter 18 has shown, the military strategists were convinced in 1914 that the next war would be won by that nation which mobilized its armies fastest and struck with concentrated power while the enemy was

still in the process of mobilization. With their military men clamouring for a speedy declaration of war the politicians ran out of time.

The murdered Archduke and his wife lying in state

On receiving the Austrian ultimatum, Serbia tried to buy a breathing space by accepting almost all Austria's terms. Austria, however, refused to be bought off and declared war on Serbia on 28 July. Sazonov, the Russian foreign minister, was not prepared to leave Serbia in the lurch but, in order not to provoke Germany, he decided that the best scheme would be to order a partial mobilization of the Russian forces aimed solely at Austria. At this point the Russian generals stepped in. If there was a partial mobilization against Austria alone, they protested, the sheer mechanics of the necessary troop movements would make a general mobilization against Germany impossible for months to come. A partial mobilization against Austria, therefore, would make Russia virtually defenceless against her most dangerous enemy, Germany. At the same time, a warning came from Germany that even a partial mobilization would mean war. The decision rested with Tsar Nicholas. For most of 29 and 30 July, he argued it out with Sazonov and the Minister of War. The Minister of War won and on 31 July Russian troop trains began rolling westwards on a general mobilization.

At once Germany prepared for war. General von Moltke and his colleagues, however, had but one plan. If they were to fight Russia, they had taken it for granted that they would fight France too. In order to win such a two-front war, France must be defeated first, quickly and completely. Only then could Germany afford to take the offensive against Russia. The German response to Russian mobilization was to prepare for an attack on France. Furthermore, the German plan of attack on France was quite inflexible and possessed certain notable characteristics. In the first place, the main line of attack must go through Belgian territory, whether the Belgians liked it or not. Secondly, in order that it should have the momentum to smash speedily through the French defences, four armies, 840,000 troops in all, had to be moved as quickly as possible to a concentrated front. The German railway network was such that all these troops had to pass through the great junction of Aachen, only a few miles from the Belgian border. Once mobilization had begun, the troop trains must move at a steady pace through Aachen and well beyond otherwise there would be chaos. Stopping at the Belgian frontier was impossible if German strategy on the western front was to be effective.

The terrible consequences of so rigid a plan became apparent on 1 August. The day before, the German government accepted Moltke's advice that Russia's actions made a general mobilization necessary and sent out preliminary orders for mobilization. The following day, the Kaiser prepared to sign the main order for the general mobilization. Before he did so, however, Sir Edward Grey, the British Foreign Secretary, made it known that if Germany refrained from attacking France, she could count upon Britain's neutrality. The Kaiser was delighted. He had no desire to fight Britain and little to fight France. 'This calls for champagne', he said, 'we must halt the march to the west.' To do so at this stage, alas, meant halting 11,000 trains. 'It is impossible', said Moltke, 'the whole army will be thrown into confusion.' As in Russia, so in Germany, the military men triumphed.

From then on, there was no hesitation on Germany's part. That same day, 1 August, Germany declared war on Russia. Two days later, German planes bombed the German city of Nuremberg and the German government, claiming that the planes were French, declared war on France. Only Britain, of the major powers, still stood aloof. Both the British public and the liberal government were in two minds whether an attack on France committed Britain to war with Germany. Only Grey, a few cabinet colleagues and

some senior military advisers knew how deeply the secret military conversations with France since 1905 had committed Britain to coming to the aid of France. The reluctance of the British government to take a firm stand both amazed and appalled the French. On the morning of 4 August, however, the Germans, true to their plan and their railway timetables, invaded Belgium despite the protests of the Belgian government. This news united British public opinion and caused the government to act. Grey sent an ultimatum to Berlin stating that, if a promise to respect the neutrality of Belgium was not received by midnight, Great Britain would be at war with Germany. No promise was received. On 6 August, Austria declared war on Russia—somewhat late in the day since the original crisis had been in the Balkans—and six days later, 12 August, the dreadful formalities were completed with the Franco-British declaration of war on Austria.

'There was a strange fever in the air', wrote Winston Churchill, First Lord of the Admiralty in 1914. 'Unsatisfied by material prosperity the nations turned restlessly towards strife.' An American visitor to Europe early in 1914, Colonel House, noted the same kind of mood. 'A militarism run mad' was how he described it. Everywhere, but above all in Germany, the military seemed dangerously outside the control of their governments. So it proved. In the frenzied days of July and August, the military machines shuddered into action almost of their own accord and the peoples of Europe, thoughtlessly rejoicing, hastened into the most frightful war in human history.

Bibliography

(Those books particularly suitable for school pupils are marked with an asterisk)

I. GENERAL

(a) Europe:

The relevant volumes of the *New Cambridge Modern History* are valuable, but indigestible.

Vol. 8, *American and French Revolutions 1763–93*.

9, *War and Peace in an Age of Upheaval 1793–1830*.

10, *The Zenith of European Power 1830–70*.

11, *Material Progress and World-wide Problems 1870–1901*.

12, *The Shifting of World Forces 1898–1945*.

Perhaps more important and certainly more stimulating is the series, edited by William L. Langer, *The Rise of Modern Europe*, the individual volumes of which are mentioned in the relevant sections of this bibliography.

Another excellent and up to date series is the Longman's *General History of Europe*, edited by Denys Hay. The relevant volumes are H. Hearder: *Europe in the Nineteenth Century 1830–80*, and J. M. Roberts, *Europe 1880–1945*.

An interesting collection of original sources, in English, is *Documents in the Political History of the European Continent 1815–1939*, edited and selected by G. A. Kertesz.

Of the many one-volume general surveys, *Europe since Napoleon* by D. Thomson is one of the most thoughtful, though not the most conveniently organized. For some outspoken, controversial interpretations, see *L. C. B. Seaman's *Vienna to Versailles*.

(b) Individual Countries:

Recommended general histories of individual European countries.

D. Mack Smith, *Italy: a Modern History*.

R. Albrecht-Carrié, *Italy from Napoleon to Mussolini*.

J. P. T. Bury, *France 1815–1940*.

*A. Cobban, *A History of Modern France* (3 vols.).

A. J. P. Taylor, *A Course of German History*.

A. J. P. Taylor, *The Habsburg Monarchy 1815–1918*.

R. Flenley, *Modern German History*.

N. Riasanovsky, *A History of Russia*.

Many of these are also useful for providing further bibliographies but the two best bibliographies on this period are:

A. Bullock and A. J. P. Taylor, *A Select List of Books on European History 1815–1914*.

W. N. Medlicott, *Modern European History 1789–1945. A Select Bibliography* (Historical Association: Helps for Students of History, No. 60).

(c) An outstanding account of the first half of the period which demonstrates the close links between the economic and political changes is E. J. Hobsbawm, *The Age of Revolution 1789–1848*.

(d) *The History of the Twentieth Century*, vol. I, originally published in magazine form, and edited by, A. J. P. Taylor and J. M. Roberts, provides a striking visual introduction to the period 1880–1914. The text is clear and sound.

II. SUGGESTIONS FOR FURTHER READING ON INDIVIDUAL CHAPTERS

1.

Most of the volumes, on individual countries, mentioned above, will provide introductions to Europe on the eve of the French Revolution, as will G. Rudé, *Revolutionary Europe 1783–1815*. *Introduction to Eighteenth Century France* by J. Lough is particularly useful, while a good survey of eighteenth-century Europe is *Absolution and Enlightenment 1660–1789* by R. W. Harris.

Relevant and interesting selections of original sources are:

J. F. Lively, *The Enlightenment*.

*S. Andrews, *Enlightened Despotism*.

2.

Selection from the mass of literature on Revolutionary and Napoleonic Europe is difficult but a good introduction is *Revolutionary Europe 1783–1815* by G. Rudé, although C. Brinton, *A Decade of Revolution* (in the Langer series) is fuller. The standard account of the revolution in France is *J. M. Thompson, *The French Revolution*, but individual aspects of it can be studied profitably in:

N. Hampson, *A Social History of the French Revolution*, which is based largely on original sources.

C. Brinton, *The Jacobins*.

M. J. Sydenham, *The Girondins*.

3.

Again Rudé (op. cit.) is of value as well as G. Bruun, *Europe and the French Imperium 1799–1814* (in the Langer series).

There are numerous biographies of Bonaparte, of which perhaps the most authoritative is *Napoleon Bonaparte—his Rise and Fall* by J. M. Thompson. An interesting and concise survey is *Napoleon and the Awakening of Europe* by F. M. H. Markham. J. C. Herold, *Bonaparte in Egypt* is a gripping account of the ambitious Egyptian campaign.

An indication of the controversies which have raged over the career of the Emperor can be found in *Napoleon—for and against* by P. Geyl, which suggests a number of historical interpretations.

4.

A brief but thoughtful introduction to the rapid growth of industry in Britain during this period is T. S. Ashton, *The Industrial Revolution 1760–1830*. E. J. Hobsbawm, *Industry and Empire* is an interesting interpretation along Marxist lines, and there are a number of versions of Karl Marx's *Das Kapital*.

351

Bibliography

The most important works on continental industrial developments are:

J. Clapham, *The Economic Development of France and Germany*.

R. E. Cameron, *France and the Economic Development of Europe*.

W. O. Henderson, *The Industrial Revolution on the Continent: Germany, France and Russia 1800–1914*.

*W. O. Henderson, *The Industrial Revolution in Europe*, which is the best general survey.

5.

Vital appreciation of the class tension generated during this period can be gained from *The Communist Manifesto* by Marx and Engels. (For a full and critical explanation of Marxism, see R. N. Carew Hunt *Theory and Practice of Communism*.) For an example of the growth of organized labour, see H. Pelling, *A History of British Trade Unionism*, which itself has a very full bibliography.

6.

The Peace Settlement of 1815 is described fully in *The Congress of Vienna* by H. Nicolson and *The Congress of Vienna* by C. K. Webster, and the diplomatic results of this restoration of the *status quo ante* are studied in *A World Restored: Metternich, Castlereagh and the Problems of Peace* by H. Kissinger. For a stimulating, non-diplomatic, and therefore less conclusive thesis, see H. G. Schenk, *The Aftermath of the Napoleonic Wars: the Concert of Europe—an experiment*.

The diplomacy of the period is embodied in the personality of Metternich and can usefully be studied from his biographies, a good example of which is A. Cecil, *Metternich*.

A sound, general survey of the earlier part of the period is F. B. Artz, *Reaction and Revolution 1814–32* (Langer series).

7.

(Books suggested in this section will also provide background material for Chapter 19).

A general introduction to the problem can be found in L. Stavrianos, *The Balkans since 1453*, although M. S. Anderson, *The Eastern Question* is altogether more analytical. The later development of Turkey is described in B. Lewis, *The Emergence of Modern Turkey*.

Other valuable books on specific topics are:

C. M. Woodhouse, *The Greek War of Independence—its Historical Setting*.

G. B. Henderson, *Crimean War Diplomacy*

*C. Woodham-Smith, *The Reason Why*.

8.

On the Second Republic and the Second Empire to 1856, the standard works are by F. A. Simpson:

The Rise of Louis Napoleon.

Louis Napoleon and the Recovery of France 1848–56.

Perhaps the most complete study is *Louis Napoleon and the Second Empire* by J. M. Thompson, but some thoughtful and controversial interpretations have been put forward by T. Zeldin in two works: *The Political System of Napoleon III*, which is an attempt at electoral analysis in the Second Empire, based on original research and *Emile Ollivier and the Liberal Empire of Napoleon III*.

9.

A sound introduction to the eventful year of 1848 is P. Robertson, *Revolutions of 1848*, supplemented by L. B. Namier's thoughtful essay *1848: The Revolution of the Intellectuals*, and I. Collins, *Liberalism in the Nineteenth Century* (Historical Association, Pamphlet G.34).

A sympathetic study of the ill-fated King of the French is ★T. E. B. Howarth, *Citizen King; the Life of Louis Philippe*.

Most popular among historians has been the Italian revolutionary movement, on which a useful collection of original sources of S. J. Woolf, *The Italian Risorgimento*. Two of the best biographies are G. O. Griffith, *Mazzini, Prophet of Modern Europe*, and E. E. Y. Hales, *Pio Nono*.

10.

R. C. Binkley, *Realism and Nationalism 1852–71* (Langer series) is a thoughtful, general survey of the period.

German Unification is very well covered from the biographical standpoint in ★A. J. P. Taylor, *Bismarck: Man and Statesman*, and in O. Pflanze *Bismarck and the Development of Germany*, which is rather less interestingly told. The best study of the diplomatic problems which arose is W. E. Mosse, *The European Powers and the German Question*.

The story of Italian Unity is well told in G. M. Trevelyan, *Garibaldi and the Thousand*, and *Garibaldi and the Making of Italy*. An interesting study of the relationship between two national heroes is D. Mack Smith *Cavour and Garibaldi in 1860*. See also Agatha Ramm: *The Risorgimento* (Hist. Assoc. pamphlet).

11.

The complex diplomacy of the period is expertly unravelled in A. J. P. Taylor, *The Struggle for Mastery in Europe 1848–1918*, and W. L. Langer, *European Alliances and Alignments 1871–90*.

On individual countries, virtually arbitrary selections from a wealth of material are:

R. D. Charques, *Twilight of Imperial Russia*.

★W. E. Mosse, *Alexander II and the Modernization of Russia*.

H. Troyat, *Daily Life in Russia under the Last Tsar*.

A. J. May, *The Habsburg Monarchy 1867–1914*.

D. W. Brogan, *Development of Modern France*.

D. Thomson, *Democracy in France*.

K. S. Pinson, *Modern Germany: its History and Civilization*.

E. Eyck, *Bismarck and the German Empire*.

12.

On the beginnings of social security in Europe see J. H. Clapham (op. cit.) chapters 10 and 11; however, histories of individual countries will give helpful information on this topic.

13.

Among the hundreds of novels which give a vivid insight into European life of the nineteenth century, the following classics are easily available in translation:

*Balzac, *Old Goriot*.
*Dostoevsky, *Crime and Punishment*.
*Flaubert, *Madame Bovary*.
*Stendhal, *Scarlet and Black*.
*Tolstoy, *War and Peace*.
*Tolstoy, *Anna Karenina*.
*Zola, *Germinal*.

A thought-provoking view of nineteenth-century urbanization and its effect on the quality of urban living is to be found in *L. Mumford, *The City in History*.

14.

In a field often neglected by historians, material of a non-specialist nature is scarce. However, W. M. McGovern, *From Luther to Hitler* is a useful study of the relationship between science and social ideas, while a good introduction to technology is J. D. Bernal, *Science and Industry in the Nineteenth Century*.

See also:

G. Himmelfarb, *Darwin and the Darwinian Revolution*.
*J. D. Bernal, *Science in History Vol. ii*.
ed. C. Singer, *A History of Technology*.
W. P. D. Wightman, *Growth of Scientific Ideas*.

15.

On the relationship between the church and the individual European states, reference should be made to histories of these countries, already mentioned. However, a notable addition is A. C. Jemolo, *Church and State in Italy*. See also:

E. E. Y. Hales, *The Catholic Church in the Modern World*.
J. N. Figgis, *Churches in the Modern State*.
*A. R. Vidler, *The Church in the Age of Revolution*.

16.

For further study of this topic, there is obviously no substitute for aquaintance with original works of art; but useful secondary works, which provide introductions to relevant artistic fields are:

B. Croce, *European Literature in the Nineteenth Century*.
*E. H. Gombrich, *The Story of Art*.
H. R. Hitchcock, *Architecture, Nineteenth and Twentieth Centuries*.
*E. Newton, *European Painting and Sculpture*.
*N. Pevsner, *History of European Architecture*.
P. Scholes, *The Oxford Companion to Music*.
*J. M. Richards, *An Introduction to Modern Architecture*.

17.

A good general survey of European Imperialism is M. E. Townsend and C. H. Peake, *European Colonial Expansion,* and the classic Marxist view on the subject is V. I. Lenin, *Imperialism: the Highest Stage of Capitalism.*

Useful studies of colonialism in particular areas are:

R. Coupland, *The Exploitation of East Africa 1856–90.*

J. T. Pratt, *The Expansion of Europe into the Far East.*

A. J. Hannan, *European Rule in Africa* (Historical Association Pamphlet G.46).

The diplomatic repercussions of colonial rivalry can be discovered in W. L. Langer, *The Diplomacy of Imperialism 1890–1902* (2 vols.).

An excellent introduction to the various interpretations of this controversial topic is D. K. Fieldhouse, *The Theory of Capitalist Imperialism.*

18.

Perhaps the most rewarding and certainly the most interesting method of studying the art of warfare is to examine individual wars and battles. An encyclopaedic approach is that of J. F. C. Fuller, *Decisive Battles of the Western World* (3 vols.). However, there are some very readable individual studies, especially:

*M. Howard, *The Franco-Prussian War.*

*C. Woodham-Smith, *The Reason Why.*

On later developments at the end of the period, see G. Ritter, *The Schlieffen Plan,* for an insight into strategy and E. L. Woodward, *Great Britain and the German Navy* on the arms race. *Field-Marshal Montgomery's *History of Warfare* is a first-class general survey.

19.

(The background to events in the Balkans is to be found in Chapter 7 and its bibliography.)

The Origins of the First World War is the title of a thoughtful Historical Association pamphlet (G.39) by B. Schmitt. But the events leading up to this war have been described in copious detail in:

S. B. Fay, *The Origins of the World War* (2 vols.).

L. Albertini, *Origins of the War 1914* (3 vols.).

The fateful assassination which triggered off the war is the subject of *Sarajevo* by R. W. Seton-Watson.

Index

357

358

Nicholas I, Tsar of Russia, 114–5, 120, 131–3, 137, 138, 162, 196–7, 218

Nicholas II, Tsar, of Russia, 219, 220–2, 330, 346–7

Nightingale, Florence, 136, 248

Nile, battle of the, 49, 50

Nonconformist churches, 228, 274–5, 282–3

Norway, 16, 108, 225

Novara, battle of, 171, 176

Novels, novelists, European, 234–9

Obrenovic, Milos, Serb leader, 126–7

Odysseus the Klepht, 128

Oersted, Danish inventor, 257–8, 265

Offenbach, composer, 149

Ohm, scientist, 258

Olympic Games, 253–4

Opium War, 308–9

Orsini, 178

Osman Pasha, Turkish commander, 329–30

Ostroleka, battle of, 120

Otho, King of Greece, 130–1

Oxford Movement, 279

Painting (1789–1914), 284–5, 290–6

Paixhans, Colonel, French artillery inventor, 325

Palacky, Czech leader, 161

Palmerston, British Foreign Secretary, 122, 131–2, 133, 138, 299

Panama scandal (1893), 214

Papal States, 17, 108, 121, 155, 169, 178, 273

Paris, 23, 26–8, 30, 36–7, 39, 53, 63, 87, 88, 98, 119, 139, 150, 151–2, 208–10, 241, 243, 244–6; Peace of, 138, 154, 340

Park, Mungo, 306

Parsons, Sir Charles, 77–8

Paskievic, Russian general, 162

Pasteur, Louis, 225–6, 260, 263, 267–9

Paxton, Joseph, 299, 300

Peasantry, in Spain and Portugal, 12–13; in France, 14, 29–30, 80, 101; in Russia, 18, 200, 218–22, 239, 243; in Europe, 72, 101–3, 174

Peguy, French writer, 282

Pellico, Italian dramatist, 167–8

Pepe, General, 112–4

Péreire, Emile and Isaac, French bankers, 86–7, 149, 150, 152

Perkin, English chemist, 261

Peter I, King of Montenegro, 125–6

Peters, Dr, German explorer, 314

Picasso, 285, 296

Piedmont, 43, 46, 82, 107, 112–3, 154, 168, 174, 176–85

Pitt, the Younger, Prime Minister of Britain, 41

Pius VII, Pope, 66

Pius IX (Pio Nono), Pope, 169–71, 172, 185, 205–6, 273, 280

Pius X, Pope, 274

Plekhanov, Russian socialist, 200–1

Plombières agreement, 178, 181

Pobedonostev, Russian churchman, 220, 221, 275

Poland, 16, 17–18, 60, 108, 114, 120, 194, 197

Polignac, French minister, 118–9

Popes, see Pius VII, Pius IX, Pius X, Leo XIII

Population growth, 72, 88–90, 220, 225, 303

Portugal, 12, 58, 112, 114, 230, 312

Prague, 162; Treaty of, 190

Press, the, 152, 249–51

Princep, Gavrilo, 345

Prussia, 16–17, 34, 36, 41, 43, 101, 107, 108, 132, 156–8, 164–7, 185–93, 229–30, 326–7; war against France, 55–6, 63, 65; industrialization of, 78–80

Public Health, 225–6

Public Utilities, 232

Pugin, A. W., architect, 297–9, 300

Quadruple Alliance, 109–10, 122

Quatre-Bras, battle of, 65

Radetsky, Austrian general, 163, 170–1, 174

Raffles, Stamford, 305

Raglan, Lord, 134, 136

Railways, building of, 73–6, 79, 81, 85, 151; financing of, 75, 87; for use in war, 327, 329

Ratazzi, Italian leader, 184

Ravel, French composer, 289

Realpolitik, 175–6, 193

Reichstadt, Duke of, 143, 144

Reign of Terror, 39–40, 264

Religion in nineteenth century, Chapter 15; see also Anglicans, Nonconformist churches, Catholic Church

Renan, French professor, 278, 281

Reuter's news agency, 251

Revolutionary War (1792–5), 39, 41–3

Revolutions of 1820–5, 112–5; of 1830–3, 116–22; reasons for failure, 172–4

Revolutions of 1848, in France, 139–43, 159, 172–4; in Austrian Empire, 160–4, 172–4; in Germany, 164–7, 172–4; in the

Italian peninsula, 167–72, 172–4

Rhigas, Greek revolutionary, 128

Rhodes, Cecil, 314

Ricascoli, Piedmontese leader, 181, 184

Richelieu, French minister, 116

Riego, General, 112–4

Rimsky-Korsakov, Russian composer, 289

Robespierre, Maximilien, leader of Jacobins, 34–5, 36, 37, 38–40

Rohe, Mies van der, architect, 301

Rome, 184–5, 273

Roon, von, 187–8, 326–7

Rossi, prime minister of Papal States, 273

Rousseau, French philosopher, 20, 38

Ruhr, the, 73, 78

Ruskin, John, 300

Russia, 16–19, 102, 108, 114–5, 218–22, 227, 239, 275, 303, 305, 308, 310, 312, 316, 327, 330, 333, 336, 338, 340–4, 346–7; Napoleonic War against France, 55–6, 60–2, 153; industrialization of, 81–2, 194, 201, 220; relations with Turkey, 123, 125, 129–38; socialism in, 200–1, 203

Russell, W. H., reporter on The Times, 136, 250

Russo-Japanese War, 196, 222, 330, 343

Sadowa (Koniggratz), battle of, 190, 191

St. Armand, British general in Crimea, 134

St. Helena, 56, 65, 66

Saint-Just, leading Jacobin, 39, 40

St. Petersburg, 220, 221, 222

St. Simon, French writer, 151

Sanitation, 225–6, 267

sans-culottes, 36–7, 40, 45

Santarosa, Italian revolutionary, 113, 114

Schleswig-Holstein, 156, 165–6, 189–91

Schonbrunn, Treaty of, 60

Schwarzenberg, Prince Felix, 162, 163, 172, 174, 176, 185

Science, growth of, 19, 231, Chapter 14; and religion, 276–8, 280–1

Scott, Sir Giles Gilbert, 297

Sebastopol, 134–6, 153

Second Coalition against France, 50, 51

Second Empire, in France, 81, 148–53, 272

Second International, 202–3

Second Republic, in France, 146–8

Sedan, battle of, 158

Serbs, 123–4, 161, 197, 218, 340–7; Serbian independence, 126–7, 138

Serfs, see Peasantry

Seven Weeks War, 156

Shaftesbury, Lord, 140, 231

Siemens, Werner, German inventor, 76, 83–5, 87, 258

Sicily, 182–3, 184

Siéyès, 24, 50, 51

Silesia, 16, 78, 98–9, 160, 161, 164

Slave trade, 70, 71, 304, 305–6

Slavs, 126–8, 173, 196–7, 340–4

Smith, Adam, 227

Smith, Sir Sidney, British naval commander, 50

Soane, Sir John, 296

Social Democratic Party, (S.P.D.), 199, 203

Socialism in Europe, 197–203, 206–7, 216, 281

Solferino, battle of, 155, 180, 326

Spain, 12, 58, 112, 113–4, 204, 230, 247; Napoleonic War against France, 58–60

Sport in nineteenth century, 252–4

Stanislas Augustus, King of Poland, 18

States-General in May 1789, 23–6

Steel, see Iron and steel

Stephenson, George, locomotive inventor, 74

Stock exchanges, 69–70, 87

Stolypin, reforms of, 102

Strauss, D. F., 277–8

Stravinsky, Igor, 285, 289–90

Suez Canal, 305, 311, 313

Suffrage, 225

Suvorov, Russian general, 50

Swan, English inventor, 258

Sweden, 16, 82, 225, 247, 248, 253; Napoleonic war against France, 60, 108

Switzerland, 19, 20, 82, 233, 248

Talleyrand, 106, 108, 119

Taxes, 23, 223–4, 233

Tchenaya, battle of River, 136

Textile industry, 70, 71–2, 73, 81, 90, 91, 92, 305

The Thousand, or 'Red Shirts', 182–3

Thiers, French President, 208

Third Coalition, 55–6

Third Estate, in France, 24–6, 30, 33, 38

Third Republic of France, 210–4

Thomas, S. Gilchrist, 76

Tibet, 316, 320

Tilak, Indian leader, 320

Tilsit, Treaty of, 56, 57, 60

Tirpitz, Admiral von, 208, 334–5

Todleben, Russian commander, 134–5, 137

Tolentino, Treaty of, 47

359